New Directions in German Studies
Vol. 26

Series Editor:
IMKE MEYER
Professor of Germanic Studies, University of Illinois at Chicago

Editorial Board:

KATHERINE ARENS
Professor of Germanic Studies, University of Texas at Austin

ROSWITHA BURWICK
Distinguished Chair of Modern Foreign Languages Emerita,
Scripps College

RICHARD ELDRIDGE
Charles and Harriett Cox McDowell Professor of Philosophy,
Swarthmore College

ERIKA FISCHER-LICHTE
Professor Emerita of Theater Studies, Freie Universität Berlin

CATRIONA MACLEOD
Edmund J. and Louise W. Kahn Term Professor in the Humanities and
Professor of German, University of Pennsylvania

STEPHAN SCHINDLER
Professor of German and Chair, University of South Florida

HEIDI SCHLIPPHACKE
Associate Professor of Germanic Studies,
University of Illinois at Chicago

ANDREW J. WEBBER
Professor of Modern German and Comparative Culture,
Cambridge University

SILKE-MARIA WEINECK
Professor of German and Comparative Literature,
University of Michigan

DAVID WELLBERY
LeRoy T. and Margaret Deffenbaugh Carlson University Professor,
University of Chicago

SABINE WILKE
Joff Hanauer Distinguished Professor for Western Civilization and
Professor of German, University of Washington

JOHN ZILCOSKY
Professor of German and Comparative Literature, University of Toronto

Volumes in the series:

Vol. 1. *Improvisation as Art: Conceptual Challenges, Historical Perspectives*
by Edgar Landgraf

Vol. 2. *The German Pícaro and Modernity: Between Underdog and Shape-Shifter*
by Bernhard Malkmus

Vol. 3. *Citation and Precedent: Conjunctions and Disjunctions of German Law and Literature*
by Thomas O. Beebee

Vol. 4. *Beyond Discontent: 'Sublimation' from Goethe to Lacan*
by Eckart Goebel

Vol. 5. *From Kafka to Sebald: Modernism and Narrative Form*
edited by Sabine Wilke

Vol. 6. *Image in Outline: Reading Lou Andreas-Salomé*
by Gisela Brinker-Gabler

Vol. 7. *Out of Place: German Realism, Displacement, and Modernity*
by John B. Lyon

Vol. 8. *Thomas Mann in English: A Study in Literary Translation*
by David Horton

Vol. 9. *The Tragedy of Fatherhood: King Laius and the Politics of Paternity in the West*
by Silke-Maria Weineck

Vol. 10. *The Poet as Phenomenologist: Rilke and the New Poems*
by Luke Fischer

Vol. 11. *The Laughter of the Thracian Woman: A Protohistory of Theory*
by Hans Blumenberg, translated by Spencer Hawkins

Vol. 12. *Roma Voices in the German-Speaking World*
by Lorely French

Vol. 13. *Vienna's Dreams of Europe: Culture and Identity beyond the Nation-State*
by Katherine Arens

Vol. 14. *Thomas Mann and Shakespeare: Something Rich and Strange*
edited by Tobias Döring and Ewan Fernie

Vol. 15. *Goethe's Families of the Heart*
by Susan E. Gustafson

Vol. 16. *German Aesthetics: Fundamental Concepts from Baumgarten to Adorno*
edited by J. D. Mininger and Jason Michael Peck

Vol. 17. *Figures of Natality: Reading the Political in the Age of Goethe*
by Joseph D. O'Neil

Vol. 18. *Readings in the Anthropocene: The Environmental Humanities, German Studies, and Beyond*
edited by Sabine Wilke and Japhet Johnstone

Vol. 19. *Building Socialism: Architecture and Urbanism in East German Literature, 1955–1973*
by Curtis Swope

Vol. 20. *Ghostwriting: W. G. Sebald's Poetics of History*
by Richard T. Gray

Vol. 21. *Stereotype and Destiny in Arthur Schnitzler's Prose: Five Psycho-Sociological Readings*
by Marie Kolkenbrock

Vol. 22. *Sissi's World: The Empress Elisabeth in Memory and Myth*
edited by Maura E. Hametz and Heidi Schlipphacke

Vol. 23. *Posthumanism in the Age of Humanism: Mind, Matter, and the Life Sciences after Kant*
edited by Edgar Landgraf, Gabriel Trop, and Leif Weatherby

Vol. 24. *Staging West German Democracy: Governmental PR Films and the Democratic Imaginary, 1953–1963*
by Jan Uelzmann

Vol. 25. *The Lever as Instrument of Reason: Technological Constructions of Knowledge around 1800*
by Jocelyn Holland

Vol. 26. *The Fontane Workshop: Manufacturing Realism in the Industrial Age of Print*
by Petra S. McGillen

The Fontane Workshop

Manufacturing Realism in the Industrial Age of Print

Petra S. McGillen

BLOOMSBURY ACADEMIC
NEW YORK • LONDON • OXFORD • NEW DELHI • SYDNEY

BLOOMSBURY ACADEMIC
Bloomsbury Publishing Inc
1385 Broadway, New York, NY 10018, USA
50 Bedford Square, London, WC1B 3DP, UK
29 Earlsfort Terrace, Dublin 2, Ireland

BLOOMSBURY, BLOOMSBURY ACADEMIC and the Diana logo
are trademarks of Bloomsbury Publishing Plc

First published in the United States of America 2019
Paperback edition first published 2021

Copyright © Petra S. McGillen, 2019

For legal purposes the Acknowledgments on pp. xvi-xvii constitute
an extension of this copyright page.

Cover design: Andrea F. Bucsi
Cover image: Theodor Fontane at his desk. Courtesy Theodor-Fontane-Archiv,
Potsdam, Germany.

All rights reserved. No part of this publication may be reproduced or
transmitted in any form or by any means, electronic or mechanical,
including photocopying, recording, or any information storage or retrieval
system, without prior permission in writing from the publishers.

Bloomsbury Publishing Inc does not have any control over, or responsibility for,
any third-party websites referred to or in this book. All internet addresses given
in this book were correct at the time of going to press. The author and publisher
regret any inconvenience caused if addresses have changed or sites have
ceased to exist, but can accept no responsibility for any such changes.

Library of Congress Cataloging-in-Publication Data
Names: McGillen, Petra (Petra S.), author.
Title: The Fontane workshop: manufacturing realism in the industrial
age of print / Petra S. McGillen.
Description: New York, NY: Bloomsbury Academic, 2019. |
Series: New directions in German studies; vol. 26 | Extensive and
substantial revision of author's thesis (doctoral—Princeton University, 2012,
titled Original compiler: notation as textual practice in Theodor Fontane. |
Includes bibliographical references and index.
Identifiers: LCCN 2019008431 (print) | LCCN 2019016631 (ebook) |
ISBN 9781501351563 (ePDF) | ISBN 9781501351570 (ePub) |
ISBN 9781501351587 (hardback: alk.paper)
Subjects: LCSH: Fontane, Theodor, 1819–1898—Criticism and interpretation. |
German literature—19th century—History and criticism. |
Realism in literature. | Creation (Literary, artistic, etc.)
Classification: LCC PT1863.Z7 (ebook) |
LCC PT1863.Z7 M34 2019 (print) | DDC 838/.709—dc23
LC record available at https://lccn.loc.gov/2019008431

ISBN: HB: 978-1-5013-5158-7
PB: 978-1-5013-7831-7
ePDF: 978-1-5013-5156-3
eBook: 978-1-5013-5157-0

Series: New Directions in German Studies

Typeset by RefineCatch Ltd, Bungay, Suffolk, UK

To find out more about our authors and books visit
www.bloomsbury.com and sign up for our newsletters.

To Michael and Henry

Contents

List of Illustrations   x
Permissions   xii
Note on Translations and Transcriptions   xiv
List of Abbreviations for Recurring Fontane Citations   xv
Acknowledgments   xvi

Introduction: Remediating Copy and Paste   1

1 Media-Historical Coordinates: Literature in the Industrial Age of Print   33

2 Biography vs. Autobiography: The Making of a Compiler   71

3 A Living Archive: Generating Input   121

4 The Manufacture of Literature: Generating Output   183

Coda: The "Uncreative" Writing of *Mathilde Möhring*   257

Bibliography   277
Index   297

Illustrations

Figure 0.1: Iconic photograph of Theodor Fontane at his desk   1

Figure 0.2: Fontane's Notebook A 11, front cover   4

Figure 1.1: Masthead of the *Gartenlaube*, 1853   49

Figure 1.2: Text-image interactions in *Ueber Land und Meer*, 1871   53

Figure 1.3: "Infinite Poetry," a caricature by Alfred Oberländer, 1888   65

Figure 2.1: Typical Fontanean "paper sleeve" with label   72

Figure 2.2: Max Schlesinger's "Englische Correspondenz" from June 22, 1861   87

Figure 2.3: Manuscript page, compiled and written by George Hesekiel, with contributions to the "France" column of the *Neue Preußische (Kreuz-)Zeitung*   89

Figure 3.1: Double-page from Fontane's Notebook A 1, showing the resemblance of his notebooks to handwritten commonplace books   138–9

Figure 3.2: Fontane's manuscript page "Figure in a Berlin Novella," with distinct graphic features   141

Figure 3.3 & 3.4: Two consecutive double-pages from Fontane's Notebook E 2, listing sources for research on the project *Before the Storm*   162–4

Figure 3.5: Double-page from Fontane's Notebook E 2, containing a cascade of topics for dialogues in *Before the Storm*   180–1

Figure 4.1: Manuscript page from Fontane's unfinished novel *Mathilde Möhring*, showing his practice of pasting notes directly into advanced drafts   188

Figure 4.2: A typical Fontanean list, in Fontane's Notebook C 1   194

Figure 4.3: Modular entries, delineated with thick pen strokes, in Fontane's Notebook A 2   197

Figure 4.4 & 4.5: Double-pages from Fontane's Notebook E 5 with topographical site plans of Tangermünde castle and Tangermünde   201

Figure 4.6: Double-page from Fontane's Notebook E 2, showing the interaction of modular entries and lists for the development of literary characters in the context of *Before the Storm*   219

Figure 4.7: Charles Dickens's Number Plan for number XVIII of *David Copperfield*   227–8

Permissions

Figures 0.2, 3.1, 3.3–3.5, and 4.2–4.6 reproduced under the Creative Commons License CC0. *Theodor Fontane: Notizbücher* (manuscript), collection of the Staatsbibliothek zu Berlin – Preußischer Kulturbesitz. *Theodor Fontane: Notizbücher. Digitale genetisch-kritische und kommentierte Edition* (digital edition), ed. Gabriele Radecke. https://fontane-nb.dariah.eu/index.html. Digital image rights owned and granted by the *Theodor Fontane: Notizbücher. Digitale genetisch-kritische und kommentierte Edition*.

Throughout the book, quotations from Theodor Fontane's Notebooks are reproduced under the Creative Commons License CC-BY-NC-ND-4.0 international. *Theodor Fontane: Notizbücher* (manuscript), collection of the Staatsbibliothek zu Berlin-Preußischer Kulturbesitz. *Theodor Fontane: Notizbücher. Digitale genetisch-kritische und kommentierte Edition* (digital edition), ed. Gabriele Radecke. https://fontane-nb.dariah.eu/index.html.

Figure 0.1 reproduced with permission of the Theodor-Fontane-Archiv Potsdam. Archival Signature TFA_AI96_33853.jpg.

Figures 1.1 and 1.2 reproduced with permission of the Universitätsbibliothek Leipzig. Archival Signatures Dt.Zs.346 and Dt.Zs.958-o.

Figure 1.3 reproduced with permission of the Universitätsbibliothek Heidelberg. "Endlose Dichtkunst," Archival Signature Fliegende Blätter – 88.1888 (Nr. 2214–2239), p. 56.

Figure 2.1 reproduced with permission of the Stiftung Stadtmuseum Berlin. Theodor Fontane: Von Zwanzig bis Dreißig. Mein Leipzig lob ich mir. Banderole 1897, Manuscript, Archival Signature V67/864,BLeipzig.

Figure 2.2 reproduced with permission of The British Library Board. German Newspaper Collection, Shelfmark LOU.LON 2 [1861], Image IS16W215270P_0002.tif.

Permissions xiii

Figure 2.3 reproduced with permission of the Staatliche Archive Bayerns, Staatsarchiv Coburg. Nachlass Hesekiel, Image NL Hesekiel 3_4.tif.

Theodor Fontane's Article "Das große Feuer und die Taschendiebe" in Chapter 2, reproduced with permission of the Staatsbibliothek zu Berlin – Preußischer Kulturbesitz. Zeitungsabteilung, *Neue Preußische (Kreuz-)Zeitung*, 30 June 1861.

Figure 3.2 reproduced with permission of the Deutsches Literaturarchiv Marbach. Nachlass A: Theodor Fontane, Prosa, Materialien, Fiche 005053, Fiche 14, Archival Signature [*Zugangsnummer*] 59.1196.

The sections "Bridging Social Distance: The Effects of a Postal Library Network" and "Material Reading Feats" in Chapter 3 develop ideas that I articulated in an earlier form in "A Creative Machine: The Media History of Theodor Fontane's Library Network and Reading Practices," *The Germanic Review* 87, no. 1 (2012): 72–90 © Taylor and Francis.

Figure 4.1 reproduced with permission of the Staatsbibliothek zu Berlin – Preußischer Kulturbesitz, Handschriftenabteilung. Nachlass Fontane, Romanmanuskript Mathilde Möhring, 263R.

Figure 4.7 reproduced with permission of the Victoria and Albert Museum, London. Forster Collection, The Charles Dickens Manuscripts.

Note on Translations and Transcriptions

Published translations of Fontane's works have been used whenever they were available and are referenced in the footnotes. Unless otherwise stated, all other translations were provided by Joe Paul Kroll. Throughout the book, English translations appear first, followed by the original German and the relevant source information.

The content of pages from Fontane's notebooks is given in German and in English. Whenever the layout of a notebook page has the status of an argument, the page is provided as a facsimile and in a simplified diplomatic transcription. These transcriptions have been checked carefully against those provided in Gabriele Radecke's digital genetic-critical edition of Fontane's notebooks and follow the text of the edition. They convey a general sense of the topography and formal organization of the page but—in contrast to the transcriptions in Radecke's edition—they do not capture every textual layer and non-textual mark. Providing transcriptions that do full justice to the extraordinary formal complexity of Fontane's note-taking would have not only exceeded the capabilities of regular word-processing software, but also gone beyond the aims and scope of this study. The priorities for this book were readability of the selected notebook pages in German and in English and serviceable representations of the key formal features. Readers who wish to analyze the specific features of Fontane's note-taking at the highest level of detail are encouraged to consult the digital genetic-critical edition at https://fontane-nb.dariah.eu/index.html.

Abbreviations for Recurring Fontane Citations

BaH	*Briefe an Wilhelm und Hans Hertz 1859–1898*. Ed. Kurt Schreinert. Stuttgart: Klett, 1972.
BaHey	*Der Briefwechsel zwischen Theodor Fontane und Paul Heyse*. Ed. Gotthard Erler. Berlin: Aufbau, 1972.
BaF	*Briefe an Georg Friedlaender*. Ed. Kurt Schreinert. Heidelberg: Quelle & Meyer, 1954.
BaR	*Briefe an Mathilde von Rohr*. Ed. Kurt Schreinert. Berlin: Propyläen, 1970. *Briefe*. Ed. Kurt Schreinert, cont. Charlotte Jolles, vol. 3.
F [vol.]	*Theodor Fontane: Fragmente. Erzählungen, Impressionen, Essays*. Ed. Christine Hehle and Hanna Delf von Wolzogen. 2 vols. Berlin: De Gruyter, 2016.
GBA [sec. vol.]	*Theodor Fontane: Große Brandenburger Ausgabe*. Ed. Gotthard Erler, cont. eds. Heinrich Detering and Gabriele Radecke. 36 vols. to date. Berlin: Aufbau, 1994–. Section I: Das erzählerische Werk; vols. 1–20. Section II: Gedichte. Zweite, erweiterte und durchgesehene Auflage; vols. 1–3. Section III: Das autobiographische Werk; vol. 3. Section V: Wanderungen durch die Mark Brandenburg; vols. 1–8. Section XI: Tage- und Reisetagebücher; vols. 1–3. Section XII: Briefe. Emilie und Theodor Fontane: Der Ehebriefwechsel; vols. 1–3.
HFA [sec. vol.]	*Theodor Fontane: Werke, Schriften und Briefe* [*Hanser-Ausgabe*]. Ed. Walter Keitel and Helmuth Nürnberger. Munich: Hanser, 1969–1997. Section I: Sämtliche Romane, Erzählungen, Gedichte, Nachgelassenes; vols. 1–7. Section III: Erinnerungen, ausgewählte Schriften und Kritiken. Aufsätze und Aufzeichnungen; vols. 1–5. Section IV: Briefe; vols. 1–5. Section V: Wanderungen, vols. 1–6.
NFA [vol.]	*Theodor Fontane: Sämtliche Werke* [*Nymphenburger Ausgabe*]. Ed. Edgar Gross et al. 24 vols. Munich: Nymphenburger, 1959–1975.

Acknowledgments

One thing I certainly learned from investigating Fontane's workshop is the value of support in the long process of writing a book. I would like to acknowledge the many wonderful individuals who constituted the intellectual community in which this book came of age.

Several colleagues and friends on both sides of the Atlantic took the time to read and comment on the entire manuscript: Ann Blair, Matt Erlin, Sean Franzel, Gerd Gemünden, Richard Kremer, Andrew McCann, Klaus Mladek—and above all, Bruce Duncan. Their incisive suggestions, along with the comments of two anonymous reviewers, improved every aspect of the argument. Nikolaus Wegmann has been a part of *The Fontane Workshop* from the beginning. Our ongoing dialogue shaped the manuscript more than he knows. Gabriele Radecke encouraged my explorations of Fontane's *Nachlass* from afar and provided invaluable expertise in deciphering his notebooks. She also gave me access to the digital genetic-critical edition while it was still being tested and developed. Heiko Christians, Heike Gfrereis, Sabine Gross, Jocelyne Kolb, Catriona MacLeod, Peer Trilcke, and Wolfgang Rasch made themselves available repeatedly for thought-provoking discussions. My research assistants, Michael Beechert, Braelyn Riner, and Dennis Wegner, dedicated many hours of their time to *The Fontane Workshop*. Joe Paul Kroll translated German primary and secondary sources into English with a Fontanean ear for nuance, while Allison Van Deventer, academic editor extraordinaire, streamlined every page of the final draft.

A great debt of thanks is also due to several institutions. Dartmouth College awarded me a year-long sabbatical to complete the book. The Leslie Center for the Humanities at Dartmouth sponsored a Manuscript Review Seminar that transformed my project. The Theodor-Fontane-Archiv, the Stiftung Stadtmuseum Berlin, the Staatsbibliothek Berlin, the Deutsches Literaturarchiv Marbach, the Bayerisches Staatsarchiv Coburg, the British Library, and the Victoria and Albert Museum made their holdings available to me, and their excellent staff—including

Klaus-Peter Möller and Peter Schaefer at the TFA and Bettina Machner at the Stiftung Stadtmuseum Berlin—helped me to track down archival objects. Above all, however, I would like to thank the Department of German Studies at Dartmouth, and in particular, Bruce Duncan, Veronika Füchtner, Gerd Gemünden, Irene Kacandes, Yuliya Komska, Klaus Mladek, and Ellis Shookman. Their mentorship, generosity, and encouragement made me feel at home in the department from my very first day there.

I feel very fortunate that the book found a home in the series New Directions in German Studies. Imke Meyer and Haaris Naqvi, the editors of the series, have been exemplarily responsive, supportive, and simply a pleasure to work with.

Finally, I would like to express my gratitude to my friends and family. Lynn Patyk, Yuliya Komska, Jennie Miller, Udi Greenberg, Meredith Kelly, and Michael Poage modeled how to stay good-humored on the tenure track, while Johannes and Katharina von Dungen reminded me that the campus is not everything. Evelyn Fleming and Steve Gordon were both lifesavers in a very non-metaphorical sense. My family, and in particular Lore, Peter, and Hans Spies, gave me their love, support, and encouragement simply by being there. My deepest gratitude, however, is to my husband, Michael McGillen, and to our son, Henry McGillen. Writing this book would not have been possible, let along meaningful, without them.

Introduction

Remediating Copy and Paste

The Great Realist at Work, or Writing with Scissors and Glue
This iconic photograph of Theodor Fontane (1819–98) (Figure 0.1) shows the great German realist at work. It conveys an image of the author as the prototypical original artist: a composed Fontane sits at his desk, pen in hand, his calm yet attentive gaze fixed on a distant and slightly elevated point that is also the light source of the scene.

Figure 0.1 Iconic photograph of Theodor Fontane at his desk.

Apparently, he is waiting quietly for inspiration in the privacy of his study. Fontane repeatedly claimed that his best writing happened in this manner. To colleagues, readers, publishers, and family members, the famous author maintained that once an observation of real life had spurred an initial creative impulse, his first drafts followed "the familiar dark urge" (HFA IV.4: 611) and unfolded on their own; his writing was "creation in the dark (*Dunkelschöpfung*), rearranged by light" (GBA XII.3: 382). Reflecting on the creative process that gave rise to his best-known novel, *Effi Briest*, he wrote to one of his publishers, Hans Hertz:

> Indeed, poor Effi! Perhaps it turned out as well as it did because I wrote the whole thing as if in a dream, almost as if through a psychograph.... It came as if of its own accord.... My patroness Lessing (of the Vossin), in answer to my question "What's *he* up to?" (an officer who was once a regular guest at the Lessing house, whom I afterwards transposed to Instetten), told me the entire story of Effi Briest, and when it came to the moment, in the second chapter, when the playing girls call "Come, Effi" through the vines, it was clear to me: "You must write *that*."
>
> *Ja, die arme Effi! Vielleicht ist es mir so gelungen, weil ich das Ganze träumerisch und fast wie mit einem Psychographen geschrieben habe. ... Es ist so wie von selbst gekommen .... Meine Gönnerin Lessing (von der Vossin) erzählte mir auf meine Frage: „Was macht denn der?" (ein Offizier, der früher viel bei Lessings verkehrte und den ich nachher in Instetten transponiert habe), die ganze Effi-Briest-Geschichte, und als die Stelle kam, 2. Kapitel, wo die spielenden Mädchen durchs Weinlaub in den Saal hineinrufen: „Effi komm", stand mir fest: „Das mußt du schreiben."*
>
> (BaH 356)

Fontane maintained that he also owed Effi's outward appearance to a "happy coincidence." In the same letter to Hans Hertz, he reported that he was sitting on the balcony of the "Hotel Zehnpfund" in Thale when two English siblings—"he 20, she 15"—stepped onto the balcony and leaned against the balustrade "barely three steps away":

> The girl was dressed in the exact manner in which I described Effi in the very first and then again in the very last chapters: a loose dress in blue-and-white striped cotton, a leather belt, and sailor's collar. I believe I could not have found a better appearance and attire for my heroine, and were it not presumptuous to regard fate as something at one's disposal for any trifle, I should like to say: this little Methodist girl was sent me by fate.

Das Mädchen war genau so gekleidet, wie ich Effi in den allerersten und dann auch wieder in den allerletzten Kapiteln geschildert habe: Hänger, blau und weiß gestreifter Kattun, Ledergürtel und Matrosenkragen. Ich glaube, daß ich für meine Heldin keine bessere Erscheinung und Einkleidung finden konnte, und wenn es nicht anmaßend wäre, das Schicksal als etwas einem für jeden Kleinkram zu Diensten stehendes Etwas anzusehen, so möchte ich beinah sagen: das Schicksal schickte mir die kl. Methodistin.

(BaH 357)

In both his poetological remarks and his official photograph, Fontane presents himself as the mere "mouthpiece" (HFA IV.4: 502) of his great muse, life, which creates the most compelling stories. His task as author, it is implied, is to be attuned to, transcribe, and perfect through stylistic refinement what "life itself" gives him in felicitous moments.

A closer look at the photograph reveals, however, that it is not at all candid, but the result of a careful *mise-en-scène*. The axial division of the image, the precision of Fontane's posture, his formal garments—in reality, he wore neither a bow tie nor crisp white shirts for writing—and the polished surface of the desk leave no doubt that the iconic shot, a typical product of early photography, was staged through and through.[1] It therefore says more about an imaginary creative process, visualized for representative purposes, than an actual one.[2]

This chasm between projected images of authorship and the material realities of late nineteenth-century literary production marks the point of departure for the present book. Its aim is to look behind the scenes and to reconstruct the great German realist's actual creative process through the triple lens of media history, material media theory, and literary poetics. To this end, the study follows Fontane into the engine room of his text production. Analyzing a wealth of unexplored archival evidence—including Fontane's sixty-seven extant notebooks (Figure 0.2), most of which have never been thoroughly studied, and

---

1 On the staging of this image, see Klaus-Peter Möller, "Preußisches Panoptikum mit Pfefferkuchen. Fontane-Porträts und -Bildnisse (2)," *Fontane Blätter* 78 (2004): 53, 58.
2 The shot first appeared in the *Berliner Illustrirte* (November 22, 1896) as part of a story about Fontane. It reappeared in the same magazine with an anonymous obituary of Fontane in October, 1898. The photograph was also the subject of the series of postage stamps, "Männer aus der Geschichte Berlins" (West Berlin, 1952–3); the source for a drawing on the title page of the *Simplicissimus* (January 1, 1920); and, for the part of it reproduced on a poster of the *Aufbau-Verlag* in 1998, a collector's item. See Möller, "Preußisches Panoptikum," 57–66.

4   The Fontane Workshop

other "paper tools,"³ such as cardboard boxes, file folders, and envelopes—the book demonstrates that Fontane produced his prose fiction, feuilleton essays, and other contributions to the press in a creative process that was the exact opposite of his self-staging as the inspired mouthpiece of the muses. Deliberate at every step, he assembled his texts from pre-mediated sources with scissors and glue, in an extraordinarily inorganic, radically intertextual, and completely conscious manner.

Specifically, Fontane applied compositional practices from the longstanding tradition of textual creation known as *compiling*: a method of text production that is predicated on practices of copy (or cut) and paste.⁴ The Latin *(com-)pilare* is translated both as "to plunder, pillage"

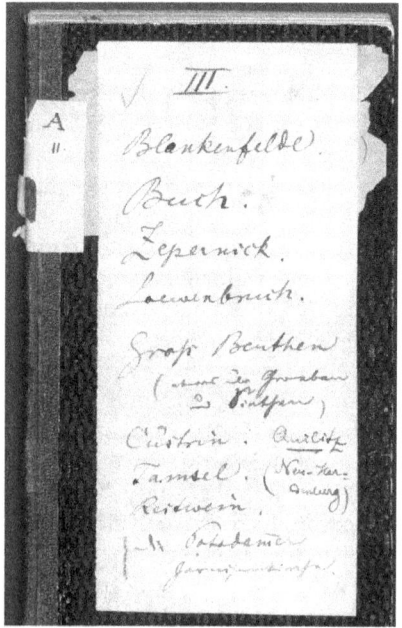

Figure 0.2 Fontane's Notebook A 11, front cover.

---

3   This coinage goes back to Ursula Klein and describes writing media that have an epistemic impact. See her essay "Paper Tools in Experimental Cultures: The Case of Berzelian Formulas," *Studies in the History and Philosophy of Science* 32 (2001): 265–312.
4   For a foundational study of compiling that includes the material media and working methods of compilers, see Ann M. Blair, *Too Much to Know: Managing Scholarly Information Before the Modern Age* (New Haven, CT: Yale University Press, 2010).

and "to excerpt," "to glean."⁵ A compiler, then, is essentially a "plunderer" who systematically scours the writings of others, breaks them down into excerpts, and reassembles these excerpts into a new text. It is a tradition that goes back to the early modern period, when compilatory practices emerged in response to the handpress as methods of knowledge organization and scholarly communication. Faced with hitherto unprecedented amounts of printed matter, early modern scholars turned to compiling as a means of dealing with the perceived "too-muchness" of circulating information, engaging in mammoth projects (e.g., encyclopedias) that were usually too vast to be undertaken alone. Compilers often collaborated or corresponded with other scholars, while family members or paid assistants, so-called *amanuenses*, helped with menial tasks such as copying.⁶ The arrangement of the excerpted sources into new works followed explicit epistemic or poetic guidelines—a classificatory system of knowledge, a defined genre, a set of rhetorical rules. The texts or text collections assembled in this fashion were then reissued under the compilers' names. Compiling thus had a mechanical side, but in the early modern period, it became a legitimate form of authorship.

Fontane's most basic modes of literary production have much in common with this textual practice. Whether he was working on a travel report, a historical essay, a book review, or a new novel, he followed a routine of scouring, excerpting, and rearranging. He amassed large quantities of source material—culled mostly from circulating newspapers and journals, but also from letters, images, historical documents, and monographs—in disconnected notebook entries and on loose folio sheets. He then surveyed these textual building blocks, outlined rearrangements with the help of lists, and combined them into a new text. This pattern of production could be surprisingly mechanical. In particular, when Fontane produced contributions to the press, which were his bread and butter, he sometimes followed set "recipes" (*Rezepten*, BaR 45; NFA XXIV: 809) for the transformation of source materials into new output. In these instances, he could outsource parts of the work process to his personal *amanuenses*, his youngest children, Martha and Friedrich, who acted as scribes and copied book passages that he had marked. Thus, when he worked on a generic piece, such as a historical essay for a newspaper, he merely had to connect the gleaned passages anew, edit as he saw fit, create a fair copy—a task that often fell to his wife, Emilie—and send off "his" essay to the press. A telling

---

5   Petra McGillen, "Kompilieren," in *Historisches Wörterbuch des Mediengebrauchs*, ed. Heiko Christians, Matthias Bickenbach, and Nikolaus Wegmann (Cologne: Böhlau, 2015), 353.
6   See Blair, *Too Much to Know*, 104–12, 173–229.

example of this mechanical mode of compiling is the essay "Das Zietensche Husarenregiment von 1730 bis 1880" (The Regiment of the Zieten Hussars from 1730 to 1880), which was published in installments in the *Vossische Zeitung* from April 11 through 14, 1880. Fontane describes its genesis to his wife as follows:

> Thank God I'm nearly done with the essay on the Zieten Hussars; I read all 670 pages of Lieutenant von Ardenne's book . . . and then Droysen and W. Hahn, too, and was compelled to make excerpts with my head growing larger and larger. Now Friedel and Martha are copying out the passages I noted. By tomorrow, I think, it should all be put in fair copy and ready to be dispatched.
>
> *Gott sei Dank bin ich mit dem Zieten-Husaren-Aufsatz so gut wie fertig; ich habe das 670 Seiten dicke Buch des Lieutenants v. Ardenne . . . danach auch noch Droysen und W. Hahn durchlesen und mit einem immer dicker werdenden Kopf Auszüge machen müssen. Nun sind Friedel und Martha beim Abschreiben der von mir notirten Stellen. Morgen Mittag ist, denk ich, alles ins Reine geschrieben und kann abgeschickt werden.*
>
> (GBA XII.3: 209)

If this seems to be a description of a straightforward process of copy-and-paste, that is exactly what it was—according to Hubertus Fischer's analysis, only one paragraph of the entire essay was noticeably shaped and reworded by Fontane; the rest of this "family product" had been simply patched together.[7] His wife and children were not the only helpers the author employed; he also turned to scores of friends and acquaintances in his vast social network to obtain source materials. The compositional process for novels was more complex, but it too was predicated on copy-and-paste, ongoing textual recombination, and input from others. His authorship, then, was a heavily paper-driven, to some extent mechanical, and often collective enterprise. Material evidence of the true nature of his authorship can even be spotted in Fontane's official portrait. On his large desk lie two pairs of scissors, a paper knife, pens, assorted crayons, manuscript sheets in different sizes, newspaper issues, tools for letter writing, and piles of letters, the everyday utensils and media of his text production. The photographed room was not what it pretended to be—the quiet study of a writer composing his next great novel in solitude. Rather, it was the material microcosm of a seasoned and well-connected compiler who spent his

---

[7] See Hubertus Fischer, "Fontanes 'Zietenhusarenschaft' – nicht nur eine Regimentsgeschichte," *Fontane Blätter* 97 (2014): 77.

working days processing printed and handwritten material in large quantities to produce a creative patchwork. The discovery that the great German realist engaged in practices of compilation when he composed his prose works is momentous, and it entails anti-canonical claims on many levels. As I will show in this book, it has far-reaching implications for our understanding of Fontane's authorial profile, originality, realist poetics, and place in the literary canon. But it also has implications that surpass the limits of Fontane's individual case. The discovery that the realist author practiced compiling calls for the revision of our established narratives about literary production in the second half of the nineteenth century, for it reinserts a textual activity and its copy-and-paste-driven mode of creativity into a period in which they have not traditionally belonged. This study is therefore more than a book about Fontane and his notebooks. Rather, it treats one of Germany's most canonical nineteenth-century authors and his working methods as the primary evidence for an alternate account of how literature was made at a formative media-historical moment, the onset of the industrial age of print.[8]

Compiling as an "Improper" Nineteenth-Century Practice

By and large, scholars do not recognize Fontane as a compiler. If this term comes up at all, it is not a compliment.[9] The reasons for this attitude run deep and stem from the poor reputation that compiling acquired as a creative practice in the modern era. Compiling was effectively erased from the ambit of legitimate textual practices and literary writing

---

8   The term "industrial age of print" has become so contested in the past years that a brief justification of its use here seems in order. Adrian Johns and, more recently, Lisa Gitelman, have pointed out that such general labels are likely to gloss over the contingencies that the processes of printing and publishing involve. I do not mean to suggest that only one kind of print existed in the second half of the nineteenth century—in fact, the first chapter will show just how many different modes, tempi, technologies, and purposes of print there were. That I nonetheless speak of an "industrial age of print" is to acknowledge the large-scale mechanization of printing methods, an increase in the number of impressions that could be made per hour, and a number of other developments that deeply influenced the material medium of literature. Following a suggestion made by Harold Love, I mobilize this term as a heuristic that frames a more specific inquiry. See Adrian Johns, *The Nature of the Book: Print and Knowledge in the Making* (Chicago: University of Chicago Press, 1998), 1–4; Lisa Gitelman, *Paper Knowledge: Towards a Media History of Documents* (Durham, NC: Duke University Press, 2014), 7–9; Harold Love, "Early Modern Print Culture: Assessing the Models," *Parergon* 20, no. 1 (2003): 53.
9   For example, the critic Conrad Wandrey disparaged Fontane's war reports as "kompilatorisch" and, in the same breath, "unoriginell" and "kompendiös." Conrad Wandrey, *Theodor Fontane* (Munich: Beck, 1919), 332–5.

techniques in the eighteenth century. From antiquity through the early Enlightenment, it was a valued textual practice and even rose to the status of an "honorable method,"[10] the material counterpart of erudition and philosophical eclecticism. The reputation of compiling took a sharp downward turn, however, when rule-based methods of invention and creation began to be devalued as "unoriginal" and the Romantic model of the inventor as creative genius emerged. "To compile" turned into a pejorative phrase and became associated with theft and a lack of poetic imagination. A popular eighteenth-century encyclopedia of deceit, the *Betrugs-Lexikon* (third edition, 1753), makes these associations plainly visible when it states that "book-writers deceive ... [w]hen from manifold books they write something together / thereupon passing it off as their own invention."[11]

It is not difficult to see why the core practices of compilers were incompatible with Romantic models of literary writing. According to Romantic aesthetics, artistic genesis happened "in the mind rather than on the page," and the work existed in perfect form only for a fleeting moment in the writer's imagination, in "pre-linguistic shape."[12] The perfect work, then, was always already a thing of the past, and the creative struggle that defined literary writing was to commit this imagined work to paper as immediately and spontaneously as possible. The more a writer labored over, supplemented, and revised the first draft, the more he or she "weakened the primacy of the original vision," as Hannah Sullivan has recently glossed Romantic attitudes toward writing.[13] Compiling, however, was an art and craft of accretion, and for a compiler, the perfect work had to be located in the future, in the form of pieces still to be gathered and material to be incorporated. Another point of friction between Romantic aesthetics and compiling consisted in the status attributed to sources and compositional rules. The original genius allegedly drew on nothing but his own imaginative faculties and stood above all rules. Paradigmatically, the eighteenth-century aesthetic theorist Johann Georg Sulzer defined the "original work" (*Originalwerk*) as follows: "In the first sense, this name befits such works as are of an essential character peculiar to them, not borrowed." Such works have

---

10 Martin Gierl, "Kompilation und die Produktion von Wissen im 18. Jahrhundert," in *Die Praktiken der Gelehrsamkeit in der frühen Neuzeit*, ed. Helmut Zedelmaier and Martin Mulsow (Tübingen: Niemeyer, 2001), 80.
11 Georg Paul Hoenn, *Betrugs-Lexikon, worinnen die meisten Betrügereyen in allen Staenden nebst denen darwieder guten Theils dienenden Mitteln entdecket* (Coburg, 1753; reprint: Leipzig, 1981), 83.
12 Hannah Sullivan, *The Work of Revision* (Cambridge, MA: Harvard University Press, 2013), 29, 3.
13 Ibid., 29.

been created "from the artistic genius's true fancy (*aus wahrem Trieb des Kunstgenies*), from real feeling that is neither feigned nor imitated."[14] It is clear that in this theoretical frame, works based on an assemblage of external sources and shaped by the imitation of generic models could never attain original status.[15] J. C. Lavater, Immanuel Kant, and other theorists argued along similar lines.[16] Of course, we know at this point that there was significant tension between Romantic theory and practice, and that the vast majority of Romantic authors relied more on existing textual sources, and did more reworking of their drafts, than they admitted.[17] Still, the Romantic conceptualization of the author as inspired genius had such an enduring impact that by the late nineteenth century, "writing with scissors and glue" had become an established catchphrase of impoverished creativity—in Otto Ladendorf's *Historisches Schlagwörterbuch* (*Historical Dictionary of Phrases*; 1906), the entry "Scissors and Paste" is explicated thus: "To work with 'scissors and paste' is considered a sign of a great lack of literary independence (*Unselbständigkeit*)."[18]

The erasure of compiling from sanctioned literary practice did not mean, however, that compilers suddenly ceased to exist after 1800. In fact, the industrialization of print brought compiling's second heyday in its wake. As the cylinders of the first rotation presses were set in motion, and the first mass media scene in the modern sense was developed, compiling had another cultural moment. The rising flood of available information, from historical data to contemporary social statistics, had to be managed; the emerging mass readership, with its

---

14 Johann Georg Sulzer, "Originalwerk," in *Allgemeine Theorie der schönen Künste* (Leipzig: Weidmann, 1774), 2:863–4.
15 Günter Butzer points out the glaring contradiction in this notion of the genius: to be above all aesthetic and discursive rules, one has to be aware of them, which presupposes a high degree of education. Contemporary theorists were well aware of this contradiction, and they resolved it through the notion of the ingenious author who has "forgotten" his education and is therefore capable of endowing his own creations with unintentional meaning. See Butzer, "Unterhaltsame Oberflächen und symbolische Tiefe. Die doppelte Codierung realistischer Literatur in Storms *Immensee*," in *Geselliges Vergnügen: Kulturelle Praktiken der Unterhaltung im langen 19. Jahrhundert*, ed. Anna Ananieva, Dorothea Böck, and Hedwig Pompe (Bielefeld: Aisthesis, 2011), 323–4.
16 See Immanuel Kant (1790), "Fine Art Is the Art of Genius (§ 46)," in *Critique of Judgment*, ed. Nicolas Walker (Oxford: Oxford University Press, 2007), 136–7; Johann Caspar Lavater, "Genie," in *Physiognomische Fragmente zur Beförderung der Menschenkenntniß und der Menschenliebe* (Leipzig: Weidmann, 1778), 4:80–99.
17 Sullivan points to the contradictions between theory and practice in *The Work of Revision*, 29–31.
18 Otto Ladendorf, *Historisches Schlagwörterbuch. Ein Versuch* (Strasbourg; Berlin: Trübner, 1906), 172.

enormous appetite for fiction, demanded to be served. In two realms in particular, both of which Fontane grew to know very well in the course of his career, compiling thrived in the second half of the nineteenth century: in every newsroom across the German-speaking countries, and at the desks of many *Kolportage* authors.[19] Newspapers were essentially compilations, assembled from dispatches of news agencies, press releases, and passages from rivaling papers.[20] Similarly, many *Kolportage* novels were based on the compilatory strategy of copying and pasting. Prolific authors engaged in compiling to produce a lot of text very quickly. Drawing on a repertoire of formulaic components, they recombined the same figures, settings, and situations in infinite permutations. Karl May, for example, discloses in his 1910 autobiography, *Mein Leben und Streben* (*My Life and My Efforts*), that he churned out his so-called Münchmeyer novels in the 1880s by basing them on a repository of preproduced topics and other formulaic elements. He allegedly built this cache by reading his way through a prison library while serving a jail sentence.[21] Upon his release, he was able to produce his novels faster than anyone else. Whereas his fellow writers had to "search for subjects laboriously," he had created "well-stocked registries" (*reichhaltige Verzeichnisse*) of subjects into which he now only had to reach: "I had only to execute; I had only to write."[22] Compiling is still a core technique in the mass production of commercial fiction (in particular that of the pornographic variety).[23]

It is somewhat ironic, then, that at a time when compiling was thriving (again), and may even have become more commonplace than

---

19 *Kolportage* novels were a particular type of popular part-issue serial that was distributed by "Kolporteure," i.e., itinerant book peddlers—*col-portare* means "to wear around the neck," referring to the hawker's tray or basket in which the peddlers carried their reading fare. This included not only sensationalist novels, but also prayer books, calendars, playing cards, encyclopedias, etc. See Reinhard Wittmann, *Geschichte des deutschen Buchhandels*, 3rd ed. (Munich: Beck, 2011), 271–4.
20 See Jörg Requate, *Journalismus als Beruf. Entstehung und Entwicklung des Journalistenberufs im 19. Jahrhundert – Deutschland im internationalen Vergleich* (Göttingen: Vandenhoeck & Ruprecht, 1995), 118.
21 Karl May, *Mein Leben und Streben* (Freiburg i. Br.: Fehsenfeld [1910]), 1:152. May's *Nachlass* contains a "Repertorium C. May" that was presumably put together during May's jail sentence at Schloß Osterstein in Zwickau. On thirty folio pages, the *Repertorium* lists more than 200 "Themenstichworte," sorted into 137 groups, and contains numerous details that May then used for *Kolportage* novels. See Hermann Wiedenroth, "XI. Fragmente, Entwürfe und Pläne," in Gert Ueding (ed.), *Karl-May-Handbuch*, 2nd ed. (Würzburg: Königshausen & Neumann, 2001), 491.
22 May, *Mein Leben und Streben*, 205.
23 See Chris Offutt, "My Dad, the Pornographer," *The New York Times Magazine*, February 8, 2015.

ever, writers who aspired to be "serious" had to hide their process more thoroughly than ever before if they wrote "with scissors and glue." The Romantic fantasy of authorship as highly subjective, inspired creation made a vigorous return in the second half of the nineteenth century, precisely when the very same media and technologies of print that facilitated compilatory practices also put pressure on the aesthetic autonomy of literary writing. Eclipsing and absorbing what had been a comparatively small and specialized literary scene, the emerging periodical industry restructured the conditions under which authors worked.[24] Periodicals turned into the main venues for the publication of literary fiction. They completely overshadowed the single-volume book, the material form on which literary authority had previously rested, and presented light and serious fiction, informational articles and entertaining ones, in a diverting mix. Moreover, periodicals employed leagues of fast-working, professional content producers and artisans who threatened to outnumber those who perceived themselves as true literary artists. The more pressure the periodical industry exerted on the aesthetic autonomy of literature, the more authors insisted on publicly upholding distinctions that the new realities of text production under industrialized conditions tore down: sophisticated literature versus light fiction, art versus craft, inspired writing versus scissors and glue.

It seems only logical, then, that numerous late nineteenth-century writers attempted to restore their authority in the very media that threatened it and staged themselves as creative geniuses in the mass press[25]—undoubtedly in full awareness that virtually nobody truly worked that way. (Behind closed doors, writers even joked about these scripted acts of staging. When Wilhelm Raabe, himself an expert on manipulating his public persona, discussed with one of his photographers how he wanted to be portrayed, he mockingly asked: "Now then, you don't really want me as if 'reading at his desk' or 'writing with the quill in hand and gazing at the clouds,' do you

---

24 For an instructive overview of the history of the periodical industry, see Andreas Graf, "Die Ursprünge der modernen Medienindustrie: Familien- und Unterhaltungszeitschriften der Kaiserzeit (1870–1918)," in *Geschichte des deutschen Buchhandels im 19. und 20. Jahrhundert*, ed. Georg Jäger, Dieter Langewiesche, and Wolfram Siemann (Frankfurt am Main: MVB, 2003), 1.2:409–522. A detailed discussion of this development and its implications for literary production follows in Chapter 1.
25 Stefan Scherer points this out in "Dichterinszenierung in der Massenpresse. Autorpraktiken in populären Zeitschriften des Realismus – Storm (C. F. Meyer)," in *Schriftstellerische Inszenierungspraktiken: Typologie und Geschichte*, ed. Christoph Jürgensen and Gerhard Kaiser (Heidelberg: Winter, 2011), 229–49.

now?"[26]). Fontane, too, had his iconic author photo made for a cover story in a popular periodical, the *Berliner Illustrirte*, which featured the celebrated writer and his home in a series about "charismatic figures" (*Charakterköpfe*) in present-day Berlin.[27] By the time he had his author photo taken, the gulf between the internal practices and external face of literary production, between what writers actually did and what they could admit, was arguably at its widest—and compiling was one of the practices that could not easily be admitted.

From Compiling to Remixing: An Alternative Historiography of Literary Production

Fontane's notebooks and the other material traces of his creative process are proof, however, that the relationship between inspired writing and compiling, art and artifact, hack-writing and sophisticated literature is more complicated and not nearly as antagonistic as Romantic projections and our usual approaches to literary production under industrialized conditions would suggest. One of the basic assumptions of this book is that if we take compiling seriously—in both its mechanical and its creative variants—as a mode of late nineteenth-century text production, a new avenue opens up for thinking not only about Fontane and his realism, but also about the period at large.

It has become customary in historiographies of German literature to conceive of the final two-thirds of the nineteenth century as a period between two peaks, after Goethe and before Modernism, and to treat it as a time when the rising middle classes took to reading and writing, yet writers also struggled to develop creative momentum.[28] By the 1820s and 1830s, art as it had been known, this (Hegelian) narrative maintains, had run its course and reached its historical end. If it had always been art's task to present the ideal state of the world in opposition to reality, post-Romantic art no longer possessed genuine poetic power because the proverbial "present prosaic conditions"—"the non-heroic, unexceptional world of ordinary life with its ever-expanding network

---

26 See Hans Müller-Brauel's reflections in *Wilhelm Raabe: Gespräche. Ein Lebensbild in Aufzeichnungen und Erinnerungen der Zeitgenossen*, ed. Rosemarie Schillemeit, *Sämtliche Werke* (Braunschweiger Ausgabe), Ergänzungsband 4 (Göttingen: Vandenhoeck & Ruprecht 1983), 219.
27 See Möller, "Preußisches Panoptikum," 57.
28 Katja Mellmann fittingly describes the prevalent view of German literary production in the mid- to late nineteenth century with the metaphor of the "Dornröschenschlaf." See Katja Mellmann, "Literarische Öffentlichkeit im mittleren 19. Jahrhundert – Zur Einführung," in *Vergessene Konstellationen literarischer Öffentlichkeit zwischen 1840 und 1885*, ed. Katja Mellmann and Jesko Reiling (Berlin: De Gruyter, 2016), 1.

of utilitarian relations"[29]—had infiltrated all elements of expression and thought. Art, then, had to re-invent itself; it had to figure out a way to embrace the quotidian without becoming pedestrian and losing its status as art, as Paul Fleming has put it. It is generally agreed, moreover, that the German literary scene felt the creative troubles of the period particularly keenly because of Germany's special status as a belated nation, in both political and literary terms. Compared to France, England, Italy, and Spain, Germany stood out because it had not experienced "a golden age prior to the rise of the middle class and the market in its modern form."[30] Additionally, the late onset of capitalism and the industrialization of print meant that "they spread through German lands more quickly and more forcefully than they had elsewhere."[31] German writers during the second half of the nineteenth century were therefore more firmly in the grip of market forces than their European colleagues. Indeed, many contemporary voices bemoaned these new conditions for literary production. Paradigmatically, Hermann Hauff, the long-term editor of Cotta's *Morgenblatt für gebildete Stände*, pointed out that the "ill-matched marriage (*Mißheirath*) between literature and industry" had drained all poetic spirit from literary production and reduced it to a "making" (*Machen*) in a completely different sense than that of *poiesis*. This new mode of making, according to Hauff, was an "*industrial* making in cold blood" in which "the mind's matter is twisted and tugged, sawn and drilled, polished and crimped, worked over hundredfold."[32]

Established accounts relate that in response to this sustained intrusion of the prosaic into art, and against the backdrop of political "belatedness," German writers developed a peculiar strand of realism, interchangeably labeled "poetic" or "bourgeois."[33] They cultivated "a persistent fascination for common life, average situations, and … mediocre protagonists," attempting to resolve the key aesthetic paradox of the period: with their writings, they tried to "step into the middle of life"[34] while also elevating it, aiming for a balance between the real and the ideal. These attempts, however, attracted substantial criticism,

---

29 Paul Fleming, *Exemplarity and Mediocrity: The Art of the Average from Bourgeois Tragedy to Realism* (Stanford, CA: Stanford University Press, 2009), 1; 121.
30 Ibid., 9.
31 John B. Lyon, *Out of Place: German Realism, Displacement, and Modernity* (London: Bloomsbury Academic, 2013), 12.
32 Hermann Hauff, "Gedanken über die moderne schöne Literatur," *Deutsche Vierteljahrs-Schrift* 11, no. 3 (1840): 275–7.
33 On the different labels and periodizations, see Todd Kontje, "Introduction: Reawakening German Realism," in *A Companion to German Realism 1848–1900*, ed. Todd Kontje (Rochester: Camden House, 2002), 5–7.
34 Fleming, *Exemplarity and Mediocrity*, 1.

especially on ideological grounds, for lacking political engagement and forceful social criticism. Compared to the English and French novelists of the mid-nineteenth century, who addressed "the impact of public social and political issues" on a large scale, the German realists concerned themselves with "small happenings, tragedies, and heroisms of humble life"[35] in regional and sentimental settings. In consequence, Germany's poetic realists have never fully shed their reputation of being somewhat parochial or even provincial by European standards.[36] In these comparative narratives, Theodor Fontane often figures as the only author whose novels are considered to be on a par with the best European mainstream fiction of the time.[37] His achievement is conventionally seen in the intriguing complexity of his portraits of Wilhelmine society. Unfolding in entertaining plots about interclass love affairs and adultery, his urbane and gently ironic social novels combine compassionate observation with narrative ambiguity and subtly nuanced dialogue to lay out "real-life" moral dilemmas that defy easy judgment.[38] Within German literary studies, it is typical to frame Fontane's achievement more specifically in terms of his position within the media landscape. The readings that have become dominant over the past two decades present him as a realist author who "survived" the market because his novels can be read on two levels at once, as entertaining fiction that conforms to the conventions of the periodical industry and as challenging works of art that self-reflexively expose the very generic and epistemic conventions on which they rest.[39] Deploying the arsenal of stereotypes, representative formulas, and commonsensical knowledge that circulated through the mass media of his time, Fontane coined his own brand of "media realism." With his prose functioning as a "medium of simulation in exchange with other media of simulation,"[40]

---

35 Lilian Furst, "Parallels and Disparities: German Literature in the Context of European Culture," in *German Literature of the Nineteenth Century, 1832–1899*, eds. Clayton Koelb and Eric Downing (Rochester, NY: Camden House, 2005), 54.
36 For a critical assessment of this view and a very accessible summary of more recent theoretical discussions of German realism, consult Lyon, *Out of Place*, 11–14.
37 Furst, "Parallels and Disparities," 55.
38 For example, see "Fontane, Theodor," in *The Oxford Companion to German Literature*, 3rd ed., ed. Henry Garland and Mary Garland (Oxford: Oxford University Press, 2005), online edition, n.p.
39 The seminal study to be mentioned here is Rudolf Helmstetter's Habilitation, *Die Geburt des Realismus aus dem Dunst des Familienblattes. Fontane und die öffentlichkeitsgeschichtlichen Rahmenbedingungen des Poetischen Realismus* (Munich: Fink, 1998); Gerhart von Graevenitz's *Theodor Fontane: ängstliche Moderne. Über das Imaginäre* (Konstanz: Konstanz University Press, 2014) represents the most recent major contribution to this strand of the scholarship.
40 Graevenitz, *Theodor Fontane: ängstliche Moderne*, 18.

he replicated but also subverted the forms of worldmaking that his readers recognized as familiar and "real" from their constant exposure to the mass press. The current assessment of Fontane's contribution to the German literary tradition, then, implies a negative stance toward the mass-media marketplace and in particular the periodical industry, for it casts the periodical industry as an adversary to be "overcome" or outsmarted[41]—a stance that is curiously partial to the self-staging of late nineteenth-century artists.

Bringing together the history of material media, media theory, and the social history of literature, this book, by contrast, treats the decades between *c.* 1860 and 1900 not as a "valley" between two peaks, but as a formative period of intense technological change, fluidity between media formats, ongoing textual reconfiguration, and loosening of entrenched distinctions. These characteristics turned the late nineteenth century into a period that not only facilitated compiling, but also enabled its modern artistic twin, the cultural practice of *remixing*. At first sight, it might seem strange to invoke remixing as a guiding concept for a redescription of the late nineteenth century, especially since much less anachronistic alternatives, including citation and montage, are readily available. A closer look at remixing and its key features reveals, however, that it is an apt concept that sheds new light on the nineteenth century and Fontane's place in it.

The beginnings of remixing as a defined artistic practice are typically located in the realm of commercial music and the disco culture of the 1970s, when the widespread use of multi-track mixers "made . . . each element of a song—vocals, drums, etc.—available for separate manipulation."[42] Artists were able to *re*-mix existing songs by swapping tracks out, changing their volume levels, playing them backwards, and integrating new ones. As a cultural practice, remixing is significant because it provides a new way of engaging creatively with massive amounts of pre-mediated ("second-hand") materials that are in cultural circulation. Like montage, remixing is often deployed in the interest of

---

41   Manuela Günter reads this negative stance toward the mass-media marketplace as a symptom of a deeper-seated bias of literary studies toward mass media. In the introduction to her study, she makes a case for treating literary history as part of media history. See Manuela Günter, *Im Vorhof der Kunst. Mediengeschichten der Literatur im 19. Jahrhundert* (Bielefeld: Transcript, 2008), 11–20.
42   Lev Manovich, "What Comes after Remix?" [Typescript, 2007], 2; http://manovich.net/content/04-projects/057-what-comes-after-remix/54_article_2007.pdf. For a brief historicization of remix, see the editors' introduction to *The Routledge Companion to Remix Studies*, ed. Eduardo Navas, Owen Gallagher, and xtine burrough (London: Routledge: 2015), 1–15.

experimentation with ready-made parts.[43] But it does differ from montage, and also from related practices such as citation, in several respects. Remixing entails rebalancing, filtering, or otherwise modifying the source materials, whereas in montage, the point is *not* to alter the sources.[44] In fact, remix artists frequently tinker with the ingredients of the mix, creating ever-new versions, until the new mix produces the desired effect. The remix artist and the tinkerer are soul mates. The effects produced through remix range from homage to parody, and they may include some friction. At the end, however, a remix is an entertaining blend that can be enjoyed.[45] This commitment to the creation of a cohesive whole, along with the emphasis on entertaining effects, makes remixing a practice that is quite distinct from montage, which is, after all, concerned with exposing "the moment of construction" and preventing "narrative and ideological closure."[46]

The precondition for remixing is a culture that is saturated with cultural production in the form of media objects. These media objects ought to be cheap and generally accessible; their use must not be negatively sanctioned; and they must be available to physical or material transformation.[47] At least on a basic level, these conditions were fulfilled earlier than has been hitherto believed—that is, with the emergence of the periodical industry. Periodicals as dynamic "storage devices"[48] collected, mixed together, and then widely disseminated the full range of cultural and informational production of the time,

---

43 On the history and function of montage in the German tradition, see Patrizia McBride, "Montage/Collage," in *German Aesthetics: Fundamental Concepts from Baumgarten to Adorno*, ed. J. D. Mininger and Jason Michael Peck (London: Bloomsbury Academic, 2016), 204–9.
44 David J. Gunkel, *Of Remixology: Ethics and Aesthetics after Remix* (Cambridge, MA: MIT Press, 2016), 15. Manovich goes so far as to characterize remix as a comprehensive and systematic reworking of the source materials, and this comprehensiveness sets remix apart from such strategies as citation and appropriation. See Manovich, "What Comes after Remix?" 3.
45 Manovich, "What Comes after Remix?" 5.
46 McBride, "Montage/Collage," 204–5.
47 These are the conditions for remix according to Felix Stalder, "Neun Thesen zur Remix-Kultur," in *Der Autor am Ende der Gutenberg Galaxis* (Zurich: Buch & Netz, 2014), 31–2.
48 On the conceptualization of the periodical as a storage device, see Sean Franzel, "Von Magazinen, Gärbottichen und Bomben: Räumliche Speichermetaphern der medialen Selbstinszenierung von Zeitschriften," in *Archiv/Fiktionen: Verfahren des Archivierens in Literatur und Kultur des langen 19. Jahrhunderts*, ed. Daniela Gretz and Nicolas Pethes (Freiburg i. Br.: Rombach, 2016), 209–31; see also the seminal essay by Gustav Frank, Madleen Podewski, and Stefan Scherer, "Kultur – Zeit – Schrift. Literatur- und Kulturzeitschriften als 'kleine Archive,'" *IASL* 34, no. 2 (2009): 1–45.

providing readers with heterogeneous media objects for relatively little money. Authors could tear from the papers what they wanted and as they saw fit; because copyright protection was haphazard in late nineteenth-century Germany, the use of periodical content—and indeed of most other printed materials—was rarely prosecuted. Authors like Fontane, who copied or pasted media content into their manuscripts and transformed them through edits, thus blurred the lines between original and derivative, their own words and the words of others, art and artifact. The textual fluidity between co-existing media formats helped create an artistic culture in which "making" increasingly became the same as "re-making." Authors encountered their own texts and the texts of others in different states and formats all the time—in manuscript, as galley proofs, as newspaper serials, as anthology chapters, or, more rarely, as single-volume books. With these format changes came textual instability: for example, when a novella that had first appeared in a periodical was slated for publication in book form, it might be reset, wholly or in part, and the author might decide to make modifications (such as giving the story a new ending). In the infinite churn of print, and with the reissuing of materials in different outlets, formats, and versions, there was always an opportunity to mix things up again. Fontane remixed not only other people's media, but also his own—he reused the same working notes and components of his own published pieces in multiple projects, pursuing a recombinant model of production.

    The periodical industry and, more generally speaking, the literary marketplace, were not just obstacles to be overcome. They also acted as creative facilitators: they enabled a new relationship between literary creativity and mass (re)production, and they provided the conditions under which the operations of copy, edit, and paste could turn into their own form of art. As a modern compiler, Fontane was the first German literary author of note to recognize the creative potential in the "massness" of print and to master the media-historical moment—he became Germany's first remix artist. In his creative process, he took what must be called a radical technical stance toward text production, for he treated the text as a mixture of elements, every one of which could be freely manipulated and adjusted. To an astonishing extent, his strategies of literary text production anticipate a provocative thought experiment that the literary scholar Michel Chaouli undertook several years ago under the programmatic title "Remix: Literatur."[49] Speculating about the future possibilities of reading and writing in the digital realm, Chaouli imagines a *Literaturcomputer*, a machine that allows the user to

---

49 Michel Chaouli, "Remix: Literatur. Ein Gedankenexperiment," *Merkur* 63 (2009): 463–76.

manipulate the linguistic features of any literary text with the help of controls. Among the controls that Chaouli envisions are an "adverb (level) control" with which the user can turn the number of adverbs up or down, a "description condenser," an amplifier/muffler for narrative voice, and so forth. The device, however, not only lets the user manipulate the features; it also suggests additions, mixing in materials from a deep reservoir of options. Ultimately, Chaouli's imagined device results in both a new kind of literature and a new kind of user, a user who values aesthetic effects that are created through constant manipulation. Fontane, a notorious tinkerer who paid much attention to the aesthetic effects of literary texts, maintained a creative apparatus of text production with which he came quite close to this vision, as we shall see later.

Exploring and reconfiguring the intersection of technology and creativity, the book reconstructs concretely how Fontane's "media realism" came into being—and "concretely" here means on the level of paper, ink, pencil, scissors, and glue. In light of the material evidence of Fontane's paper tools, it provides a link between two concepts that the Fontane scholarship has researched individually but not sufficiently connected, namely, the media-historical conditions under which he worked and his poetics of the novel.[50] (This connection is missing not only in Fontane's case; as Hannah Sullivan has recently noted, studies that link a text's thematic or formal concerns to its genesis are generally rare.[51]) In previous inquiries, the connections between Fontane's output and the periodical press have been drawn mostly in terms of the relationship between the literary text and the surrounding architext, that is, in terms of Fontane's preference for certain discursive modes, topics, and aesthetic devices, as well as his strategic negotiations with editors. These studies are based on Fontane's finished and published writings. This present study, in contrast, demonstrates how Fontane's entire work *process*—from his archive to his practices of

---

50 Roland Berbig's *Theodor Fontane im literarischen Leben. Zeitungen und Zeitschriften, Verlage und Vereine* (Berlin: De Gruyter, 2000) and his monumental *Theodor Fontane Chronik* (5 vols., Berlin: De Gruyter, 2010) provide extremely insightful background on the publishing conditions under which Fontane worked, but as historical studies and reference works, they are not intended to carry these findings into the realm of poetics. Helmstetter's *Die Geburt des Realismus*, which is situated precisely on the interface between the history of the public sphere and Fontane's poetics of the novel, has a blind spot when it comes to his creative process—Helmstetter even declares that researching Fontane's working methods is unnecessary because they can be fully deduced from Fontane's self-descriptions in letters (83–4). Graevenitz's recent study of Fontane's poetics is also not concerned with his creative process.

51 Sullivan, *The Work of Revision*, 5.

revision—emerged in interaction with the contemporary media landscape. It thus provides a textual-genetic foundation for the acclaimed double quality of Fontane's authorship and the twofold readability of his prose works as "periodical-oriented entertainment for everyone" and "art for sophisticated readers." The notebooks demonstrate that Fontane worked at once like an infinitely tinkering remix artist and like a mass producer of *Kolportage* fiction. He perfected the aesthetic effectiveness of his novels through endless revision, but he also preproduced, modularized, and reused generic components of text, many of which he gleaned liberally from elsewhere. The analysis of the notebooks and other paper tools thus brings (back) into focus a side of Fontane that is typically not emphasized in the current scholarship, presenting an author who had surprisingly much in common with late nineteenth-century mass-producers of fiction.[52] Accordingly, Fontane is flanked in this book not just by the usual suspects from the nineteenth-century canon—Heine, Keller, Raabe, and Dickens, to name but a few—but also by writers from the so-called second and even third tiers, such as George Hesekiel and Hermann Goedsche, two polygraphers whom Fontane knew well from his years at the *Kreuzzeitung*.

Fontane's work with mass-mediated sources—the ways he gathered, enhanced, and remixed them—shows that his answer to the aesthetic troubles of his time was different than scholars have until now believed.

---

52 There was a great deal of scholarly interest in Fontane as an author of popular or "trivial" fiction in the 1970s (above all, Peter Demetz comes to mind), but that interest has long since faded. Manuela Günter's *Im Vorhof der Kunst* is among the few more recent studies that have begun to reverse that trend. She treats Fontane's poetics of entertainment not as the "unavoidable" other side of his oeuvre, but as the realm in which we must locate his literary innovativeness. My own inquiry adopts this view as far as the connection between entertainment and innovativeness is concerned (and I find her readings of *L'Adultera* and *Effi Briest* as new forms of literary "infotainment" illuminating), but I disagree with her complete subsuming of Fontane under this category and, by extension, her equation of late nineteenth-century literature with entertainment (*Im Vorhof der Kunst,* 25ff.; 33–42). In her conceptualization of the mass-media marketplace, there is no space left for an autonomous literary function. I agree with her critics that her radical stance toward entertainment and mass media simplifies matters. In the words of Katja Mellmann, one of the disadvantages of Günter's conceptualization is that she attributes from the very beginning "Systemcharakter" to the mass media, as if with one big switch, all communicative codes had been rewritten. It seems more historically accurate not to assume a sudden switch, but the coexistence of different communicative codes, media subsystems, and functions of literature, with entertainment representing the dominant one—but certainly not the only one. See Mellmann, "Literarische Öffentlichkeit im mittleren 19. Jahrhundert," 2.

Fontane's realism consisted not in the mimetic *reconstruction* of the mass-mediated world of the late nineteenth century, but in the *emulation* of this world with its own resources. Emulation implies competition; in the rhetorical tradition, it is the attempt to remake an existing text, transpose it into a different form, and outdo it in beauty or effectiveness.[53] This is precisely what Fontane's novels did with the mass media that surrounded them, and this is where his art so clearly exceeded that of his contemporaries. Fontane did not just "integrate" media content into his realist prose (as many realists did); he put entire representational modes—indeed, entire competing media—into his novels, which he consciously designed to become highly effective media hybrids. Amazingly, his novels nonetheless make for seamless reading. They maintain a carefully mixed middle style, blended from the media sources that Fontane sampled. To arrive at the perfect blend, he not only filtered and enhanced his source material—a process that is revealed in his notebooks—but also subjected his drafts to continual rounds of remixing, moved text passages around, swapped them out, condensed, expanded, deleted, and rephrased them.

Fontane's achievement as an artist lies therefore in two innovations: in his development of an artistic practice and notion of "making" that reconciled individual creation with mass production, and in the radical model of material textuality operant in his work. Fontane's practices of remix hinged on material sources. In a way, however, he treated the material text as if it were not material at all, in that he never let material resistance get in the way of his attempts to design an effect. He did with manuscript sheets, ink, pencil, scissors, and glue what today we do so effortlessly with our word-processing software. The story of his authorship is therefore also an opportunity to de-familiarize the textual practices that in many ways define our own cultural moment.[54] Our practices of copying and pasting, which remediate the "paper-and-scissors era," have become one of the "central command routines of modernity"[55] and are now completely commonplace. (I cannot tell you how many times I moved passages around while writing this introduction.) Fontane's case puts us in touch with the forgotten

---

53 Heinrich Lausberg (1973), *Handbook of Literary Rhetoric: A Foundation for Literary Study*, ed. David E. Orton and R. Dean Anderson, trans. Matthew T. Bliss, Annemiek Jansen, and David E. Orton (Leiden: Brill, 1998), §1101–2.
54 On the textual practices in the era of word processing, see Matthew Kirschenbaum, *Track Changes: A Literary History of Word Processing* (Cambridge, MA: Belknap, 2016), especially 235–47.
55 Jussi Parikka, "Copy," in *Software Studies: A Lexicon*, ed. Matthew Fuller (Cambridge, MA: MIT Press, 2008), 74, 70.

backstory of these practices, the story of compiling, and provides us with a new vantage point to historicize what we do when we write "with scissors and glue."

On Method: How to Reconstruct a Creative Process

As Fontane's author photo has already made clear, stories about creative processes and "the writer at work" are never free from imaginative projections. Over time, these projections can take on a life of their own, and even become extreme. Consider the case of young Georges Simenon, who signed on to an unheard-of PR stunt roughly thirty years after Fontane's death that made him, in the words of his biographer, "into a phenomenon forever after."[56] At the suggestion of his Paris publisher, the notorious Eugène Merle, 23-year-old Simenon agreed to hammer out his next novel in public, within no more than a week, at the improbable rate of one feuilleton per hour, while sitting in a glass cage suspended from the Moulin Rouge. A contract spelling out the details of the acrobatic act was drawn up, and announcements went out. Parisians were first entranced, then enraged upon hearing that a man of letters would be debased in this manner, reduced to the status of a circus performer. As work on the glass cage began and Simenon was busy fending off criticism, Merle went bankrupt, and the whole event was suddenly called off. Strangely, however, the episode entered literary histories (even scholarly ones) as if it had actually taken place: "The most incredible thing about this whole story is that Georges Simenon would forever after be known as 'the man who wrote a novel locked in a glass cage.'"[57]

In accounts of authorship and creative work, then, theatricality and fantasy are always at play. This finding has implications for the kind of historical reconstruction that this book attempts. For one thing, it calls for heightened awareness on the historian's part that she is dealing with freighted subject matter when she tries to piece together a creative process. It also encourages her to zoom in on the circulating projections, dismantle the staging, and contrast the faux representations with material evidence of the actual, "untheatrical" work processes that took place backstage. The material evidence to be considered includes inconspicuous tools, such as the everyday utensils that the writer used, and traces of the writer's gestures and activities. It also entails larger, more obvious media of writing and self-administration, such as

---

56 Pierre Assouline, *Simenon: A Biography*, trans. Jon Rothschild (New York: Knopf, 1997), 76.
57 Ibid., 81.

notebooks, other working notes, draft materials, and folders, and even the chair, desk, and study where the author worked.⁵⁸

Until recently, the Fontane scholarship had not paid much attention to this material evidence. Many of Fontane's media of text production have never been properly edited and published. For a fully canonized author, such neglect is curious and cannot be attributed simply to his clever self-fashioning as a "mouthpiece" of the muses. The other reason for this neglect is the archival situation. Fontane's *Nachlass* is scattered across sixty public institutions, not all of which have inventoried their holdings.⁵⁹ Additionally, in the case of the notebooks, the history of the divided Germany played a role—the sixty-seven extant notebooks were preserved in the former East Germany and were not freely accessible to all scholars until reunification.⁶⁰ Even then, their evaluation remained challenging for several reasons. Fontane's working notes were intended for his eyes only and can therefore be extremely difficult to read. Furthermore, his status in the field of German literary studies has contributed to the overlooking of the notebooks and other documents of his creative process. Because Fontane never laid out an explicit poetics or a theory of writing, he is not considered an intellectual author.⁶¹ Scholars have never attempted to read his notebooks as "brainscapes" in the same way that they have examined the notebooks of Lichtenberg, Goethe, Kafka, Mann, or Musil. Fontane's papers have commonly been mined for commentaries to the standard editions of his

---

58 Rüdiger Campe coined the influential term "scene of writing" (*Schreibszene*) to describe the ensemble of media and archival objects that ought to be considered in the historicization of writing processes. See his essay "Die Schreibszene. Schreiben," in *Paradoxien, Dissonanzen, Zusammenbrüche. Situationen offener Epistemologie*, ed. Hans-Ulrich Gumbrecht and Karl Ludwig Pfeiffer (Frankfurt a. M.: Suhrkamp, 1991), 759–72. His definition of the "scene of writing" also includes the self-reflexive moments in the written text in which the act of writing draws attention to itself. The coda of this study will explore this dimension.

59 *Vermißte Bestände des Theodor Fontane Archivs. Eine Dokumentation im Auftrag des Theodor-Fontane-Archivs*, ed. Manfred Horlitz (Theodor-Fontane-Archiv, Potsdam, 1999), 11.

60 Theodor Fontane's son Friedrich offered sixty-seven notebooks and other archival materials for sale at an auction, held by the Berlin-based autograph dealer Meyer & Ernst, in 1933. For this sale, the autograph dealer divided up the booklets into five groups, labeled A–E, and assigned ascending numbers to the booklets in each group. To this day, this nomenclature has been retained. The *Preußische Staatsbibliothek zu Berlin* (East Berlin) purchased the notebooks and gave them to the *Theodor-Fontane-Archiv*, Potsdam, as a permanent loan in 1965. Gabriele Radecke, "Schneiden, Kleben und Skizzieren. Theodor Fontanes Notizbücher," in *'Gedanken Reisen, Einfälle kommen an.' Die Welt der Notiz*, eds. Marcel Atze and Volker Kaukoreit (Vienna: Praesens, 2017), 214–15.

61 Ibid., 211.

work, in particular the *Große Brandenburger Ausgabe*. But in the commentaries, the notes figure merely as spadework on the way to the seemingly superior aesthetic form of the finished text.[62] These philological circumstances are finally changing, mostly because of the efforts of a few scholars who have made a case in their work for the inclusion of more manuscript materials—and especially the notebooks—in Fontane scholarship.[63] Fortunately, the first edition of the notebooks, a groundbreaking undertaking spearheaded by Gabriele Radecke, is now close to completion,[64] and it is slowly becoming clear what a unique body of evidence they offer. Fontane used the light and portable notebooks, which measure *c*. 10 by 17 cm, from the early 1850s to the late 1880s, with the earliest extant booklet dating back to 1859/60.[65] Bound in simple cardboard covers and held together with thread stitching, the notebooks amount to approximately 10,000 pages in all, and contain traces of almost every aspect of his authorship.[66] In them, he jotted down ideas, spontaneous observations, and drawings when he went on research trips, to theater performances, and to art exhibitions. He also resorted to these media of writing for deskwork; to plan out and

---

62 An exception is the Fontane philology of the 1910s to circa 1940. During this period, there was a noticeable interest in Fontane's manuscripts, including his notebooks. The studies by Fürstenau and Rost are good examples, yet they are largely forgotten today. For a succinct overview of the research on Fontane's manuscripts, see Gabriele Radecke, *Vom Schreiben zum Erzählen. Eine textgenetische Studie zu Theodor Fontanes 'L'Adultera'* (Würzburg: Königshausen & Neumann, 2002), 17–30.

63 See Roland Berbig, "'aber zuletzt – [. . .] schreibt man doch sich selbst zu Liebe.' Mediale Textprozesse. Theodor Fontanes Romanerstling *Vor dem Sturm*," in *Theodorus Victor: Theodor Fontane, der Schriftsteller des 19. am Ende des 20. Jahrhunderts. Eine Sammlung von Beiträgen*, ed. Roland Berbig (Frankfurt a M.: Lang, 1999) 99–120; Christine Hehle and Hanna Delf von Wolzogen (eds.), *Theodor Fontane: Fragmente. Erzählungen, Impressionen, Essays* (2 vols., Berlin: De Gruyter, 2016); Walter Hettche, "Die Handschriften zu Theodor Fontanes *Vor dem Sturm*. Erste Ergebnisse ihrer Auswertung," in *Fontane Blätter* 58 (1994): 193–212; "'Die erste Skizze wundervoll.' Zu einem Kapitel aus Theodor Fontanes Roman *Vor dem Sturm*," in *Schrift – Text – Edition. Hans Walter Gabler zum 65. Geburtstag*, ed. Christiane Henkes et al. (Tübingen: Niemeyer, 2003), 213–20; Radecke, *Vom Schreiben zum Erzählen*.

64 For an overview of the "born digital" edition, its underlying principles, digital facsimiles, and transcriptions of the notebooks, see the official online portal, *Theodor Fontane: Notizbücher. Digitale genetisch-kritische und kommentierte Edition*, at https://fontane-nb.dariah.eu/index.html.

65 Letters by Fontane document that he possessed at least one notebook as early as 1852, and there are compelling reasons to believe that already at that time he used notebooks routinely. See Radecke, "Schneiden, Kleben und Skizzieren. Theodor Fontanes Notizbücher," 200–1.

66 Ibid., 201–2.

draft novel chapters, poems, letters, travelogue episodes and book reviews; to excerpt readings; to store newspaper clippings; to write down addresses and travel connections; and to calculate honoraria. While it is not necessarily remarkable that such a wide spectrum of Fontane's writerly activities is documented in the booklets (after all, countless writers had notebooks and used them in a similarly comprehensive fashion), the breadth of the content becomes significant in conjunction with the peculiar material features of the notebooks. They evince how literally Fontane understood text as process. He made entries in the form of running lists and easily movable blocks; he left wide margins to give himself space for additions and revision; he added tabs to pages for better orientation; and he pasted snippets of other texts into his notes. He also systematically designed entire booklets for cutting and pasting—leaving the verso pages intentionally blank, he prepared the recto pages with a vertical line along the gutter and was careful not to write above it, ensuring that when he later cut out the pages along that line, he would not cut into the text.[67] His notebooks were designed for two-way traffic among his different writing projects, but also between his writing projects and the surrounding media landscape, testifying to a model of authorship in which textual materials could always be reused, converted across genres, and remixed.

    These features of the working notes, however, have not been sufficiently addressed by the few previous inquiries into Fontane's papers. In fact, his use of the notebooks and other paper tools as a textual practice *sui generis*, one that has powerful poetological consequences, has not yet been studied.[68] This book is intended to

---

[67] I owe this observation about the vertical lines to Radecke, "Schneiden, Kleben und Skizzieren," 205. Radecke and her team have begun tracking the materials that Fontane tore or cut out of his notebooks (just in Notebook E 1, these amount to more than seventy pages) and have discovered some of them in manuscripts of novels. For example, they have identified seven pages of notes that Fontane took during a trip to the Harz mountains in 1879 in the manuscript of the 1884 novel *Graf Petöfy*.

[68] A recent exception is Hehle and Delf von Wolzogen's new edition of Fontane's *Fragmente*. In the introduction, the editors use a rhetorical perspective to approach Fontane's "fragments" wholesale, as a flexible "arsenal" that could be mobilized for different purposes. Their approach takes up initial suggestions that I made in my Ph.D. dissertation, "Original Compiler: Notation as Textual Practice in Theodor Fontane" (Princeton University, 2012), and in my essay "A Creative Machine: The Media History of Theodor Fontane's Library Network and Reading Practices," *The Germanic Review* 87, no. 1 (2012): 72–90. Their approach differs from mine, however, insofar as they are concerned with the characterization of one particular stage in Fontane's creative process, and they do not draw out the implications of Fontane's note-taking practices for his overall poetics, whereas my research emphasizes these implications.

address this gap. Focusing on the creative implications of Fontane's note-taking, it looks at the notes from a perspective that is at once media-theoretical, historical, and poetological—it treats them as an *interface* between Fontane's creativity and his interactions with the mass-media marketplace. From a media-theoretical point of view, the function of interfaces is to join different elements together; they structure access to systems and enable and condition workflows (a classic example of an interface is a search engine that allows a computer user to retrieve data). But interfaces also make the user readable, for example "by means of records of patterns of search terms and choices."[69] If the notebooks and other writing media allowed Fontane to access the media landscape around him and to navigate his compilatory world, they also permit us to access and read his authorship.

In placing so much argumentative weight on the notebooks, it is important to keep one thing in mind. Notebooks (and by extension other kinds of notational media) are loaded objects in their own right, and their evaluation poses significant challenges. As highly personal, auratic, and often perplexing writing media, authors' notebooks invite speculation and all sorts of projections on the philologist's part, simply because it can be so hard to make sense of them. It is far from obvious what the philologist or media historian should do with notes. When entries are disconnected, when there is no apparent context for a scribbled remark, and when there are literally thousands of entries, the philologist trying to "read" them is likely to oscillate between interpretive excess and denial. After all, if anything may be important, what could keep the interpretation of an author's mindlessly drawn doodle in check? At the same time, if we read teleologically and assume that the notes are mere preparatory material or byproducts on the way to the real work, why should we care?

Recent methodological developments in material or "German" media theory, book history, and the history of science provide a way out of this impasse. These fields have put forth practice-driven approaches that can be fruitfully applied to the analysis of writers' notebooks.[70]

---

69 Florian Cramer and Matthew Fuller, "Interface," in *Software Studies: A Lexicon*, 151.
70 Key reference points for the practice-driven approach, especially in the context of notebook studies and the history of writing, are Ann M. Blair, "Note Taking as an Art of Transmission," *Critical Inquiry* 31 (2004): 85–107; Lorraine Daston, "Taking Note(s)," *Isis* 95, no. 3 (2004): 443–8; Campe, "Die Schreibszene, Schreiben"; Karin Krauthausen, "Vom Nutzen des Notierens. Verfahren des Entwurfs," in *Notieren, Skizzieren. Schreiben und Zeichnen als Verfahren des Entwurfs*, ed. Karin Krauthausen and Omar Nasim (Zurich: Diaphanes, 2010), 7–26; Bernhard Siegert, *Cultural Techniques: Grids, Filters, Doors, and Other Articulations of the Real*, trans. Geoffrey Winthrop-Young (New York: Fordham, 2015); and Cornelia Vismann, "Cultural Techniques and Sovereignty," *Theory, Culture and Society* 6 (2013): 83–93.

Rather than immediately focusing on the content of a given notebook, the practice-driven approach first asks what happens when a writer takes notes in particular ways. It focuses on recurring procedures and notational routines that emerge *across* individual entries, through the practices that a note-taker repeatedly performs—regardless of whether the notes can be attributed to a "work." Implicit in this approach is the idea that notational procedures—and indeed all cultural practices—have an epistemic "life of their own" (*Eigenleben*), which is to say that they both enable and foreclose further practical and intellectual operations.[71] To give a simple example, Fontane's preferred notational practice, list-making, facilitated his creative mixing of diverse source materials. With the help of lists, he was easily able to bring completely different materials together while drafting portrayals of his fictional characters. At the same time, lists are very reductive forms, so that when he sketched out a chapter with the help of a list, it limited his options for the development of complex narrative connections. The example makes clear that when one applies the practice-driven approach to understanding a medium, the materiality of the medium matters profoundly in determining its use. The material features of a notebook—its size and weight, the number of pages it contains, the nature of the paper, the binding, the stiffness of the cover, etc.—directly influence what the user can and cannot do with it. But the converse also applies. The usage, in its specific historical context, turns a mere material object into a medium in the first place. In the words of Bernhard Siegert, not every history of paper is already a media history: "The history of paper only turns into a media history if it serves as a reference system for the analysis of bureaucratic or scientific data processing."[72] To apply this to the case at hand, we can observe that a Fontanean paper sleeve on its own does not constitute a medium; it is no more than a simple, large-format wrapper folded around a bunch of manuscript pages. But if we look at the ways Fontane used the paper sleeves as storage devices with which he archived his material and (haphazardly) organized the revision process of his manuscripts, they turn into powerful media with agency that at once enabled and limited his actions. According to the practice-driven approach, material medium and cultural usage must be considered together because they generate each other.

Which practices emerge in an individual case is a matter of overlapping personal, functional, intellectual, and historical contexts. Modern (that is, post-1800) note-taking can easily appear completely unregulated and individualized. Yet there is always more to it than

---

71 Siegert, *Cultural Techniques*, 10–11.
72 Ibid., 5.

idiosyncrasy. As Karin Krauthausen explains, "the idiosyncratic stamp imprinted on notes and sketches (*die idiosynkratische Ausprägung des Notierens*), rather than replacing their instrumental character, opens them up to a multiplicity of uses."[73] The highly formalized practice of learned note-taking may coalesce with more individual and context-specific practices, gradually emerging into a stable routine that is as personal as it is functional. For Fontane, one important context was, of course, his career in journalism. Nineteenth-century journalists carried affordable notebooks around with them to "keep pace with the cascade of events"[74] and note the fleeting impressions of the everyday. Fontane's notebooks are visibly shaped by the emerging mode of journalistic topicality. He often scribbled down observations and thoughts with the unsystematic pragmatism characteristic of journalistic note-taking, which focuses more on short-term productivity than on long-term archiving. The ample margins around Fontane's entries, too, can be related to the news trade; using such margins was standard practice in the dispatches that professional news agencies disseminated, because doing so made it much easier for editors to select and excise whatever they needed for their publications. Fontane adopted this and other conventions in his note-taking. These conventions come into view only if one heeds the different contexts and traditions in which his individual case takes part.

Finally, the practice-driven approach calls for the contextualization of the notebooks in the note-taker's larger working environment.[75] Note-taking is usually just one step (albeit a crucial one) within a whole range of interrelated intellectual or creative practices, and its epistemic ripple effects can be seen only if one views it as embedded in these practices. This book therefore situates Fontane's notebooks and other paper tools in the wide ambit of his interactions with the media landscape. This scope includes practices of research, composition, and revision; exchanges with family members, colleagues, and editors; self-reflections in his diaries on the state of the art; activities as a critic; and his attempts to influence the reception of his works. In assembling all of these aspects, I reconstruct what one might term the poetics of "the Fontane workshop," to adopt a felicitous coinage by Stephan

---

73 Krauthausen, "Vom Nutzen des Notierens," 18.
74 Lothar Müller, *White Magic: The Age of Paper*, trans. Jessica Spengler (Cambridge/Malden, MA: Polity Press, 2014), 145–6.
75 See Christoph Hoffmann, "Umgebungen. Über Ort und Materialität von Ernst Machs Notizbüchern," in *Portable Media. Schreibszenen in Bewegung zwischen Peripatetik und Mobiltelefon,* ed. Martin Stingelin and Matthias Thiele (Munich: Fink, 2010), 89–107.

Porombka.⁷⁶ A "workshop poetics" exceeds the reconstruction of an individual author's scene of writing and creative process, for it also considers the logistics of production and distribution, the network of colleagues and helpers, and the communicative logic of the media environment with which the author interacted. It treats all of these factors as central to the production procedure. The concept of "workshop poetics" is therefore well suited to the analysis of late nineteenth-century literary production and its technical contexts. It acknowledges that authors outsourced and mechanized parts of their creative process, and that they observed poetological rules that were prescribed by the literary market when they produced their work. At the same time, it focuses on sources that come as close to the creative process in action as possible and are capable of showing how a literary work in the making adapted and bent the poetological rules.⁷⁷ A "workshop poetics" thus avoids the false choice between treating the creative process as guided either by a merely technical poetics based on rules (*Regelpoetik*) or by an inspired individual genius. It opens up a space in which art and craft, the individual and the mechanical, the personal and the collective dimensions of nineteenth-century literary production can interact.

In this conceptual space, and in the context of a workshop poetics, literary rhetoric acquires an important function. In the discussions of Fontane's poetics, terms from the tradition of classical literary rhetoric (*copia, inventio*, emulation, etc.) will continually appear. This is by design—I have decided to mobilize the age-old arsenal of rhetorical knowledge because it seems uniquely suited to studying Fontane's realism both in the making and in action. For one thing, rhetoric conceives of poetics as a practice or set of interlocking practices that can be learned and applied. The manuals of rhetoric by Cicero, Quintilian, and others thus provide us with a technical optic to reverse-engineer the concrete making of a text and assess its complexity, mapping it onto the full spectrum between the mechanical and the virtuosic. But there is another reason why rhetoric is a helpful analytical tool for the study of Fontane's realist poetics. It is to be found in the category of the effect. As the art of persuasion, rhetoric is naturally concerned with the effects a text has on its audience. In fact, rhetoric can be understood as cultural history's most refined inventory of applied literary means and the corresponding aesthetic effects. As briefly discussed earlier, Fontane invested a major share of his artistic energies into perfecting reality

---

76 Stephan Porombka, "Der Eckermann-Workshop. Die *Gespräche mit Goethe* als Einübung in die Literatur der Gegenwart," *Politische Künste. Jahrbuch für Kulturwissenschaften und ästhetische Praxis* (2007): 183–218.
77 Ibid., 185, 192.

effects in his novels; rhetorically speaking, he attempted to emulate fictional worlds in which the reader forgets about the rift that runs through every representational project, the rift between *res* (things) and *verba* (words). The domain of rhetoric thus enables us to observe, analyze, and appreciate this important dimension of Fontane's realist prose.

Organization of This Book and Chapter Summaries

According to Wolfgang Ernst, studies based on archival work are prone to becoming archives themselves.[78] This insight applies all the more to a study that follows a prolific compiler into the shifting, bottomless repository of material snippets from which he drew his texts together. The systematic problem of how to turn the many snippets into a narrative is complicated further by the particular nature of Fontane's notes. These notes belong to myriad contexts, and they were often used for more than one project, which makes their one-to-one allocation to individual published "works" difficult. What is more, there are entries in various stages of literary development; the scale runs from just a few isolated words to multiple pages of fully formulated prose. Notes explicitly taken for individual novels—what one might assume to be the most interesting material—account for a small portion of entries. The bulk of the notes, it seems, were initially taken for Fontane's *magnum opus*, the multi-volume series of feuilleton essays that he published as *Wanderungen durch die Mark Brandenburg* (*Walks through Mark Brandenburg*), but then again, these are often the materials that Fontane also used for his fiction. If Fontane's other working notes are added, such as the portions of prepared draft materials that he stored in paper sleeves, it becomes even more complicated to decide which material evidence to choose and how to organize it.

Following the practice-driven approach, this book argues that it is the recurring notational procedures that lend the notes coherence. They keep the heterogeneous source materials of Fontane's literary production together—across differences in context, function, genre, biographical stage (the "early" versus the "late" Fontane), and writing medium. In light of recurring procedures, the material underside of his creative process emerges as a corpus that one can study, in which source materials are formatted and put to use in stable, describable ways. Accordingly, this analysis is structured by Fontane's path to becoming a compiler and the arc of the textual practices in which he engaged

---

78 Wolfgang Ernst, "Nicht Organismus und Geist, sondern Organisation und Apparat. Plädoyer für archiv- und bibliothekswissenschaftliche Aufklärung über Gedächtnistechniken," *Sichtungen* 2 (1999): 130.

across his various realist prose projects.[79] Rather than tracing the development of a single work from "notes" to "novel," I analyze Fontane's working methods on a broader plane, focusing on a series of salient moments in the creative process at which Fontane's tools and technologies of writing interacted with the surrounding media landscape, and demonstrating with a range of examples how this interaction gave rise to some of the most characteristic features of his realist practice. With the exception of the coda, I do not offer traditional readings of Fontane's works (although I do draw connections between notational practices and his published writings throughout). What this study has to offer instead is a reading of the relationship between material tools, poetics, and literary creativity.

Chapter 1, "Media-Historical Coordinates: Literature in the Industrial Age of Print," situates Fontane's compilatory enterprise in the German media landscape of the second half of the nineteenth century. Taking its cue from a well-informed satire, Hauff's "Die Bücher und die Lesewelt" ("Books and the World of Reading"), the chapter provides a historical and systematic account of the complex relationship between mass media and literary production. It shows how the co-evolution of the printing press and the periodical industry created conditions of fragmented textuality and saturation that put pressure on literary autonomy, causing writers such as von Droste-Hülshoff, Keller, and Raabe to turn away from mass media. For a compiler like Fontane, however, these conditions proved stimulating and even led to a different perception of the period: whereas many of his colleagues felt like mere epigones, Fontane interpreted the cultural climate of epigonism in terms of a liberation from tradition, as a license to exploit and mix the overabundance of existing textual sources ad libitum.

Chapter 2, "Biography vs. Autobiography: The Making of a Compiler," reconstructs how Fontane acquired his basic compilatory skill set. It follows him to the sites where he was trained for his first two careers, the mid-nineteenth-century pharmacy and the newsroom, and shows how he internalized material practices of mixing, storing, cutting, and pasting at these sites that proved formative for his literary career. Focusing on Fontane's "false foreign correspondence" (*unechte Korrespondenzen*), newspaper articles that pretended to have been sent

---

79 That said, one realm of his production had to remain excluded from this analysis: Fontane's poetry. While this is of course a very important dimension of his oeuvre, its inclusion would have made my source base—which, as things stand, already entails thousands of pages of notes and manuscript materials—entirely unmanageable. I have therefore limited myself to studying the nexus between Fontane's compilatory practices and his poetics in the context of his novellas, novels, and journalistic writings.

in from abroad but were actually assembled in the Berlin newsroom of the *Kreuzzeitung*, the chapter demonstrates how he learned to piece together reports from published articles through cut-and-paste. The compiled reports were fake in many ways, and yet they seemed utterly realist to readers, for they replicated worldviews with which readers were already familiar from their constant consumption of mass media. The "media realism" that Fontane practiced as a journalist carried over into his literary realism, which was also based on the collocation of mass-media sources. The chapter traces this overall mode of production in the working methods of polygraphers, to which Fontane's methods are briefly compared, and concludes with a discussion of how he attempted to hide his compilatory activities in his autobiography, *Von Zwanzig bis Dreißig* (*From Twenty to Thirty*).

After this reconstruction of the historical and biographical formations that enabled compiling both in the media landscape more generally and in Fontane's authorship in particular, the following two chapters turn to the major steps in his practice of literary compiling. The chapters proceed from the "input end" to the "output end" of the enterprise, treating the notebooks and other paper tools as the mediating agents in between.

Chapter 3, "A Living Archive: Generating Input," reconstructs the emergence of the material archive on which Fontane's versatile authorship rested, arguing that two nineteenth-century "crowdsourcing" devices—amateur collecting and the Prussian postal system—were crucial to this process. Branding his first sizeable literary project, *Wanderungen durch die Mark Brandenburg*, a "collection" in need of completion, Fontane incentivized readers to send him material or even entire episodes for inclusion. The *Wanderungen* thus turned into a material-generating apparatus that ran for decades and produced thousands of pages of text for future writing projects. Beyond the *Wanderungen*, Fontane deployed the capacities of the Prussian postal service, turning his social network into a postal lending library and requesting books, maps, and gossip from acquaintances. The chapter analyzes the administrative technologies and the infrastructure that enabled this network to reach into geographically and socially remote areas, and it discusses the epistemic features of the surprisingly slapdash storage media with which Fontane tried to manage a constant influx of material. In contrast to the systematic archives of such authors as Goethe and Raabe, his assemblage of slips, notebooks, and boxes remained a fluid contact zone between the media landscape and his own output, a quality that had significant implications for his authorship and modes of productivity.

Chapter 4, "The Manufacture of Literature: Generating Output," investigates Fontane's material poetics of production by tracing the interaction between his writing tools, his recurring notational forms, and the surrounding mass media landscape. The chapter argues that his preferred forms and media of notation—lists and modular entries, scribbled onto single notebook pages and slips—facilitated a recombinant, building-block-like mode of compiling that could be practiced mechanically, as a form of literary mass production, or creatively, as a complex form of media art. Analyzing the early working notes for *Before the Storm* (*Vor dem Sturm*) and *A Man of Honor* (*Schach von Wuthenow*), the chapter shows how Fontane based his novels on a remix of media that produced effects of verisimilitude. Blending, for instance, the familiar imagery of domestic genre painting with snippets of current newspaper discourse in the portrait of a fictional character, he built his drafts around aesthetic effects (atmospheric scenes, discursive sounds, and credible social types) before he gave thought to the plot. The chapter contrasts this compositional method with Dickens's drafting of novels with the help of "number plans." Applying recent theories of writing, it argues that Fontane's deployment of writing as a nonlinear recording medium enabled him to develop a poetics of realism as media remix that differed markedly from that of fellow realists: his creative practice culminated not in the mimetic reconstruction of the mass-mediated world of late nineteenth-century Germany, but in the virtuosic emulation of this world with its own resources.

A brief coda, "The Calculated Novel: The 'Uncreative' Writing of *Mathilde Möhring*," explores the self-reflexive dimension of Fontane's creative process, reprising some of the central themes with which this study is concerned. It reads one of his last prose works, the unfinished *Mathilde Möhring* (1891/96), as an ironic reflection of the ambivalent status of compiling. The novel's title character, a woman from Berlin's lower stratum named Mathilde, appears as a figurative compiler who embodies several of Fontane's working methods. Determined to ascend to the middle class, she patches together a false newspaper article that helps her apathetic husband impress his superiors. While successful in her textual strategies, Mathilde remains a coldly calculating character, and the reader develops little appreciation for her skills. The novel as a whole, however, is a display of finesse and calculated poetic effects. Remixing central topics from Fontane's previous production in self-aware fashion, it turns into art precisely the kind of calculation that the title character executes prosaically. The coda concludes by resituating Fontane in the larger context of German nineteenth-century realism and describes the so-called "valley between two peaks" as an era of innovative textual practices.

One Media-Historical Coordinates: Literature in the Industrial Age of Print

An Instructive Case of Literary Mass Production
In 1827, the novelist Wilhelm Hauff published a satire titled "Die Bücher und die Lesewelt" ("Books and the World of Reading").[1] Its unnamed protagonist, who aspires to become a bestselling author, sets out to unlock the secret of literary success. In contrast to Balzac's Lucien de Rubempré in *Lost Illusions* (1837/43), Hauff's protagonist is free of idealistic motivation and has no illusions about the literary market. To articulate his straightforward intentions, he uses the vocabulary of craftsmanship instead of the language of aesthetic creativity, and he takes it for granted that for debuting authors like him, the standard mode of text production ought to be imitation:

> I did not yet have any particular object or purpose, and was still quite undecided about which great master my first piece should be modeled upon . . . ; yet it seemed to me that no task was as great and necessary to one intending to produce a book than to study people; not to gain knowledge of human nature, which now is learned from books, but rather to glean what meets with the greatest applause among the populace, being read often and gladly. Here, too, I thought, vox populi, vox dei would obtain.
>
> [I]*ch hatte noch keinen besonderen Gegenstand oder Zweck, und war noch sehr unentschieden, nach welchem großen Meister ich mein erstes Stück verfertigen sollte . . . ; doch schien mir das Größte und Notwendigste für einen, der ein Buch machen will, daß er die Menschen studiere; nicht um Menschenkenntnis zu sammeln, die lernt man jetzt*

---

1   Wilhelm Hauff, "Die Bücher und die Lesewelt," in *Sämtliche Werke*, ed. Sibylle von Steinsdorf (Munich: Winkler, 1970), 3:55–71.

in Büchern, sondern um den Leuten abzusehen, was etwa am meisten Beifall finde, oft und gern gelesen werde. Vox populi, vox dei, dachte ich, gilt auch hier.

(55)

For Hauff's protagonist, the obvious question is not *whether* he should invoke a great master but *which* master to invoke. He also assumes that the highest purpose of a book is to be read frequently and with pleasure. In his view, craftsmanship, epigonism, and popularity are the default objectives of literary writing.

Hauff's satire is part of the mediated self-observation that characterizes the nineteenth century as an epoch,[2] and it merits a closer look. Written by a "virtuoso"[3] of the German literary scene when it was on the cusp of mass production, it combines a sociology of reading, a history of technology, an economic analysis of publishing, and a knowledge of poetics to tell a multifaceted story of literature's entrance into the industrial age of print. The result is an amusing lampoon, but its anti-canonical image of nineteenth-century literary production is too well informed to be dismissed as mere satire. Rather than applying the simplifying tropes of cultural criticism, Hauff's account provides a practitioner's view of the media infrastructure and conditions under which the vast majority of literary authors, from Adalbert Stifter to Theodor Fontane and Karl May, worked during the second half of the nineteenth century.

Hauff's would-be bestselling author discovers that the conditions for literary production are determined by the interacting components of a proto-entertainment industry. He learns that there is an enormous demand for entertaining novels because readers from all social strata read chiefly for diversion, "like a horse when it gets flighty" (57), and they devour installment after installment of light fiction. He also discovers two ways to cater to the demands of these insatiable readers: one can either mix novels together, like a chef creating an appetizing dish, to strike a balance between ingredients that will "create the most effect" and those that will easily appeal to the common palate; or one can simply translate successful foreign-language fiction as efficiently as possible. To his astonishment, he learns that precisely this kind of

---

2   See Jürgen Osterhammel, *The Transformation of the World: A Global History of the Nineteenth Century*, trans. Patrick Camiller (Princeton, NJ: Princeton University Press, 2014), 3.
3   Andrea Polaschegg, "Hauff im Fokus. Eine Einleitung," in *Wilhelm Hauff oder Die Virtuosität der Einbildungskraft*, ed. Ernst Osterkamp et al. (Göttingen: Wallstein, 2005), 7.

rationalized translation work is already happening at a "translation factory" (*Übersetzungsfabrik*) in the town of Scheerau, where a labor force of thirty-four translators churns out fifteen sheets of new Walter Scott translations every day. The production process is governed by the principles of mechanization and the division of labor into highly specialized tasks, as one of the protagonist's interlocutors explains:

"At the back of the yard is the paper-mill, which produces *endless paper* that rolls, (already) dry, like a stream of lava onto the main building's ground floor; there, a mechanism cuts it up into sheets and pushes it right underneath the printing presses. Fifteen presses are in operation, each of which produces twenty thousand copies per day. They are dried next door, where the binders' workshop may also be found. It has been calculated that the pulp that is still liquid at five o'clock one morning is an elegant little book by eleven o'clock the next, that is, within thirty hours."

„Hinten im Hof ist die Papiermühle, welche unendliches Papier macht, das schon getrocknet wie ein Lavastrom in das Erdgeschoß des Hauptgebäudes herüberrollt; dort wird es durch einen Mechanismus in Bogen zerschnitten, und in die Druckerei bis unter die Pressen geschoben. Fünfzehn Pressen sind im Gang, wovon jede täglich zwanzigtausend Abdrücke macht. Nebenan ist der Trockenplatz und die Buchbinderwerkstätte. Man hat berechnet, daß der Papierbrei, welcher morgens fünf Uhr noch flüssig ist, den andern Morgen um eilf Uhr, also innerhalb dreißig Stunden, ein elegantes Büchlein wird."

(62)

On the first floor of the factory, "workmen" generate the content for this rapid mass production. They turn out rough drafts of translations that a few "stylists" polish and even fewer "poetic workmen" embellish with epigraphs. As a result, the Scheerau factory is able to flood the market with Scott volumes at rock-bottom prices and keep them coming.

Armed with these insights, the protagonist joins forces with a bookseller named Salzer to mass-produce a German Walter Scott— "original" German works written in the style of Walter Scott. Their literature factory combines individually fabricated parts in a recipe-style procedure of text production and refines them through a series of manipulations. The process is made efficient through the division of labor, taking the principles of rationalized manufacture used in the Scheerau translation factory to another level. Salzer suggests hiring six accomplished novelists who will together embody the German Walter Scott and make the basic decisions about plot lines and main characters. The protagonist eagerly develops this idea further. He suggests they erect a "factory, much like that at Scherau," in which twenty-four content producers, under the direction of the six experienced novelists, write conversations and draw towns, regions, and buildings "from nature," using etchings (*Kupferstiche*) of Germany's romantic regions, "costumes of the days of yore," and legends from *The Youth's Magic Horn* and other anthologies as templates. Because all members of the workforce have specialized skills—"one's gifts may incline more toward landscape painting, those of the other to costumes, the third to conversations, . . . others more to tragic"—the protagonist proposes the following division of labor:

> "[T]he young artists are thus divided into landscape painters, costume tailors, conversationalists, comedians, and tragedians, and each novel passes through the hands of all in the manner of the paintings at Campe's in Nuremberg, where one draws the sky, another the earth, this one roofs, the other soldiers, where the first paints the green, the second the blue, the third red, the fourth yellow, each after the other."
>
> „[S]o werden die jungen Künstler in Gegendmaler, Kostümschneider, Gesprächsführer, Komiker und Tragiker eingeteilt und jeder Roman läuft durch aller Hände wie die Bilder bei Campe in Nürnberg, wo der eine den Himmel, der andere die Erde, jener Dächer, dieser Soldaten zeichnet, wo der erste das Grüne, der zweite das Blaue, der dritte Rot, der vierte Gelb malen muß nach der Reihe."
>
> (68)

In Hauff's satire, the novel is no different from Marx's wire in the manufacture of needles; it is an "article" (*Machwerk*) that goes "through a series of processes step by step," passing through the hands of several workers.[4] Ironically, the protagonist, instead of becoming the co-owner of the factory, embarks on a career as one of the twenty-four specialized content producers; he embodies what Marx and Engels would term the "detail labourer" who is riveted to a single fractional task. It is precisely this absorption in the machinery that finally makes the protagonist happy: "I had become a limb, a finger of that new and unknown body, I was able to write according to my fancy and to read in print what I had written" (69). In less than two years, the factory successfully issues seventy-five volumes of German historical fiction. In a final bow to the economic forces it has honored, it closes down when novels in the style of Scott go out of fashion.

---

4   Karl Marx (1867), *Capital: A Critical Analysis of Capitalist Production*, trans. from the third German edition by Samuel Moore and Edward Aveling, ed. Frederick Engels (Moscow: Foreign Language Publishing House, 1958), 1:343–4.

Rotational Presses, Outpaced Books, and New Reading Habits

Hauff's satirical account proves insightful on several levels. Obviously, it leverages the comic potential of the clash between literary creation and mass production, subjecting what is considered the realm of the spirit and aesthetic intuition to the rules of rationalization and economic calculation. The mass production of literary texts by unskilled writers was by no means a new concern; as early as the 1760s, intellectuals voiced complaints that "factory-made literature" was swamping the market. Indeed, according to the social historian Richard Biernacki, the production of fiction became "one of the first livelihoods to be commercialized as lowly wage work outside the institutions of guild, estate, or community custom" in the second half of the eighteenth century.[5] The concern about literary mass production acquired a new urgency in the first third of the nineteenth century. As the demand for fiction rapidly grew, more and more people joined the ranks of professional writers, and publishing companies began to speculate with mass production—in fact, Hauff based his satire on a real-life enterprise, the so-called "translation factory" run by the Schumann Brothers in Zwickau, which had issued a low-cost paperback edition of Scott's works.[6] Through an ironic lens, Hauff's account precisely depicts the economic anxieties of authors who understood themselves as artists, not mass-producers, and who grew increasingly concerned in the course of the nineteenth century about their ability to make a living with sophisticated literature. Among these concerned authors was Theodor Fontane. In correspondence with Hermann Kletke, the editor of the *Vossische Zeitung*, Fontane predicted that the already mediocre "cotton cloth of novellas" (*Novellenkattun*) that was published all around him would deteriorate further, along with the audience's ability to distinguish between high- and low-quality literary writings. "And the ones who end up footing the bill are *those* who, rather than opening a factory, persisted quietly in their honest labors," he remarked, pointing out that he was simply not capable of competing with "an average and mass manufacturer" (*Durchschnitts- und Massen-Fabrikanten*, HFA IV.3: 50) because he could not possibly write more than two respectable novellas per year and thus had to ask much higher prices in order to feed his family.

What makes Hauff's satirical account so illuminating is not, however, merely the description of economic anxieties. Rather, its most instructive

---

5 Richard Biernacki, "The Social Manufacture of Private Ideas in Germany and Britain, 1750–1830," in *Wissenschaftskolleg zu Berlin. Jahrbuch 1998/99*, ed. Wolf Lepenies (Berlin: Wissenschaftskolleg zu Berlin, 2000), 221.
6 See the editorial commentary in Hauff, *Sämtliche Werke*, 451.

aspect lies in its concept of literature. The satire rests upon the unspoken, compelling assumption that literature is a medium with a material basis and that *everything* about this medium changes when the basis shifts from limited reproduction to mass reproducibility.[7] In 1827, the true quantitative leap in print runs was still to come, but enough mass reproduction had already occurred to induce a qualitative change in the relationship between literature and its material basis. This change was what fascinated Hauff.[8] If, as Friedrich Kittler claims, the key question in the discourse network of 1800 had been how to distribute a text to reach the maximum number of addresses,[9] the industrialization of print turned this question on its head. The problem now was how to produce enough discourse in the first place to provide content to all of the addresses that the mass media had constituted. Hauff's satire emphasizes, then, that in the course of the nineteenth century, literature became a function of the new technological possibilities of mass production. Hence the order in which Hauff's satire describes the production process: it first lists the machinery of the paper mill, the printing presses, cutting devices, etc., that churn out sheet after sheet after sheet, and then it describes the fleet of content producers who work in shifts to feed the running machinery.

In 1827, the final product in Hauff's satire was still a bound book. This format was about to change. Over the next two decades, literature increasingly left the single-volume book form behind and migrated into mass media such as the newspaper and the illustrated journal, which provided the conditions for a true mass reproducibility that for Hauff was still a fantasy.[10] In the second half of the nineteenth century, the

---

7   Walter Benjamin provides the canonical media-historical analysis of this shift in his 1936 essay "The Work of Art in the Age of Its Technological Reproducibility" (Second Version), in *Walter Benjamin: Selected Writings*, ed. Howard Eiland and Michael W. Jennings, vol. 3: 1935–1938, trans. Edmund Jephcott (Cambridge, MA: Belknap Press of Harvard University Press, 2002), 101–33.
8   Benjamin makes this argument about a quantitative development that leads to a qualitative change for the impact of lithography on image reproduction ("The Work of Art in the Age of Its Technological Reproducibility," 102), yet Manuela Günter shows how it can also be applied to the reproduction of literature. See Manuela Günter, *Im Vorhof der Kunst: Mediengeschichten der Literatur im 19. Jahrhundert*. (Bielefeld: Transcript, 2008), 12.
9   Friedrich Kittler, *Discourse Networks 1800/1900*, trans. Michael Metteer, with Chris Cullens (Stanford, CA: Stanford University Press, 1990), 70.
10 For a detailed account of this process, see Reinhard Wittmann, *Geschichte des deutschen Buchhandels*, 3rd ed. (Munich: C.H. Beck, 2011), 257–94; for an analysis that emphasizes the implications for Fontane and the modes of poetic realism, see Rudolf Helmstetter, *Die Geburt des Realismus aus dem Dunst des Familienblattes. Fontane und die öffentlichkeitsgeschichtlichen Rahmenbedingungen des Poetischen Realimus* (Munich: Fink, 1998), 37–95.

mass media absorbed literature—and, in the multiple senses of the word, "employed" it. The external conditions for this employment were provided by the Prussian state. When, on January 1, 1850, Prussia surrendered its advertising monopoly in newspapers and journals, these mass media entities entered into a competition for advertisers in which they aggressively sought to increase their readerships; like network television a century later, they tried to "capture eyeballs" for advertisers by attracting regular viewers.[11] One way to do this was, of course, through literature, especially serialized fiction, which was an effective means to bind readers and for which the mass media could now pay lucrative honoraria.[12] In the same year that Prussia relinquished the advertising monopoly, Karl Gutzkow's *Die Ritter vom Geiste* (*The Knights of the Spirit*) appeared as one of the first German novels to be published in serialized form in a newspaper, the *Deutsche Allgemeine Zeitung*.[13] Other states—and other papers—quickly followed suit, and literature took up residency in the budding entertainment industry and its most important medium, the periodical, the first "time-stamped commodity"[14] of modernity.

The book as a material medium "limped along behind"[15] in this process, for it was the periodical press that pushed for and financed virtually all of the technological advancements in industrialized production processes that resulted in greater, faster, and cheaper print runs. In their recent historiographies of papermaking and printing, Lothar Müller and Helmut Müller-Sievers have characterized the process by which printing became industrialized as one of increasing

---

11 See Wittmann, *Geschichte des deutschen Buchhandels*, 278.
12 How quickly the periodical industry grew in size and spending power becomes clear from the steep increase in advertising space that periodicals were able to lease out: ten years after the advertising monopoly had been lifted, a given issue of the *Vossische Zeitung*, for example, contained "16 pages of editorial material compared with 56 pages of advertising." See Gideon Reuveni, *Reading Germany: Literature and the Consumer Culture in Germany before 1933* (New York: Berghahn, 2006), 126.
13 See Charlotte Woodford, introduction to *The German Bestseller in the Late Nineteenth Century*, ed. Charlotte Woodford and Benedict Schofield (Rochester, NY: Camden House, 2012), 4.
14 Margaret Beetham, "Towards a Theory of the Periodical as a Publishing Genre," in *Investigating Victorian Journalism*, ed. Laurel Brake et al. (Basingstoke: Palgrave Macmillan, 1990), 21.
15 Rob Banham, "The Industrialization of the Book 1800–1970," in *Companion to the History of the Book*, ed. Simon Eliot and Jonathan Rose (Malden, MA: Blackwell, 2007), 277.

"cylindrification."[16] While Gutenberg's letterpress had relied on the principle of "flat surface against flat surface,"[17] or platen against sheet, the use of the cylinder in Friedrich Koenig's 1814 high-speed press introduced rotary motion into the printing process. The form of type now shuttled underneath two revolving cylinders, one of which smeared the form with ink before the other pressed the sheet to the inked form. This principle was refined to full continuity of motion by William Bullock's 1865 web-fed rotational press, which no longer printed from a flat form but rather from curved stereos.[18] Such fully rotational presses sped up the printing process exponentially. Consisting of nothing but interacting cylinders, they superseded even the most advanced early-nineteenth century models, which were based on oscillating motion.[19] The production of paper, too, was "cylindrified." Papermaking, until the beginning of the nineteenth century, happened on a sheet-by-sheet basis and was an elaborate art, but with Louis-Nicolas Robert's invention of a continuous papermaking machine, it became possible to produce a perpetual roll of paper by cranking a handle.[20] Yet again, the increase in production speed was enormous. Zedler's *Universal-Lexicon Aller Wissenschafften und Künste* (*Universal Encyclopedia of All Sciences and Arts*) states in the entry on "paper maker" from 1740 that each sheet of (rag-based) paper had to "pass thirty-two times through the hand . . . before it can be used for writing"[21] and that papermakers received more than four years of professional training. With the continuous papermaking machine, such highly skilled labor was no longer needed, and the machine produced "more paper in a day than a single vat for hand production could make in a week."[22] Continuous papermaking machines were introduced to Germany in 1818, and although they "spread rapidly from the 1820s, paper production did not reach industrial dimensions until the late nineteenth

---

16 Lothar Müller, *White Magic: The Age of Paper*, trans. Jessica Spengler (Cambridge; Malden, MA: Polity, 2014), 182, 196–200; Helmut Müller-Sievers, *The Cylinder: Kinematics of the Nineteenth Century* (Berkeley: University of California Press, 2012), 73–7.
17 Müller, *White Magic*, 197.
18 See Müller-Sievers, *The Cylinder*, 75.
19 Müller-Sievers writes that "by 1866, the fully cylindrical Walter Press printed six thousand sheets per hour" (*The Cylinder*, 76), as opposed to the three hundred sheets per hour that, according to Banham, could be printed on an iron handpress ("The Industrialization of the Book 1800–1970," 276).
20 See Müller, *White Magic*, 137–40.
21 Johann Heinrich Zedler, "Papiermacher," in *Großes vollständiges Universal-Lexicon Aller Wissenschafften und Künste . . .*, vol. 26 (P–Pd) (Halle and Leipzig, 1740), col. 646–7.
22 Banham, "The Industrialization of the Book 1800–1970," 274.

century."²³ In his satire, Hauff anticipates the effects of the continuous papermaking machine when he links his description of a "paper-mill, which produces *endless* paper" to an overall decrease in the cost of printing. The continuous papermaking machine amplified the effect of the fully rotational printing press, and it helped to replace "the combination of the manual press and hand-made paper," which had been "stable for centuries,"²⁴ with a much more effective machine.

In all of these instances, however, the new technologies found their first adopters in newspaper companies. In London, John Walter, the owner of *The Times*, was the first to invest in Koenig's high-speed presses, in 1814; similarly, the first company to use Bullock's rotary press was the *Philadelphia Public Ledger*.²⁵ In Germany, the publishing giant Cotta purchased a steam-powered high-speed press in 1823, using it initially not for book production, but for the production of the *Allgemeine Zeitung* in Augsburg.²⁶ Even the development of paper itself—the leap from rag-based paper to paper based on wood pulp— put the periodical industry at an advantage, simply because mass-produced paper based on wood pulp disintegrated much faster than rag-based paper and was thus better suited for ephemeral forms of publication than for books.²⁷ By the end of the nineteenth century, then, nearly all of the steps in the printing process—including casting and setting type—had been mechanized and industrialized, resulting in printing machines that could churn out 24,000 copies of a complete newspaper, cut and folded, in just one hour.²⁸ The bound book had been left in the dust, largely because the fully industrialized printing presses required greater financial investments than book publishers were prepared to make. In fact, Friedrich Koenig and his business partner, Bauer, recognized early on that their presses were not suitable for most book publishers, and they made efforts to reverse some of the gains in speed for the sake of a higher quality, developing models that were profitable with lower print runs.²⁹ Even these presses remained the exception until the mass-market paperback at the turn of the twentieth century encouraged book publishers to acquire industrial-scale printing

---

23 Müller, *White Magic*, 140.
24 Ibid., 182.
25 See Banham, "The Industrialization of the Book 1800–1970," 276.
26 See Peter Neumann, "Industrielle Buchproduktion," in *Geschichte des deutschen Buchhandels im 19. und 20. Jahrhundert*, ed. Georg Jäger, Dieter Langewiesche, and Wolfram Siemann (Frankfurt am Main: MVB, 2001), 1.1:170.
27 See Müller, *White Magic*, 190–2.
28 See Banham, "The Industrialization of the Book 1800–1970," 277.
29 See Koenig and Bauer's advertisement, "Pressen der HHrn. Bauer und König in Oberzell bei Würzburg," *Polytechnisches Journal* 21, no. 114 (1826): 474–6.

presses and to invest in other equipment to mechanize typesetting, folding, book binding, and the production of covers and jackets.[30] Hauff's satirical vision of a machinery that produced and printed unlimited amounts of paper, in short, was first fully realized not in a "book factory" but in the emerging periodical industry. It is more than fitting, then, that Hauff's satire itself initially appeared in serialized form, in the periodical *Morgenblatt für gebildete Stände*.

Some of the implications of these technological developments for the history of literature are obvious: with periodicals publishing literary and non-literary, light and dense texts side by side in enormous print runs, a mass readership emerged that formed new reading habits. The "mass" in mass readership must first and foremost be understood quantitatively, as a historically unprecedented increase in audience size that coincided with two other socio-demographic developments: the growth of the population on the territory of the *Kaiserreich* from 33 to 45 million between 1848 and 1880, and governmental campaigns for mass literacy.[31] Social historians estimate that by 1830, about thirty percent of all Germans who were at least six years old could read, and with each decade, this rate increased by an additional ten percent.[32] More people than ever, then, became able to read after 1830, constituting what has been termed the "second reading revolution."[33] During the first reading revolution, in the eighteenth century, the middle classes had gained access to more newspapers, journals, and books and supplemented their intensive reading of a small canon of works with extensive reading of current print products. In the nineteenth century, this process repeated itself, but this time it included a wider spectrum of social classes.[34] And if purchasing bound single-volume books had already

---

30 See Banham, "The Industrialization of the Book 1800–1970," 277; Neumann, "Industrielle Buchproduktion," 172–4, 177.
31 On increasing literacy, see Osterhammel, *The Transformation of the World*, 788–91. It is worth noting that recent scholarship has questioned the effectiveness of governmental intervention and stresses "the rising opportunity cost of *not* knowing how to read" as the truly decisive factor in the increase of mass literacy. See Leah Price, "Victorian Reading," in *The Cambridge History of Victorian Literature*, ed. Kate Flint (Cambridge: Cambridge University Press, 2012), 40.
32 See Monika Estermann and Georg Jäger, "Geschichtliche Grundlagen und Entwicklung des Buchhandels im Deutschen Reich bis 1871," in *Geschichte des deutschen Buchhandels im 19. und 20. Jahrhundert*, ed. Georg Jäger et al. (Frankfurt a. M.: MVB, 2001), 1.1:21–2.
33 See Wolfgang Langenbucher, "Die Demokratisierung des Lesens in der zweiten Leserevolution," in *Lesen und Leben*, ed. Herbert G. Göpfert et al. (Frankfurt a. M.: Buchhändler-Vereinigung, 1975), 12–35.
34 Ibid., 16. The terminology of intensive and extensive reading goes back to Rolf Engelsing, *Der Bürger als Leser: Lesergeschichte in Deutschland 1500–1800*

been unusual during the first reading revolution, in which lending libraries, reading circles, and cheap part-issue publications catered to the rising demand, bound single-volume books now receded even further into the background, as they were financially out of reach for all but a few wealthy readers.[35] The new reading masses formed their textual habits by reading the newly available periodicals, inducing what Günter Butzer has termed the society-wide "change in media" (*Medienwechsel*) from books to periodicals.[36]

The emerging reading habits can be only partly captured with the term "extensive." They entailed a whole new stance toward printed matter, a stance shaped as much by the nature of the periodical as by the legal framework of the German press law and the business models it engendered. Readers of periodicals broadly defined, from newspapers to part-issue novels, *consumed* printed matter, seeking gratification on the first reading (which often, but not always, remained the only reading).[37] Consumption was made convenient and easy by the German authorities' insistence on subscription rather than street sale as the

---

(Stuttgart: Metzler, 1974), 183. The distinction between "intensive" and "extensive" reading has been called into question since the late 1980s; more recent scholarship has brought it back into use, however, to describe the strong correlation between the emergence of new reading habits, such as skimming, and the rise of ephemeral genres, such as the periodical. See Price, "Victorian Reading," 37 and David Vincent, *The Rise of Mass Literacy: Reading and Writing in Modern Europe* (Cambridge: Polity Press, 2000), 103.

35 See Wittmann, *Geschichte des deutschen Buchhandels*, 288–90.
36 Günter Butzer, "Von der Popularisierung zum Pop. Literarische Massenkommunikation in der zweiten Hälfte des 19. Jahrhunderts," in *Popularisierung und Popularität*, ed. Gereon Blaseio, Hedwig Pompe, and Jens Ruchatz (Cologne: DuMont, 2005), 115. Butzer's formulation implies a binary distinction between the book and the periodical, yet the forms actually marked the opposite ends of a spectrum. Periodicals gravitated to the book form when they were collected and bound together, while "books" issued in parts shared key characteristics of periodicals. More precisely, then, one should speak of the society-wide switch from the monograph to the periodical. See Nicola Kaminski, Nora Ramtke, and Carsten Zelle, "Zeitschriftenliteratur/Fortsetzungsliteratur: Problemaufriß," in *Zeitschriftenliteratur/Fortsetzungsliteratur*, ed. Nicola Kaminski, Nora Ramtke, and Carsten Zelle (Hannover: Wehrhahn, 2014), 11.
37 Drawing on Luhmann's systems theory, Butzer provides an accessible explanation of how and why periodicals and other media of mass communication immediately grow "old" after the first reading. See Günter Butzer, "Unterhaltsame Oberflächen und symbolische Tiefe: Die doppelte Codierung realistischer Literatur in Storms *Immensee*," in *Geselliges Vergnügen. Kulturelle Praktiken der Unterhaltung im langen 19. Jahrhundert*, ed. Anna Ananieva, Dorothea Böck, and Hedwig Popme (Bielefeld: Aisthesis, 2011), 326–32. Indeed, one hardly ever reads a newspaper twice—and if one does, one typically reads with a different interest or focus, e.g., as a collector.

default mode for obtaining periodicals. Anxious to retain control over the mass market, German press law by and large prohibited the selling of periodicals in the street, as happened in England and France; rather, German readers had to subscribe to newspapers and journals, and the subscriptions had to be managed by licensed mediating agents, such as the post office, bookstores, and registered colporteurs.[38] The latter in particular—the itinerant salesmen and book peddlers (*Kolporteure*) who carried periodicals and other print products such as calendars and cookbooks from door to door—provided easy access to the products of the press. They visited a huge variety of households, even in remote areas, and significantly lowered the hurdles for first-generation readers, who no longer had to cross the threshold of a bookstore or lending library to access journals and books.[39] The business model of subscription and home delivery in turn influenced the ways publishers designed and priced their products. To meet the needs of a broad spectrum of households, publishers programmatically mixed light and sophisticated contents in periodicals, and they offered a variety of subscription models to suit all pockets. The same periodicals were available in variably priced editions. The cheapest editions could be afforded by even the lower working classes, while the many available pricing options encouraged middle-class readers to subscribe to more than one periodical at a time.[40] Readers of periodicals thus learned to ignore boundaries of genre; they read multiple papers to stay informed; and they read "hastily, changeably, inconstantly—in great quantities, yet in small bites, enjoyed and digested in passing (*im Flug*),"[41] as a critical observer noted gloomily in 1865.

---

38 Graf explains these laws, from the "Stempelsteuer" to the "Postzwang." Andreas Graf, "Die Ursprünge der modernen Medienindustrie: Familien- und Unterhaltungszeitschriften der Kaiserzeit (1870–1918)," in *Geschichte des deutschen Buchhandels im 19. und 20. Jahrhundert*, ed. Georg Jäger, Dieter Langewiesche, and Wolfram Siemann (Frankfurt a. M.: MVB, 2003), 1.2:416–23.
39 Graf, "Die Ursprünge der modernen Medienindustrie," 420–1. *Kolporteure* increasingly sold subscriptions rather than the actual periodicals at the door, applying at times aggressive marketing strategies. As Kosch and Nagl detail in the excellent introduction to their comprehensive *Kolportage* bibliography, the reputation of *Kolporteure* declined in the 1880s and 1890s in keeping with the extent to which their business succeeded. At the end of the century, traditional booksellers waged a war against *Kolporteure*, which were eventually banned. See Günter Kosch and Manfred Nagl, introduction to *Der Kolportage-Roman: Bibliographie 1850–1960* (Stuttgart: Metzler, 1993), 11–26; 42–46.
40 For examples of subscription models, see Graf, "Die Ursprünge der modernen Medienindustrie," 412–13.
41 Franz Dingelstedt, "Die deutsche Schillerstiftung," *Allgemeine Zeitung* 1865, qtd. in Wittmann, *Geschichte des deutschen Buchhandels*, 292.

Above all, however, readers of periodicals across the board read for entertainment. Hans-Otto Hügel has shown that reading for entertainment is an "attitude of reception . . . in which a particular use of media is assumed, and no particular object."[42] He has further qualified this mode of media usage by what he calls "partial" concentration. While the reception of a text (or other cultural product) as art requires that a fully focused reader engage with it ever more deeply, the reception of a text as entertainment allows a measure of equanimity and distance, and it may "be broken off at any detail, any step, without the imperfection of the process of reception becoming apparent."[43] At the same time, the reader *may* become fascinated if the text strikes a particular chord or maps well onto a preexisting interest. According to Hügel, reading for entertainment is a mode of reception that is characterized by seriousness and levity in equal measure. It is not the same as mere distraction, nor does it operate without attentiveness. Rather, it operates with a different kind of attentiveness, one that does justice to life under the conditions of modernization, such as the experience of acceleration.[44]

While this mode of reading did not require a specific object, it found an ideal match in two kinds of periodicals: the illustrated family magazine and the universal culture magazine (*Rundschauzeitschrift*), in which virtually all literary writers in late nineteenth-century Germany initially published their works. Programmatically a mixed form, these magazines were modeled on several predecessors—including the *Moralische Wochenschrift*, the penny magazine, and English and French journals such as the *Magasin pittoresque* (1833), the *Illustrated London News* (1842), and Dickens's *Household News* (1842)—and combined images, prose fiction, popularized news stories, and educational articles to offer the reader a panoramic view of the world that catered to diverse interests.[45] Just how panoramic this view was becomes apparent from the editorial in the first issue of the *Gartenlaube*, the prototypical and most widely circulated family magazine of the period. The editors

---

42 Hans-Otto Hügel, "Unterhaltung durch Literatur: Kritik, Geschichte, Lesevergnügen," in *Medien zwischen Kultur und Kult: Zur Bedeutung der Medien in Kultur und Bildung. Festschrift für Heribert Heinrichs*, ed. Rudolf Keck and Walter Thissen (Bad Heilbrunn: Klinkhardt, 1987), 96.
43 Hügel, "Unterhaltung durch Literatur," 107.
44 Walter Benjamin makes this point in his "Artwork" essay. See Günter, *Im Vorhof der Kunst*, 38.
45 For a thorough, historically informed theoreticization of these forms, see Gerhart von Graevenitz, *Theodor Fontane: ängstliche Moderne. Über das Imaginäre* (Konstanz: Konstanz University Press, 2014), 341–505; Beetham, "Towards a Theory of the Periodical"; and Helmstetter, *Die Geburt des Realismus*, 47–95.

announced that it would cover "the history of the human heart and of the peoples" and "the struggles of human passions and times past" in the fictional stories, while in the educational articles, they promised insight into "the workshops of human knowledge," "open nature," "the woods and the earth's entrails," "the build of man and his organs," and "what else there is of interest in the doing of men."[46] The articles would be informative enough to be taken seriously, but the most important purpose of the illustrated family magazine was to entertain. The same editorial also emphasized that all contributions, regardless of the topic, would be flavored with a "hint of poetry" (*Hauch von Poesie*), and it stated that the magazine's goal was "to entertain and instruct entertainingly," with entertainment clearly coming first.[47] It would be a misunderstanding to conclude, however, that the contents of family and culture magazines were always "trivial." Rather, they typically constituted a "gray area"[48] (*Grauzone*), in which entertainment, education, and art, light and serious materials appeared together. Different magazines had different accents. *Ueber Land und Meer*, for example, presented itself as more sophisticated than the *Gartenlaube*.[49] In general, the term "entertainment" should not be taken to mean simplistic contents. If anything, the measure of good entertainment went *up* over the course of the nineteenth century, not only because of competition in the media marketplace, but also because cheap part-issue publications of German classics and foreign-language fiction in translation set high standards. Family and culture magazines, then, were not only ideally suited for a mode of reception that oscillated between seriousness and levity; they were also structured around entertainment, resulting in a "programming" of the contents that made it possible to perceive the *entire* journal as entertainment.[50] Yet again anticipating the programming practices of network TV stations approximately one century later, family magazines provided the first truly modern mass media in which entertainment had become an autonomous function and the primary *raison d'être*.[51] If the entertainment industry had been in a nascent state in Hauff's "Die Bücher und die

---

46 Ernst Keil and Ferdinand Stolle, "An unsere Freunde und Leser!" *Die Gartenlaube* 1 (1853): 1.
47 Ibid.
48 Günter, *Im Vorhof der Kunst*, 42.
49 See Helmstetter, *Die Geburt des Realismus*, 54–5.
50 See Hügel, "Unterhaltung durch Literatur," 104.
51 Ibid., 105; Hans-Jürgen Schrader, "Autorfedern unter Preß-Autorität: Mitformende Marktfaktoren der realistischen Erzählkunst – an Beispielen Storms, Raabes und Kellers," *Jahrbuch der Raabe-Gesellschaft* (2001): 3.

Lesewelt," it reached maturity after 1860 in the illustrated family and culture magazines, which in turn became the industry's most important products. The print runs of the best-known titles confirm this historiography, especially when contrasted with those of novels. The ordinary print run of an average novel was calculated based on the needs of lending libraries and typically did not exceed 1,000 to 1,500 copies. For novellas, the default was sometimes even lower—Fontane learned this the hard way and apologized for his presumptuousness after he had unsuccessfully approached his publisher, Hertz, about an initial print run of 1,500 copies for a volume of novellas (BaH 189). By contrast, the *Gartenlaube* started with 5,000 copies per issue in 1853, peaking at 382,000 in 1875. The *Ueber Land und Meer*, mentioned earlier, reported selling 130,000 copies by 1886; the conservative *Daheim* saw an increase from 24,000 copies in the first year (1864) to 39,000 in 1870; and even *Westermanns Monatshefte*, the most intellectually ambitious of the journals, sold 15,000 copies per issue.[52] Considering that one copy usually circulated to multiple readers—subscriptions were often shared beyond individual households—and that there were anywhere between 50 and 100 magazines,[53] it is fair to assume that these print media easily reached more than a million reader-consumers. Literature was an integral part of the magazines and the entertainment industry that they propelled, but of course not the only part. If, in the eighteenth and early nineteenth centuries, those who read books and journals had constituted the first sizeable literary public, those who read illustrated family and

---

52 Figures taken from Eva Becker, "Literaturverbreitung 1850 bis 1890," in *Literarisches Leben: Umschreibungen der Literaturgeschichte* (St. Ingberg: Röhrig, 1994), 110; Graf, "Die Ursprünge der modernen Medienindustrie," 424–37, 470; Wittmann, *Geschichte des deutschen Buchhandels*, 278–9. The figures vary considerably depending on the source and mode of quantification (most magazines appeared in a number of editions, which makes it difficult to calculate how many copies of a given issue circulated). The point nonetheless stands that these magazines operated on an entirely different scale compared with their eighteenth-century forerunners, which rarely went beyond a few hundred copies per issue, and the entire magazine industry grew at an unprecedented pace. Lynne Tatlock writes that "from 1826 to 1927, the number of [journal] titles multiplied eighteenfold—that is, more than doubled every twenty-five years." Lynne Tatlock, introduction to *Publishing Culture and the "Reading Nation." German Book History in the Long Nineteenth Century*, ed. Lynne Tatlock (Rochester, NY: Camden House, 2010), 6–7.

53 Graf, "Die Ursprünge der modernen Medienindustrie," 423–24. Hügel gives a much higher figure, speaking of 200 to 350 family magazines ("Unterhaltung durch Literatur," 103), yet that figure seems to be based on a rather loose definition of what counts as a family magazine.

culture magazines constituted a true mass public that was "no longer exclusively literary."[54]

Reformatting Literature: The Authority of the Periodical

Through the marginalization of the single-volume book form, the relocation of literature to the periodical, and the textual habits of the new mass readership, the mediality of literature changed in fundamental ways. These changes exceeded individual adjustments to publishing policies; rather, literature had to be reformatted wholesale to remain compatible with the periodical as a mass medium.[55] Mass media operate with specific communicative parameters: their audience is large, socially diffuse rather than distinct, scattered, anonymous, and aware of its anonymity.[56] Mass audiences, moreover, typically trend toward disintegration and differentiation into interest groups that must be addressed for the medium to remain effective.[57] Periodicals responded to this communicative situation with several strategies, all of which shaped the modes of literature in the mass press.

Among the most important strategies was the creation of "continuities of format, shape and pattern of content"[58] from one number to the next. While the periodical was (and is) a various form, it had to provide a somewhat predictable mixture in the interest of "offering readers a recognizable position in successive numbers" and "creating a consistent 'reader' within the text."[59] Periodicals addressed readers as individuals but positioned them as members of clearly defined social groups: "[T]his positioning [was] effected by all aspects of the periodical: price, content, form and tone," and, one ought to add, the title and programmatic design features, such as the masthead. For culture magazines such as *Die Gegenwart*, the invoked reader was well-educated, affluent, supportive of Bismarck, urbane, and slightly polemical.[60] For family magazines

---

54 Helmstetter, *Die Geburt des Realismus*, 44.
55 See Butzer, "Von der Popularisierung zum Pop," 117.
56 See Günter, *Im Vorhof der Kunst*, 13.
57 As Graf points out, family magazines were by and large unable to bind the diversifying mass audience together beyond the centennial threshold. At the beginning of the twentieth century, the readership had diversified so much that the family magazines' standing rubrics turned into thematically focused magazines of their own (e.g., "Modeblätter," "Rätselzeitschriften," and "Kriminalzeitschriften"), which catered to defined interest groups rather than a mass audience. See "Die Ursprünge der modernen Medienindustrie," 426–7.
58 Beetham, "Towards a Theory of the Periodical," 28.
59 Ibid., 29.
60 Roland Berbig, "2.21 Die Gegenwart," in *Theodor Fontane im literarischen Leben: Zeitungen und Zeitschriften, Verlage und Vereine*, ed. Roland Berbig and Bettina Hartz (Berlin: De Gruyter, 2000), 212–13.

Literature in the Industrial Age of Print

Figure 1.1 Masthead of the *Gartenlaube*, 1853.

such as the *Gartenlaube*, which were typically conservative, the implied reader—as the name suggests—was the intact middle-class family. The position that this magazine offers its readers is that of a family member and friend; as modeled in the masthead (Figure 1.1), the reader is invited to step into a domestic circle and join the pleasant conversation, which unfolds around an issue of the magazine and in an idyllic, enclosed space.

The *Gartenlaube* and other periodicals of the same mold thus reframed the communicative situation of mass media. They created an illusion of direct face-to-face communication in a medium that actually reached hundreds of thousands.[61] To this end, the magazines cultivated a diction of familiarity, directly addressing their readers with "Du" or "ihr" and soliciting an auditory mode of reception,[62] as displayed in the *Gartenlaube* masthead. Keil and Stolle emphasized the auditory reception of the contents when they announced in their editorial that the *Gartenlaube* readers should "hear"—not read—about the various topics covered in the magazine.[63]

This comprehensive communicative framing impacted literature insofar as the magazines' editors favored textual genres suited to the emulation of oral face-to-face communication, such as the letter and the dialogue-driven novella.[64] In the case of family magazines, moreover, the idea that the magazines would be enjoyed by the whole family had a profound impact on the moral codes with which the magazines operated and even led to what Helmstetter has termed the "normative secret 'poetics' of the family magazine novel (*Familienblattroman*)."[65] A whole range of topics and stylistic registers was off-limits. Keil and Stolle of the *Gartenlaube*, for example, promised to deliver contents tailored to anyone who still had "an appetite for that which is good and noble," which meant staying away "from all contentious politics and all conflict of opinion in religious and other affairs."[66] The often-quoted writing directive that the *Gartenlaube* is said to have circulated internally, which was leaked by a disgruntled contributing author in 1898, further specifies the moral code:

---

61 See Butzer, "Von der Popularisierung zum Pop," 119–20.
62 Ibid., 119.
63 Keil and Stolle, "An unsere Freunde und Leser!" 1.
64 See Butzer, "Von der Popularisierung zum Pop," 119.
65 Helmstetter, *Die Geburt des Realismus*, 71.
66 Keil and Stolle, "An unsere Freunde und Leser!" 1. One should not conclude, however, that the *Gartenlaube* was therefore apolitical. For an analysis of the political dimension of the *Gartenlaube*, see Kirsten Belgum, *Popularizing the Nation: Audience, Representation, and the Production of Identity in "Die Gartenlaube," 1853–1900* (Lincoln: University of Nebraska Press, 1998).

The articles deemed fit for publication in our paper may contain neither a political nor a religious tendency and must, with respect to eroticism (*in erotischer Hinsicht*), maintain such a tone as can be read among the family in the presence even of the younger members. Nor may divorce or suicide be mentioned. ... The ending must be a happy one, leaving a pleasing impression.[67]

The directive makes reference to the family's "younger members," yet the moral codes were designed with (young) women in mind, as Helmstetter has shown.[68] The mass audience became largely female in the final third of the nineteenth century. These reading women not only determined what literature ought to look like, but also were determined by it, because they internalized the opinions and social codes that their preferred literature conveyed. Women and young women were "connected to the control circuit of text distribution, to the circulation of information and opinions, practicing reading as a social behavior ..., yet editorial projections are an important factor in this control system, for the image that editors form of their audience itself molds and rallies that audience."[69] The projections of magazines and the resulting selective mechanisms to include certain topics and exclude others for the sake of young women affected literary production as a whole, simply because there was no equal alternative to the family magazine for authors who wanted to be published on a large scale.

Because family and cultural magazines strove to offer panoramic or "universal" contents within this normative framework to reach their mass audiences, literary articles appeared in a challenging media environment of competing semiotic systems with fluid boundaries.[70] A short story might share the page with an informational article, an advertisement, and, most importantly, an image or even several images.[71] Thomas Carlyle fittingly remarked that publishing literature in periodicals was like publishing among firecrackers exploding "distractively and

---

67 Arthur Zapp, "Schriftstellerleiden," *Die Zukunft*, November 12, 1898, 304.
68 Helmstetter, *Die Geburt des Realismus*, 73–5. The German family magazines thus performed a regulatory function that in Great Britain was undertaken by Mudie's circulating library, which treated "a hypothetical girl" as "the lowest common denominator against whose supposed sensitivities every new publication was measured." Price, "Victorian Reading," 51.
69 Helmstetter, *Die Geburt des Realismus*, 73–4.
70 Ibid., 48.
71 On the permeable boundaries between literature and advertisements, see Ilinca Iurascu's insightful analysis in "Annoncenliteratur: Kleist, Fontane, and the Rustle of Paper," *Oxford German Studies* 43, no. 3 (2014): 246–61.

destructively"[72] around the reader. His observation, though directed at the English media landscape, fully applied to the German scene, as a spot check in a randomly chosen magazine issue from 1871 confirms (Figure 1.2).

In this sample from *Ueber Land und Meer*, the text in columns belongs to Levin Schücking's novella *Der Dämon* (*The Demon*), but it is broken up and pushed to the margins by a rather crude comic strip about a doctor's unorthodox cholera treatment. (The example also illustrates that journals had different thresholds for acceptable topics; the same comic strip would certainly not have been published in the *Gartenlaube*.) Literature was literally pushed to the margins in the final third of the nineteenth century, as the amount of space dedicated to images within a given journal issue increased sharply. The *Gartenlaube* had an average image density of 15 percent by 1865, which became 45 percent by 1895; other journals underwent a similar development.[73] Writers had to make do with the space left. Accordingly, Salomon's *Geschichte des deutschen Zeitungswesens* (*History of the German Press*) praises the novelist F. W. Hackländer as "a highly useful contributor" to *Ueber Land und Meer*, because he was able to write his novellas "around . . . acquired woodcuts, often in a carefree and merry way."[74]

The presence of multiple textual and visual forms with their competing semiotic systems had implications not only for the amount of space left for literary writings, but also for the way these writings were perceived. Since the "universal" contents were understood by and large as entertainment, readers processed these contents through the distinctions of new/old and interesting/boring,[75] regardless of whether a given item was an educational article on, say, Galileo,[76] a crossword

---

72 Thomas Carlyle, *Sartor Resartus*: *The Life and Opinions of Herr Teufelsdröckh*, ed. Charles Frederick Herold (New York: Odyssey Press, 1937), 11.
73 See Graf, "Die Ursprünge der modernen Medienindustrie," 472. One notable exception is the *Deutsche Rundschau*, whose editor—Julius Rodenberg—consciously decided against illustrations to make his journal stand out as highbrow. Yet as Graevenitz explains with reference to the journal's visually connoted title ("Rund-Schau"), "Bilderlosigkeit" does not equal "Bild- und Anschauungslosigkeit" in the style of the articles. See Graevenitz, *Theodor Fontane: ängstliche Moderne*, 207.
74 Ludwig Salomon, *Geschichte des deutschen Zeitungswesens: Von den ersten Anfängen bis zur Wiederaufrichtung des deutschen Reiches*, vol. 3: Das Zeitungswesen seit 1814 (Aalen: Scientia Verlag, 1973), 674.
75 Building on Luhmann, Günter calls "interessant/langweilig" the central code of entertainment within mass media. See Günter, *Im Vorhof der Kunst*, 41–2.
76 See G. H-r. and H. B., "Und sie bewegt sich doch. Zum Jubelgedächtniß eines Erlösers der Wissenschaft," *Die Gartenlaube* 7 (1864): 100–4. Tellingly, the article is introduced by a "schwungvollen Gedicht" that provides the reader with some levity before delving into the explanation of Galileo's discoveries.

Figure 1.2 Text-image interactions in *Ueber Land und Meer*, 1871.

puzzle, or a novella chapter. What is more, all writings, including literary texts, became connected to the world of genre images[77] in the family and culture magazines: painted or drawn scenes of everyday life with titles such as "The Convalescent Child,"[78] "Walking to Midnight Mass in the Tyrolean Alps,"[79] and "At the Dog Kennel,"[80] to name three examples that appeared in the same year in *Die Gartenlaube*. It would be an oversimplification to equate visuals in the periodical press with genre images (for example, magazines also carried modern technical drawings and diagrams, as Graevenitz has pointed out).[81] However, genre images, the "staple products of the bourgeois [art] market since the early decades of the [nineteenth] century,"[82] constituted the largest waves of the "image flood" in nineteenth-century mass media. Omnipresent not just in periodicals, but on all sorts of surfaces, they helped to collectivize the subjective imagination and its symbolic repository, providing a visual vocabulary that literature could hardly ignore.[83]

Literature, then, was surrounded by and gradually sucked into a comprehensive image world, a world that not only extended well beyond the magazines but was also fully industrialized in its own right.

---

77 While the exact meaning of the term "genre image" has been subject to art-historical debates since the term arose in the late eighteenth century, the overlap between the many attempted definitions is this: "Die Genremalerei wird in Lexika des 20. Jahrhunderts übereinstimmend als eine Gattung beschrieben, die Szenen aus dem täglichen Leben wiedergibt. ... im Gegensatz zur Historienmalerei mit ihren Themen aus Geschichte, Mythologie und Religion charakterisiert 'Genre' eine andere ...untergeordnete Gattung der Malerei, in der keine heroischen Taten und historische Ereignisse, keine bekannten und bedeutenden Persönlichkeiten, sondern anonyme, 'unhistorische' Figuren in ihrem individuellen Lebensbereich, ihrem zuständlichen Dasein oder bei unspektakulären Ereignissen dargestellt werden." Barbara Gaethgens, introduction to *Genremalerei*, ed. Barbara Gaethgens (Berlin: Reimer, 2002), 13.
78 "Das genesende Kind. Nach dem eignen Oelgemälde auf Holz gezeichnet von Ernst Fischer," *Die Gartenlaube* 15 (1865): 229. This image illustrates the article "Auf der Landarztpraxis."
79 "Der Gang zur Mitternachtschristmesse in den Tiroler Alpen. Nach der Natur aufgenommen von Stauber," *Die Gartenlaube* 3 (1865): 37. This image illustrates the article "Eine Weihnacht in Tirol."
80 "Vor der Hundehütte. Originalzeichnung von L. Beckmann," *Die Gartenlaube* 20 (1865): 309. This image illustrates the brief article "Gute Freunde und getreue Nachbarn."
81 See Graevenitz, *Theodor Fontane: ängstliche Moderne*, 22–5.
82 Robin Lenman, "From 'Brown Sauce' to 'Plein Air': Taste and the Art Market in Germany, 1889–1910," in *Imagining Modern German Culture: 1889–1910*, ed. Françoise Forster-Hahn (Hanover, NH: University Press of New England; Washington: National Gallery of Art, 1996), 55.
83 Graevenitz, *Theodor Fontane: ängstliche Moderne*, 29–33.

The comparatively inexpensive method of xylography enabled the mass production of genre images that appeared in journals, yet the same images and the same stereotypical motifs also appeared in popular calendars, in art exhibitions and catalogs, as wall décor, and even on cookie tins and coffee mugs.[84] Wilhelm Hauff correctly anticipated the formative influence that mass-produced images would have on literary production. After all, the protagonists of his satire envision the rapid production of novels on the basis of circulating etchings (*Kupferstiche*) that the writers consult for landscape descriptions. The protagonists, moreover, refer to the assembly line in an image factory that churns out genre paintings to model how the novels in their text factory should be put together. Indeed, literary authors responded to the permeating presence of the genre image by emulating its aesthetic modes in writing, such as in highly pictorial and scenic descriptions. (Fontane, as we will see in Chapter 4, was an expert in this kind of media emulation.) The ubiquitous references to genre scenes and "little pictures" (*kleinen Bildern*) in popular book titles of the period also testify to the omnipresence of this visual form in literary texts.[85] Conversely, genre images in journals were often narrativized, evincing the mutual influence of the two media forms. It is clear from these interactions and attempts at emulation that literature in family magazines could not decouple its aesthetic profile from the mass-mediated image.

Finally, literature's existence in the mass press was influenced by the periodicals' special relationship to time, and the consequences of this relationship for production and reception. Periodicity implies that new content must be available at regular intervals to fill the pages and the standing rubrics of a given paper.[86] To meet this challenge, journal editors resorted to serializing the content. From their perspective, publishing in installments offered several advantages: the content could be distributed more flexibly while enticing readers to keep

---

84 See Birgit Wildmeister, *Die Bilderwelt der Gartenlaube. Ein Beitrag zur Kulturgeschichte des bürgerlichen Lebens in der zweiten Hälfte des 19. Jahrhunderts* (Würzburg: Bayerische Blätter für Volkskunde, 1998), 12, 31.
85 Examples from different decades include Ludwig Anzengruber, *Bekannte von der Straße. Genre-Bilder* (Leipzig, 1881); Fanny Lewald, *Zwölf Bilder aus dem Leben* (Berlin, 1888); Carl Arnold Schloenbach, *Originale: Genre-Bilder aus der Wirklichkeit* (Breslau, 1853); Amalia Schoppe, *Erinnerungen aus meinem Leben, in kleinen Bildern* (Altona, 1838); Ottilie Wildermuth, *Genre-Bilder aus einer kleinen Stadt* (Stuttgart, 1862).
86 Accordingly, Scherer and Stockinger treat the deadline as the "wichtigste Strukturvorgabe" of periodicals. See Stefan Scherer and Claudia Stockinger, "Archive in Serie. Kulturzeitschriften des 19. Jahrhunderts," in *Archiv/Fiktionen: Verfahren des Archivierens in Literatur und Kultur des langen 19. Jahrhunderts*, ed. Daniela Gretz and Nicolas Pethes (Freiburg im Breisgau: Rombach, 2016), 263.

reading; the overall financial risk was lower because a series that proved unpopular could be discontinued or swapped out quickly; and publishing many texts in small portions increased the variety that a periodical could offer.[87] Indeed, during the course of the nineteenth century, serialization became the norm in periodicals across genres.[88] What appeared piece by piece was not just sensationalist literature but also complex fiction, scientific articles, political treatises, philosophical writings, and even images. The comic strip in Figure 1.2 illustrates the pervasiveness of the serial form. The strip, too, is serialized; it is the second of three installments that appeared in *Ueber Land und Meer*.

For authors, this scattered mode of publication made it harder to be perceived as autonomous entities. If Jean Paul had already bemoaned in 1815, "I keep breaking myself up (*versplittere mich*) into these damned magazine pieces,"[89] authors in the serial-driven mass-media marketplace felt all the more fragmented. Their already precarious authority was further threatened by the collective of editors, or as Fontane called it, the "nebulous and impersonal editorial office" (*Redaktion*, BaH 18), that took over some of the author's functions and retained the final word on all text-related decisions. As Vance Byrd has recently shown with the example of Annette von Droste-Hülshoff's *The Jew's Beech*, authors therefore often lacked control over the paratextual environment in which their writings appeared.[90] One indeed wonders how Schücking, one of the most popular literary writers in late-nineteenth century journals, felt about the placement of *Der Dämon* next to gagging cartoon figures. But it was not only editors who participated in the construction of the text. Readers, too, were involved in this process. Many periodicals invited reader feedback, especially on serial narratives that were still

---

87 This is not to say that serialization was limited to the periodical. The whole genre of *Kolportageliteratur* was, of course, based on part-issue publication of cheap, collectible booklets that itinerant book peddlers sold, and publishers such as Carl Joseph Meyer exploited the advantages of the installment principle for the production and dissemination of affordable encyclopedias and anthologies, e.g., Meyer's famous *Konversationslexikon* and *Miniaturbibliothek deutscher Klassiker*. Part-issue publication was attractive not only because of the financing model, but also because it allowed book publishers to exploit loopholes in copyright law and avoid censorship. See Wittmann, *Geschichte des deutschen Buchhandels*, Chapters 7 and 8, for details, especially 229–32 and 270–4.
88 Mark W. Turner, "The Unruliness of Serials in the Nineteenth Century (and in the Digital Age)," in *Serialization in Popular Culture*, ed. Rob Allen and Thijs van den Berg (New York: Routledge, 2014), 20.
89 Qtd. in Ludwig Fertig, "Ein Kaufladen voll Manuskripte. Jean Paul und seine Verleger," *Archiv für Geschichte des Buchwesens* 32 (1989): 334.
90 Vance Byrd, "Epigraphs and the Journal Edition of Droste-Hülshoff's *Judenbuche*," *Colloquia Germanica* 49, no. 3–4 (2016): 178–9.

evolving, which editors relayed to authors. Even periodicals that made no direct attempts to involve their audiences were "co-written" by readers in the long run through sales figures.[91]

In addition to these general challenges to authorship, serialization created concrete difficulties for writers' day-to-day production. A text had to lend itself to being cut up according to the preferred installment length and other formal requirements, which varied greatly from outlet to outlet; for example, the *Gartenlaube* typically published texts in much smaller segments than did the *Rundschau*. Fontane's novellas and novels, which appeared in periodicals across the full spectrum, were at times divided into as few as two installments, at times into as many as thirty-six, and the installments varied in length from two to fifty pages.[92] Authors internalized the importance of such formal requirements and often approached new projects through considerations of length. When Adolf Glaser, the editor of *Westermanns Monatshefte*, asked Wilhelm Raabe to provide more details about his current novel in the making, *Hunger-Pastor* (*Der Hungerpastor*), Raabe replied: "The work will again consist of three volumes, and each volume will contain twenty of my writing sheets, as with *Die Leute aus dem Walde*. What might make the volumes a little thicker is that my handwriting was narrower this time around."[93] The form, in short, had to follow the format, and the format was always on the writer's mind.[94] The priority of the format resulted in considerable pressure on writers to deliver, especially those who worked in serial, from installment to installment. They had to keep content coming, regardless of whether they had enough ideas at hand or were snowed under with other work. Yet again, a prominent example is Wilhelm Raabe, who had a miserable experience with the serialized publication of *Hunger-Pastor* because of the formal pressures. On a whim, he sold the unfinished novel to Otto Janke for the newly founded *Romanzeitung* rather than following up with his friend Glaser. Janke, eager to open the new journal with Raabe's work, sent the first part to the typesetters while Raabe was still hard at work on the second and

---

91 See Beetham, "Towards a Theory of the Periodical," 26.
92 For instance, Fontane's *L'Adultera* appeared in just two issues of *Nord und Süd* (vol. 13, 1880, no. 39, 299–349; vol. 14, 1880, no. 40, 47–95), whereas *Vor dem Sturm* was divided into 65 chapters and published in 36 issues of *Daheim* (vol. 14, 1878, nos. 14–51).
93 Letter to Adolf Glaser, July 3, 1863, in *Wilhelm Raabe: Briefe 1842–1870*, ed. William Webster (Berlin: Erich Schmidt, 2004), 185.
94 Occasionally, editors made exceptions and bent over backwards to accommodate a (famous) writer's needs, as was the case with the *Deutsche Rundschau* and Gottfried Keller's late work. Yet special arrangements remained the exception. See Chapter 4.

third parts. Between reading the proofs of the first part and producing the drafts of the second, Raabe lost track of the big picture and became increasingly schematic and clichéd in his narrative.[95] In the midst of the difficult production process, he declared his disgust with serialized publishing and confided to Glaser:

> My *Hunger-Pastor* still weighs heavily upon me, but two volumes have thankfully been dispatched and the third will, God willing, be finished in early December. Then, however, I shall have to relax for a few months . . . . I may contentedly tell myself that my ambition is becoming ever more serious, and that all manner of factory-like literary productions is increasingly hateful to me.[96]

> *Mein Hungerpastor liegt mir noch schwer auf den Armen, doch sind zwei Bände glücklich abgeschickt und der dritte wird Deo volente Anfangs December fertig. Dann aber werde ich mich einige Monate auf die Bärenhaut legen müssen . . . . Ich darf mir mit Genugthuung sagen, daß mein Streben immer ernster, und daß mir alles literarische Fabrikwesen immer verhaßter wird.*[97]

Although *Hunger-Pastor* proved a stunning success, Raabe never made peace with the way the novel had come into the world and subsequently tried to keep the forces of the literary market at arm's length.[98] But even for writers who did not work in serial, production schedules could be constraining and rigid. Because periodicals were eager to offer their readers new novels during the typical sales seasons, such as holidays and summer vacation, writers had to make sure not to miss these opportunities. They often tried to improve their chances by synchronizing the narratives of their novels with "real-world" time to the best of their abilities. Fontane's *Before the Storm*, for instance, opens with an atmospheric chapter about a snowy Christmas Eve, which was published as the novel's first installment in the journal *Daheim* in early January 1878, just a few days after the Christmas holiday. The dark-humored Wilhelm Raabe commented in his cynical way on the implications of seasonal production schedules for the development of literary narratives, ironically subtitling *The Lar*, one of his novellas, *A Story of Easter, Whitsuntide, Christmas, and New Year* (*Eine Oster-, Pfingst-, Weihnachts- und Neujahrsgeschichte*).[99]

---

95 See Schrader's analysis in "Autorfedern unter Preß-Autorität," 25.
96 Raabe to Glaser, October 10, 1863, *Briefe 1842–1870*, 205.
97 Ibid.
98 See Schrader, "Autorfedern unter Preß-Autorität," 26–7.
99 Eckhardt Meyer-Krentler, "'Wir vom Handwerk.' Wilhelm Raabe als Berufsschriftsteller," in *Vom Wert der 'Arbeit' in der deutschen Literatur (1770–1930)*, ed. Harro Segeberg (Tübingen: Niemeyer, 1991), 209.

The Poet at the Loom and the Compiler's Moment

As Raabe's example of *Hunger-Pastor* shows, the impact of formatting was intensified by what I will term the "heavy materiality" of the writing process, which contrasted sharply with the ephemerality of the mass-produced periodical. Writers like Raabe, Stifter, and Fontane experienced this contrast in its acutest form—while the means of reproduction had been fully industrialized, these authors still wrote by hand, with a quill pen, steel pen, or pencil, in a comparatively slow and exhausting process. The quill pen in particular required physical mastery, notably a flexible wrist, good control of grip and finger pressure, and stamina—a writer's arm could easily tire just from holding the pen and shuttling back and forth between inkwell and sheet, as Heinrich Bosse points out.[100] And while these writers' younger colleagues, such as Paul Lindau and Mark Twain, had the "production means of the printing press on their desks" in the form of the typewriter and were thus able to "fuse"[101] composition and publication, writers of the older generation produced unique manuscripts, frequently only making one fair copy that they sent to a journal. To be sure, for journals, the difference between manuscripts and printed texts was unimportant; they received texts in both forms from their contributors all the time. Newspaper editors called everything that had not been set for their own purposes "manuscript," even printed source materials.[102] It was on the writers' side that the difference carried weight.

The clash between the heavy materiality from the writer's end and the speed with which written text could be multiplied skewed the relationship between original and reproduction. By Goethe's death in 1832, German cultural critics had already lost confidence in the possibility of original German literature because of the perception that all aesthetic options had been exhausted, so that whatever was to come would be characterized by epigonism, a technical, imitative, and lifeless play with existing forms.[103] The problems of the epigones became so pressing during the nineteenth century that they turned into topics for

---

100 Heinrich Bosse, "Schreiben," in *Historisches Wörterbuch des Mediengebrauchs*, ed. Heiko Christians, Matthias Bickenbach, and Nikolaus Wegmann (Cologne: Böhlau, 2015), 490.
101 Kittler, *Discourse Networks*, 259.
102 See Joseph Kürschner, *Handbuch der Presse für Schriftsteller, Redaktionen, Verleger [und] überhaupt Alle, die mit der Presse in Beziehung stehen* (Berlin: Hillger, 1902), col. 1563.
103 According to Philipp Theisohn, nineteenth-century cultural criticism defined the literary production of epigones as characterized by four flaws: it was "massenhaft," "massiv publikumsorientiert," and "ohne ein echtes Qualitätskriterium," and it bore the "Kainsmal der Unselbständigkeit." Theisohn's analysis continues: "Ihr Vergehen [i.e., das Vergehen der Epigonen]

literary writing itself. Karl Immermann's novel *Die Epigonen* (*The Epigones*; 1836) gave the cultural moment its name and, in its now canonical passage, defined the epigones' dilemma as a search for originality stymied by the "too much" of already circulating material:

> We are, to express the entire misery in *one* word, epigones, and bear part of the burden that tends to stick to every generation that is born late and lives on its inheritance. The great movement in the realm of spirit, which our fathers undertook from their cottages and little huts, has provided us with many treasures that now lay upon the market tables. Without particular effort, even the least ability can at least acquire the token coins of every form of art and science. But it proceeds with borrowed ideas as it does with borrowed money: the one who carelessly does business with others' possessions only gets poorer.[104]

In the words of Paul Fleming, Immermann characterizes the post-Goethean age as one in which the treasures of the past were readily available, yet "such riches equally hinder the ability to produce something new, something original."[105] Other literary narratives, such as Gottfried Keller's 1860 novella *Die mißbrauchten Liebesbriefe* (*The Misused Love Letters*), picked up on the troubles of the epigones in more overtly humorous terms, yet they too put their finger on the problematic relationship between originality and reproduction. For instance, the waiter Georg Nase becomes a popular author because he succeeds at two things: imitating the epigonal hack writers who stay at his hotel and reissuing passages gleaned from classic writers as new contributions under his own name.[106] In the second half of the nineteenth century, the

---

liegt ... nicht in der Rückwendung auf Symbolik, Rhetorik und Stilistik ihrer Vorgänger, sondern vielmehr darin, dass sie diese Formen nur noch sammeln, aber nicht wiederbeleben können." See Philipp Theisohn, *Plagiat: Eine unoriginelle Literaturgeschichte* (Stuttgart: Kröner, 2009), 357, 361.

104 Karl Immermann, *Die Epigonen. Familienmemoiren in neun Büchern* (= *Werke in fünf Bänden*, vol. 2), ed. Benno von Wiese (Frankfurt a. M.: Athenäum, 1971), 121; translation from Fleming, *Exemplarity and Mediocrity: The Art of the Average from Bourgeois Tragedy to Realism* (Stanford, CA: Stanford University Press, 2009), 125–6.

105 Fleming, *Exemplarity and Mediocrity*, 126.

106 See Gottfried Keller, *Die mißbrauchten Liebesbriefe*, in *Sämtliche Werke. Historisch-Kritische Ausgabe*, ed. Walter Morgenthaler (Basel: Stroemfeld, 2000), 5.2:101–6. Fittingly, Georg Nase explains that he always had the "Genugthuung, das Ding [i.e., a given piece from his output] munter durch die ganze Presse zirkulieren zu sehen" (105).

mechanisms of the mass-media marketplace and the technologies of reproduction promoted imitative practices and provided the conditions under which a limited set of very similar forms and contents became extremely visible, while diverse, genuinely original contents were marginalized. There was, in other words, a great deal of mutual imitation and redundancy built into the mass-media system—a system that nevertheless strove to uphold some semblance of originality, as we shall see.

To begin, popular and widespread works of fiction were often inherently formulaic, following the same narrative schemas, as an extensive body of research on light fiction has shown.[107] Moreover, translations of a few fashionable foreign-language authors, such as Cooper, Dickens, Dumas, Scott, and George Sand (just as depicted in Hauff's "Die Bücher und die Lesewelt"), swamped the literary scene after 1820 and trumped the print runs of original German works.[108] The technology of stereotyping based on light and transportable *papier-mâché* mats or "flongs," developed by Claude Genoux in 1829, helped to fuel an increasingly international trade in stock images and stock texts.[109] This breakthrough in reproduction technology not only led to the mass circulation of the same content items through different media; it also provided the historical reality behind the modern figurative notions of the "stereotype" and the "cliché" as overused images and phrases[110]—journals practiced what Salomon's *Geschichte des deutschen Zeitungswesens* plainly terms "buying clichés."[111] At the same time, copyright law had not yet caught up to these new technological standards, which invited the imitation and plagiarizing of texts and images as a lucrative artistic mode. Even though in 1837 Prussia

---

107 Among the numerous sources, one that is particularly pertinent in the context of "Konventionalisierung" of fiction through narrative and visual means in family magazines is Gerhart von Graevenitz, "Memoria und Realismus. Erzählende Literatur in der deutschen 'Bildungspresse' des 19. Jahrhunderts," in *Memoria: Vergessen und Erinnern*, ed. Anselm Haverkamp and Renate Lachmann (Munich: Fink, 1993), 283–304. For an excellent literature review and problematization of the fields of "Unterhaltungs- und Populärkultur," see Hans-Otto Hügel, "Forschungsfeld Populäre Kultur: eine Einführung," in *Lob des Mainstreams. Zu Begriff und Geschichte von Unterhaltung und Populärer Kultur* (Cologne: von Halem, 2007), 58–94.
108 See Wittmann, *Geschichte des deutschen Buchhandels*, 239.
109 See Banham, "The Industrialization of the Book 1800–1970," 280.
110 According to the *DWB*, the adjective "stereotype" was coined as a technical printing term around 1800, but gained traction as a figurative term in the final third of the nineteenth century. See "stereotype, *adj.*," *Deutsches Wörterbuch von Jacob Grimm und Wilhelm Grimm*, vol. 18 (Leipzig: Hirzel, 1941), col. 2455.
111 Salomon, *Geschichte des deutschen Zeitungswesens*, 674.

promulgated the "Gesetz zum Schutze des Eigenthums an Werken der Wissenschaft und Kunst gegen Nachdruck und Nachbildung" ("Law for the Protection of Property in Works of Scholarship and Art from Reprinting and Imitation"), which was celebrated as the beginning of intellectual property rights for German authors, enforcement was difficult because there was too much ambiguity surrounding the questions of what an intellectual object was and how to define its theft.[112] As a result, only the most blatant cases—such as the publication of someone else's work under one's own name—were punished, and plagiarizing practices such as copying and imitating passages without proper references remained free of legal consequences.[113] Legal copyright protection was not established until 1886, and even after its implementation, "image factories" (*Bilderfabriken*) continued to copy popular motifs. They simply resorted to the strategy of the "second and third brew" (*zweiter and dritter Aufguss*); that is, they recreated successful images with minor variations.[114]

These reproduction practices, especially those pertaining to image reproduction, introduced doubleness into the notion of the "original" and eroded the original's claim to ontological uniqueness. Outwardly, periodicals played up the notion of originality and encouraged readers to think that the images they encountered in a given issue were unique to the outlet. "The illustrations in our newspaper are wood engravings," the *Leipziger Illustrirte Zeitung* explained to readers in a virtual tour of its drawing studio and xylographic workshop, adding that a wood engraving required "a drawing on wood, and this in turn a preceding original drawing (*Originalzeichnung*). These originals are sent to our offices by artistic contributors and now consist partly of original wood drawings, partly of photographs . . ., partly of sketches or watercolors from nature, made on the spot (*an Ort und Stelle*)."[115] In reality, only a fraction of the "original drawings" was as unique as the *Leipziger Illustrirte* led its readers to believe. Far more often than this quotation

---

112 Theisohn provides a detailed discussion of Prussian copyright law and its loopholes in *Plagiat*, 333–54. On the global stage, there were no comprehensive regulations until the Berne Convention of 1887. See Tatlock, introduction to *Publishing Culture and the "Reading Nation,"* 8.
113 See Theisohn, *Plagiat*, 341.
114 See Wolfgang Brückner, "Trivialisierungsprozesse in der bildenden Kunst zu Ende des 19. Jahrhunderts, dargestellt an der 'Gartenlaube,'" in *Das Triviale in Literatur, Musik und bildender Kunst,* ed. Helga de la Motte-Haber (Frankfurt am Main: Klostermann, 1972), 230.
115 "Wie die Illustrirte Zeitung entsteht," *Leipziger Illustrirte Zeitung* no. 1000, August 30, 1862, 146.

admits, the drawings were slightly modified copies of existing images (oil paintings, photographs) and even of images that had already been reproduced thousands of times (e.g., engravings that had already appeared in other periodicals). In a complex, multi-step copying process that involved tracing paper and several other media, these so-called "originals" were transferred onto woodblocks, where they were turned into wood-end engravings from which images could be printed *en masse* on the printing press. As a technical reality, then, an "original" simply designated a template (*Vorlage*) for reproduction. This template could be anything from a genuinely new and unique image that a professional illustrator or artist had created from scratch for the outlet to a generic image. The captions underneath the images reflect both this ambiguity and the outlets' attempts to emphasize the uniqueness of their visual material whenever possible. Papers frequently resorted to vague formulations such as "Serbian Family Fleeing from Belgrade to Semlin [Zemun]. After an original drawing," which provided only limited information about the image's provenance but still evoked notions of ontological uniqueness.[116]

Redundancy and imitation also lay at the heart of the news business and were practiced with an intensity that most journalists preferred not make public. Newspapers routinely copied topics and even stole entire articles from one another—or, to be more precise, the smaller papers usually copied content from a few very well-established papers that set the agenda. With a few clever tweaks, the gleaned content could easily be dressed up as a paper's own production. As Kürschner's *Handbuch der Presse* aptly put it, "Large established newspapers are often the principal source (*vornehmste Quelle*) for smaller ones. Since a piece of news as such, an event of the day, is not protected by copyright, it is standard procedure to lift such items from other papers, and ultimately, it is inevitable that they should do so."[117] Professional agencies such as the *Depeschenbureau*, the *Telegraphenbureau*, and the *Korrespondenz* contributed systemically to this kind of redundancy because it was their business model to disseminate the same content, ranging from news stories to feuilleton articles, to multiple papers at once.[118] The practice was so widespread that some agencies, especially those dealing in serialized fiction, had to make conscious efforts to limit their scope so

---

116 This caption is taken from the *Leipziger Illustrirte Zeitung* no. 993, July 12, 1862, 29.
117 Kürschner, *Handbuch der Presse*, col. 1573.
118 See ibid., col. 1555–63.

that their subscribers would be able to perceive at least a semblance of originality.[119]

Finally, the general structure of the mass-media marketplace was conducive to redundancy because it rewarded authors for pursuing what Lee Erickson, in a different context, calls an "additive strategy"[120] of publishing. Because it was most profitable for authors to appear in print frequently, they benefited from self-anthologizing, prepublishing while letting a corpus grow, and publishing revised versions. The best possible scenario was, of course, to publish the same work in multiple venues at the same time. Friedrich Spielhagen's *The Breaking of the Storm* (*Sturmflut*) simultaneously appeared in the *Petersburger Herold*, *Berliner Tageblatt*, *Hannover'schen Courier*, *Breslauer Zeitung*, and *Elberfelder Zeitung*.[121] For some, in short, the media market opened the doors to previously unheard-of fame. Authors such as Spielhagen, Felix Dahn, and Gustav Freytag, whose novel *Debit and Credit* (*Soll und Haben*) passed through seventy-four editions between 1855 and 1910, defined the notion of the modern bestseller.[122] Yet the omnipresence of such bestsellers also diminished the space left for original works.

Indeed, only a lucky few sold as well as Spielhagen. The majority of writers perceived the discrepancy between the speeds of production and reproduction, along with the pressure on originality, as stifling. A caricature by Alfred Oberländer in the *Fliegende Blätter* of 1888, published with the title "Endlose Dichtkunst" ("Infinite Poetry"), aptly captures this perception (Figure 1.3).

According to the subtitle, the caricature shows "the Spanish author of romances, Don Smieros de los Papiros, in his workroom." The loom-like construction at which the poet is sitting, featuring an infinite roll of paper and a foot pedal, comically clashes with the quill pen, the Don's serious facial expression, and the gesture of exquisiteness with which he puts his hand to his heart. A close look reveals, of course, that the poetry produced by the Don is not so exquisite after all—all of his poems follow exactly the same format; they are three lines long and

---

119 Ibid., col. 1563.
120 Lee Erickson, *The Economy of Literary Form: English Literature and the Industrialization of Publishing, 1800–1850* (Baltimore: Johns Hopkins University Press, 1996), 39.
121 See Wittmann, *Geschichte des deutschen Buchhandels*, 282.
122 Wittmann explains that the second half of the nineteenth century enabled a literary economy of scale, making a handful of authors very wealthy. Freytag, for example, earned royalties of 440,000 Goldmark just with *Die Ahnen* and became what one would nowadays call a multi-millionaire. See Wittmann, *Geschichte des deutschen Buchhandels*, 281.

Literature in the Industrial Age of Print 65

Figure 1.3 "Infinite Poetry," a caricature by Alfred Oberländer, 1888.

spaced out at regular intervals with truly mechanistic regularity. If we are to believe this caricature, literature's migration into mass media was detrimental to art, because a production process capable of keeping up with the industrialization of print came at the expense of originality. Indeed, this narrative of unoriginality, a "stencil-like character" (*Schablonenhaftigkeit*), and a loss of poetic quality was echoed by writers, publishers, and critics alike and reverberated through the entire nineteenth century.[123]

Some contemporary writers were so appalled or so anxious that they refused to participate in the market and its mechanisms of endless productivity. When the journal editor Julius Niedner tried to pressure Raabe into a contract for "a running series of any number of little volumes titled 'Tales from German Cities and Towns,'" the writer firmly declined; similarly, Theodor Storm turned down the offer to write poetry in serial fashion as accompanying text for an image sequence because he simply did not want to become part of the serial machinery.[124]

Theodor Fontane shared this negative attitude toward mass production and the market—yet only to a certain extent. As the passage about the "cotton-cloth of novellas" cited earlier indicates, he did not want to be a text factory, and on bad days, he seemed just as depressed as his colleagues about the reading public's lack of appreciation for quality. He felt that it was of no consequence whether he was alive or not, he once wrote to his wife, and perhaps of even less consequence whether he wrote a novel entitled *Peter der Große*, *Peter in der Fremde*, or *Struwelpeter*, for they all consisted of "the same 24 [sic] letters, and they all go into the lending library where they are read for 1 *Silbergroschen* per volume and deemed alternately good or bad on a whim" (HFA IV.3: 204). In general, however, Fontane took a much more pragmatic stance toward his profession, literary production, and the mass-media marketplace. In an early letter to Theodor Storm, he called himself a *Praktikus* and expressed his conviction that snobbery toward the market was shortsighted, perhaps even reprehensible, because the literary preferences of "tailors and glovers" (*Gevatter Schneider und Handschuhmacher*)—that is, common people—deserved to be taken to heart much more than most authors assumed (HFA IV.1: 355–6). What was more, by deploying the textual practice of compiling, Fontane developed rationalized working methods that allowed him to benefit from the very same material and communicative conditions that his colleagues perceived as stifling. For him, the redundancy inherent in the mass press was useful: it provided the backdrop of familiarity against which he learned to create realist effects. Fontane relied on the readers' knowledge of current topics, household names,

---

[123] From the nineteenth century, one of the most iconic pieces of criticism is Friedrich Christoph Perthes' "Die Bedeutung des deutschen Buchhandels, besonders in der neuesten Zeit," with which the *Börsenblatt für den deutschen Buchhandel* opened on January 3, 1834. See Friedrich Perthes, *Der deutsche Buchhandel als Bedingung des Daseins einer deutschen Literatur. Schriften*, ed. Gerd Schulz (Stuttgart: Reclam, 1995), 49–53.

[124] See Schrader, "Autorfedern unter Preß-Autorität," 24.

and images—in short, of everything that circulated widely—when he reworked mass-mediated materials in his own writings. These were precisely the elements that gave his readers the feeling that they "knew" the fictional characters, plots, and settings to which Fontane's works introduced them. His working methods, then, made redundancy programmatic in more than one way. Not only did he glean from the very same mass media in which he himself would publish, but he also used the gleaned materials for several distinct projects, as we shall see later.

The fragmented textuality of the periodical press was also a condition that a compiler could embrace. For most writers, textual material cut up into pieces connoted destruction and loss; for instance, when the mean-spirited parrot in Immermann's *Die Epigonen* rips apart the Countess's personal writings and drops them into a wastebasket, Hermann desperately picks up the shreds and tries to put them back together, pressing the remnants of his beloved's text to his heart.[125] Fontane, by contrast, realized the creative potential that such destruction entails. For him, fragmented texts were no reason to mourn. On the contrary, he preferred to receive them cut to size. In letter exchanges with his informants, he requested repeatedly that they send him their input "on slips" (*auf Zetteln*, HFA IV.2: 425). These instructions underscore Fontane's fondness for moving textual building blocks around and arranging them into patchwork, as opposed to writing everything from scratch.

The cultural climate of epigonism, the leveling of generic hierarchies in the mass press, and the *de facto* absence of copyright law also created a setting in which all materials were *gleich-gültig*—in-different, indistinguishable in terms of value—in the literal sense of the word. Such a setting was likely unsettling for many writers. To a seasoned compiler, it proved stimulating. Fontane viewed printed matter (*Drucksachen*) as "a well-spread table from which all may help themselves, and the more the merrier; nor do I care for the citation of sources or names by which others set so much store."[126] Note yet again how sharply his metaphorics differ from Immermann's: whereas

---

125 Immermann, *Die Epigonen*, 257–8.
126 Fontane made this bold statement in a letter with which he defended himself against accusations of plagiarism. Eduard Handtmann, who had published the volume *Neue Sagen aus der Mark Brandenburg* (Berlin, 1883), reproached Fontane for appropriating passages from this volume in the essay "Die Eldenburger Quitzows" without citing the source. The letter has only recently been discovered. See Klaus-Peter Möller, "Eduard Handtmann – der Pfarrer von Seedorf," *Jahrbuch Ostprignitz–Ruppin* (2005): 52.

Immermann had seen the textual situation of the epigones as a market table on which treasures were laid out that would hamper creativity and eventually become mismanaged, Fontane saw nothing but opportunities for a collective and guilt-free feast. In brief, Immermann characterized his epoch from the position of "the copy*right*," while Fontane looked at it from that of "the copy*left*."[127] To him, the myriad things in circulation invited creative recombination across a hitherto unknown spectrum of topics, genres, and types of sources. With everything up for grabs, the compiler could proceed as he saw fit and be as disrespectful as only an epigone at peace with his inherited riches could be. Even Schiller could furnish material for experimentation with ironic sound bites: "Der Mensch ist frei, und wär' er in Köthen geboren," Fontane punned in one of his textual building blocks.[128]

His compilation-based working methods overlap to a stunning extent with Hauff's satirical program of literary mass production in "Die Bücher und die Lesewelt." It could almost be said that he unwittingly realized Hauff's satire: like the unnamed protagonist, he applied a work process that relied heavily on the sources in circulation and that was partly modular. Even the templates on which Hauff's protagonist draws—historical novels, etchings, songs, historical costumes, collections of folk tales—were actually used by Fontane. It was precisely these compilatory strategies and this general stance toward textuality, however, that enabled Fontane to alleviate the "heavy materiality" of producing by hand in an industrialized setting in which formal requirements loomed large. For a compiler, it is comparatively easy to turn a novella into a novel or shrink a novel into a series of freestanding scenes, because all he or she needs to do is add or take away elements to scale up or down.[129] Moreover, the rationalized working methods that he developed for the quick production of bread-and-butter articles for the mass press could segue into a virtuosic form of remix for more complex literary writings on the basis of the same set of notes. Fontane thus possessed the versatility, the "quill cut for all purposes" (*für Alles zugeschnittene Feder*),"[130] that publishing in late

---

127 On the conceptual opposition of copyright and copyleft, see David J. Gunkel, *Of Remixology: Ethics and Aesthetics after Remix* (Cambridge, MA: MIT Press, 2016), xix–xx.
128 In translation, the pun requires an explanation: Fontane plays with the well-known line "Man is free, though he were born in shackles" from Schiller's poem "Die Worte des Glaubens," replacing the German word for "shackles," *Ketten*, with the similar-sounding name of a provincial town, *Köthen*.
129 On Fontane's methods of scaling up and compressing projects, see Chapter 4 of this study.
130 As according to an anonymous contemporary "observer" qtd. in Wittmann, *Geschichte des deutschen Buchhandels*, 248. Fontane's versatility was indeed

nineteenth-century mass media required. All told, his particular work process proved remarkably productive: Within the roughly six decades of his journalistic and literary career, he published at least 2,700 individual contributions to newspapers and journals. This output included the release of almost one novel or novella per year during the last two decades of his life.[131] In contrast to the works "written" by Hauff's protagonist, however, Fontane's novels have not yet gone out of fashion. It must be considered his particular achievement that his compilation-based work process yielded unique and original results.

---

remarkable; his literary output included such different genres as ballads, travel sketches, war reports, criminal novellas, historical and contemporary novels, literature and theater reviews, and art criticism. (A more extensive discussion of his versatility, including the wide spectrum of media in which he managed to publish, will follow in the course of this book.)

131 This figure is taken from Wolfgang Rasch's *Theodor Fontane Bibliographie*, which lists all of the Fontane contributions that have hitherto been identified, covering the period 1839 to 1898. See Chapter 7 of Wolfgang Rasch, *Theodor Fontane Bibliographie. Werk und Forschung*, ed. Ernst Osterkamp and Hanna Delf von Wolzogen (Berlin: De Gruyter, 2006), 1:275–834.

Two Biography vs. Autobiography: The Making of a Compiler

Unwrapping an Early Modern Figure

In 1902, some three years after Fontane's death, a moving crew lugged his bulky desk into the *Märkisches Provinzialmuseum* (now the *Stiftung Stadtmuseum Berlin*), together with its contents—bundles and bundles of manuscripts, many of which were wrapped in newspaper to form curious packets.[1] Half a dozen of these packets, one of which is shown in Figure 2.1, contained drafts and fair copies of Fontane's autobiography, *Von Zwanzig bis Dreißig* (*From Twenty to Thirty*).[2]

Fontane liked to fold sheets of newsprint into envelopes or sleeves—he called them "bundles" (*Bündel*) or "packets" (*Pa[c]kete*), while the German scholarship confusingly speaks of "banderoles" (*Banderolen*)—and use them to store source materials, drafts, and fair copies. He often labeled these packets and closed them with a few drops of homemade glue or red sealing wax before putting them away in his desk. The packets provide a powerful symbol of this chapter's topic: the story of how Fontane became a compiler. In immaterial terms, Fontane's autobiography appears as one cohesive trajectory, proceeding from his first publication to his difficult yet rewarding existence as a fully fledged poet. In material terms, however, it emerges as bundles of loose sheets, a set of moveable episodes, assembled from varied sources and enveloped by the very medium in which the author, through his career as a newspaper editor, professionalized the act of compiling.

---

1   See Bettina Machner, "Der Dichternachlaß," in *Fontane und sein Jahrhundert*, ed. Stiftung Stadtmuseum (Berlin: Henschel, 1998), 254.
2   All six packets are described in detail in Wolfgang Rasch's editorial commentary on *Theodor Fontane: Von Zwanzig bis Dreißig*, GBA III.3: 505–7.

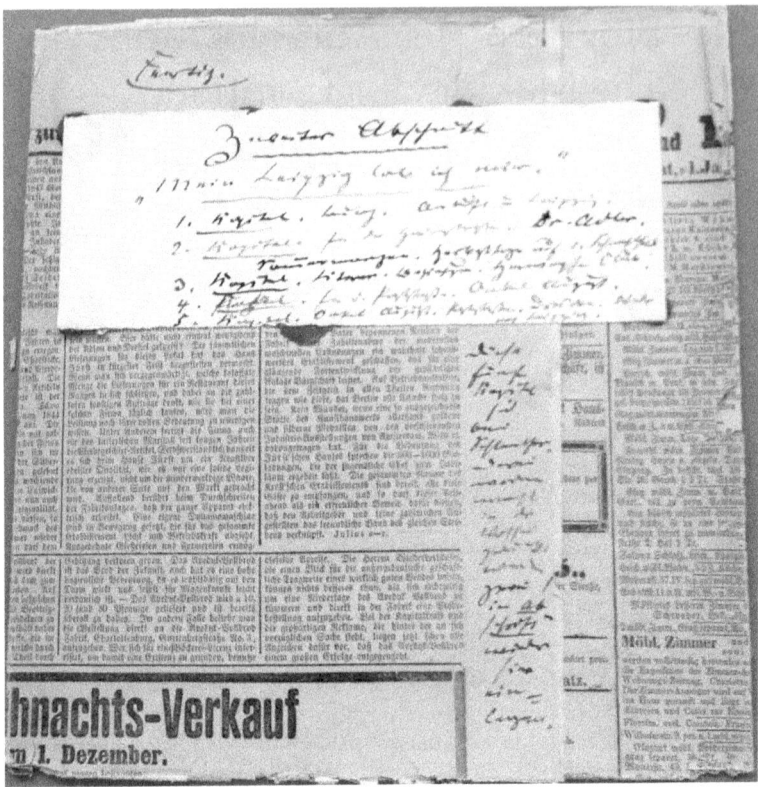

Figure 2.1 Typical Fontanean "paper sleeve" with label.

Scholarship has by and large overlooked these packets; with only a few exceptions, Fontane is not known as a compiler. In part, this has to do with the packets' suggestive content—in his autobiographical writings, Fontane creates an authorial presence that distracts the readers from the seemingly mundane wrapping, leaving no room for traces of compiling. (I will return to this problem in more detail later.) Another reason is that the author as compiler is not included among the official *dramatis personae* of nineteenth-century literary history. That figure was much more familiar during the Renaissance, when compiling—that is, the collocation of textual excerpts from multiple sources in a new, bounded text—enjoyed its first heyday.[3]

---

3 Ann M. Blair discusses the early modern period as an age of compiling from a historical and comparative perspective in *Too Much to Know: Managing Scholarly Information Before the Modern Age* (New Haven: Yale University Press, 2010), 11–61.

In fact, the early modern period provides the prototype for the nineteenth century's tacit rearticulation of the compiler. A number of similar textual-historical conditions mark the early modern period as the prelude to the compiler's moment in the latter half of the nineteenth century. Renaissance compiling thrived in response to the handpress and the subsequent proliferation of print, which encouraged premodern scholars and authors to deal pragmatically and creatively with an unprecedented excess of printed matter. This scenario repeated itself with even greater force in the nineteenth century, when print became a modern mass medium. In both ages, moreover, printed matter circulated unbound. The handpress came without standards for book production, as Jeffrey Todd Knight has recently pointed out.[4] Printed texts in the Renaissance, especially vernacular writings, were often sold as stacks of loose sheets, and readers, collectors, and writers bound texts together in myriad ways (or not at all). This textual condition, too, returned in the nineteenth century—if the early modern period must be understood as an age in which large amounts of printed matter were *not yet* wedged between solid book covers and stitched to spines, the later nineteenth century was an age in which the same was *no longer* the case. To be sure, standards for book production had been developed in the meantime. Yet the fragmenting effects on textuality of the periodical press and the principles of part-issue publication limited the impact of these standards. For example, consider the unsettling effect that the leap from journal printing to book publication, one of the standard maneuvers of nineteenth-century publishing, could have on a literary text.[5] When authors made this leap, they often changed the text in response to the demands of readers and publishers or took the opportunity to restore ideas and passages that had been lost in the journal version, as was the case with Wilhelm Raabe's 1885 novel *Restless Guests* (*Unruhige Gäste*) in the *Gartenlaube*. In the words of Manuela Günter, the dual existence of literary writings as both journal printings and books thus opened up a "space for interaction"[6] among writers, readers, and publishers in which

---

4   Jeffrey T. Knight, *Bound to Read: Compilations, Collections, and the Making of Renaissance Literature* (Philadelphia: University of Pennsylvania Press, 2013), 4–5.
5   As Hannah Sullivan puts it, "significant format change," either between serial publication and the initial book edition, or between a first edition and a cheaper reset one, provided the most common opportunity for authorial revision in the nineteenth century and thus introduced fluidity into the notion of the text. See Hannah Sullivan, *The Work of Revision* (Cambridge, MA: Harvard University Press, 2013), 36–7.
6   Manuela Günter, "Die Medien des Realismus," in *Realismus: Epoche – Autoren – Werke*, ed. Christian Begemann (Darmstadt: Wissenschaftliche Buchgesellschaft, 2007), 50.

the text was available for modification. Both periods, then, featured a lack of textual and epistemic "fixity," inviting readers, writers, and most importantly compilers to take (written) matters into their own hands.[7]

Well-studied sample cases from the early modern period give the scholar of nineteenth-century literature a clear picture of what this means: immersed in a setting of ongoing "textual reconfiguration,"[8] compilers emerged as literary craftsmen who treated the written text as adaptable. Amassing excerpts from all kinds of sources for their own projects, both literary and scholarly, they applied practices of knowledge organization that increased the fluidity between topics and genres.[9] It was perfectly normal to cut up, reconfigure, augment, and reissue a project that someone else had already put forth, as the often unwieldy book titles from the early modern period plainly demonstrate.[10] In addition, the early modern prequel teaches us that the textual practices of compilers were emphatically physical and "embodied." According to Knight, literary scholarship is still struggling to assimilate this insight. He writes, "While our metaphors are insistently material, ... we imagine this particular, habitual intertextuality in Renaissance letters unfolding discursively," as if it happened only in the realm of ideas.[11] Yet he insists that the "Renaissance inclination to 'gather' and 'patch' was a more physical, ingrained thing than our assumptions about practice have allowed." Knight therefore concludes that a revised understanding of intertextuality, allusion, and imitation is in order, one that considers these concepts not merely discursively, but also in terms of a material reality.

The early modern craftsman and information worker who gathered and patched with scissors (or paper knife) and glue lived on in at least

---

7 Referencing "fixity" (6), Knight positions himself against Elizabeth Eisenstein's argument in *The Printing Press as an Agent of Change* (Cambridge: Cambridge University Press, 1979) that the onset of print led to a textual culture in which printed matter was standardized and its contents were "fixed," an argument that has also been refuted in compelling form by Adrian Johns in *The Nature of the Book: Print and Knowledge in the Making* (Chicago: Chicago University Press, 1998), 10–40. While I agree with both studies' problematization of fixity, I disagree with their treatment of the nineteenth century as the age that finally established fixity via the industrially bound, standardized, and self-contained book. Such a historiography overlooks the unsettling effect that nineteenth century periodicals, ephemera, and serialized forms had on textual and material fixity.
8 Knight, *Bound to Read*, 7.
9 Petra McGillen, "Kompilieren," in *Historisches Wörterbuch des Mediengebrauchs*, ed. Heiko Christians, Matthias Bickenbach, and Nikolaus Wegmann (Cologne: Böhlau, 2015), 358.
10 Knight, *Bound to Read*, 6–7.
11 Ibid., 8.

two forms in the nineteenth century: the newspaper editor and the producer of *Kolportage* novels.[12] Both figures habitually performed the particular material intertextuality that Knight describes as characteristic of the early modern compiler. To patch together their texts—newspaper articles or installments of serialized fiction—they first amassed and then fluidly moved between source materials on a wide generic spectrum, treating texts as material objects that could be cut up, adapted, and quickly (re)published. For biographical, sociological, and media-historical reasons, both types of producers became crucial parts of Fontane's multifaceted authorial profile, as we shall see later.

Acknowledging that Fontane was a compiler leads to a fundamental shift in perspective. When treated as a compiler, he joins a literary tradition quite different from canonical German realism; his output seems more akin to that of newspaper editors, modern information workers, mass producers of light entertainment, and, via *Kolportage*, modern remix artists. If, moreover, we are to take seriously the insights of scholarship on the early modern period and remix studies, this output ought to be evaluated anew, with revised notions of intertextuality and its related concepts (such as originality and epigonism). All of these concepts must be grounded in the material realities of late nineteenth-century compiling.

Bringing the hidden compiler in Fontane to light, however, requires three things. First, it requires a careful reconstruction of the two sites at which the author learned how to gather and patch: the mid-nineteenth-century pharmacy and the newsroom of a daily paper, the *Kreuzzeitung*,[13] in Berlin. While in his first career as a pharmacist, Fontane acquired material practices foundational to his compilatory working methods, such as cutting, organizing, and composing, his second career as a newspaper editor taught him to perform compiling as a sophisticated and professional textual practice. Second, the re-evaluation of Fontane's authorial profile calls for an analysis of the curious products that he patched together as a newspaper editor. Typically, Fontane's journalistic

---

12 I am purposefully not including the nineteenth-century anthologist in this typology because anthologists produce collections of individual texts, not textual patchwork.

13 The newspaper was officially called *Neue Preußische Zeitung* [*New Prussian Newspaper*]. It insisted on referring to itself as *Kreuzzeitung* [*Cross-newspaper*] in the masthead, though, to avoid confusion with the *Preußische Zeitung*, which was also based in Berlin. See Heide Streiter-Buscher, introduction to *Theodor Fontane: Unechte Korrespondenzen 1860–1865* (Berlin: De Gruyter, 1996), 1. Because *Kreuzzeitung* has become the far more familiar name in the scholarship, I will continue to use it throughout this book. In references, it will be abbreviated in accordance with the scholarship as *NP(K)Z*.

career is seen as distinct from his career as a literary author, overlapping at best in a reservoir of shared subject matter and a few poetic strategies. If one analyzes the articles that Fontane compiled at the *Kreuzzeitung*, however, it becomes evident that journalistic compiling shaped core areas of the author's literary poetics, such as his modes of originality and realism. Third, this comprehensive reconstruction requires a reading of Fontane's autobiographical writings that teases out material traces of his textual practices that frequently undermine the lofty image that he tried to establish. What awaits at the end of this reconstructive process is a completely different Fontane, now the paradigm of a new authorial figure: the nineteenth-century compiler as a precursor to the modern remix artist.

The Pharmacy as Storehouse: Boxes and Material Practices

Fontane's first career as a pharmacist lasted well over a decade, but the scholarship has not attributed a substantial formative influence to it. Born in the *Löwenapotheke* in Neuruppin, which his father ran, Fontane joined a Berlin pharmacy as a sixteen-year-old apprentice in April 1836, at his father's suggestion. He completed the vocational training in early 1840 and subsequently worked, interrupted by his one-year military service, a few illnesses, and his first trip to England, in various positions as a pharmacist until he transitioned into a full-time post at the Press Office, or *Literarisches Cabinet*, of the Prussian Department of the Interior in 1850.[14] Accepting Fontane's self-fashioning in his autobiographical writings at face value, the standard biographical accounts consider this time as formative only in terms of the literary connections he forged, political circles he entered, observations about society he made, and literary dreams he nourished.[15] It is usually

---

14 For a helpful summary of Fontane's biography, see Helmuth Nürnberger, "Theodor Fontane: Leben und Persönlichkeit," in *Fontane-Handbuch*, ed. Christian Grawe and Helmuth Nürnberger (Stuttgart: Kröner, 2000), 25–40.

15 See, in chronological order, Joachim Schobess, "Fontanes Apothekerlaufbahn und ihr Einfluss auf sein literarisches Schaffen," *Die Pharmazie* 9 (1958): 588–94; Hans-Heinrich Reuter, *Fontane* (Munich: Nymphenburger Verlagshandlung, 1968): 1:122–6; Helmuth Nürnberger, *Fontanes Welt* (Berlin: Siedler, 1997), 62–122; Wolfang Hädecke, *Theodor Fontane: Biographie* (Munich: Hanser, 1998), 54–60. While Schobess concedes that Fontane's first occupation provided "einen nicht unwesentlichen Grundstein zu dem gesellschaftskritischen, unübertroffen realistischen Prosawerk des alten ... Fontane" (589), Schobess provides the model for later biographers in that he confines his analysis to the "Menschenkenntnis" that the future writer developed as a pharmacist. As for self-fashioning, Fontane begins his autobiography with an anecdote about his final exam as a pharmaceutical apprentice, which happened to coincide exactly with the appearance of his first substantial poetic work, the novella

assessed as a period in which Fontane unenthusiastically carried out his day job (a "disillusionment," according to Nürnberger) only to pursue his literary ambitions after hours.[16] These accounts, however, do not acknowledge that a profound *déformation professionelle* may take place on the level of practice, in the shape of embodied working routines, regardless of whether one self-identifies with a profession. That such a transformation occurred is particularly plausible considering that well into the nineteenth century, pharmaceutical training emphasized the acquisition of practical skills, following the pattern of other traditional German trades.[17] Evidence from Fontane's *Nachlass*, in conjunction with several remarks he made in passing, suggests that Fontane did in fact internalize material practices at the pharmacy that would become conducive to his activities as a compiler. Above all else, he learned how to store his materials in separate receptacles. This was a mode of storage that many compilers systematically used beginning in the early modern period because it opened up rich combinatorial and organizational possibilities.[18]

The connection between pharmaceutical training and the basic compilatory skills of gathering and storing is not as farfetched as it may seem. The preindustrialized pharmacy has a deep historical affinity with the early modern natural-curiosity cabinet and the natural-scientific collection, because pharmacists and doctors between the sixteenth and late eighteenth centuries derived their *materia medica* predominantly from plants, animals, soil, and rocks. In pharmacies and natural-curiosity cabinets alike, the collected specimens were put on display, which at times involved dangling spectacular showpieces such as stuffed crocodiles and other exotic animals from the ceiling.[19] Fontane

---

Geschwisterliebe (*Sibling Affection*), in the *Berliner Figaro*. The latter is far more important an event for the narrating "I" than the former, and so the opening chapter of *Von Zwanzig bis Dreißig* establishes the theme of Fontane's overcoming his existence as a pharmacist to find his true calling as a writer. Wolfgang Rasch's excellent commentary conclusively proves, however, that the exam and the publication did not happen on the same day and that the fudging of dates is due to a "erzählerische[n] Dramaturgie . . ., die auf das Ende der Lehrzeit den Beginn einer öffentlichen Dichterlaufbahn folgen lassen will" (536).

16 Nürnberger, *Fontanes Welt*, 64.
17 See Elisabeth Huwer, *Das deutsche Apotheken-Museum. Schätze aus zwei Jahrtausenden Kultur- und Pharmaziegeschichte*, 2nd ed. (Regensburg: Schnell und Steiner, 2008), 46–8.
18 A famous example is Vincent Placcius' "Note Closet." For a detailed description of this and other devices of famous compilers that includes illustrations, see Blair, *Too Much to Know*, 93–102.
19 See Peter Dilg, "Apotheker als Sammler," in *Macrocosmos in Microcosmo: Die Welt in der Stube. Zur Geschichte des Sammelns 1450 bis 1800*, ed. Andreas Grote (Opladen: Leske und Budrich, 1994), 453–4.

pays tribute to this history in *Meine Kinderjahre* (*My Childhood Years*) when he describes his father's pharmacy in Swinemünde in terms evocative of a provincial curiosity cabinet: the slightly uncanny house is "furnished with a world of things," swallows and butterflies fly back and forth between "great herb planters" (*Kräuterkisten*), and "the laboratory with its alembics and spirit stills (between which a dried halibut hung from the vaulted ceiling)" appears to the young Fontane as "a perfectly alchemistic room, wherein Faust might easily have intoned his 'Now I have studied'" (*ein vollkommen alchimistischer Raum, darin Faust sein 'Habe nun, ach' ohne weitres hätte beginnen können*, HFA III.4: 35–6; 39).

Indeed, pharmacies, or *Apotheken*, are literally "storehouses" for drugs. Accordingly, among the first tasks that apprentices such as Fontane had to learn was how to effectively store the many materials, ingredients, and instruments of a pharmaceutical practice. The best-known nineteenth-century textbooks, such as Trommsdorff's *Systematisches Handbuch der Pharmacie für angehende Aerzte und Apotheker* (*Systematic Handbook for Trainee Physicians and Pharmacists*, Vienna, 1816) and Hagen's *Lehrbuch der Apothekerkunst* (*Textbook of the Pharmacist's Art*, 8th ed., 1828), preface the discussion of chemical processes with detailed descriptions of the interior design of the pharmacy. Trommsdorff states in the second chapter that the pharmacy "must be a house well furnished for the gathering, storage, preparation, and sale of drugs."[20] Concretely, this requirement translated into a central workroom, or *Offizin*, in which ensembles of differently sized cabinets and tall shelves were arranged around a large *Rezepturtisch*, the desk on which the pharmacist spread out ingredients and utensils for mixing medicines.[21] The shelves accommodated myriad receptacles. Among them, *Kasten* were key because they allowed for the separate storage of perishable raw materials and drugs in dry and airy conditions. *Kasten* came in two forms: freestanding boxes made of wood, tin, or cardboard, and wooden drawers, or *Schubkasten*, which were built directly into the shelves and the work desk. In essence, the pharmacist worked in an environment filled with receptacles that kept everything he or she needed at hand.

Fontane, who mentions Hagen's textbook in *Von Zwanzig bis Dreißig*, adopted important principles of this design in the study in his last

---

20 Trommsdorff, *Systematisches Handbuch der Pharmacie für angehende Aerzte und Apotheker*, 2nd. rev. ed. (Vienna: Aloys Doll, 1816), 11–12.
21 For descriptions, with excellent reproductions, of the interior design of pharmacies in different historical settings, complete with receptacles and "Rezepturtischen," see Elisabeth Huwer, "Arbeitsplatz Apotheke," in *Das deutsche Apotheken-Museum*, 46–99.

apartment in Potsdamer Straße 134c, to which he moved in 1872 and where he produced the majority of the literary texts for which he is known today. From descriptions by his son Friedel and others, and from various photographs and drawings, it is clear that the author's massive desk was flanked by several pieces of furniture for the storage of writing utensils and textual materials in all sizes (e.g., newspapers, books, maps, folders, letters, and fair copies of manuscripts).[22] This furniture included a shelf fitted with a deep bottom, drawers, and pigeonholes; another tall shelf; a cabinet (*Vertikow*); and a ledge holding stashes of manuscripts. Strikingly, the desk itself closely resembled a *Rezepturtisch*. It had a huge work surface and was equipped with drawers at the front and back, as Friedel points out: "However, what I wish particularly to emphasize is that the front of the table facing the windows also displays numerous drawers. Hence, it could be used from two sides."[23] Precisely this design peculiarity can be found in the pharmaceutical work desks on display at the German Pharmacy Museum in Heidelberg. Fontane purchased the desk secondhand in 1861 from his friend Wilhelm Lübke, a prolific art historian.[24] It is

---

22 My reconstruction of Fontane's working environment is based on the following sources: Hans-Werner Klünner, "Theodor Fontanes Wohnstätten in Berlin," *Fontane Blätter* 4, no. 2 (1977): 107–34; Machner, "Der Dichternachlaß," 251–68; Klaus-Peter Möller, "Preußisches Panoptikum mit Pfefferkuchen: Fontane-Porträts und –Bildnisse (2)," *Fontane Blätter* 78 (2004): 52–74; and the anecdotes by Ottomar Beta ("Er hat mich bis zueltzt geottomart"), Friedrich Fontane ("Potsdamer Straße 134c"), and Gertrud Schacht ("'Kind, du darfts kommen!'") in *"Erschrecken Sie nicht, ich bin es selbst,"* ed. Wolfgang Rasch and Christine Hehle (Berlin: Aufbau, 2003), 34–43, 80–6, 260–4. The photographs and drawings are as follows: the photographs taken by the Berlin studio Zander und Labisch in 1896 (Theodor-Fontane-Archiv, file no. TFA_AI 96_33853; fig 0.1); a wood engraving by Georg Dreher showing Fontane at his desk; a floor plan of Fontane's study drawn by his son Friedrich; and a portrait of Fontane by Hanns Fechner from 1893 known as the *Wolkenschaubild*. All of these images are printed in Möller, "Preußisches Panoptikum mit Pfefferkuchen," and in Hans-Werner Klünner, "Theodor Fontane im Bildnis," in *Festschrift der Landesgeschichtlichen Vereinigung für die Mark Brandenburg*, ed. Eckart Henning and Werner Vogel (Berlin: n.p., 1984), 279–307.
23 Qtd. in Machner, "Potsdamer Straße 134c," 80. Hermann Fricke's account of Fontane's *Nachlass* provides a specific number of drawers; he describes the desk as "rechts und links auf Vorder- und Rückfront mit je zehn Schubkästen, breit und geräumig [ausgestattet]." See Hermann Fricke, "Das Theodor-Fontane-Archiv. Einst und jetzt," *Jahrbuch für brandenburgische Landesgeschichte* 15 (1964): 168.
24 A replica of the desk is preserved at the *Stadtmuseum Berlin*, but because its measurements are slightly inaccurate, it is not officially on view. The original desk has been considered lost since the Second World War. See Machner, "Potsdamer Straße 134c," 267.

unlikely that Lübke had acquired the desk from a pharmacy; rather, the important point is that Fontane chose a desk with an inbuilt mode of storage—numerous drawers—that he knew from his pharmacy work, and that he used it throughout his career.

The author's correspondence is full of remarks that demonstrate how intensely he used his *Kasten*. For example, when he was about to begin proofreading the second volume of *Der Deutsche Krieg 1866* (*The German War of 1866*) while being held as a prisoner of war in France, he wrote to his wife, Emilie, to request manuscript sheets from one of his drawers:

> To this end, I shall also require one or two manuscript sheets, which are to be found in the *middle* of the three drawers to the right of my seat at the desk. The nethermost drawer contains the novel's manuscript [*Before the Storm*, PM], so I mean the drawer *above* it; in the right-hand part of the drawer itself. It is [a] draft in pencil, titled "Closing Remarks" or suchlike.

> *Ich gebrauche dazu auch noch einen oder zwei Manuskriptbogen, die in dem* mittleren *der drei Kästen liegen, die zur rechten meines Platzes am Schreibtisch sind. Im untersten Kasten liegt das Roman-Manuskript* [Vor dem Sturm, PM], *also in dem Kasten darüber; im Kasten selbst rechts. Es ist Bleistiftschreiberei, trägt die Ueberschrift "Schlußbemerkung" oder so ähnlich.*
>
> (October 25, 1870; GBA XII.2: 530)

Numerous other examples could be cited.[25] The various references in Fontane's letters indicate, moreover, that the author used not only drawers, but also the freestanding kind of pharmaceutical *Kasten* to store textual materials. In fact, an anecdote about Fontane suggests that he indeed internalized the use of these receptacles as part of his vocational training. One of the typical tasks of apprentices in

---

25 See, for example, the letters to Bernhard van Lepel, January 2, 1857; to Julius Grosser, January 31, 1882; to Emil Dominik, January 25, 1887; to Emilie, October 2, 1888; to Friedlaender, May 22, 1893. The catalog for the 1933 auction in which Friedrich Fontane sold off his father's belongings, moreover, lists as Item No. 662 a small "Erinnerungs-Kästchen," which contained various notes, excerpts, and a few items of personal paraphernalia. In a note that was kept in the lid, Fontane designated it as "mein Stoffkästchen." Meyer & Ernst, *Theodor Fontane. August von Kotzebue. Zwei deutsche Dichternachlässe. Katalog 35* (Berlin, 1933), 112. I am very grateful to Wolfgang Rasch for pointing me to this auction catalog.

nineteenth-century pharmacies was gluing together receptacles made of cardboard.²⁶ Fontane's acquaintance Ottomar Beta reports that he once encountered the author at home, doing precisely that (*er klebte*), and adds that Fontane possessed a "great adeptness (*große Handfertigkeit*) at making boxes."²⁷ In response to Beta's sudden appearance, Fontane purportedly blushed with embarrassment and explained that this was "a mechanical pastime (*Beschäftigung*) . . . , it has been second nature to me (*ist mir zur zweiten Natur geworden*) since my days as a pharmacist. It distracts me or, failing that, makes for agreeable thinking." Fontane himself, then, considered his "pharmaceutical period" formative on the level of the practical, the habitual, and the deeply ingrained. While no homemade cardboard boxes have been preserved, they surface in descriptions of Fontane's study; Friedel mentions an "entire assortment of specially made little cardboard boxes"²⁸ (*extra angefertigten Pappkästen*) on the tall shelf, in which the author kept letters, and another "four boxes" on the smaller shelf that contained "all manner of things." There can be no doubt, then, that the author adopted the pharmaceutical use of *Kasten* for the storage of his correspondence, sources, notes, drafts, and utensils. As a compiler, he benefited poetologically from this use of separate receptacles, as a more detailed analysis in Chapter 3 will demonstrate.

The peculiar paper envelopes that Fontane created from newspaper, the labels that he affixed, and the type of glue with which he worked further testify to the pharmaceutical influence on his material working methods. Early nineteenth-century pharmacies were paper-based enterprises; the material played an important role in many administrative, organizational, and production-related processes. Pharmacists routinely folded paper around goods that they stored and sold. Apprentices had to produce the so-called *Faltbriefchen*, little paper wrappers or envelopes in which powders and pills were dispensed in small quantities.²⁹ As a compiler, Fontane continued this practice on a larger scale. Many of his large newspaper envelopes have descriptive labels, which may yet again have been a result of his vocational training,

---

26 E-mail exchange with Elisabeth Huwer, Director of the *Deutsches Apotheken-Museum* Heidelberg, June 15, 2011. I am indebted to Dr. Huwer for sharing her expertise and reference materials on this topic with me.
27 Beta, "Er hat mich bis zuletzt geottomart: Gespräche in London und Berlin," in '*Erschrecken Sie nicht, ich bin es selbst,*' 38. Fontane also mentions *Papparbeit*, the creation of cardboard figures and settings with the help of scissors, glue, and paint, as one of his favorite childhood pastimes in *Meine Kinderjahre* (HFA III.4: 139–40).
28 Friedrich Fontane, qtd. in Machner, "Potsdamer Straße 134c," 253.
29 See Huwer, *Das deutsche Apotheken-Museum*, 188.

because pharmaceutical handbooks always emphasized the importance of labeling. The glue he used was certainly a product of the pharmacy: Fontane worked with *Mehlpapp*, a mixture of water and flour, and Hagen's pharmaceutical textbook recommends the exact same mixture in various chemical processes.

Beyond storage, the pharmacy gave Fontane the opportunity to practice the general compositional principle of any compilatory process: cutting up the gathered ingredients and combining them into a new mixture. Hagen's textbook distinguishes four mechanical operations, all of which translate easily into the cut-and-paste activities of compilers: the "division and separation" (*Theilung und Zertrennung*) of raw materials into "parts of equal nature," the "breaking down" (*Zersetzung*) into "component parts," the "mixing (*Vermischung*) of crude drugs . . . or the component parts of various such substances with each other," and the "transplantation (*Versetzung*), when a substance's components are alternately inserted into another."[30]

The precision and constant adjustments that the compositional process required on the pharmacist's part may even have led Fontane to develop a "pharmaceutical" working style. Fontane is well known for his endless, even pedantic tweaking of his literary compositions, provided that he was not pressed for time.[31] This aspect of his poetics has plausible roots in the pharmaceutical laboratory. Fontane himself found this connection quite likely. He called the process "laboratory work" (*Laboratoriumsarbeit*, HFA IV.3, 535) and reflected on it with mixed feelings. This ambivalence is evident in an 1898 letter to his daughter Mete about Henrik Ibsen, a fellow pharmacist-turned-poet. In this letter, Fontane quotes a critic who had remarked that Ibsen never cast off the pharmacist, who now haunted his plays and his conversation: "He is ever the little pharmacist (*ein kleiner Apotheker*), biding his time and tiptoeing about (*der dribbelt*) and lying in wait (*und auf der Lauer liegt*)." Fontane agrees with the critic, adding: "I had to laugh out loud, if only to hide my own fear behind the big guffaw" (HFA IV.3, 726). The thought that his pharmaceutical training might have influenced his output was obviously as uncomfortable for him as it was plausible.

---

30 Karl Gottfried Hagen, *Lehrbuch der Apothekerkunst*, 3rd ed. (Königsberg; Leipzig: Hartung, 1786), 494–6 (§204).

31 For an excellent analysis of Fontane's stylistic refinements, see Gabriele Radecke, *Vom Schreiben zum Erzählen. Eine textgenetische Studie zu Theodor Fontanes 'L'Adultera'* (Würzburg: Königshausen & Neumann, 2002), 83–9. More recently, Clarissa Blomqvist has analyzed Fontane's late-stage revision strategies in "'Dreiviertel ist corrigiren und feilen gewesen.' Theodor Fontanes Bearbeitung eigener Texte," *Euphorion* 111, no. 1 (2017): 75–91.

The pharmacy, then, shaped the basic material practices that the author acquired as routines and that permeated his working methods, influencing even his compositional style. These practices were not yet concretely embodied in the making of text, however. Their translation into modes of textual productivity happened elsewhere: in the Berlin newsroom of the *Kreuzzeitung*, which Fontane joined on May 30, 1860, and where he learned how to compile professionally—and how to cover his tracks.

The Editor's Patchwork of Commonplaces: Compiling "False Foreign Correspondences"

Editors (*Redakteure*) have always been compilers. The earliest modern newspapers, the *avvisi*, were the products of scissors and glue: preprofessional "journalists" such as postmasters and printers collected news stories from various sources and patched them together in newsletters that they then disseminated.[32] Even as newspapers became more professionalized in the years leading up to the March Revolution and as the so-called "editorial (*redaktioneller*) journalism"[33] emerged, compilatory practices remained paramount. Editorial journalism was built upon the principle of what contemporaries called *Räsonnement*, that is, the critical evaluation of news items and their sources. Rather

---

32 See Jörg Requate, *Journalismus als Beruf. Entstehung und Entwicklung des Journalistenberufs im 19. Jahrhundert – Deutschland im internationalen Vergleich* (Göttingen: Vandenhoeck & Ruprecht, 1995), 118. For a more detailed European history of the *avvisi*, see Andrew Pettegree, *The Invention of News: How the World Came to Know about Itself* (New Haven, CT: Yale University Press, 2014), 107–13; 182–207.

33 I follow Requate's useful distinction between three overlapping periods in modern German journalism history. According to this periodicization, which goes back to Dieter Baumert's 1928 *Die Entstehung des deutschen Journalismus*, modern journalism began with "corresponding journalism" in the middle of the sixteenth century, after which came the phase of "literary journalism" from the middle of the eighteenth century on, finally to give way to "editorial journalism" after 1830. Each period had its own characteristic practices and media. In the case of corresponding journalism, the journalists' role comprised collecting and (re)publishing news items, which they had received in the form of correspondence and hearsay, in *avvisi*. Censorship and lack of sufficient training led to the largely uncritical publication of news; the "Bewertung der Meldungen oder 'Räsonnement' blieben in den 'Avisenzeitungen' aus" (Requate, *Journalismus als Beruf*, 118). "Literary journalism," by contrast, is characterized by the intense evaluation of the published content, and its main medium is the "Herausgeberzeitung," a paper led and often even run by a single person (such as Wieland's *Deutscher Merkur*). "Editorial journalism" replaces the one-man model with that of the "Redaktion," and its main medium is the "Verlegerzeitung," i.e., a newspaper whose editor-in-chief is backed by a publishing house (119–20).

than patching all kinds of news stories together, papers such as Cotta's *Neueste Weltkunde* and its successor, the *Allgemeine Zeitung*, strove to present a well-organized and comprehensive selection of "true facts."[34] This task called for full-time professionals, *Redakteure*, who worked in salaried positions and gradually replaced the rotating rosters of high-school teachers, pastors, lawyers, and doctors who had previously helped the newspaper owners as freelancers.[35] These *Redakteure* required access to large reservoirs of source materials—mainly reports from news agencies and correspondents, official announcements, letters from informants, and of course other newspapers—to compare and critique. Accordingly, Kürschner describes the main tasks of the *Redakteur* as first assessing the incoming material in terms of its usability for printing, and second, lending the usable material its final form, in which it was set and printed. He concludes that writing is only the editor's secondary calling: "His foremost task is to appraise, redact, rework, arrange."[36] This emphasis on editing resulted in completely malleable texts: the *Redakteure* essentially cut up the source materials to edit and rearrange them for their newspapers, producing combinations of foreign and "home-made" texts that were better verified and better researched than the contents of the *avvisi*, but which were nonetheless still based on compiling. In short, the sophistication of the editors and the resources available determined the extent to which a newspaper was "a mere compilation from other papers"[37] or ran its own exclusive articles. The medium-sized and ultra-conservative *Kreuzzeitung*, which Fontane joined as "editor for English affairs" (*Redakteur des englischen Artikels*) on May 30, 1860, did both.[38]

By the time the forty-year-old Fontane took over the England desk in the paper's Berlin newsroom, he had already been a serious journalist for several years and had contributed to a number of publications, the *Kreuzzeitung* included.[39] His journalistic work ranged from news reports

---

34 Ibid., 122–3.
35 Ibid., 121–30.
36 Joseph Kürschner, *Handbuch der Presse für Schriftsteller, Redaktionen, Verleger [und] überhaupt Alle, die mit der Presse in Beziehung stehen* (Berlin: Hillger, 1902), col. 1575.
37 Requate, *Journalismus als Beruf*, 153.
38 Cofounded by Bismarck and other conservatives in 1848, the *Kreuzzeitung* was a highly partisan paper. It was expressly intended as an "Instrument zur Bekämpfung liberaler, fortschrittlicher Ideen und zur Unterstützung der gefährdeten Monarchie." Luise Berg-Ehlers, *Theodor Fontane und die Literaturkritik: Zur Rezeption eines Autors in der zeitgenössischen konservativen und liberalen Berliner Tagespresse* (Bonn: Winkler, 1990), 27.
39 For a complete summary of Fontane's journalistic *curriculum vitae*, see Streiter-Buscher, "Die politische Journalistik," in *Fontane-Handbuch*, ed. Christian Grawe

sent from abroad to political articles, cultural criticism, historical essays, travel writings, war reporting, and literary portraits.[40] One can assume that text production in several of these genres involved compilatory practices, especially in the case of texts that Fontane assembled for the Prussian Communications Department of the Manteuffel government. The Department had hired him in 1850 to influence public opinion by excerpting current newspapers, imbuing the excerpts with the desired political tinge, and sending them as so-called *Privatkorrespondenzen* to the offices of smaller local papers.[41] I focus on Fontane's decade at the *Kreuzzeitung* to study how he became a compiler for two reasons. First, his work at the *Kreuzzeitung* has been better researched than any of his other journalistic employments, despite a challenging archival situation.[42] Moreover, while Fontane was compiling at the *Kreuzzeitung*, he also started working on his first significant prose texts, namely, the earliest episodes of the *Wanderungen durch die Mark Brandenburg* (*Walks through Mark Brandenburg*) and drafts of his first novel, *Before the Storm*. The years at the *Kreuzzeitung* thus lend themselves particularly well to examining the crossover between modes of journalistic and literary text production.

Fontane signed on to be in the *Kreuzzeitung* newsroom for three hours a day, from 9:30 a.m. to 12:30 p.m. (although in reality, he often stayed until the newsroom closed around 2:00 p.m.).[43] Together with four colleagues, and supervised by one editor-in-chief, he helped to fill the pages of the Berlin daily for 900 *Thaler*, later 1,000 *Thaler*, per month, a typical salary for an editor.[44] His main responsibility, the England desk, called for two forms of compiling, one simple and the other more

---

and Helmuth Nürnberger (Stuttgart: Kröner, 2000), 788–806. His motivations for joining the *Kreuzzeitung* are discussed conclusively in Streiter-Buscher's introduction to her edition of *Theodor Fontane: Unechte Korrespondenzen*, 8–9.

40 See Charlotte Jolles, "Fontane als Journalist und Essayist," *Jahrbuch für internationale Germanistik* 7, no. 2 (1975): 104.
41 See Streiter-Buscher, "Die politische Journalistik," 795–6.
42 In addition to Streiter-Buscher and Berg-Ehlers, see Roland Berbig and Bettina Hartz, eds., *Theodor Fontane im literarischen Leben: Zeitungen und Zeitschriften, Verlage und Vereine* (Berlin: De Gruyter, 2000), 61–70, and Dorothee Krings, *Theodor Fontane als Journalist – Selbstverständnis und Werk* (Cologne: von Halem, 2008) 15–20, 63–9, 173–4. Apropos of the archival situation, Streiter-Buscher points out that no Fontane diaries from the *Kreuzzeitung* years have been preserved; furthermore, the archive of the newspaper is lost. See Streiter-Buscher, introduction, *Theodor Fontane: Unechte Korrespondenzen*, 31.
43 Ibid., 13.
44 Streiter-Buscher calls this salary fully in line with what other papers paid. See "'...und dann wieder jahrelang unechter Korrespondent': Der Kreuzzeitungsredakteur Theodor Fontane." *Fontane Blätter* 58 (1994): 90.

sophisticated. Both are worth analyzing because they reveal what happens to source texts when compilers rework them and suggest the implications of this practice for the poetics of the compiled text.

Fontane's comparatively simple first task was to fill the daily rubric "Great Britain," located on pages 2 and 3 of the paper, with news. He had to survey and choose from the source materials, collocate the most striking passages, connect them with a few words of his own, and at times put them in the desired perspective through brief introductory or concluding phrases that he added as the "head" or the "tail"[45] of a news item. One gets a clear sense of the material dimensions of this process from looking at one of Fontane's typical sources, a correspondence (*Korrespondenz*) sent by Max Schlesinger's news bureau (Figure 2.2), and the compilation that this source became.

An Austrian-born émigré, Schlesinger was the London correspondent of the day, and a number of important German dailies—including the *Kreuzzeitung*—subscribed to his well-informed news service and received lithographed sheets such as the one shown in the reproduction.[46] "Correspondences" such as this were designed to make the editors' business "as comfortable as possible," as Wuttke's 1866 study *Die deutschen Zeitschriften* (*German Periodicals*) put it,[47] which is to say that they facilitated compiling through specific material features.

Beginning with a dateline ("London, Saturday, June 22, 1861"), this example brings a variety of ready-made news items together in two columns, from which the editor could choose as he saw fit.[48] To make it easier to select from the topics, which in this example include "Parliament News" and a comprehensive review of the English press, the central names and topics in each article are underlined. The most

---

45 This reconstruction of Fontane's work process and of the features of the source materials is indebted to Streiter-Buscher, introduction, *Theodor Fontane: Unechte Korrespondenzen*, 1: 35–7.

46 Hubert Reitterer, "Schlesinger, Max(imilian)," *Österreichisches Biographisches Lexikon und biographische Dokumentation 1815–1950* (Vienna: Verlag der Österreichischen Akademie der Wissenschaften, 1992), 10: 197–8. That Schlesinger wrote the "Correspondences" by hand and had them lithographed was common for this kind of medium because typesetting would have been too slow and costly. See Heinrich Wuttke, *Die deutschen Zeitschriften und die Entstehung der öffentlichen Meinung. Ein Beitrag zur Geschichte des Zeitungswesens*, 3rd ed. (Leipzig: Krüger, 1875) 124–6.

47 Wuttke, *Die deutschen Zeitschriften*, 125.

48 Later, the two-column design gave way to a four-column design on larger sheets (*c.* 50 × 60 cm), as a correspondence piece by Schlesinger's news bureau from 1874 indicates (reproduced in Streiter-Buscher's study). Other material features—dateline, margins, keywords, clearly bounded sections—remained the same. See Streiter-Buscher, introduction, *Unechte Korrespondenzen*, 1: 42–3.

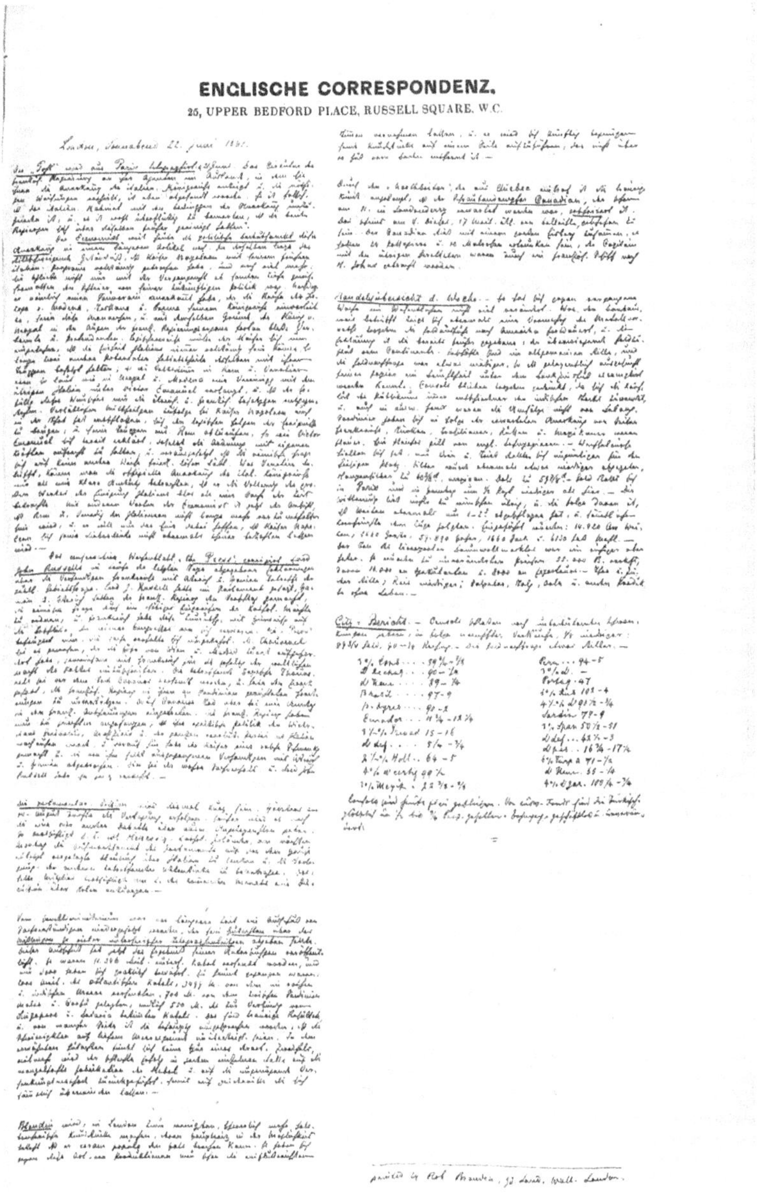

ENGLISCHE CORRESPONDENZ.

25, UPPER BEDFORD PLACE, RUSSELL SQUARE, W.C.

London, Sonnabend 22. Juni 1861.

Figure 2.2 Max Schlesinger's "Englische Correspondenz" from June 22, 1861.

important feature, however, is the margin that surrounds each article. Through the margin, every article is clearly bounded, takes on a modular appearance, and becomes easy to excise. The editor could thus copy or snip out only the items he needed and paste them together with England news from other sources onto a new blank sheet.

The resulting document was a compilation, a thematically motivated collocation of gathered items that were transformed in the editing process. While no such compiled documents written in Fontane's hand have survived, one produced by his colleague George Hesekiel can serve as an adequate substitute (Figure 2.3).[49] Hesekiel and Fontane had nearly identical jobs at the *Kreuzzeitung*, except that Hesekiel was responsible for different countries, mainly France and Spain. Hesekiel's manuscript sheet illustrates the compiling practices that editors at the foreign desks used to fill their news columns: they appropriated, edited, and repurposed the gleaned materials to arrive at a document that was visibly glued together and that presented news items clipped directly from other papers (or from "correspondences") mixed with news items written out or copied by hand.

The underlying processes of compiling changed the nature of the original articles, as Hesekiel's example shows. They are no longer whole, as the editor has cut out only those sections that he has deemed relevant for his own column. The transposition into a new context also necessitates semantic adjustments. In the third article, the editor has cut off a portion of the sentence with which the excised section begins, and has inserted a specific time adverb (*vorgestern*, the day before yesterday) that synchronizes the described event with the publication rhythm of the *Kreuzzeitung*. In the next step, such a compiled pastiche would be marked up by the supervising editor and then given to the typesetter, who would add it to the form for the printed newspaper page. Once printed, any traces of compilation would no longer be visible: the homogenizing face of print would make the seams of this "patchwork" disappear.

The second task of editors at the foreign desks was to produce "false foreign correspondences" (*unechte Korrespondenzen*), the medium for a more sophisticated form of compiling. This form was highly relevant to Fontane's literary poetics because of the way the compiler manufactured authenticity in these articles, a method he would use in his realist literary projects. A widespread phenomenon in late nineteenth-century journalism, "false foreign correspondences" consisted of relatively long

---

49 The credit for finding this sheet goes to Streiter-Buscher, who located this and other manuscripts in the *Nachlass* of the Hesekiel family in the *Staatsarchiv Coburg*, Germany. The manuscript shown in Figure 2.3 is not reproduced in Streiter-Buscher's study.

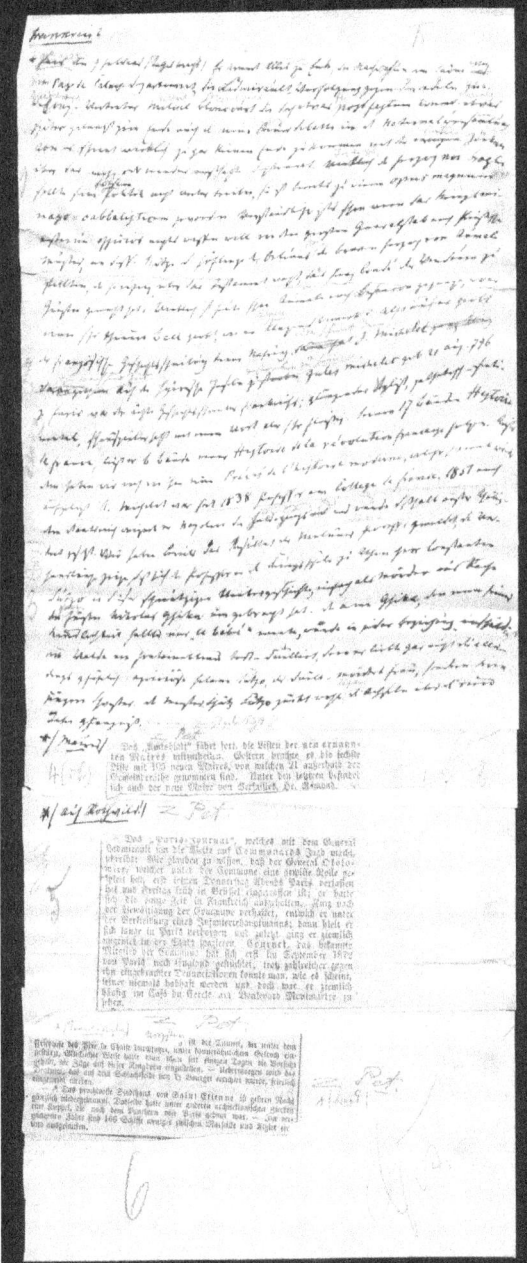

Figure 2.3 Manuscript page, compiled and written by George Hesekiel, with contributions to the "France" column of the *Neue Preußische (Kreuz-)Zeitung*.

and analytical news articles or opinion pieces written in the style of letters, ostensibly by correspondents reporting from abroad.[50] Like a regular article, each piece had a dateline indicating "when" and "from where" it had supposedly been written, and a logogram (*Sigle*) at the beginning established the sense of a particular authorial identity, even though this identity was not publicly revealed. Such articles were works of fiction, however. They were produced not by foreign correspondents, but by an editor who patched them together at his Berlin desk in much the same way as he assembled the news column.[51] The reader, of course, was supposed to believe that he or she was reading an authentic first-hand account produced by an individual reporter at a foreign site.

Analysis of Fontane's "false foreign correspondences" reveals the method by which the reader is being led on. The editor compiles news articles that toggle between trading in stereotypical knowledge and establishing their own aesthetic codes. The stereotypical content makes a given account credible because the reader can recognize it as familiar;[52] in contrast, the unique aesthetic code that surfaces in carefully regulated doses in each article helps to "personalize" the account and corroborate the impression that an individual reporter with a unique worldview is writing. In combination, these two textual strategies create an impression of authenticity.[53] There are no manuscript sheets from Fontane's archives

---

50 See Streiter-Buscher, introduction, *Theodor Fontane: Unechte Korrespondenzen*, 49. Günter and Homberg emphasize that the phenomenon of "false foreign correspondence" must be seen as a response to the rise of modern news agencies, which dispatched ever-more anonymous news articles written in a neutral voice. "Authentication" through an individual reporter's first-person narratives, as in the "false foreign correspondence," thus became a particularly effective (albeit unethical) strategy to make a given article stand out. See Manuela Günter and Michael Homberg, "'cut & paste' im 'Archiv der Massenmedien'? Theodor Fontanes *Unechte Korrespondenzen* und die Poesie der Zeitung," in *Archiv/Fiktionen. Verfahren des Archivierens in Literatur und Kultur des langen 19. Jahrhunderts*, ed. Daniela Gretz and Nicolas Pethes (Freiburg i. Br.: Rombach, 2016), 241–2.
51 Dotzler rightly points out that the fictionality of these articles did not foreclose the possibility of their being "objective" (*sachhaltig*)—although they had not been written abroad, they could still contain correct information. See Bernhard Dotzler, "Genuine Correspondences. Fontane's World Literature," trans. Chris Chiasson, *The Yearbook of Comparative Literature* 55 (2009): 266.
52 It is worth pointing out that Fontane exploits the communicative principle at the heart of all mass media for his purposes. Newspapers always standardize their reporting to some extent; they select "bestimmte Ereignismuster" and have a preference for "bestimmte – stereotype – Themen" to make their contents communicable and accessible, as Günter and Homberg point out in "'cut & paste' im 'Archiv der Massenmedien,'" 237.
53 For a polar opposite understanding of authenticity in Fontane's writings, see Robert Vellusig, "'Ein Widerspiel *des* Lebens, das wir führen.' Fontane und die

that would allow for a genetic reconstruction of the way these articles were written. It is possible, however, to reverse-engineer examples of published "false foreign correspondences" and compare them to the array of sources from which the author regularly gleaned his material.[54] Fontane's "false foreign correspondence" with the title "Das große Feuer und die Taschendiebe" ("The Great Fire and the Pickpockets"), purportedly written in London on June 26, 1861, lends itself well to such an exercise and evinces multiple facets of Fontane's sophisticated compilatory practice. The text was published in the *Kreuzzeitung* on June 30, 1861 and covered the so-called "Tooley Street Fire," later known as the "Great Fire" of 1861, which raged in Cotton's Wharf near London Bridge for well over a week, starting on June 22, 1861. The *Kreuzzeitung* had already published three articles about the fire based on (real) correspondence pieces by Schlesinger and his staff.[55] These articles had been written in a more or less neutral news style.[56] A topic as dramatic as a city fire, however, begged to be exploited further through an "eyewitness" piece. To put the fudged story together, Fontane turned not only to his usual sources, but also to the articles that had already been published in the *Kreuzzeitung*. In a brief commentary on Fontane's text, Streiter-Buscher states that "the correspondence is essentially a summary of the facts conveyed in the previous articles."[57] This characterization is not precise. Fontane's compiling involved not just summarizing facts, but also remixing the most pertinent commonplaces with which the fire and the surrounding scenery had already been described repeatedly in the previous articles (e.g., man's helplessness

---

Authentizität des poetischen Realismus," *Zeitschrift für deutsche Philologie* 125, no. 1 (2006): 215–18. Vellusig defines authenticity as a "reality of life" (*Lebenswirklichkeit*) and "quality of impression" (*Eindrucksqualität*), yet he makes efforts to keep these concepts free from mass media, which seems problematic in light of the overall saturation of Fontane's writings and the readers' world with mass-media content.

54 According to Streiter-Buscher, these sources include Max Schlesinger's news service, mentioned above, along with several of the bigger English and German newspapers, such as the *Times, Standard, Kölnische Zeitung, Allgemeine Zeitung, Weser-Zeitung, Hamburger Nachrichten,* and *Norddeutsche Allgemeine Zeitung.* See Streiter-Buscher, introduction, *Theodor Fontane: Unechte Korrespondenzen,* 36.

55 See Schlesinger's "Englische Correspondenzen," June 24–26, 1861, The British Library, German Collections, LOU.LON 2 [1861].

56 "Großes City=Feuer," *NP(K)Z* 147, June 27, 1861: S3; "Zum City=Brande," *NP(K)Z* 148, June 28, 1861: S3; "Zum City=Feuer," *NP(K)Z* 149, June 29, 1861: S3. The three articles will henceforth be cited as Sources A, B, and C.

57 See Streiter-Buscher's editorial commentary in *Theodor Fontane: 'Eine Zeitungsnummer lebt nur 12 Stunden.' Londoner Korrespondenzen aus Berlin,* ed. Heide Streiter-Buscher (Berlin: De Gruyter, 1998), 184.

when fighting the elements; the danger of being hit by collapsing walls). Additionally, Fontane incorporated an allusion to a book title and a cultural reference (to the Tower of Babel) and drew on a police report that had appeared in *The Times* to round off his piece. In his "false foreign correspondence," Fontane brought all of these gleaned elements into a new order and "authenticated" them through skillful dramatization in a first-person voice.

A full transcription of the resulting article as it appeared in print, with all of the gleaned elements highlighted and linked to their sources, provides ample evidence of this textual strategy. It shows that the compiler recycled old information from previous reporting in every major sentence of his article. Indeed, the connections to the "old" news about the fire are so crucial to the credibility of Fontane's armchair reporting that he explicitly reminds the readers of their knowledge in the opening sentence—he begins by saying, "news of the great fire . . ., which broke out around noon two days ago . . ., will already have reached you (see Nos. 147, 148, and 149)," referring to the previous three issues of the *Kreuzzeitung*. The only passages that are not obviously gleaned from previous articles are those conveying historical background information; they were easy enough to write up with access to a standard history reference. Fontane, however, almost never copied his sources' exact formulations. That he avoided replicating the exact wording makes the example particularly revelatory; it displays the skilled compiler's "glean and hide" strategy:

> *†* London, June 26. [The Great Fire and the Pickpockets.] The news of the great fire, which broke out at midday two days ago at Cotton Wharf in Southwark and destroyed a number of lofts and warehouses (the best and most fireproof London possessed, it is said[58]), will already have reached you (see nos. 147, 148, and 149). I was there today, my curiosity not to be outdone by hundreds of thousands[59] [of onlookers]. My companion had a pass of sorts, and we were thus able to approach quite closely[60] despite the cordon barring access to the scene. The sight is dreadful, and one looks upon the scene of the conflagration as upon a city of craters; yet the craters' fire is not exhausted;[61] there is uncanny life in the deeps, and a new blaze [*Lohe*] might shoot forth at any time from

---

58 B: "The warehouses . . . were among . . . London's best-built."
59 B: "The fire's site near London Bridge is . . . so heavily thronged with onlookers that the police has trouble . . . keeping them away."
60 B: "without being able to come close to the source of the fire because of the great heat".
61 A: "in which it continues to burn dangerously".

any one of the ashen mounds.[62] Ghostly is the aspect of the walls, some of which stand blanched by fire,[63] some blackened by smoke, some tilting precipitously and ready at any moment to come crashing down upon the ashen mounds and the smoldering vaults beneath.[64] It is the most dreadful fire by which London has been visited in many a year,[65] and as you may imagine, there has been no shortage of comparisons with the Great Fire, which in 1666 destroyed five-sixths of the old City of London (just across [the river] from the scene of the present fire). Indeed it can be ascribed only to a stroke of Divine mercy that not all of the borough of Southwark, with about half a million inhabitants, burned down as the old City did nearly two hundred years ago. All man's art and wit proved altogether powerless,[66] and all machines of rescue and protection would not have frustrated the borough's ruin if, instead of a complete calm,[67] a moderate northeasterly wind had animated the air and swept the column of fire[68] across the scalding hot roofs. I speak not of the human sacrifices the fire claimed, nor of Mr. Braidwood,[69] London's "Director of Fires," as you might call him in Berlin, nor even of those foolhardy wretches who, sailing up and down the burning embankment, skimmed the molten tallow off the water's surface and are likely to have perished[70] more numerously than has hitherto been supposed; I wish only to mention how these events have once again warned us against conceit and admonished us to

---

62 A: "All these massed lofts . . . are now but a steaming pile of rubble, from which flames continue to burst forth"; C: "from the cellars beneath . . . flames burst forth unceasingly."
63 B: "Partly because of the burnt-out and incandescent walls, which may collapse at the wind's slightest stirring".
64 C: "for many of the six-story high walls still stand erect, with some inclined and threatening to bury anybody audacious enough to come too close."
65 A: "Since Sunday afternoon, London has been visited by a blaze of an enormity such as has not been witnessed in many years."
66 B: "The pumps . . . could do nothing more than to stay the fire, and that too would have exceeded their power had the merest draught . . ."; C: "Foundations of vaulted stone, uncommonly solid brick walls, iron beams! What little use they all were!"
67 A: "Thanks to the calm".
68 C: "Throughout the night, the rising column of fire remains visible for miles".
69 A: "alas, several people met their death, the widely respected Braidwood, superintendent of the London Fire Engine Establishment, among them."
70 B: "Already in the night of Saturday . . . boatmen were close to, indeed amid the fire of the tallow streaming into the river, risking their lives in busily scooping it up. Several of these foolhardy men are said to have perished in doing so."

humility, which has become as rare in this age of "mechanical miracles"⁷¹ as it was in the days of Babel's tower. In this fire, the elements were all; man, who so enjoys acting their lord, was nothing. Neighboring lofts and cellars, in which were stored vats of ardent spirits and turpentine,⁷² were spared as if by a miracle. Had they too been seized by the flames, the fire would have taken on gigantic proportions, the lull notwithstanding. The damage is enormous, 2 million pounds,⁷³ some say, a vast sum, though it seems slight against the destruction wrought by the fire of 1666. The estimate at the time (when money was worth perhaps six times its present value) was 10 million pounds of damage. More than 10,000 houses were destroyed, and the smoke drew its black trail some 50 English miles into the countryside. It is in such figures that the present finds consolation. Incidentally, the pickpockets made one of their finest hauls during and after the fire. At the City Police Court alone, 20 stood accused of "pickpocketing during the great fire," 11 of whom were sentenced for theft of watches.⁷⁴ As you see, everything here tends to greatness, or at least sheer mass.⁷⁵

† London, 26. Juni. [Das große Feuer und die Taschendiebe.] Die Nachricht von dem großen Feuer, das vorgestern mittag am Cotton-Wharf in Southwark ausbrach und eine Reihe Speicher und Warenhäuser (man sagt, die besten und feuerfestesten, die London besaß⁷⁶) zerstörte, wird bereits zu Ihnen gekommen sein (s. Nr. 147, 148 und 149). Ich war heute dort, um mit meiner Neugierde hinter Hunderttausenden⁷⁷ nicht

---

71 Here Fontane perhaps alludes to the book *Die Wunder der Mechanik, Arithmetik, Chemie, Optik und Physik* (ed. Albanus, Naumburg, 1858). See Streiter-Buscher's commentary in *"Eine Zeitungsnummer lebt nur 12 Stunden,"* 184.
72 A: "In this and adjacent warehouses were stored . . . thousands of tea chests and bales of silk, whereas the lower rooms were filled with tallow, saltpeter, tar, oil, cotton, and grain."
73 C: "Even today, the damage is still estimated at around £ 2 million."
74 "Upwards of 20 . . . men and lads were charged during the sitting [= of the court; PM] with picking the pockets, chiefly of watches, of people in the crowd who had assembled to see the fire on Saturday night and Sunday. Of these 11 were convicted and sentenced to various terms of imprisonment with hard labour." *The Times* [London], June 25, 1861, 11.
75 "Massness" has been a commonplace in writings about London since Lichtenberg and Heine. See Braese, "Im Labyrinth des Fortschritts," *Realien des Realismus*, 28.
76 B: "Die Waarenhäuser . . . gehörten . . . zu den bestgebauten Londons."
77 B: "Die Brandstätte bei Londonbridge ist . . . von Neugierigen so dicht belagert, daß die Polizei Mühe hat, sie . . . fern zu halten."

The Making of a Compiler 95

zurückzubleiben. Mein Begleiter hatte eine Art Passepartout, und so konnten wir, trotz der Kordonlinie, die den Schauplatz absperrt, bis in eine gewisse Nähe[78] vordringen. Der Anblick ist furchtbar, und man sieht auf die Brandstätte wie auf eine Kraterstadt; aber die Krater sind nicht ausgebrannt;[79] unheimlich lebt es in der Tiefe, und aus jedem Aschenkegel kann jeden Augenblick eine neue Lohe emporschießen.[80] Gespenstisch stehen die teils weißgebrannten, teils vom Qualm geschwärzten Mauern[81] da, einige weit vorgebogen und jeden Augenblick auf dem Punkt, auf die Aschenkegel und die glühenden Kellergewölbe niederzustürzen.[82] Es ist das furchtbarste Feuer, von dem London seit einer langen Reihe von Jahren heimgesucht wurde,[83] und wie Sie sich denken können, hat es an Vergleichen mit dem großen City-Feuer nicht gefehlt, das 1666 Fünfsechstel der ganzen Londoner Altstadt (dem Schauplatz des jetzigen Feuers gerade gegenüber gelegen) zerstörte. In der Tat ist es allein einer gnädigen Fügung Gottes zuzuschreiben, daß der ganze Stadtteil Southwark, mit etwa einer halben Million Einwohner, nicht genau in derselben Weise niederbrannte, wie vor fast zweihundert Jahren die alte City. Menschenkunst und Menschenwitz erwiesen sich als völlig ohnmächtig,[84] und alle Schutz- und Rettungsmaschinen würden den Ruin des Stadtteils nicht hintertrieben haben, wenn etwa, statt einer absoluten Windstille,[85] die herrschte, ein mäßiger Nordost die Lüfte belebt und die Feuersäule[86] über die sengend heißen Dächer hingefegt hätte. Ich spreche nicht von den Menschenopfern, die dieses Feuer gefordert hat,

---

78 B: "ohne daß man dem Feuer-Herde der großen Hitze wegen nahe kommen kann"; C: "der Heerd der Brandstätte bleibt der großen Hitze wegen vorerst unzugänglich. Nur an den äußersten Rändern ist es möglich".
79 A: "aus dem es in gefährlicher Weise fortbrennt".
80 A: "Diese ganze Masse von Speichern . . . sind heute nur noch ein dampfender Schutthaufen, aus dem noch fortwährend Flammen aufschlagen . . .;" C: "aus den Kelleröffnungen . . . schlagen ununterbrochen hohe Flammen auf".
81 B: "Theils wegen der weißglühenden und ausgebrannten Mauern, die beim leisesten Windhauch zusammen brechen können".
82 C: "denn noch immer stehen viele der sechs Stock hohen Mauern aufrecht und drohen in theils überhangender Stellung Jeden zu begraben, der ihnen vorwitzig nahe tritt."
83 A: "Seit Sonntag Nachmittag ist London von einer Feuersbrunst heimgesucht, wie sie in solcher Furchtbarkeit seit vielen Jahren nicht erlebt worden ist."
84 B: "Die Spritzen . . . vermochten nichts weiter als den Brand zu begrenzen, und auch dazu wären sie ohnmächtig gewesen, hätte auch nur der leiseste Luftzug". C: "Steinerne Grundgewölbe, ungewöhnlich feste Ziegelmauern, eiserne Zwischenbalken! Wie wenig hat das alles genutzt!"
85 A: "Dank der Windstille".
86 C: "Die Nacht über ist die aufsteigende Feuersäule noch immer meilenweit hin sichtbar".

nicht von Mr. Braidwood,[87] *dem „Londoner Branddirektor", wie Sie in Berlin sagen würden, auch nicht von jenen armseligen Wagehälsen, die, an dem brennenden Ufer auf- und abfahrend, das geschmolzene Talg von der Oberfläche des Wassers abschöpften und wahrscheinlich viel zahlreicher ums Leben gekommen sind,*[88] *als bisher vermutet wurde; nur darauf möchte ich hinweisen, wie dieser Vorgang mal wieder vor Überhebung gewarnt und zur Demut gemahnt hat, die in unserem Zeitalter der „Wunder der Mechanik"*[89] *so rar geworden ist wie zu den Tagen des Babelturms. Die Elemente waren bei diesem Feuer alles; der Mensch, der sich so gern als ihr Herr gebärdet, war nichts. Nachbarspeicher und Kellerräume, in denen Fässer mit Sprit und Terpentinöl lagen,*[90] *sind wie durch ein Wunder gerettet worden. Wurden auch sie von den Flammen ergriffen, so gewann das Feuer riesige Dimensionen trotz der Windstille. Der Verlust ist enorm, man spricht von 2 Millionen Pfund,*[91] *eine riesige Summe, die aber doch verschwindet neben dem, was das Feuer von 1666 vernichtete. Man schätzte damals (wo das Geld einen vielleicht sechsfach höheren Wert hatte) den Schaden auf zehn Millionen Pfund. Über 10.000 Häuser waren zerstört und der Qualm zog wie eine schwarze Fahne 50 englische Meilen weit ins Land hinein. An diesen Zahlen richtet sich die Gegenwart wieder auf. Übrigens haben, während und nach dem Feuer, die Taschendiebe einen ihrer glänzendsten Fischzüge ausgeführt. Nur allein vor dem City-Polizeigericht standen gestern 20 auf „Taschendiebstahl beim großen Feuer" Angeklagte und 11 von ihnen wurden wegen gestohlener Uhren verurteilt.*[92] *Sie sehen, es geht hier alles in Große, wenigstens ins Massenhafte.*[93]

---

87 A: "aber leider sind auch mehrere Menschen zu Grunde gegangen, unter ihnen der allgemein geschätzte Braidwood, Chef der Londoner Lösch=Anstalten."
88 B: "Schon in der Nacht vom Sonnabend auf den Sonntag... sah man Schifferleute hart an der Brandstätte, ja mitten im Feuer des in den Fluß strömenden Talgs, beschäftigt, ihn mit Lebensgefahr aufzufischen. Mehrere dieser Wagehälse sollen dabei ums Leben gekommen sein."
89 Fontane perhaps alludes to the book, *Die Wunder der Mechanik, Arithmetik, Chemie, Optik und Physik* (ed. Albanus, Naumburg, 1858). See Streiter-Buscher's commentary in *"Eine Zeitungsnummer lebt nur 12 Stunden,"* 184.
90 A: "In diesem und in den anstoßenden Magazinen lagen... Tausende von Theekisten und Seidenballen, während die unteren und Kellerräume mit Talg, Salpeter, Theer, Oel, Baumwolle und Getreide gefüllt waren."
91 C: "Der Schaden wird auch heute noch auf ungefähr 2 Mill. £tr. veranschlagt."
92 "Upwards of 20... men and lads were charged during the sitting [= of the court; PM] with picking the pockets, chiefly of watches, of people in the crowd who had assembled to see the fire on Saturday night and Sunday. Of these 11 were convicted and sentenced to various terms of imprisonment with hard labour." *The Times* [London], June 25, 1861, 11.
93 "Massenhaftigkeit" has been a commonplace in writings about London since Lichtenberg and Heine. See Braese, "Im Labyrinth des Fortschritts," *Realien des Realismus,* 28.

Thanks to Fontane's clever adaptation of the established information and stereotypical descriptions, one could never tell without prior knowledge that this "eyewitness" account was produced in a Berlin newsroom. Indeed, the pre-mediated elements provide the basic material—I am consciously avoiding the term "raw materials," for "raw" is precisely what they are not—that Fontane manipulates for the sake of credibility, increased aesthetic effectiveness, heightened drama, and the sending of a moral message.[94] A few localized instances suffice to analyze how this manipulation works. Take Fontane's adaptation of the commonplace of "getting close to the scene," a standard component of reporting on catastrophic events. The reader knows from two of the previous articles (Sources B and C) or simply from common sense that no one can get very close to a raging fire, so the fact that the "correspondent" writing under the logogram of *†* was able to get a good look at the scene calls for an explanation. Fontane provides one; he swiftly invents a "companion" (*Begleiter*) with special privileges who helped him break through the police cordon so that he could approach the horrific site "quite closely" (*bis in eine gewisse Nähe*). "Quite" closely is tellingly vague, yet it was likely specific enough to make the following account of the fire credible to an unsuspecting reader. The evocation of this commonplace thus fulfills a double function: it enables Fontane to connect to an already well-known fact about the fire while also establishing his "personal" perspective as plausible.

The author uses this method throughout the article. After he has rendered his personal perspective plausible, he "authenticates" it further by modifying the formulaic description of the fire. His sources speak simply of "flames" (*Flammen*) that keep flaring up from the "cellars beneath" (*Kelleröffnungen*) and "piles of rubble" (*Schutthaufen*);

---

94 In their analysis of Fontane's armchair reporting, Günter and Homberg make a very similar point: they use the terms "Nachrichtenrecycling" (recycling of news) and "Sekundärrohstoff" (secondary raw material) to emphasize that Fontane worked with past media content to launch his own account into mass-media circulation. Their analysis differs from mine, however, insofar as they focus not on Fontane's specific textual practices, but on contrasting the communicative modes of the nineteenth-century newspaper with that of the archive through the lens of false foreign correspondence. While Günter and Homberg's juxtaposition of newspaper and archive is illuminating, their conclusion that Fontane's material practices of "copy and paste" left no traces in his *Nachlass* does not hold up. To be sure, there is no archival evidence of his work in the newsroom of the *NP(K)Z* , but most of his extant notebooks and countless literary manuscripts testify to his methods of cutting, copying, and pasting for writing projects across the board. See Günter and Homberg, "'copy and paste' im Archiv der Massenmedien," 240, 252n44.

Fontane finds a more evocative image that marks his perspective as unique. He turns the whole scene into a *Kraterstadt*, a city of craters, and replaces the general term *Flammen* with *Lohe*, a much more powerful and literary word that does not belong to the standard German of newspapers.[95] This semantic choice not only individualizes the generic description, but also dramatizes it (one thinks of *lodern*, to blaze, when one hears *Lohe*, and Fontane also makes sure that the *Lohe* "shoots forth" as opposed to merely flaring up). In a similar vein, Fontane engages with the commonplace of human powerlessness. He amplifies the insufficiency of the pumps and other technical means of firefighting to reach universal dimensions, speaking of "all man's art and wit which had proved altogether powerless (*völlig ohnmächtig*)." This commonplace finally paves the way for a message that, in its moralizing tone, bolsters the impression of an individual correspondent with strong opinions that are fully compatible with the conservatism of the *Kreuzzeitung*: "I wish only to mention how these events have once again warned us against conceit and admonished us to humility (*zur Demut gemahnt*)." Add a fake dateline and several direct addresses to the reader, along with ostentatious familiarity with the readers' horizon of knowledge, and the impression of a credible, London-based correspondent who regularly communicates with his Berlin audience is complete. Significantly, the final judgment of this "expert" voice on the incident—"As you see, everything here tends to greatness, or at least sheer mass (*ins Massenhafte*)"—is highly unoriginal in its simplistic cultural criticism. After all, London as an epitome of "massness" was a prominent *idée reçue* of the mid-nineteenth century.[96] Precisely because of its unoriginal quality, however, the conclusion fulfills an important purpose: it ensures that the message of the manufactured article confirms the readers' worldview.

Fontane's calculated efforts to sell his readers a manufactured article as authentic did not trouble him much. On the contrary, in his explanation of the "false foreign correspondence" as a medium, he emphasizes that *all* products of journalism rely on pre-mediated sources, and that in this scenario, manufactured authenticity is at times even better than "the evidence of one's own eyes" (*persönlicher Augenschein*):

---

95 Indeed, these terms do not appear anywhere in Fontane's sources—neither in Schlesinger's correspondence pieces nor in the *NP(K)Z* articles.
96 On this commonplace in Fontane's writing, see Stephan Braese, "Im Labyrinth des Fortschritts. Fontanes *Ein Sommer in London*," in *Realien des Realismus*, ed. Stephan Braese and Anne-Kathrin Reulecke (Berlin: Vorwerk 8, 2010), 27–30.

The Making of a Compiler 99

I may be permitted to add to the foregoing a note on the subject of "real" and "false correspondences." The difference between the two, if one is familiar with a language, a country, and its people, is not great. It is much as with the anecdotes concerning Frederick the Great—the false ones are as good as the real, and sometimes even a little better. I was myself a real correspondent for years and then a false one for years again, and I speak from experience. One takes one's wisdom from the *Times* or the *Standard* etc., and it is of little consequence whether one reproduces it in Hampstead-Highgate or in Steglitz-Friedenau. Fifteen kilometers or one hundred fifty miles make no difference at all. Of course it may happen that the evidence of one's own eyes is better than reproducing what another has seen. But here, too, a necessary condition is that he who would see for himself have very good eyes indeed and know how to write. If not, work translated from well-informed journals will always be superior to the originals.

Es mag mir gestattet sein, an das Vorstehende noch eine Bemerkung über „echte" und „unechte Korrespondenzen" zu knüpfen. Der Unterschied zwischen beiden, wenn man Sprache, Land und Leute kennt, ist nicht groß. Es ist damit wie mit den Fridericianischen Anekdoten, die unechten sind gerade so gut wie die echten und mitunter noch ein bißchen besser. Ich bin selbst jahrelang echter und dann wieder jahrelang unechter Korrespondent gewesen und kann aus Erfahrung mitsprechen. Man nimmt seine Weisheit aus der „Times" oder dem „Standard" etc., und es bedeutet dabei wenig, ob man den Reproduktionsprozeß in Hampstead-Highgate oder in Steglitz-Friedenau vornimmt. Fünfzehn Kilometer oder hundertfünfzig Meilen machen gar keinen Unterschied. Natürlich kann es einmal vorkommen, daß persönlicher Augenschein besser ist als Wiedergabe dessen, was ein anderer gesehen hat. Aber auch hier ist notwendige Voraussetzung, daß der, der durchaus selber sehen will, sehr gute Augen hat und gut zu schreiben versteht. Sonst wird die aus wohl informierten Blättern übersetzte Arbeit immer besser sein als die originale.

(GBA III.3: 282)

The telling comparison with anecdotes about Frederick the Great helps tease out what Fontane means by "better" in the context of "false foreign correspondences." A "false correspondence" is preferable to an original account whenever it is better able to entertain the readers or characterize a particular phenomenon, for this is what one expects from a good anecdote. The compiler's task, then, is to obtain materials from "well-informed journals" and then to create a patchwork from these sources that displays entertaining or illustrative qualities.

Inventio, Originality, and Media Realism: Poetic Features of Fontane's Compiling

The texts that were generated through this compilatory procedure defy easy categorization. Because "false foreign correspondences" were based on the writings of others and were often extremely generic, Fontane scholars argue over whether these articles are "real Fontane" and should be included in his oeuvre.[97] The debate sparked by the "false correspondence" is symptomatic of the difficulties that ensue when posterity faces cleverly assembled compilations. Yet it is precisely the puzzling authorial and aesthetic status of compiled texts such as "Das große Feuer" that helps to make visible certain patterns in Fontane's compilatory poetics outside the journalistic context. Two elements in particular surface in "Das große Feuer" that are also relevant to Fontane's literary projects: the understanding of originality and the notion of manufactured authenticity, both of which became operative in his realist poetics.

The originality pattern that emerges in the news article—the individualization of widely circulating commonplaces and pre-mediated knowledge—repeats itself in Fontane's novellas and novels. They, too, are based on the careful adaptation of commonplaces, stereotypes, topics, and discursive modes of the mass press, as Rudolf Helmstetter has demonstrated in his groundbreaking 1998 study. Without mentioning compiling or journalistic textual practices, Helmstetter describes Fontane's novels as "composed from topical literary elements and stereotyped set pieces (*Versatzstücken*)."[98] He points out that the author used "newspapers and society's talk of the day as a kind of (no longer codified) catalog of *topoi* of the life-world (*Topik der Lebenswelt*)" in order to import "tittle-tattle" (*kolportierte Geschichten*), "society scandals," and "social typology" into his narratives, only to individualize and subvert them in the next step. Fontane's novels, then, feed on the "temporalized commonplaces" of the periodical press, which furnished him with materials in the same way that a traditional catalog of rhetorical commonplaces provided materials, the difference being that the "catalogs" of the nineteenth-century press were always in flux.

Helmstetter rightly associates the foundation of this mode of text production with the age-old rhetorical principle of *inventio*, the practice

---

97 See Rudolf Muhs, "*Unechte Korrespondenzen*, aber alles echter Fontane? Zur Edition von Heide Streiter-Buscher," *Fontane Blätter* 64 (1997): 200–20, and Streiter-Buscher's convincing rejoinder, "Gebundener Journalismus oder freies Dichterleben? Erwiderung auf ein Mißverständnis," *Fontane Blätter* 64 (1997): 221–44.

98 Rudolf Helmstetter, *Die Geburt des Realismus aus dem Dunst des Familienblattes. Fontane und die öffentlichkeitsgeschichtlichen Rahmenbedingungen des Poetischen Realimus* (Munich: Fink, 1998), 97.

of "finding" (rather than creating from scratch) suitable subject matter and arguments in an ordered rhetorical inventory. As a generative principle and poetic strategy, *inventio* was crucial to compilers; it legitimized their methods of assembling textual patchwork and encouraged recombination as a valid form of authorship.[99] Just like compiling in general, however, it receded into the backstage areas of intellectual and literary production once the notion of the original genius took hold around 1800.[100] According to the ideals of classical aesthetics, writers were supposed to take out of themselves (and not out of the papers) whatever was necessary for the creation of original texts. Compiling, a material technique that openly relied on sources in large quantities, stood completely at odds with the idealization of the creative process, an idealization reinforced by Romantic notions of writing (as discussed in the Introduction). Consequently, the reputation of compiling became so problematic that even compilers themselves derided the practice. Georg Christoph Lichtenberg, himself an avid plunderer of the textual sources of others, called compiling "an occupation that melts all powers of thought"[101] and associated it with the mindless mass production of texts. Although the technique remained crucial throughout the late eighteenth and the nineteenth centuries and shaped the working methods of numerous intellectuals and writers (Winckelmann, Fichte, Goethe, and Jean Paul, to name a few), it was considered fundamentally unoriginal and second-rate in the realms of "serious" literary production and culture. Not even the new understanding of writing as intellectual work (*geistige Arbeit*) that emerged after 1850 could change this view, for literary authors still felt compelled to distinguish themselves from those who treated text production as a "mere" craft or industry based on material techniques.[102]

---

99 On the role of *inventio* in literary poetics, see Manfred Kienpointner, "inventio," in *Historisches Wörterbuch der Rhetorik*, ed. Gert Ueding (Tübingen: Niemeyer, 1998), 4:577–8.
100 Paradigmatically, Edward Young stated in "Conjectures on Original Composition" (1759) that the true genius had no need for "crutches" such as compositional rules and inventories of material, which were only good for mechanical "manufacture" and imitation, but not for "original" production. The essay is reprinted in *Critical Theory Since Plato*, ed. Hazard Adams (New York: Harcourt Brace Jovanovich, 1971), 329–37. For a multifaceted historicization of the concept of the original genius, see Günter Peters, "Genie," in *Historisches Wörterbuch der Rhetorik*, ed. Gert Ueding (Tübingen: Niemeyer, 1996), 3:737–50.
101 Georg C. Lichtenberg, *Sudelbücher*, ed. Wolfgang Promies (Munich: Deutscher Taschenbuchverlag, 2005), 1:815–16 (J 1155).
102 On authorship as "intellectual work" and the self-stylizing of German writers, see Rolf Parr, *Autorschaft. Eine kurze Sozialgeschichte der literarischen Intelligenz in Deutschland zwischen 1860 und 1930* (Heidelberg: Synchron, 2008), 22–37.

Editors like Fontane, however, were untroubled by such aesthetic demands, at least to the extent that they operated with completely different licenses in matters of originality. To recall Kürschner's insightful handbook of the press, editors were not only allowed but actually expected to recombine circulating materials, work with generic language elements that were accessible to a wide readership, and use imagery to which everyone could easily relate. As an editor, Fontane was thus able to embrace, practice, and carry into his literary projects a mode of text production that had officially become anachronistic for writers. This technique, however, turned out to be beneficial in the media-historical situation of his day. In an era when redundancy had begun to dominate the media scene, the same literary commonplaces and generic imagery rippled through the various media channels, and the enforcement of anti-plagiarism legislation was lax (see Chapter 1), Fontane made redundancy work to his advantage. His compiling fostered a mode of originality that did not rely on the novelty of his topics, characters, plots, scenery, or underlying ideas. Rather, his originality was found in *how* he recombined the generic forms, the commonplaces, and the schemas that he took over from the surrounding mass media and adapted for increased aesthetic effectiveness—just as in "Das große Feuer."

The second, related phenomenon that is thrown into sharp relief in "Das große Feuer" is a crucial aspect of what literary studies scholars term Fontane's realism. The article shows that in essence, Fontane's realism must be understood as a media-based effect. Exploiting imagery and stereotypical descriptions with which the readers were already familiar from mass media, the article bridges the gap between the view of the world that it presents and the readers' medially pre-encoded, habitual ways of world-making. Some twenty-five years after Fontane, Roman Jakobson would famously theorize this kind of realism as "meaning B" in "On Realism in Art": "A work may be called realistic if I, the person judging it, *perceive it* as true to life." According to Jakobson, this judgment depends upon the work's compatibility with the artistic conventions, knowledge, and linguistic codes in which the reader has been steeped.[103] Roland Barthes later fleshed out this insight with his description of the "reality effect" and suggested that the meaning of a "realist" description "depends on conformity not to the model but to

---

103 Roman Jakobson, "On Realism in Art" (1921), in *Readings in Russian Poetics: Formalist and Structuralist Views*, ed. Ladislav Matejka and Krystyna Pomorska (Cambridge, MA: MIT Press, 1971), 38, italics my own.

the cultural rules of representation."[104] This is exactly what one can observe in "Das große Feuer," a text adhering so closely to the rules applicable to the mass-media coverage of catastrophic events that it appears completely credible. Fontane's realism, then, emerges first and foremost as a media realism, notwithstanding the many ways one might qualify it further (e.g., as bourgeois, critical, conversational, poetic, or transfigured). Characterizing it as a calculated effect opens up fruitful avenues for further discussion. One might ask, for example, how an author designs a given "reality effect." Fontane provides a compelling example; he resorted to a number of aesthetic strategies to calibrate precisely the effects that would increase the verisimilitude of his literary writings (see Chapter 4).

The primacy of media in Fontane's textual practices has attracted considerable scholarly attention over the past decade, but it has not yet become an interpretative standard in Fontane scholarship, despite Helmstetter's comprehensive study.[105] There are still discussions of the author's realism that are either oblivious to the role of media content or that confuse mass media with the "real world"[106] (*wirkliche Welt*). In part, the author's own take on realism might be to blame here. Whenever Fontane wrote as a theorist, he proclaimed a naïve understanding

---

104 Roland Barthes, "The Reality Effect," in *The Rustle of Language*, trans. Richard Howard (Oxford: Blackwell, 1986), 145. See also Barthes' "Inaugural Lecture," in *A Barthes Reader*, ed. Susan Sontag (New York: Hill and Wang, 1982), 461–7. Readers of Barthes will be aware that this is only the first step in Barthes's argument about the reality effect, for Barthes also discusses how the realist text, through the evocation of excessive and superfluous details, *disrupts* conventions of making meaning. I will return to this self-conscious, conflictual nature of the realist enterprise in Chapter 4. For a succinct discussion of Jakobson and Barthes, see Eric Downing, *Double Exposures: Repetition and Realism in Nineteenth-Century German Fiction* (Stanford, CA: Stanford University Press, 2000), 2–6.

105 In addition to the sources already cited in this chapter, pertinent contributions that focus on the interactions between media and realist poetics in Fontane's writings include Manuela Günter, *Im Vorhof der Kunst: Mediengeschichten der Literatur im 19. Jahrhundert*. (Bielefeld: Transcript, 2008), 209–37; Manuela Günter, "Realismus in Medien. Zu Fontanes Frauenromanen," in *Medialer Realismus*, ed. Daniela Gretz (Freiburg: Rombach, 2011), 167–90; Gerhart von Graevenitz, *Theodor Fontane: ängstliche Moderne. Über das Imaginäre* (Konstanz: Konstanz University Press, 2014); Christian Thomas, *Theodor Fontane: Autonomie und Telegraphie in den Gesellschaftsromanen* (Berlin: Logos, 2015).

106 For example, see Katharina Grätz, *Alles kommt auf die Beleuchtung an. Theodor Fontane – Leben und Werk* (Stuttgart: Reclam, 2015). While Grätz acknowledges the mediality of Fontane's sources (e.g., newspapers and gossip), she does not apply this insight to her discussion of the author's realist poetics and speaks of "aus der Realität bezogene[m] Material" (55) that becomes poeticized.

of realism that was not nearly as sophisticated as his textual practice.[107] In "Unsere lyrische und epische Poesie seit 1848" ("Our lyric and epic poetry since 1848"), one of the central programmatic texts of realism, he dubs realism "that which is fresh and full of life" (*das Frische, Lebensfähige*), associates it with being "not infected (*unangekränkelt*) by the pallor of thought," and insists that the poet write not "by the *book*" (*nach dem Buche*) but "from *life*" (*nach dem Leben*; HFA III.1: 237–39; 260). Accordingly, he summarizes realism as the "reflection of all real life, all true powers and interests in the element of art . . . . It encompasses the wealth of life, in its greatest and smallest aspects: Columbus, who gifted the world a new one, and the little aquatic creature, whose universe is a droplet" (*Widerspiegelung alles wirklichen Lebens, aller wahren Kräfte und Interessen im Elemente der Kunst . . . . Er umfängt das ganze reiche Leben, das Größte wie das Kleinste: den Columbus, der der Welt eine neue zum Geschenk machte, und das Wasserthierchen, dessen Weltall der Tropfen ist*). To be sure, Fontane is careful to distinguish realism from the "the naked reproductions (*nackte Wiedergeben*) of daily life" and, in particular, "its misery and dark sides" and demands "purification" (*Läuterung*) of realist subject matter from the poet.[108] But, citing Goethe, he urges the poet to reach into "the whole of life (*volle Menschenleben*) / And wherever you get hold of it, it's interesting," establishing life, *das Wirkliche*, as the "marble quarry" that provides the material for the realist poet. What he fails to acknowledge is that the processes of "purification" and "transfiguration" start not with the "real" world but with subject matter that has already been mediated. Fontane's own examples—Columbus and the "little aquatic creature"—illustrate this situation perfectly. Although Fontane treats them as instances of reality, or *Wirklichkeit*, the vast majority of Fontane's readers could only know them from mass media, such as illustrated family journals,

---

107 Peter James Bowman remarks that this observation, which goes back to Thomas Mann's essay "Der alte Fontane," has since been repeated multiple times in the scholarship. See Peter J. Bowman, "Fontane and the Programmatic Realists: Contrasting Theories of the Novel," *Modern Language Review* 103.1 (2008): 129–30. Bowman himself puts forth a contrasting view, arguing that Fontane's theoretical writings develop a complex notion of realism.

108 Fontane shared this idea of "Läuterung" (purification) with other programmatic realists, such as Julian Schmidt, Gustav Freytag, and Robert Prutz, who all insisted that "realism" should not be construed as mimetic copying but should be understood as the further idealization of those elements of "life" that were "objectively" already beautiful. Subjects such as a "sterbende[r] Proletarier, den hungernde Kinder umstehen," to cite Fontane's essay, were thus not appropriate for realist writers. For a discussion of the ideological dimension of realism, see Gerhard Plumpe, introduction to *Bürgerlicher Realismus und Gründerzeit*, ed. Edward McInnes and Gerhard Plumpe (Munich: Hanser, 1996), 61–83.

general-reference encyclopedias, and textbooks used in school. Gerhard Plumpe explains this blind spot in programmatic positions such as Fontane's when he argues that "realism [had to] invent the very 'reality' . . ., as whose 'transfiguration' it then regarded itself."[109]

As a practitioner, however, Fontane worked with a much more sophisticated understanding of realism, one that acknowledged the implicit media constructivism and the constitutive role of media templates in the creation of realist effects. If the example of the "false correspondence" has already demonstrated this point in the journalistic realm, a parallel example can show how this understanding of realism plays out in Fontane's poetic production. It appears in an inconspicuous place, an 1893 letter exchange with Georg Friedlaender in which Fontane—sleeves rolled up, tie loosened—instructs his informant and friend on how to help him with the research for a short story that he planned to write. Several years prior to the exchange, Friedlaender had told Fontane about a local man named Pohl, who owned an inn on top of the Schneekoppe Mountain in the Riesengebirge. Now, in 1893, Fontane finally wanted to use that material to write a story in which Pohl died in an upstairs bedroom of his inn while his guests enjoyed a lively summer night downstairs.[110] Pohl's last wish provided the story's central motif: that his corpse be silently carried down the mountain so as not to disturb the merriment of the raucous crowd. To flesh out this story with more details, Fontane turned to Friedlaender for help. The material that Friedlaender sent, however, had gaps. Fontane's attempts to fill in these *lacunae* help to define his notion of media realism. Invoking a popular poem as a media template, he instructed Friedlaender as follows:

> The beginning is good and the end is good . . ., only the middle section, which in the beginning seemed the most promising, still leaves much to be desired. That is [the part about] getting the dead Pohl down from the mountain to the valley. I imagine that it happened the same night, as silently and with as little ado as possible, so as not to disturb the couples dancing to the strains of the harpist. But how then was it, step by step, the downhill transport? There is a famous poem by Platen, "Lament of Emperor Otto the Third," in which the young dead emperor is borne, coming from Rome, northward across the Alps. It must be possible to tell such a story about Pohl I. Where did they rest? Who

---

109 Ibid., 83.
110 Fontane published the story in September, 1893, under the title "Eine Nacht auf der Koppe" as part of the series "Aus dem Riesengebirge" in der *Deutschen Rundschau*. It is reprinted in HFA I.7, 89–94.

accompanied him? Was it pitch dark or did they carry lanterns on sticks? What happened when they reached the bottom? etc. etc. I daren't attempt it *without* these things. The magic is always in the detail. So please, direct your attention *there*. In particular, however, I suppose that as much is known in Schmiedeberg and among the persons living in the valley as up on the mountain, the 100th ascent of which I . . . would like to spare you.

Der Anfang ist gut und der Schluß ist gut . . ., nur das Mittelstück, von dem ich mir anfänglich am meisten versprach, läßt noch viel zu wünschen übrig. Das ist das Herabschaffen des todten Pohl von der Koppe zu Thal. Ich denke mir, daß es in derselben Nacht stattfand, möglichst still und verschwiegen, um die nach dem Spiel der Harfenistinnen tanzenden Paare nicht zu stören. Aber wie war nun, etappenweise, dieser Transport bergab? Es giebt ein berühmtes Gedicht von Platen „Klagelied Kaiser Otto des Dritten", wo sie den jugendlichen todten Kaiser, von Rom her, nordwärts über die Alpen tragen. So was muß sich auch von Pohl I. erzählen lassen. Wo machten sie Rast? Wie war die Begleitung? Stockduster oder mit Stocklaternen? Wie ging es weiter als sie unten waren? etc. etc. Ohne *diese Dinge bringe ich die Forsche nicht recht 'raus. Der Zauber steckt immer im Detail. Also bitte, richten Sie* hierauf Ihr Auge. *Von dem allem aber weiß man muthmaßlich in Schmiedeberg und bei zu Thal wohnenden Personen ebenso viel, wie oben auf der Koppe, die zum 100. Mal zu besteigen ich Ihnen . . . gern ersparen möchte.*

(BaF 221)

August von Platen's popular "Lament," written in 1833, becomes the template for Fontane's poetic imagination, and Fontane charges Friedlaender with finding locals whose memories of the real, historical Pohl can be mobilized to confirm what Fontane has already imagined via Platen. The procedure—looking into "life" with a lens shaped by a literary template—illustrates how realism first invents the "reality" that it then ventures to render poetic. To a considerable extent, the process is self-referential and circular.

Fontane justifies his poetic method to Friedlaender with the argument of increased entertainment value already familiar from his reference to the "false anecdotes concerning Frederick the Great." In another letter to his friend, he wrote, "I shall let the story about Pohl stand as it stands, and everybody will prefer my story (night-time transport, torch-lit) to leathery reality." If Pohl's son were to make a fuss and insist that his family's history was actually quite different, Friedlaender was to remind him of the monetary advantages of an entertaining story: "But if you then tell him: 'Pohl, don't be an ass (*seien*

Sie kein Schaf), it's good advertising (*es macht Reklame*) and may well sell you an extra 100 cups of coffee a day,' I expect him to calm down" (BaF 222). For both the literary writer and the editor Fontane, "reality" needed to be assembled from pre-mediated elements, which in turn had to be aesthetically enhanced.

In other words, the narrative of what Fontane learned as a journalist and then applied to his literary production has to be rewritten. Until now, the overlap between his journalistic and literary writing has been seen mostly in terms of materials, or "Stoffliches."[111] Admittedly, a few scholars have acknowledged more substantial connections, arguing that Fontane's journalistic practice affected individual aspects of his literary poetics. These include the accumulation of large amounts of source materials and the art of allusion, the latter of which was a crucial journalistic skill in times of censorship.[112] The example of the "false foreign correspondence" analyzed in this chapter suggests, however, that the compiling method that Fontane practiced at the *Kreuzzeitung* influenced his literary poetics on a more fundamental level. Two key aspects of his literary poetics were affected, as we have seen: the particular notion of originality that arose from the adaptation of commonplace materials, and the reality effect that his compilations produced.[113] Fontane's textual practices, then, cut across professional roles that were just beginning to emerge as different on the contemporary media scene. If the editor and the literary writer were beginning to develop distinct professional practices, both sets of practices converged in Fontane's compiling.

Keeping Company with *Kolportage* Writers and Remix Artists

As a compositional principle, compiling slashed through even more distinctions than that between the editor (or information manager) and the literary writer. The practice was also essential for polygraphers and, in particular, the producers of *Kolportage* novels, the most sensationalist form in the literary mass market of mid- to late nineteenth-century Germany. Foregrounding Fontane's work as a compiler thus opens up an additional perspective from which to approach his output. Typically,

---

111 For example, Jolles speaks of Fontane's journalistic work as the "Stoffreservoir seiner Romane" in "Fontane als Journalist und Essayist," 112–13.
112 See Jolles, "Fontane als Journalist und Essayist," 106, and Streiter-Buscher, introduction, *Theodor Fontane: Unechte Korrespondenzen*, 1: 44–5.
113 Concerning the reality effect, Dotzler, Günter, and Homberg are (to my knowledge) the only other scholars who connect the "false correspondence" with Fontane's poetic realism at all. Because their respective essays do not focus on material processes, however, they do not demonstrate concretely *how* Fontane constructs his particular media realism.

Fontane is treated as part of the high literary canon, pigeonholed next to Stifter, Raabe, Keller, and other poetic realists who published in family magazines and referenced popular culture but were not a part of it. If one considers, however, which types of authors compiled in the second half of the nineteenth century, one can look at Fontane anew, from a perspective that emphasizes light fiction, literary entertainment, and the art of creative recombination.[114] Fontane thus receives a whole new set of literary companions, which sharpens his profile as both an entertainment writer and a mass media artist and sensitizes the reader to new poetological problems.

The *Kolportage* novel is one of the most understudied phenomena of the second half of the nineteenth century. Not much is known about it, for "scarcely another chapter of fictional literature ... has been as radically expunged from society's cultural memory,"[115] as the authors of the one (!) comprehensive bibliography of German-language *Kolportage* novels, Günter Kosch and Manfred Nagl, state in the introduction. The biographies, material practices, and poetic strategies of *Kolportage* producers are poorly researched. Not even the novels themselves are accessible in libraries and archives; Kosch and Nagl had to skim secondhand bookstores and turn to fellow collectors for help in hunting down at least a fraction of what once circulated in the mass-media marketplace. With the exception of Karl May's serials, the scholarship has ignored *Kolportage* novels as unworthy of serious analysis. The little that is known, however, suggests a strong sociological and poetological affinity between the mass-media compiler à la Fontane and the producer of *Kolportage* novels. The overlap extends from biographical factors to textual practices and aesthetic principles. Indeed, much of Fontane's realism converges in form with the *Kolportage* novel, as we shall see in a moment.

From the limited materials that were available to Kosch and Nagl, they deduced the typical *curriculum vitae* of a *Kolportage* writer. Born around 1830 in the provinces, the archetypical *Kolportage* writer switched multiple times between different vocational trainings or courses of study, self-identified with the democratic side in the 1848 revolution, gained experience abroad, and worked in media, and

---

114 Manuela Günter has already made a case for taking entertainment in Fontane much more seriously than has hitherto been done. See "Realismus in Medien. Zu Fontanes Frauenromanen" and the Introduction.

115 Günter Kosch and Manfred Nagl, introduction to *Der Kolportage-Roman: Bibliographie 1850–1960* (Stuttgart: Metzler, 1993), 1–2. Symptomatically, Rolf Parr's otherwise extensive socio-historical survey of types of authorship in Germany between 1860 and 1930 does not mention *Kolportage* authors. See Parr, *Autorschaft*, 75–100.

occasionally also in the theater, before or during his writerly career, as a reporter, newspaper editor, book editor, or founder of a journal.[116] Kosch and Nagl conclude: "We seem then to be dealing with a type of modern, journalistically skilled writer of workaday literature"[117] (*journalistisch versierten Gebrauchsschriftsteller*).

The genre in which these writers worked displays several core poetic features and compositional principles.[118] Among these features, the claim to authenticity ranks first. *Kolportage* novels were advertised as true stories, yet their "authenticity" was based on media constructivism. Authors culled familiar social and political topics from mass media, especially from newspapers, and then declared that "life" itself had provided them with subject matter that they merely had to gather up and shape. An advertisement for the 1898 *Kolportage* novel *Auf ewig getrennt? oder: Kapitän Dreyfus und seiner Gattin ergreifende Erlebnisse, Schicksale und fürchterliche Verbannung* (*Separated forever? or: Captain Dreyfus and His Wife's Stirring Experience, Fate, and Terrible Banishment*) by Victor von Falk (the pen name of Heinrich Sochaczewsky) accordingly declares, "Life, truth has given us a novel such as is unlikely ever to have unraveled as stirringly. One of Germany's finest authors addressed this subject matter with alacrity and spun it into a tale."[119] In truth, however, the subject matter of von Falk's serial stems not from "life" in some pure and unmediated form, but from reporting in the mass media. (Indeed, in this particular case, one of the biggest media spectacles of the late nineteenth century—the Dreyfus affair—provided the subject matter, and von Falk's novel skillfully tapped the media frenzy that followed the publication of Émile Zola's article "*J'accuse*" in January 1898.)

When they had assembled and fleshed out their materials, *Kolportage* authors spun out their narratives in scenes, according to "the principle of episodic seriality and the techniques of narrative-associative repetition and compilation."[120] The fate of one protagonist or family provided the axis around which episodes loosely revolved, putting a

---

116 Kosch and Nagl, *Der Kolportage-Roman*, 39.
117 Ibid.
118 In what follows, I am relying on Kosch and Nagl's preliminary characterization of the *Kolportage* novel as a genre in *Der Kolportage-Roman*, 39–42. Kosch and Nagl themselves point out that their characterization must be taken with an (un)healthy grain of salt since they did not have the opportunity to carry out detailed autopsies of the 1,500 novels in their corpus. No studies could be found, however, that analyze a representative set of *Kolportage* novels in light of generic features. Due to their unparalleled expertise, Kosch and Nagl still provide the best source.
119 The advertisement is reprinted in Kosch and Nagl, *Der Kolportage-Roman*, 27.
120 Ibid., 40.

cast of characters through situations and events in endless permutations. This loose structuring resulted in texts that were "of indeterminate genre." A remarkably flexible medium, the late nineteenth-century *Kolportage* novel could accommodate a mixture of readymade elements from all kinds of genres, such as historical and sentimental novels, memoirs, crime fiction, etc. Providing a compelling *Kolportage* novel was all about mastering the "art of the mixture"[121] (*Kunst der Mischung*), as the contemporary critic Otto Glagau put it. As hybrids, *Kolportage* novels were then marketed to entire households of readers.[122]

Aesthetically, *Kolportage* authors emulated the representation practices of popular theater to bring the episodes of a given novel to life. The protagonists are frequently modeled upon stock theatrical characters. Dressed in historical costumes or in contemporary clothing replete with status markers, they typify clearly recognizable social strata. In addition, *Kolportage* authors transferred the orality of popular theater into their writings, which, as Kosch and Nagl assume, not only rendered episodes dynamic but also made them easier for novice readers to digest. As if on stage, the protagonists constantly converse with one another, and even when they are alone, they soliloquize, mutter, and shout. Some *Kolportage* authors, such as Robert Kraft, Karl May, and Paul Walter, purportedly also composed or revised orally, which is to say that they acted out scenes before they wrote them down, or that they had an assistant read out their drafts to them.

In his biography, poetic strategies, and textual practices, Fontane bears surprising similarities to Kosch and Nagl's archetypical *Kolportage* writer. Born in Neuruppin in the first third of the nineteenth century, he, too, came from the provinces and toyed with a number of careers. (In addition to the professions discussed in this chapter, Fontane worked as an English tutor, acted as secretary to the Prussian Academy of the Arts in Berlin, briefly ran a boarding house for high school students, and was at one point even drawn to a position as reader to the royal court.)[123] At least temporarily he stood with the democrats in the revolution of 1848; he gained extensive international experience through his years in England and his trips to Scotland, Denmark, France, Italy, and elsewhere; and he played a multitude of roles in the

---

121 Otto Glagau (1870), "Der Colportage-Roman, oder 'Gift und Dolch, Verrath und Rache,'" *Realismus und Gründerzeit. Manifeste und Dokumente zur deutschen Literatur 1848–1880*, ed. Max Bucher (Stuttgart: Metzler, 1981), 2:663. Kosch and Nagl also speak of the "Mischungsprinzip" of *Kolportage* novels.
122 Kosch and Nagl, *Der Kolportage-Roman*, 40.
123 The one biographical aspect that does not seem to fit is the "difficult childhood" that Kosch and Nagl attribute to the typical *Kolportage* writer. The Fontane scholarship does not assume that Fontane's childhood was overly troubled.

media scene of his era—reporter, news editor, editor of a yearbook, critic, balladeer, etc. In terms of Fontane's poetics, his programmatic dictum to treat "life" as the quarry for novels resonates with the principle of the "true story" that underlies the *Kolportage* novel and its media constructivism.

Moreover, the compositional and aesthetic principles that Fontane applied converge with those of *Kolportage*. His novels, too, are "scenically arranged"[124] (*angelegt*). With the help of the flexible notational form of the list (see Chapter 4), he strung scenes together in variable sequences that were organized loosely by situations and protagonists.[125] This list-driven composition practice kept Fontane's texts as generically open as *Kolportage* novels while they were in the draft stage, which made them well-suited to publication in the periodical press, a medium characterized by textual heterogeneity. Concerning the question of genre, scholars therefore have concluded that the question of genre was, with regard to Fontane's fictional work, ultimately "settled by posterity."[126] And just as in a *Kolportage* novel, Fontane's protagonists emerge as types, embodying their social milieus with the help of fashion tokens, furniture or other props, and characteristic modes of speech (for example, consider Friederike's working-class dialect in *Die Poggenpuhls*). His subject matter also displays an affinity to *Kolportage*. Plot elements such as adultery, murder, suicide, and duels occur across the board, not to mention the many erotic allusions, which were at times significantly more explicit than those in the writings of his fellow poetic realists. If Wilhelm Raabe's novels were said to be so morally proper that they would never make a decent "German matron"[127] blush, the thinly veiled sexual remarks in some of Fontane's narratives embarrass even his own protagonists. For instance, in *On Tangled Paths* (*Irrungen, Wirrungen*) Frau Dörr draws Lene into a conversation about the recent Berlin fashion of stuffing mattresses with the catkins of black poplar trees. Lene innocently remarks that this

---

124 Grawe, "Der Fontanesche Roman," in *Fontane-Handbuch*, ed. Christian Grawe and Helmut Nürnberger (Stuttgart: Kröner, 2000), 472.
125 For a case study, see Petra McGillen, "Poetische Mobilmachung im Textbaukasten. Fontanes Listen und die Kunst der Weiterverwendung—der Fall 'Allerlei Glück'," in *Formen ins Offene. Zur Produktivität des Unvollendeten*, ed. Hanna Delf von Wolzogen and Christine Hehle (Berlin: De Gruyter, 2018), 97–119.
126 Grawe, "Der Fontanesche Roman," 471.
127 Horst Denkler cites this characterization of Raabe in *Wilhelm Raabe. Legende – Leben – Literatur* (Tübingen: Niemeyer, 1989), 125. The absence of *explicit* sexuality in Raabe's novels should not be misconstrued as a complete absence of all matters sexual, however. As Denkler is careful to add, undercurrents of repressed sexual drives run through Raabe's writings; they become visible only through hermeneutic work.

fashion would not suit Frau Dörr, to which the chatty woman responds: "You are right there. I like it nice an' firm, horsehair an' springs, so that if you really toss up and down..."[128] (*Da hast Du Recht. Ich bin so mehr fürs Feste, für Pferdehaar und Sprungfedern und wenn es denn so wuppt...*, GBA I.10: 59), at which point Lene anxiously cuts in and changes the topic to the weather. The predominance of dialogue and other oral forms such as anecdotes, songs, and poems in Fontane's novels, moreover, is such a well-known hallmark that it hardly needs to be pointed out here. Fontane's production process, too, was driven by orality—while revising, he would read passages aloud to himself and fine-tune by ear (see Chapter 4). From biography to aesthetic principles, (some) topics, and textual practices, then, Fontane had much more in common with *Kolportage* authors than has hitherto been acknowledged.

Perhaps coincidentally, Fontane's *Kreuzzeitung* colleague Hermann Goedsche (1815–78) was one of the most prolific and successful *Kolportage* writers of the later nineteenth century. One of the few *Kolportage* authors whose output has been studied, he illustrates the company that Fontane kept as a compiler.[129] To place Goedsche in Fontane's company might seem a step too far in the eyes of some scholars, and it certainly would have offended Fontane, for in terms of subject matter (but not of narrative skill), Goedsche represented the lowest rung of literary sensationalism.[130] In charge of the notorious gossip and local crime column "Berliner Zuschauer" ("Berlin Spectator") at the *Kreuzzeitung*, under the pseudonym "Sir John Retcliffe" he published novels that modern criticism has unambiguously labeled sadistic and openly anti-Semitic.[131] With titles such as *Nena Sahib, oder Die Empörung in Indien* (*Nena Sahib, or the Indian Revolt*), the novels were marketed as treating contemporary world-historical topics such as the Indian Rebellion of 1857. In this guise, they delivered an

---

128 Theodor Fontane, *On Tangled Paths*, trans. Peter James Bowman (London: Penguin, 2013), 56.
129 Volker Neuhaus's *Habilitationsschrift* analyzes the extremely extensive corpus of Goedsche's so-called "Sir-John-Retcliffe" novels. See Volker Neuhaus, *Der zeitgeschichtliche Sensationsroman in Deutschland 1855–1878. 'Sir John Retcliffe' und seine Schule* (Berlin: Erich Schmidt, 1980).
130 Indeed, in a recent analysis of Fontane's serialized novels, Hans Ester is careful to separate Fontane from the likes of Goedsche: "Ein Sacher-Masoch oder Sir John Retcliffe ... war Fontane bestimmt nicht." See "Fontane und der Fortsetzungsroman," in *Formen ins Offene. Zur Produktivität des Unvollendeten*, ed. Hanna Delf von Wolzogen and Christine Hehle (Berlin: De Gruyter, 2018), 75.
131 See Neuhaus, *Der zeitgeschichtliche Sensationsroman*, 52–5. Fontane mentions the violence in Goedsche's novels, but he portrays the writer in harmless terms, as a "Quelle ständiger Erheiterung für uns" [i.e., for his friend Hesekiel and himself]. GBA III.3: 291.

encyclopedic collection of pornographic and otherwise violent scenes. Goedsche churned out the 16,000 pages, or thirty-five volumes, of his "Retcliffe" novels over the course of twenty-three years, from 1855 to 1878. This profuse productivity left no time for extensive revisions. By contrast, Fontane prided himself on the care with which he revised and polished his output, which, in his self-understanding, set him miles apart from polygraphers like Goedsche.[132] But if one suspends these objections and admits the observation that Fontane and Goedsche overlap in their compilatory working methods, one can extrapolate from the analytical work that has already been done on Goedsche to see Fontane in a new light, as an innovative entertainment artist.

The most intriguing idea is based on Volker Neuhaus's observation that Goedsche's thirty-five novels constitute one endless and ever-shifting text. During Goedsche's lifetime, the novels appeared in seven distinct series, yet later editions completely reorganized the sequencing.[133] In so doing, editors never went so far as to distill the individual volumes, let alone the chapters, into their basic components. According to Neuhaus, however, such a "dissolution into the smallest parts," followed by a "rigorously executed rewriting" (*Neukomposition*) of Goedsche's "Retcliffe" novels, would have been possible, revealing the works' true character: "It is a single novel in 35 volumes, left incomplete,"[134] in which the building blocks—primarily figures, but also situations, sites, and motifs—are interconnected in myriad ways. Applied to Fontane's output, this is an intriguing perspective. Seeing his output as connected not only to mass media but also to itself, as the topical recombination of a vast set of elements, one can begin to ask new questions. Previous studies of Fontane's poetics have often attempted to catalog instances in which the author "cited" existing textual sources (and focused mostly on references to high culture), but Goedsche's case and the general affinity with *Kolportage* invite us to think more broadly.[135] In other words, if Fontane assembled his output, at least at base, from a growing yet largely stable repertoire, one should

---

132 See, for example, Fontane's well-known letter to Gustav Karpeles from March 3, 1881, in which he underscores that he is a stylist, not one of those "unerträglichen Glattschreibern, die für alles nur *einen* Ton und *eine* Form haben". HFA IV.3, 120.
133 See Neuhaus, *Der zeitgeschichtliche Sensationsroman*, 44. The website AbLit Abenteuerliteratur provides an overview of the shifts in sequencing at http://www.retcliffe.ablit.de/bib/uebersicht/uebersicht.htm.
134 See Neuhaus, Der zeitgeschichtliche Sensationsroman, 44–5 and 81–2.
135 See Lieselotte Voss, *Literarische Präfiguration dargestellter Wirklichkeit bei Fontane. Zur Zitatstruktur seines Romanwerks* (Munich: Fink, 1985); Bettina Plett, *Die Kunst der Allusion. Formen literarischer Anspielungen in den Romanen Theodor Fontanes* (Cologne: Böhlau, 1986); Julia Encke, *Kopierwerke. Bürgerliche Zitierkultur in den späten Romanen Fontanes und Flauberts* (Frankfurt am Main: Lang, 1998).

try to characterize this repertoire, as opposed to enumerating single instances of citation.

If, furthermore, *Kolportage* is all about the "art of mixing" generic elements, it is worth studying *how* Fontane—the trained pharmacist—mixed his compilations together. *Kolportage*, then, nudges us toward a perspective from which Fontane appears more as a modern remix artist than as a nineteenth-century writer. The poetological problems that arise from this perspective can shed new light on Fontane's output. Contemporary media studies defines remix as the "act of using preexisting materials to create something new as desired by the creator."[136] To understand the activity of remix artists, however, it is crucial not to think of materials in terms of "itemizable sources," for this kind of thinking "usually devolves into making inventories of 'originals,' 'copies,' and 'derivations'" and fundamentally misrecognizes the product thus created.[137] Rather, remix artists proceed on the basis of *samples*, material snippets chosen for their "aesthetic appropriateness," their capacities to represent genres, and their "cultural connotations."[138] The poetological problems that remix artists face when working with samples can alert readers of Fontane to similar problems in the compiler's output. Remix artists try to combine samples into palatable and coherent wholes; to this end, they rely on repetition to mimic the structure of pop music (think looping baselines and refrains) and thus to create a feeling of familiarity in the audience.[139] Obvious clashes, then, are not desired; joints need to be smooth, the song danceable. At the same time, too much repetition induces tedium. The remixed samples need to sustain the listeners' attention, "leverage the audience's understanding of the samples in their original contexts,"[140] and provide surprises. The question immediately arises of how Fontane chose his samples, balanced repetition with surprises, and dealt with friction. At this point, the perspective of remix becomes fully compatible with Fontane's endless stylistic tinkering: the tinkering appears as a strategy to avoid heavy clashes between samples while balancing out aesthetic effects. (Fontane's work with samples is discussed in detail in Chapter 4.)

---

136 Eduardo Navas, Owen Gallagher, and xtine burrough, introduction to *The Routledge Companion to Remix Studies*, ed. Eduardo Navas et al. (New York: Routledge, 2015), 1. The editors of the volume point out that remix culture grew out of New York pop music culture of the late 1970s, but the term is now used for "acts of recombination in all forms of media" (3).
137 Martin Irvine, "Remix and the Dialogic Engine of Culture: A Model for Generative Combinatoriality," in *The Routledge Companion to Remix Studies*, 17.
138 Scott H. Church, "A Rhetoric of Remix," in *The Routledge Companion to Remix Studies*, 46–7.
139 Ibid., 47.
140 Ibid., 44.

Finally, the perspective of *Kolportage*/remix allows us to add one more touch to the sketch of Fontane's authorial type, distinguishing him from a figure with whom he should *not* be associated: the modern collage artist. The reason lies in different aesthetic agendas. To adapt Eisenstein's famous dictum, collage is conflict; the reader (or beholder) is supposed to be aware at all times of the heterogeneity of the collaged pieces.[141] Fontane's *Nachlass* contains numerous manuscript pages that look like collages, yet for publication, he strove to arrive at smooth, polished textual surfaces and carefully limited the amount of obvious friction. The collage artist and the mass-media compiler thus worked toward different goals: if the former attempted to shock the beholder into consciousness, the latter sought to provide fine entertainment for a broad spectrum of journal readers.

Wrapping Up, or How the Compiler Went into Hiding

It has not gone entirely unnoticed in literary criticism that compiling played a role in Fontane's work process. As early as 1858, when the author lived in England as a "real" correspondent for the Prussian government, his friend Wilhelm von Merckel asked him (with a palpable sense of annoyance) whether he was the reporter of the *Kreuzzeitung* who always built with "English chunks" (*Brocken*) a "compilation of 1001 things, in order to *write long* letters, which elsewhere may well already be *printed*, and more completely, too."[142] Additionally, a few scholars have made passing references to compiling in studies of both Fontane's journalistic and his literary writings.[143] Yet any knowledge of Fontane's compilatory activities has effectively been repressed in reception history, and the extent to which the collocation of textual sources in large quantities provided the core condition of Fontane's poetic productivity has not yet been recognized. Two related reasons account for this repression. As indicated in the introduction to this chapter, the first reason lies with the author himself. Fontane actively tried to curate an authorial image directly opposed to that of a compiler. The second reason is that the scholarship, adhering to an

---

141 The seminal theoretical contribution on the collage aesthetic is Peter Bürger's 1974 *Theory of the Avant-Garde*, which treats collage as an art form full of subversive energy. Peter Bürger, *Theory of the Avant-Garde*, trans. Michael Shaw (Manchester: Manchester University Press; Minneapolis: University of Minnesota Press, 1984), 77.
142 Letter from January 27, 1858. *Die Fontanes und die Merckels. Ein Familienbriefwechsel 1850–1870*, ed. Gotthard Erler. (Berlin: Aufbau, 1987), 1:261.
143 For example, see Conrad Wandrey, *Theodor Fontane* (Munich: C.H. Beck, 1919), 33–4; Fricke, "Fontanes Historik," *Jahrbuch für Brandenburgische Landesgeschichte* 5 (1954), 13–22; Dotzler, "Genuine Correspondences," 266. None of these sources treats compiling as a poetic principle, however.

idealized understanding of the creative process, became complicit in this endeavor of authorial image-fashioning over a period of several decades and tried to dissociate Fontane from "unoriginal" writing techniques.

Fontane's self-fashioning left no room for compiling because in his autobiographical writings, he downplayed the importance of precisely those sites and intellectual contexts in which he had learned how to compile. If, as we have already seen, this was the case for Fontane's training in the pharmacy, it was even more the case for his job in the newsroom. According to Streiter-Buscher, the author's efforts to belittle this part of his past were motivated by reputational concerns (which is to say that they had nothing to do with compiling per se). When Fontane committed the memories of his life to paper in the fall of 1894 and the spring of 1896, the reputation of the *Kreuzzeitung* was at a historical all-time low—not only had the paper become increasingly extreme in its anti-Semitic and pro-Christian propaganda, but its role in Bismarck's removal from power had also been revealed. On top of everything else, the editor-in-chief was sentenced to three years in prison for embezzlement and the forgery of documents in a highly publicized trial.[144] Uncomfortable about having a past at a paper that his contemporaries described as "church upstairs, brothel downstairs,"[145] Fontane painted an idyllic picture of his years at the *Kreuzzeitung*, one that rendered harmless what he had done there.[146] In *Von Zwanzig bis Dreißig*, he counts the decade in the service of the paper among the "very happiest years" of his life and leaves the impression of an essentially carefree job that neither stressed nor challenged him:

> These were, with a view to England, quiet times . . ., and it thus happened that for a while, the editor-in-chief would approach my desk and whisper to me in his quiet voice: "If at all possible, only a few lines today; the fewer the better." I could not have agreed more and had a comfortable time of it. Ultimately of course, just counting down the hours bored me, and—a minor argument also having taken place—I made to retire from the paper.
>
> *Es waren, auf England hin angesehen, stille Zeiten . . . , und so kam es, daß zeitweilig jeden Morgen der Chefredakteur an meinen Platz trat und mir mit seiner leisen Stimme zuflüsterte: „Wenn irgend möglich,*

---

144 See Streiter-Buscher, introduction, *Theodor Fontane: Unechte Korrespondenzen*, 20–1.
145 The description is attributed to Franz Chassot von Florencourt, quoted in Neuhaus, *Der zeitgeschichtliche Sensationsroman*, 24.
146 Streiter-Buscher therefore speaks of Fontane's "Selbstzensur" of his past. "'Und dann wieder jahrelang unechter Korrespondent. . .,'" 91.

The Making of a Compiler 117

> *heute nur ein paar Zeilen; je weniger, desto besser." Ich war immer ganz einverstanden damit und hatte bequeme Tage. Zuletzt freilich wurde mir das bloße Stundenabsitzen langweilig, und ich trat – ein kleiner Streit kam hinzu – meinen Rückzug von der Zeitung an.*
>
> (GBA III.3: 293)

This nostalgic description belies the realities of text production in the newsroom, and it falsifies the reason Fontane quit. Fontane did not resign out of boredom—the *Kreuzzeitung* kept its editors busy[147]—but because of the terms of his employment, which did not include any retirement benefits. In the letter in which Fontane revealed to his wife that he had quit the *Kreuzzeitung*, he speaks of "the cruelty (*Brutalität*) of exploiting our freedom and intellectual resources without having the care and humanity of thinking about our dotage." It was this "cruelty" that he was no longer willing to bear, and in the follow-up letter, he characterizes his job as an "outwardly attractive, but at heart treacherous position" (*aber in ihrem Kern perfiden Stellung*)—so much for the "very happiest years" (GBA XII.2: 475–76, 481). Because the author did his best, however, to present the decade at the *Kreuzzeitung* in retrospect as a time during which he did little, the work he did do—cutting and pasting, copying, editing, reframing, compiling—was never apparent to readers of his autobiography.

The terms and images with which Fontane described his work process also brushed the realities of compiling aside. The author stylized himself in letters to colleagues, publishers, and readers as writing "as with a psychograph (the boundless tinkering comes in only later)" who followed, once he had determined his plan and goal, "the well-known 'dark urge' in a natural process (*Naturprozeß*)." He went on, "It sounds a little conceited, but I am honest and sincere in saying this: it is natural, unconscious growth [of the texts, PM] (*Es klingt ein bischen arrogant, aber ich darf ehrlich und aufrichtig sagen: es ist ein natürliches, unbewußtes Wachsen*)."[148] This description, with its references to organicity, inexplicability, and mystery, could not be further from a

---

147 Streiter-Buscher cites numerous letters that Fontane wrote during the *Kreuzzeitung* decade in which the author depicts his job as taxing (the key words are "Tortur," "Tretmühle," "Lahmlegung aller Kräfte," etc.). See Streiter-Buscher, "Gebundener Journalismus oder freies Dichterleben?", 28.
148 Letter to Paul Schlenther from June 13, 1888, HFA IV.3, 611. For parallel passages, see the letter to Emilie from May 14, 1884 ("My entire production is psychography and criticism, creations of the dark straightened out by daylight") in GBA XII.3: 382; the letter to Hans Hertz from March 2, 1895 in BaH, 356–7; and the letter to Paul Schlenther from November 11, 1895 in HFA IV.4, 502.

production process as inorganic, modular, porous, and deliberate as compiling.[149]

Whether Fontane actually believed in these descriptions is impossible to tell and ultimately irrelevant. The much more important observation is that substantial parts of the scholarship accepted this authorial image, which was unsympathetic to compiling, for several decades. Thomas Mann's seminal 1910 essay "The Old Fontane" ("Der alte Fontane") established a standard when it emphasized the "naturalness" (*Echtheit*) and "immediacy of feeling" evident in Fontane's commentaries on his own creative process and claimed that they afforded a glimpse into "the workshop of a keen and passionate artist" who preferred "life in all its charm" (*das liebenswürdige Leben*) to any kind of artifice (and, as is implicit in this statement, to media sources).[150] As polemical and insightful as ever, Helmstetter has sketched how this idealized *Autor-Imago* of Fontane as the sensitive novelist of "real" life inflected a whole period of German studies scholarship, contributing to a self-referential body of research literature that forgot to question the problematic premises under which it operated—premises that neglected the material media and conditions of publishing that were formative for Fontane's work process.[151]

Even though the contemporary Fontane scholarship is aware of the constructedness of Fontane's authorial self-image, the long-term ripple effects of this image and the bias against compiling are still felt quite keenly. In fact, scholars and publishers alike have attempted to exclude that which is "merely compiled" from Fontane's poetic oeuvre. If the debate around the "false correspondences" has already provided a case in point, the publication history of Fontane's best-known work, the *Wanderungen durch die Mark Brandenburg*, can serve as an even more instructive example of the desire to detach the author from "unoriginal" production techniques. In *Wanderungen* editions of selected episodes, the long passages that Fontane copied directly from foreign sources are frequently clipped.[152] The rhetoric used by more recent studies that describe the author's work process still bespeaks bias against compiling. In an essay on Fontane's use of textual sources for the *Wanderungen*, Manfred Horlitz contrasts "creative development" (*eigenschöpferische*

---

149 Radecke emphasizes the difference between Fontane's self-stylizing and his actual work process in *Vom Schreiben zum Erzählen*, 89.
150 Mann, "The Old Fontane," in *Thomas Mann: Essays of Three Decades*, trans. H. T. Lowe-Porter (New York: Knopf, 1947), 296.
151 Helmstetter, *Die Geburt des Realismus*, 13–37.
152 Jens Bisky, "Zur Verlagsgeschichte der 'Wanderungen durch die Mark Brandenburg' 1860–1945. Mit einer kommentierten Bibliographie," *Berliner Hefte zur Geschichte des literarischen Lebens* 1 (1996): 116–17.

Gestaltung) with such terms as "cannibalize" (*ausschlachten*) and "adopt verbatim with no citation,"[153] an opposition that leaves no doubt about which textual practice is considered more valuable.

There is no need to keep Fontane artificially clean, though. Compiling, as this chapter has revealed, was a historical and biographical reality in the author's text production. It also functioned as a foundational poetic principle in Fontane's output, made possible by the skills he acquired through his professional training and his first two careers as a pharmacist and an editor at a newspaper. Fontane's authorial profile thus emerges in the dynamic space between high poetic realism and sensationalist *Kolportage*. He filled this space skillfully, with aesthetic strategies that anticipate the art of remix. These strategies enabled him to succeed in the literary marketplace without dividing his output into "authentic" and "inauthentic" work, as so many of his fellow writers had to do in the latter part of the nineteenth century (e.g., Wilhelm Raabe and, later, Arno Holz).[154] In Fontane's writing, everything is connected to itself; his work appears as one long textual patchwork whose blocks the compiler shifts around in response to the media scene of his time. His authorship, then, rests on practices of recombination and aesthetic effect design that lend coherence to his oeuvre. The innovative potential of these practices can come to light only if one fully acknowledges that Fontane worked as a compiler, albeit a compiler in hiding.

---

153 Manfred Horlitz, "Fontanes Quellennutzung für seine Wanderungen-Texte," in *"Geschichte und Geschichten aus Mark Brandenburg." Fontanes Wanderungen durch die Mark Brandenburg im Kontext der europäischen Reiseliteratur*, ed. Hanna Delf von Wolzogen (Würzburg: Königshausen & Neumann, 2003), 274, 281.

154 See Parr, *Autorschaft*, 19–20. Parr points out that Raabe increasingly alternated between "marktgerechten und experimentellen Texten," while Holz even operated under two different names—he founded the so-called "Volkmarfirma" with Oskar Jerschke in order to write crowd-pleasing and lucrative plays under a pseudonym.

Three A Living Archive: Generating Input

On the Hunt for Material

For a compiler, access to textual material is everything. After all, having suitable material at hand is the minimal requirement for any kind of compiling. Compilers, therefore, are usually on the hunt for sources. Famous historical cases suggest that these hunts can consist of large-scale reading and organized note-taking. Exemplars like Theodor Zwinger (1533–88) and Johann Jacob Moser (1701–85), described by their contemporaries as "busy bees," "bookworms," and "hamsters,"[1] tirelessly scoured books and other written sources for gargantuan intellectual projects such as Zwinger's *Theatrum vitae humanae*, a compilation of moral examples of human behavior that added up to a whopping 4,500 folio pages in the final edition.[2] They obtained their sources from obvious places, such as libraries and print shops, and also through expansive correspondence networks. Typically, they did not work alone. Paid research assistants, or even the writers' wives and children, helped with the menial aspects of the research, such as copying passages and ordering books.[3] Compilers methodically stored the cuttings in personal archives, using scholarly receptacles—commonplace books, note closets, and boxes of paper

---

1. On the metaphorics surrounding the activities of compilers, see Ann M. Blair and Peter Stallybrass, "Mediating Information, 1450–1800," in *This Is Enlightenment*, ed. Clifford Siskin and William B. Warner (Chicago: University of Chicago Press, 2010), 150, and Michael Cahn, "Hamster: Wissenschafts- und mediengeschichtliche Grundlagen der sammelnden Lektüre," in *Lesen und Schreiben im 17. und 18. Jahrhundert. Studien zu ihrer Bewertung in Deutschland, England, Frankreich*, ed. Paul Goetsch (Tübingen: Narr, 1994), 63–77.
2. See Ann M. Blair, *Too Much to Know: Managing Scholarly Information Before the Modern Age* (New Haven: Yale University Press, 2010), 131–2.
3. Ibid., 104–12.

slips, to name but a few—designed to systematize the materials with the help of alphabetical indices or other such search aids.[4] In brief, their note-taking practices and storage media allowed them to decompose large quantities of textual sources into disconnected parts, from which new compilations could be assembled in accordance with a higher order of knowledge.

To a large extent, Fontane followed this tradition. He, too, usually encountered his sources through remarkable feats of reading and note-taking. He began his career with a mammoth project, the patriotic *Wanderungen durch die Mark Brandenburg* (*Walks Through Mark Brandenburg*, 1856–92),[5] a multi-volume collection of episodic travel sketches of the history, people, and landscape of the eponymous German region. He realized this project with scores of helpers, among them several family members, who excerpted sources on his behalf and sent him material. Cleverly applying the principles of crowdsourcing, he also invited the readers of the initial *Wanderungen* episodes to contribute to the project and thus set a constant stream of material (newspaper articles, historical sources, anecdotes, etc.) into motion. After cutting up this material, he gathered it into a growing repository from which he pieced together new episodes. He first published these episodes in carefully selected conservative newspapers and journals and then bundled them up and republished them in volume form, selling the volumes as parts of an increasingly comprehensive, curated

---

4   The term "archive" can be defined in so many ways that a brief explanation of how I use it seems in order. I follow Daniela Gretz and Nicolas Pethes in their twofold understanding of the term as a metaphor for processes of selection, transformation, and tradition that determine discursive formations (in the Foucauldian sense) and as the tangible storage media in which the metaphor becomes real. See Daniela Gretz and Nicolas Pethes, introduction to *Archiv/Fiktionen. Verfahren des Archivierens in Literatur und Kultur des langen 19. Jahrhunderts*, ed. Daniela Gretz and Nicolas Pethes (Freiburg i. Br.: Rombach, 2016), 11–12. For instructive case studies of archiving with different storage media, see Markus Krajewski, *Paper Machines: On Cards & Catalogs, 1548–1929*, trans. Peter Krapp (Cambridge, MA: MIT Press, 2011), 40–56; and Blair, *Too Much to Know*, 206–29.

5   This time frame spans from the first-known notes on the project to the publication of episodic *Wanderungen* texts in journals and magazines from 1859 to 1892. During this time, Fontane also published selected *Wanderungen* episodes in a four-volume book set (1862–82), individual volumes of which continued to appear in revised editions. An overview of the complicated publication history can be found in Jens Bisky, "Zur Verlagsgeschichte der 'Wanderungen durch die Mark Brandenburg' 1860–1945. Mit einer kommentierten Bibliographie," *Berliner Hefte zur Geschichte des literarischen Lebens* 1 (1996): 112–32.

collection intended to foster the readers' "love and affection for their native land"[6] (*Liebe und Anhänglichkeit an die Heimath*).

At the same time, however, Fontane's material repository deviated markedly from the historical template established by the likes of Zwinger: it lacked an overarching order. Fontane's storage media, including notebooks, file folders, cardboard boxes, and the peculiar "paper sleeves" mentioned in the previous chapter, amounted to a dynamic storage space, not a systematic archive. In it, all kinds of materials—from excerpts, newspaper clippings, and drafts to published episodes—were jumbled together; the headings under which they were stored often shifted; and there were no reliable indices or other search aids, much less a discernable higher order of knowledge. Rather than systematizing and perpetuating the deposited content, Fontane's "archive" followed an ongoing circulation pattern: materials constantly piled up, were assembled into new episodes, were published in periodicals or in volume form, and then returned to the archive, where the published pieces could yet again be reconstituted into material for other projects. The archive was as much a tool of ad-hoc production as of storage, and it was directly plugged into the material circulation among newspapers, journals, and books in the mass-media marketplace, to which it also contributed.

The account of how Fontane's peculiar "living" archive was generated begins with a closer look at the *Wanderungen* project. Fontane scholarship has long since established that this extended publishing endeavor was foundational to his authorship. For one thing, it provided financial stability—the honoraria that he received for the publication of *Wanderungen* episodes in the periodical press and for the book volumes proved to be the highest revenue source in his family's budget.[7] Furthermore, as several source studies have demonstrated, the plethora of material that the project generated, including detailed landscape descriptions, historical anecdotes about locals, and inventories of notable buildings, built the basis for his future creative fictional output. But while the Fontane scholarship accepts that the *Wanderungen* served as an archive, it has not yet explored how this archive emerged, what its insides looked like, or which epistemic principles sustained its rapid

---

6   Theodor Fontane, preface to *Wanderungen durch die Mark Brandenburg* (Berlin: Hertz, 1862), viii.
7   Peter Wruck, "Fontane als Erfolgsautor: Zur Schlüsselstellung der Makrostruktur in der Produktions- und Rezeptionsgeschichte der Wanderungen," in *"Geschichte und Geschichten aus Mark Brandenburg." Fontanes "Wanderungen durch die Mark Brandenburg" im Kontext der europäischen Reiseliteratur*, ed. Hanna Delf von Wolzogen (Würzburg: Königshausen & Neumann, 2003), 377.

growth. It remains to be seen how Fontane's stylization of the *Wanderungen* as a patriotic, open-ended collection in need of expansion created an optic through which ever more local-historical materials could be identified, and how it provided an interactive publishing framework that encouraged readers to contribute. A closer inspection of the process reveals a strong contrast between the curated, carefully aestheticized surface of the growing *Wanderungen* text and its unruly archival underside. The fluidity inherent in Fontane's archive, as beneficial as it was for his productivity in the fast-paced literary market, created challenges for his authorship and legacy.

Fontane strategically expanded the scope of his crowdsourcing efforts with a proliferating epistolary network that furnished material for more than just the *Wanderungen*. A media-historical reconstruction of this network shows how an effective mix of direct and indirect contacts allowed him to communicate with informants from all walks of life, including people well above and below his own social rank. Reaching into socially distant places with the help of his network, Fontane enriched the local-historical materials in his archive with an influx of contemporary sources, extending from professorial expertise on technical inventions to political rumors and piquant societal gossip. His research activities generated materials covering the full spectrum of antiquarianism, popular contemporary topics, and sensationalism. A brief survey of the content of Fontane's notebooks confirms that these descriptors—antiquarian, popular, and sensationalist—usefully characterize the bulk of the notes taken for literary prose projects and expose key ingredients with which he later compiled his realist novels.

It will also be useful to analyze the reading techniques with which Fontane traversed the influx of material generated by his research. Fontane performed "discontinuous" reading, a mode encouraged by the journal form, in which the reader leaped from article to article (or source to source), freely constellating the text portions according to his interests.[8] A virtuosic reader, he applied this technique with so much sophistication that it generated poetic momentum and turned his dynamic archive into a motor of creative literary production.

---

8   The basic principle of discontinuous reading is explained in Peter Stallybrass, "Books and Scrolls: Navigating the Bible," in *Books and Readers in Early Modern England: Material Studies*, ed. Jennifer Andersen and Elizabeth Sauer (Philadelphia: University of Pennsylvania Press, 2002), 42–79. Nicola Kaminski, Nora Ramtke, and Carsten Zelle provide an account of journal reading as "zapping" in "Zeitschriftenliteratur/Fortsetzungsliteratur: Problemaufriß," in *Zeitschriftenliteratur/Fortsetzungsliteratur*, ed. Nicola Kaminski, Nora Ramtke, and Carsten Zelle (Hannover: Wehrhahn, 2014), 7–40.

Crowdsourcing the *Wanderungen*

Upon his return from London in 1859, Fontane was fiercely determined to establish himself as a literary writer and gain recognition in Prussia's conservative circles.[9] He turned to a promising patriotic project that had been on the back burner for several years: a comprehensive study of the landscape and history of Prussia. This study, Fontane hoped, would keep its author occupied for "approximately ten years" and would fill "twenty volumes."[10] From the very beginning, the colossal project, eventually named the *Wanderungen durch die Mark Brandenburg*, figured as both an archive and a work. Its earliest trace, a brief diary entry from 1856, envisions a hybrid form that would simultaneously enable future poetic production and appear as an authored work. Here Fontane wrote:

> Made a plan. "*The Marches*, their Men and their History. Collected and Edited, for the Benefit of the Fatherland's Literature and That to Come, by Th. Fontane." The things themselves I shall render alphabetically. If I find time to write *that* book, I shall not have lived in vain and can lay my bones to sleep in peace of mind.
>
> *Einen Plan gemacht. „Die Marken, ihre Männer u. ihre Geschichte. Um Vaterlands- u. künftiger Dichtung willen gesammelt u. herausgegeben von Th. Fontane." Die Dinge selbst geb' ich alphabetisch. Wenn ich noch dazu komme das Buch zu schreiben, so hab' ich nicht umsonst gelebt u. kann meine Gebeine ruhig schlafen legen.*
>
> (GBA XI.1: 161)

The tension between archive and work is expressed in the central verbs, "to collect and edit," or *sammeln* and *herausgeben*, contrasting with "to write," *schreiben*, and the emphatic reference to posterity. Even though Fontane envisioned a volume with itemized contents in alphabetical order, he called its production an act of *writing*. To be precise, he would write "*that* book," a formulation charged with notions of his life's work and posthumous fame. This tension between archival mode and finished work would continue to drive the project, and it is essential to understanding the astounding productivity of the project as a material-generating apparatus.

---

9 See Roland Berbig, "Das Ganze als Ganzes oder: Pastor Schmutz und Geheimrat Stiehl. Zur Rezeptionssteuerung der 'Wanderungen' durch Fontane," *Berliner Hefte zur Geschichte des literarischen Lebens* 2 (1998): 75.

10 Undated letter to Theodor Storm, written prior to August 1, 1860. See *Theodor Storm–Theodor Fontane: Briefwechsel. Kritische Ausgabe*, ed. Gabriele Radecke (Berlin: Erich Schmidt, 2011), 119.

The project was also intended as a contribution to a popular cultural activity: local-historical collecting. Referencing the great men of the Mark Brandenburg and the literary heritage of the "fatherland" (*Vaterland*), Fontane aligned himself with a trend that had begun in the early decades of the nineteenth century, when individuals interested in history (antiquarians, philologists, scholars of law, amateur historians, etc.) attempted to collect and preserve their experiences of the past and make them available to others.[11] During these years, historical collecting turned from a predominantly personal passion into a shared cultural practice intended to "awaken" the rich historical heritage slumbering everywhere in the homeland, to encourage the public to value the past, and to fuel conservative ideals.[12] By the time Fontane became serious about the *Wanderungen* project, the practice was in full swing. A large infrastructure of historical associations, journals, and correspondence networks had already emerged and was ready to be tapped by Fontane. Moreover, Arnim's and Brentano's *The Youth's Magic Horn* (*Des Knaben Wunderhorn*, 1806–8) and the Brothers' Grimm *Children and Household Tales* (*Kinder- und Hausmärchen*, 1812/1815) provided influential models that showed how to gather, inventory, edit, and popularize cultural relics.

Just how closely Fontane aligned his project with these collectors' endeavors becomes clear from a reference letter that he requested in 1860 from the respected art historian Karl Schnaase as part of a funding proposal that he submitted to the Prussian Ministry for Affairs of Religion, Education, and Medicine. (The proposal was successful, and Fontane was awarded an annual stipend of 300 *Thaler* over a period of eight years for his project).[13] Schnaase, likely instructed by Fontane on what he should emphasize,[14] described the proposed historical collecting as a means to patriotic awakening. At the same time, the reference letter lays out the general research parameters that would guide Fontane's hunt for material and determine what kind of sources would eventually enter his archive through the *Wanderungen*. Schnaase opened his letter with the claim that the project arose from the Fontane's

---

11 In what follows, I am relying on Susan A. Crane's narrative of the emergence of historical collecting, *Collecting and Historical Consciousness in Early Nineteenth-Century Germany* (Ithaca, NY: Cornell University Press, 2000).
12 Ibid., 13–19; 62–3.
13 See Wruck, "Fontane als Erfolgsautor," 388; Henrik Karge, "Poesie und Wissenschaft. Fontane und die Kunstgeschichte," in *Fontane und die bildende Kunst*, ed. Claude Keisch, Peter-Klaus Schuster, and Moritz Wullen (Berlin: Henschel, 1998), 274.
14 Karge assumes that Schnaase had been briefed thoroughly by Fontane on "die Umstände und die Zielsetzung der 'Wanderungen.'" See "Poesie und Wissenschaft. Fontane und die Kunstgeschichte," 274.

"faithful attachment to his native Marches (*märkisches Heimathland*)" and aimed at providing a depiction of the region that was "not merely readable, but attractive and patriotically inspiring."[15] While scholarly historiography, such as Ernst Fidicin's *Die Territorien der Mark Brandenburg*,[16] which developed the topographic and legal conditions of times past from ancient documents and "monosyllabic chronicles," was "praiseworthy," it was unlikely to contribute to "living historical sentiment" and "an understanding of the peculiarities of one's native land." In this regard, Fontane's project promised to stand out:

> Yet no means is likely to be more effective to that end than historical and topographical accounts of the kind intended by Mr. Fontane, which, departing from an appraisal of present conditions and localities, bring back to life the past both proximate and remote, accord a place to tradition and legend alongside proven historic facts, and throughout pay particular attention to the personal, individual element, considering not only the great heroes of history, but also representatives of popular life and manners.[17]

As Schnaase underscored, Fontane's project would be based on "solid historical facts" and would require "complete and examined material" (*vollständiges und gesichtetes Material*). To this end, it would include exhaustive antiquarian details, gathered from archival sources, scholarly accounts, and fieldwork in numerous Brandenburgian towns and villages. At the same time, these sources would be complemented and enlivened through anything that a broad audience might find appealing, from historical curiosities to popular-literary stories and anecdotes about individual people.

As we saw in Chapter 1, however, the book format that Fontane envisioned and that Schnaase's letter supported had ceased to be the general norm for publication by the mid-nineteenth century. With literature's migration into mass media—above all, periodicals—book sales dwindled throughout the latter half of the century to the point that

---

15 Untitled Reference Letter, June 25, 1860. Staatsbibliothek zu Berlin – Preußischer Kulturbesitz, Handschriftenabteilung, Slg. Darmst. 2 I 1834, Schnaase, Karl. Printed in Karge, "Poesie und Wissenschaft. Fontane und die Kunstgeschichte," 276.

16 Ernst Fidicin, *Die Territorien der Mark Brandenburg oder Geschichte der einzelnen Kreise, Städte, Rittergüter als Fortsetzung des Landbuchs Kaiser Karls IV*, 4 vols. (Berlin: Guttentag, 1857–64).

17 Untitled Reference Letter, June 25, 1860. Printed in Karge, "Poesie und Wissenschaft. Fontane und die Kunstgeschichte," 277.

the *Preußische Jahrbücher* laconically stated in 1884, "A German buying a book is a special man indeed."[18] Instead of single-volume books, readers purchased subscriptions to newspapers, family-oriented magazines, literary journals, and part-issue editions. Writers had to establish their names in these media before they could dream of being (re)published in book form. Accordingly, Fontane dispatched the first episodes of his undertaking to the *Kreuzzeitung* and other conservative mass media, considering these episodes to be "visiting cards" (*Visitenkarten*, GBA XII.2: 175–6) with which to publicize his name and his topic.[19]

From these first episodes on, the author strove to ensure that his writings would be well received and that he, in turn, would receive further material to compile.[20] Indeed, Fontane established a self-reinforcing dynamic, a reciprocal relationship between production and reception that fueled his productivity. He carefully chose like-minded companions, or *Wandergefährten*, such as the conservative collector of local folktales Wilhelm Schwartz, and invited them to accompany him on research trips through the Mark. (These trips were usually not *Wanderungen*, "walks," but meticulously planned carriage rides—the distances to be covered were too great for walking.[21]) As Roland Berbig writes, Fontane selected these travel companions not only for their expertise in local history, but also for the potential readership that they represented.[22] They often had access to the noble families around which many of the episodes revolved and who were Fontane's primary target audience. Methodically, Fontane thus enlarged his initially small circle of readers, and whenever he could, turned readers into contributors, inviting them to add their share to—and recognize themselves in—the historiography.[23] The same held true for Fontane's exchanges with local pastors, teachers, Prussian civil servants, and professional historians,

---

18 Quoted in Reinhard Wittmann, *Geschichte des deutschen Buchhandels*, 3rd ed. (Munich: C.H. Beck, 2011), 289.
19 Fontane realized early on, however, that this publication strategy had significant downsides. In an 1859 letter to his friend Henriette von Merckel, he emphasized his dissatisfaction with having to sell the episodes off "bit by bit, here today, there tomorrow." See *Die Fontanes und die Merckels. Ein Familienbriefwechsel*, ed. Gotthard Erler (Berlin: Aufbau, 1987), 2:204.
20 Roland Berbig analyzes how Fontane took control of the initial reception of the *Wanderungen* episodes in "Das Ganze als Ganzes." I am gratefully building on Berbig's analysis here.
21 Jutta Fürstenau, *Fontane und die märkische Heimat* (Berlin: Ebering, 1941), 46–9. To my knowledge, Fürstenau's study provides the first systematic evaluation of Fontane's research methods and crowdsourcing efforts in the context of the *Wanderungen* (46–84).
22 Berbig, "Das Ganze als Ganzes," 82.
23 Ibid., 80.

whom he sought out with the help of local historical associations such as the "Verein für die Geschichte der Mark Brandenburg" (Association for the History of the Brandenburg Marches). In her pioneering study of the *Wanderungen*, Jutta Fürstenau aptly describes Fontane's strategy as an instance of collective scholarship,[24] yet an even better term may be—as noted earlier—"crowdsourcing," for it highlights the participatory aspects of the strategy. After all, Fontane did not hesitate to tap the talents of his growing crowd and to publish entire episodes that his contributors sent him, at times with only minimal edits.

The "visiting card" strategy proved effective. Roughly eighteen months into the project, Fontane made the leap to the desired book form through Wilhelm Hertz, a publisher whose agenda and typical audience matched those of Fontane's preferred publication venue, the conservative mass media.[25] Fontane had proposed the project to Hertz repeatedly and even simulated the book form as part of his pitch: he pasted some of the published episodes into a cutting book and sent it to Hertz, along with a comprehensive table of contents, "so that the whole may appear as 'a whole'" (*damit das Ganze als 'ein Ganzes' erscheint*, BaH 25). In February 1861, Hertz and Fontane agreed on a contract for one volume of episodic travel sketches with an option for a second one (BaH 28).

But now the author faced a problem. How could he realize two forms of publication at once—that is, make the leap to the form of the complete book without bringing the topic to a close, so that he could continue to churn out more episodes in the serial media? By this time, he was contributing episodes to several daily papers and weekly journals in various series with titles such as "Märkische Bilder" ("Pictures from the Marches," *Kreuzzeitung*), "Bilder und Geschichten aus Mark Brandenburg" ("Pictures and Tales from the Brandenburg Marches," *Morgenblatt für gebildete Leser*) and "Aus Stadt und Grafschaft Ruppin" ("From the Town and County of Ruppin," in *Wochenblatt der Johanniter Ordens-Balley Brandenburg*).[26] He was not ready to limit his focus or stop. Fontane's case complicated the typical nineteenth-century

---

24 Fürstenau, Fontane und die märkische Heimat, 59.
25 Berbig points out that Hertz's publishing agenda revolved around state and Church, contemporary politics, schools, religion, history, and archeology, and that the publishing house can be seen as one of the main sources of published support for the forces of the Prussian reaction. See "Das Ganze als Ganzes," 76–7.
26 For details, see the editorial commentary to the *Große Brandenburger Ausgabe* of the *Wanderungen*, which states for each episode whether and where it had initially been published in the periodical press. Hertz insisted that Fontane produce some episodes exclusively for the book edition, which was a constant point of contention between the author and the publisher.

scenario of "republication into a single book"²⁷ (*nachgeordneter Werksynthese*) insofar as his work was far from complete when he began assembling the first volume. In terms of formal complexity, his *Wanderungen* project was not unlike Heine's popular *Reisebilder* endeavor (1826–31/1856), which also unfolded in series of episodes in the periodical press while Heine assembled the first *Reisebilder* monographs. Two editorial decisions ensured that Fontane would be able to issue a book volume *and* continue writing more episodes. He developed a catch-all title for his book project, applying a strategy that had already worked well for Heine. With Hertz, he named the project *Wanderungen*, which was an established umbrella term for all sorts of cultural, historical, and proto-ethnographic writings and thus enabled a continuing production with considerable generic and thematic leeway.²⁸ His second editorial decision, however, deviated decidedly from Heine's framing of his undertaking. If Heine had conceived of the *Reisebilder* as a "haphazard patchwork"²⁹ (*zusammengewürfeltes Lappenwerk*) and exploited the friction between the individual episodes for critical, satirical, and provocative purposes, Fontane used a far more conservative and holistic concept to join the pieces: in the preface to the first *Wanderungen* book volume, he explicitly connected his project to the contemporary discourse of historical collecting.³⁰ This connection was so important to Fontane that he repeatedly invoked the rhetoric and imagery of collecting in the preface. Resorting to the familiar trope of hidden "wealth," Fontane wrote:

> I wandered across my native country and found it to be richer than I had dared to hope. Every patch of earth came to life

---

27 See Kaminski et al., "Zeitschriftenliteratur/Fortsetzungsliteratur," 8.
28 On "Wanderliteratur" as a genre and a paradigm for cultural, sociological, and ethnographic research, see Andrew Cusack, *The Wanderer in Nineteenth-Century German Literature: Intellectual History and Cultural Criticism* (Rochester, NY: Camden House, 2008), 1–12.
29 Heine used these terms in a letter to Moser dated January 11, 1825. See *Briefe 1815–1831*, ed. Fritz Eisner and Fritz Mende, vol. 20, Säkularausgabe (Berlin: Akademie-Verlag, 1975), 184. On the conception and structure of the *Reisebilder*, see Gerhard Höhn, "Die Reisebilder: Das Gesamtprojekt," in *Heine-Handbuch. Zeit, Person, Werk*, 3rd ed. (Stuttgart: Metzler, 2004), 180–91.
30 Günter Häntzschel's recent study on literary collecting also situates Fontane's *Wanderungen* as a *Sammelwerk* in this overall historical context. His treatment of the topic does not discuss the consequences that arise from this discursive framing, however. See Günter Häntzschel, *Sammel(l)ei(denschaft). Literarisches Sammeln im neunzehnten Jahrhundert* (Freiburg: Königshausen & Neumann, 2014), 160–2.

and offered up characters.... I was comforted by a fullness, a wealth, which I quite surely feel unable ever to master even by approximation; for the copious matter presented in the following was gathered within the space of a few miles: on the shores of Ruppin Lake and outside the gates of Berlin. And I collected it casually, too, not like one going to harvest with a sickle, but like a passer-by pulling the occasional ear from a rich field.[31]

Ich bin die Heimath durchzogen und ich habe sie reicher gefunden, als ich zu hoffen gewagt hatte. Jeder Fußbreit Erde belebte sich und gab Gestalten heraus.... Eine Fülle, ein Reichthum sind mir entgegen getreten, denen gegenüber ich die bestimmte Empfindung habe, ihrer niemals, auch nur annähernd, Herr werden zu können; denn das immerhin Umfangreiche, das ich in Nachstehendem biete, ist auf wenig Meilen eingesammelt: am Ruppiner See und vor den Thoren Berlins. Und sorglos hab' ich es gesammelt, nicht wie einer, der mit der Sichel zur Erndte geht, sondern wie ein Spaziergänger, der einzelne Aehren aus dem reichen Felde zieht.

The idea that Fontane had gathered his materials "casually" like a "passer-by" from a cornfield was obviously bogus, yet these tropes helped to convey the impression that the presented materials were "natural" and authentic, as opposed to strategically collected and edited. In the preface to the *Children- and Household Tales*, the Grimms had constructed a similar myth about their project, which was much more contemporary with the *Wanderungen* than it may seem—the tenth edition of the Grimms' *Tales* had appeared in 1858, shortly before Fontane began the *Wanderungen*. Fontane adopted their stance in his own preface and even appropriated their metaphor: the Grimms, too, had compared collecting to picking up individual ears (*Ähren*) by hand, not with a sickle.[32] Finally, Fontane characterized what he had gathered as "something colorful and manifold"[33] (*ein Buntes, Mannigfaches*). He thus referred to the discourse of collecting, as the aesthetic concept of "manifoldness" was typically used by collectors

---

31 Fontane, preface to *Wanderungen durch die Mark Brandenburg* (1862), viii. From the fourth edition on, "Heimath" in the first line of the quotation is replaced by "die Mark."
32 Jacob and Wilhelm Grimm, "Vorrede," in *Kinder- und Hausmärchen. Gesammelt durch die Brüder Grimm*, vol. 1, vergrößerter Nachdruck der zweibändigen Erstausgabe von 1812 und 1815, ed. Heinz Rölleke (Göttingen: Vandenhoeck & Ruprecht, 1986), v.
33 Fontane, preface to *Wanderungen durch die Mark Brandenburg* (1862), viii.

to distinguish their collections from mere accumulations of material.[34] He closed with a patriotic statement that had already figured prominently in Schnaase's letter of reference, namely, that all of the episodes were born of "love and affection" for his "native land" (*Liebe und Anhänglichkeit an die Heimath*) and that he hoped to kindle similar feelings in others.

The collection thus provided the conceptual string with which Fontane bundled up the episodes that had already appeared scattered across several media. The concept also retrofitted his project with a distinct beginning, while signaling that more was still to come.[35] Framed in this way, his project entered the book market under the title *Wanderungen durch die Mark Brandenburg*, just in time for the Christmas sales in mid-November 1861.[36] In the following decades, as the project grew to four volumes that appeared in revised editions, Fontane continued to insist on using collecting as a framing device. The epilogue to the final volume, *Spreeland. Beskow⸗Storkow und Barnim⸗Teltow* (Berlin, 1881), still stressed this activity, thus defining the expandable space in which the *Wanderungen* episodes were presented as a single work.

Considering the genesis of the project, Fontane's mobilization of "collecting" was a logical and, from a publishing perspective, a pragmatic choice. Yet it was also the public staging of a cultural and archival practice with epistemic consequences. It turned the *Wanderungen* project into a productive tool for the absorption of ever more material. Only after the publication of the scattered episodes in volume form could the project be perceived as benefiting from the epistemic work that the collection, as an organizing medium, can carry out.

The Concept of Collecting

Collections come into being through a posited frame of reference.[37] This frame—typically defined by the collector's passion ("Cookbooks from

---

34 In his review of Arnim and Brentano's *The Youth's Magic Horn*, Goethe famously praised the song collection for its "Mannigfaltigkeit." See Goethe, "A. v. Arnim; C. Brentano, Des Knaben Wunderhorn," *Jenaische Allgemeine Literatur-Zeitung* 3.18 and 3.19 (January 21 and 22, 1806): 137–8.
35 Wruck also notes in his excellent analysis that the macro-structure of the *Wanderungen* project was "kumulativ" and geared toward gradual expansion and completion. He does not, however, discuss the role of the collection as an organizing medium. See Wruck, "Fontane als Erfolgsautor," 388–9.
36 The volume is predated to 1862, according to contemporary publishing custom.
37 This abstract description of the logic of the collection as medium is based on Nikolaus Wegmann, *Bücherlabyrinthe. Suchen und Finden im alexandrinischen Zeitalter* (Cologne: Böhlau, 2000), 158–81, and Manfred Sommer, *Sammeln. Ein philosophischer Versuch* (Frankfurt: Suhrkamp, 1999), 17–32.

Victorian Britain"), professional interests ("Wildlife in Indonesia"), or cultural-political priorities ("Early Netherlandish Painters")—provides the context in which a mere object is transformed into a collectible. The frame introduces the distinctions that separate what belongs in the collection from the mass of materials that clutter the modern world. As soon as this frame of reference has been posited, the first selection criteria are formulated, and the process of collecting sets in motion a recursive operation that identifies and absorbs into the collection new objects, which in turn refine the context—and so forth. As we have already seen, the frame of reference that Fontane's *Wanderungen* explicitly posited was "love and affection for one's native land." This might seem too elusive a category to define a collection, but it was exactly what made the *Wanderungen* into such a productive tool. Its ingenuity lies in its scope: "love and affection for one's native land" provides what systems theory calls a second-order distinction (*sekundäre Unterscheidung*), that is, a distinction without a clearly defined opposite and without reference to anything concrete. There are no objective criteria for distinguishing what does and does not belong to "love and affection for one's native land."[38] All the phrase does is imbue the topic with importance. To find this taxonomy banal, however, would be to miss the vast thematic inclusion that "love and affection for one's native land" enables. With this criterion, *anything* can be meaningfully included.

A contrastive glance at *Wien und die Wiener, in Bildern aus dem Leben* (*Vienna and the Viennese in Pictures Drawn from Life*, 1841–4), a set of feuilleton essays edited by Adalbert Stifter, clarifies the epistemological impact of Fontane's taxonomy. Stifter's project is similar, insofar as it is composed of a series of episodes concerning the history, people, and landscape (or rather cityscape) of a particular locale. The episodes, twelve of which Stifter wrote himself, were first published as part-issues and then republished as a book volume. The project differed markedly, however, in the organization of its contents. In his preface, Stifter uses the metaphor of the kaleidoscope to explain how the episodes are connected: "The purpose and aim of these pages is ... to let pass [before the spectator's eye] pictures both gay and serious, as in a kaleidoscope, of this capital city"[39] (*wie in einem Kaleidoskop Scenen dieser Hauptstadt vorüber zu führen*). While Fontane resorts to an extremely inclusive concept, Stifter presupposes a limited number

---

38 Wegmann analyzes the epistemological impact of second-order distinctions on collecting projects in *Bücherlabyrinthe*, 178.
39 Adalbert Stifter, *Wien und die Wiener, in Bildern aus dem Leben. Adalbert Stifter: Werke und Briefe. Historisch-kritische Gesamtausgabe*, ed. Alfred Doppler and Hartmut Laufhütte (Stuttgart: Kohlhammer, 2005), 9.1:v.

of elements that create shifting pictures of the chosen locale for the readers' enjoyment and edification. Furthermore, Stifter's project revolves around a concrete reference point, St. Stephen's Cathedral, as its organizing figure: the introductory episode, "Aussicht und Betrachtungen von der Spitze des St. Stephansthurmes" ("Prospect and Reflections from the Steeple of St. Stephen's"), provides a "perspective from the cathedral tower" that is "mobilized to map the Viennese topography, emergent industrialization, modernization efforts, and then to reflect on the terms of memory."[40] When an episode written by one of Stifter's co-contributors did not fit into this perspective, Stifter rewrote it or excluded it altogether from the project, as the correspondence with his publisher, Gustav Heckenast, reveals.[41] By contrast, Fontane's *Wanderungen* project had no such restrictive reference point. Indeed, the preface to the second edition of the first *Wanderungen* volume openly renounces selectivity. The ideal traveler in the Mark Brandenburg, Fontane writes, "must have the good will to find good what is good, instead of wearing it down by means of pedantic comparisons (*anstatt es durch krittliche Vergleiche tot zu machen*)."[42] "Love and affection for one's native land" could, in other words, function everywhere, regardless of the landscape.

While this unselective criterion at the heart of the *Wanderungen* made it conceptually easy to add to the project, publication in volume form increased its visibility. As a result, Fontane began to receive "Nachtrage-Stoffe," or unsolicited supplementary materials from his readers that they hoped to see included in future editions. Just a few weeks after the publication of the first volume, he sent an urgent request to Hertz, asking him for a copy of the *Wanderungen* interleaved with blank pages on which he could note or paste the additions: "I would not dream of inconveniencing you thus," Fontane wrote, "were it not that the supplementary material keeps on multiplying" (*wenn nicht der Nachtrage-Stoff sich rapide mehrte*, BaH 64).

Of course, this rapid accumulation of new material was entirely in the author's interest, and he added steps to intensify the process and increase both the visibility of the *Wanderungen* and his crowdsourcing

---

40 Vance Byrd, "The Politics of Commemoration in *Wien und die Wiener* (1841–44)," *Journal of Austrian Studies* 47, no. 1 (2014): 15.
41 See Agathe Gisela Muth, "Stifters Briefe an Gustav Heckenast im Zusammenhang mit ihrem ersten gemeinsame Unternehmen, *Wien und die Wiener*. . .," in *Der Brief in der österreichischen und ungarischen Literatur*, ed. András F. Balogh and Helga Mitterbauer (Budapest: Elte, 2005), 132–34.
42 Theodor Fontane, preface to *Wanderungen durch die Mark Brandenburg. Erster Theil* (Berlin: Hertz, 1865), v.

efforts. He sent a large number of free book copies to critics and other influential players on the cultural and political scene, including well-known historians (e.g., Johann Gustav Droysen and Leopold von Ranke), members of the Ministry of Culture, and staff writers of the *Neue Preußische (Kreuz-)Zeitung*.[43] Shortly thereafter, Fontane proudly reported to Hertz that thanks to the *Kreuzzeitung*, the *Wanderungen* had become fashionable "among the aristocracy and the officer corps" and that they were also being read "at *court*" (BaH 68–9), where they had met with acclaim. Moreover, the author and publisher developed a set of targeted advertisements for a wide range of local papers to alert readers to *Wanderungen* episodes that treated their specific villages.[44] Fontane also posted survey questions in journals—for example, about the presence and design of "carved altarpieces" in local churches—and concluded an episode on the "Yew Tree" (*Eibenbaum*) in the *Kreuzzeitung* with an explicit invitation to his readers to send him more local tales: "The yew tree has experienced far, far more than told here. . . . Any further correspondence (care of this newspaper) would be most welcome."[45] Last but not least, he developed questionnaires with long lists of queries about specific topics or sites that he needed to research, handed them out to his helpers, and collected their answers.[46] The commitment of Fontane's helpers to the project becomes clear in the numerous acknowledgments that the author made over the years. About one of his most loyal contributors, Mathilde von Rohr, he wrote that he owed "likely a dozen of the most readable chapters" to her "unflagging industry" and that her work had supplied numerous "contributions, many of which were ready to print . . ., needing only a little pruning (*mitunter*

---

43 Berbig speaks of sixty-three copies (of an initial print run of 1,065 copies) that Fontane sent out. See "Das Ganze als Ganzes," 85–6.
44 The advertisements are reprinted in BaH 443–4. I owe this reference to Berbig, "Das Ganze als Ganzes."
45 He posted the survey about carved altar pieces ("Schnitzaltäre") in the *Schulblatt für die Provinz Brandenburg* 28, no. 5/6 (1863): 400, and he published the one about the "Yew Tree" in *NP(K)Z* 302, December 25, 1862. Both examples are quoted in Fürstenau, *Fontane und die märkische Heimat*, 70.
46 Fontane pasted one such questionnaire, completed by his wife Emilie, into his Notebook A8, 7RAV. The precision with which the author formulated his questions ("3. Wo stammen die Böller her, die an der Eintrittshalle des Schlosses [Schloss Gusow; PM] stehen?") emphasizes how invested he was in accumulating detailed knowledge about the region. Fürstenau refers to several similar questionnaires that she encountered in the *Schriftenarchiv*, now *Theodor Fontane Archiv*. See Fürstenau, *Fontane und die märkische Heimat*, 258–9, notes 120–6. Since the *TFA* is still in the process of indexing its holdings, precise archival signatures cannot be given here.

fix und fertige Beiträge . . ., die nur ein wenig Zurechtstutzung bedurften)."[47] In the epilogue to the final *Wanderungen* volume, Fontane expressed his gratitude for the "encouragement and assistance from my contributors dispersed across half the province" and included such a long list of people that he divided it into three groups: noble families, country pastors, and school teachers.[48]

What had started with a handful of individual episodes about the "Prussian core" of the author's homeland gradually became a history of an entire region.[49] For three decades, Fontane continued to publish episodes in the periodical press while negotiating new volumes and editions with Hertz. As a nineteenth-century collecting project and semi-scholarly undertaking, the *Wanderungen* were driven by the ideal of completeness, or *Vollständigkeit*, which had been part of the earliest project proposals, and the author periodically restated his ambition to treat his topic "in an exhaustive fashion."[50] As he prepared for the third edition of the first volume, Fontane reported to Wilhelm Schwartz that he planned "over the course of the next half-year to travel the Ruppin country three or four times, a week at a time, and while doing so to wander from village to village, such that at the end, no church and no castle, no house of the Lord and no lord's house, will be left into which I have not cast a curious glance and on which I have not made a note" (HFA IV.2: 424). At the same time, because a *complete* account of "love and affection for one's native land" was of course impossible to produce (at what point would one call such an account complete?), the project continued to generate new material.

Fontane's Storage Media

The ceaseless influx of material put a strain on Fontane's storage media. Underneath the increasingly aestheticized textual surface, the *Wanderungen* project posed huge challenges. Archiving the different kinds of sources that were added to the project every day proved difficult because of a problem inherent in any storage system: an ongoing influx of new material exerts constant pressure on the

---

47 GBA V.6:115. Qtd. in Berbig, "Das Ganze als Ganzes," 80–1.
48 Theodor Fontane, *Wanderungen durch die Mark Brandenburg. Vierter Theil. Spreeland. Beeskow⸗Storkow und Barnim⸗Teltow* (Berlin: Hertz, 1882), 451.
49 See Erhart, "Die Wanderungen durch die Mark Brandenburg," 844.
50 Indeed, "Vollständigkeit" figured as one of the unquestioned ideals of late nineteenth-century scholarship. For an incisive contemporary problematization of the concept from a philologist's perspective, see Richard M. Meyer, "'Vollständigkeit.' Eine methodologische Skizze," *Euphorion* 14 (1907): 1–17. I am indebted to Nikolaus Wegmann for this reference.

categories pre-established to sort and code it for later retrieval. Fontane must have grasped this difficulty early on. Although he must have initially thought he could accommodate the additional material with the interleaved *Wanderungen* volumes that he had requested from Hertz, he made little use of this method, presumably because it was insufficiently flexible.[51] Copious archival evidence suggests that rather than trying to force the incoming material into one predetermined organizational scheme, Fontane used an assemblage of interacting storage media that realized several different kinds of order, all of which were changeable and to some extent tentative. This dynamic assemblage included Fontane's notebooks and "paper sleeves" (*Banderolen*), as well as assorted folders (*Mappen*), drawers, and boxes (*Kasten*). The ordering categories of these media frequently changed on the fly, in response to the new material being added, as revisions and additions to labels on several notebooks and paper sleeves indicate.[52] What is more, the storage media acted on the new content in such a way as to decrease the cohesion among the already accumulated items. This prepared the material for flexible use in the *Wanderungen* project, whose macrostructure shifted when a volume was revised or a new one added, and for Fontane's productions in general.

The notebooks provided a storage space that operated independently of the order of the published *Wanderungen* volumes, making room for methods of notation that were not bound to specific moments in the textual fabric of the project. They enhanced the maneuverability of the stored material by introducing two general systems of order: one organized by location and the other by year, which at times occurred in combination, as the label of Notebook A 15 indicates: "Havelland. / Mostly (*Meist*) 1869."[53] Within these ordering systems, Fontane often stored his material according to the places, sites, and people to which

---

51 The interleaved copy of the first edition of volume 1 is lost, but the TFA holds the interleaved copies of the second edition of volume 1 (archival signature Q10) and of the first edition of volume 2 (archival signature Q11). Fontane made fewer than fifty annotations in these volumes in total and added only very specific pieces of information, such as corrective remarks on factual errors. One gets the impression that these storage media were a bad fit for Fontane and his project.
52 For example, Fontane superimposed the original label on notebook A 11 with a new one (fig. 0.2); to a paper sleeve labeled "Marquardt" in black ink, he added, "Herrn Hofrath Herrlich" with a blue crayon in the top-left corner (*Stadtmuseum Berlin*, archival file no. V 67_869_B, Marquardt); and he canceled out the town "Groß Glinike" on the label of a paper sleeve reading "Pichelsdorf / Groß Glinike" (*Stadtmuseum Berlin*, archival file no. 48_522 R_B,Pichelsdorf).
53 There are, however, also some notebooks with thematic labels such as "Arbeits≠Notizen" (A 12).

the individual entries referred, and he used the names of places (or people or sites) as headings. The organizational appearance of numerous notebooks is thus loosely reminiscent of a commonplace book, as a page from Notebook A 1 illustrates (Figure 3.1):

Figure 3.1 Double-page from Fontane's Notebook A 1, showing the resemblance of his notebooks to handwritten commonplace books.

	52
Die alten Burgen im Ruppinschen waren: Alt-Ruppin. Wildberg. Metzelthin (siehe das letzte Blatt) Krentzlin (draußen am Dorf) Der Burgwall gegenüber Carwe. wahrscheinlich noch viele andre; nur die beiden ersten waren von Belang. (Siehe Bratring.)	Binenwalte und Koepernitz. An Herrn v. Zeuner schreiben oder einen benachbarten Geistlichen von Binenwalde. Walsleben. Im Bratring. – Herr Gentz wegen des Denkmals in der Kirche. Wildberg. Im Bratring. – Die Knochen wahrscheinlich aus Kriegs⸗ oder Pestzeit.

	52
The old castles in the Ruppin country were: Alt-Ruppin. Wildberg. Metzelthin (see the last sheet) Krentzlin (at the edge of the village) The castle ramparts opposite Carwe. Probably many others; only the first two were of consequence. (See Bratring.)	Binenwalte and Koepernitz. Write to Mr. von Zeuner or a neighboring cleric from Binenwalde. Walsleben. In Bratring. – Mr. Gentz about the monument in the church. Wildberg. In Bratring. – The bones probably dating back to wartime or the plague.

The notebook, which Fontane labeled "1864. / Summer Journey through the Ruppin County" (*Sommerreise durchs Ruppinsche*), was likely used for research for the second edition of the first *Wanderungen* volume. Like a commonplace book, the transcribed notebook page 52R gathers various pieces of information and allocates them to topics, figuring here as names of villages: under the heading "Wildberg," for example, Fontane combined a note on one of his standard reference works, F. A. W. Bratring's *Statistisch-topographische Beschreibung der gesammten Mark Brandenburg* (Berlin 1809), with a detail about a local historical curiosity, a large number of bones that had been found on the site of Wilsberg Castle, that he had learned of from another source.[54] Such topic-based notational systems facilitated the processing and reworking of material.[55] As page 52R illustrates, the individual entries are not interconnected and are thus suited to easy access and quick retrieval. The underlined topic headings also helped to identify entries and make them searchable. (A closer analysis of the formatting of Fontane's notebook entries will follow in the next chapter.) Similarly, the entry on 51V—a list of "The Old Castles in Ruppin County"—condenses under a single thematic heading information that is scattered across different places, thus making it available as a bundle for inquiries about this topic.

The various drawers, boxes, folders, and paper sleeves (Figure 2.1, see Chapter 2) that littered Fontane's study served first and foremost as

---

54 Fontane mentions the mysterious bones in his description of Wilsberg in "Dörfer und Flecken im Lande Ruppin," GBA V.6: 70.
55 See Blair, *Too Much to Know*, 131–2.

extensions of the notebooks, turning the two-dimensional, script-based order of the notebook pages into the three-dimensional order of real— not just figurative—containers. These storage media further increased the flexible use of Fontane's archival items, because they allowed all kinds of differently sized material to be kept on loose sheets in unbound form. Receptacles filled with discrete textual objects, such as note closets (*Zettelschränke*) and slip boxes (*Zettelkasten*), are advantageous storage media for compilers, for they invite the generative process of reshuffling sources and creating textual patchwork from new combinations.[56] In fact, Fontane used his paper sleeves like a large-format slip box. In them, he stored material for the *Wanderungen*, but also for novels, novellas, and autobiographical writings on individual sheets.[57] The example "Figur in einer Berliner Novelle" ("Character in a Berlin Novella"), a folio sheet from Fontane's *Nachlass*, provides a glimpse of how he formatted his material and indicates how important he found it to keep it in slip-like form (Figure 3.2).

The author made visible efforts to put everything down on one page, leaving a generous left-hand margin, presumably to facilitate surveying and expanding the content. He equipped the page with a circled heading in the upper left corner and hence in an easily identifiable spot that allowed for efficient retrieval. In this way, he turned his notes into mobile textual units—an excerpt from a historical source, a newspaper clipping, the sketch of a literary character, a part of a dialogue, etc.— that could then be pulled out like slips from a slip box.

The archival evidence suggests that Fontane's most important methods for storing his massive amounts of material were the paper sleeves, boxes, and folders, with their slip-box effect. Little has been noted about this aspect in the scholarship to date, likely because only a few dozen sleeves, a few folders—and none of the cardboard boxes—are extant.[58] Yet they

---

56 Anke te Heesen uses the examples of the type case and the slip box to explain how the basic act of putting things into boxes and taking them out can be a generative step in a productive process. See te Heesen, *Weltkasten. Die Geschichte einer Bildenzyklopädie aus dem 18. Jahrhundert* (Göttingen: Wallstein, 1997), 157–61.

57 The eighteen paper sleeves that I was able to evaluate in detail for this study are preserved at the Stadtmuseum Berlin. From their labels, it is evident that Fontane used them for the *Wanderungen*; two autobiographical writings, *Meine Kinderjahre* and *Von Zwanzig bis Dreißig*; the novel *L'Adultera*; and the short story *Onkel Dodo*. One paper sleeve, labeled *Allerlei*, contained miscellaneous items and could not be attributed to any one project.

58 According to Klaus-Peter Möller, an archivist at the Theodor-Fontane-Archiv, thirty-five paper sleeves can be identified as part of the TFA's current holdings (on the basis of the catalog). How many "folders" ("Mappen") are preserved is a question of definition—the archive holds "several" cardboard folders as well as numerous simple paper sheets that Fontane used as folders. E-mail exchange with Klaus-Peter Möller, Archivist, Theodor Fontane Archiv (December 1, 2017). I am indebted to Klaus-Peter Möller for sharing this information with me.

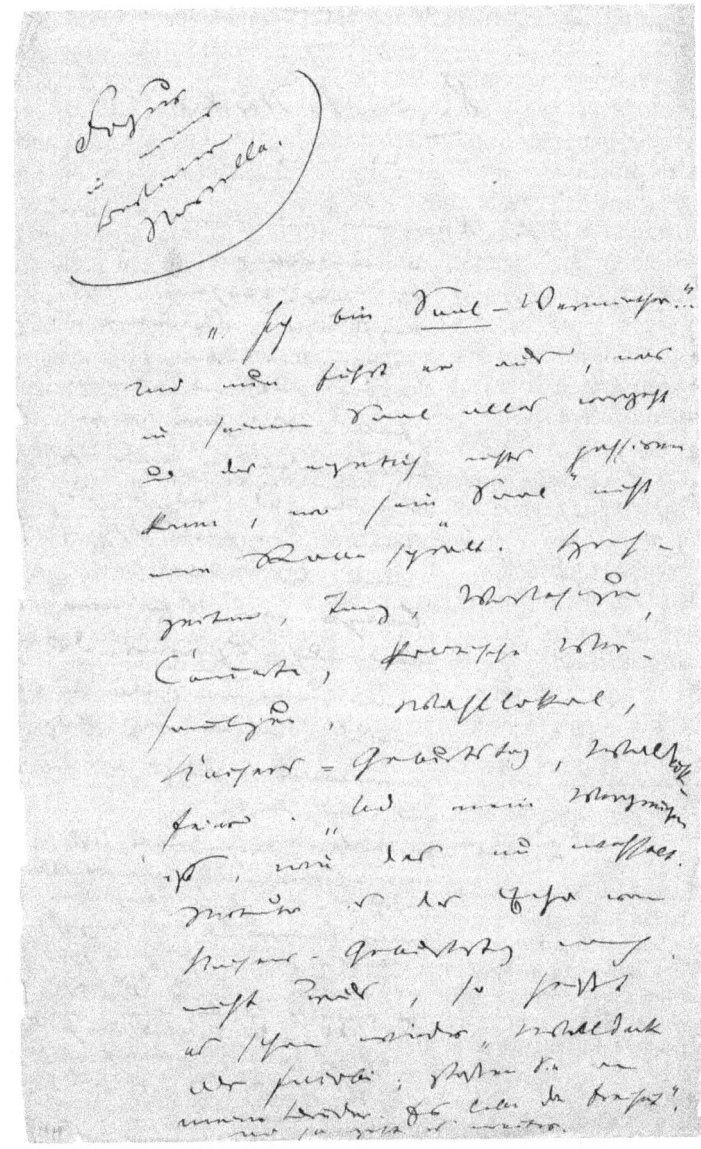

Figure 3.2 Fontane's manuscript page "Figure in a Berlin Novella," with distinct graphic features.

must have been abundant. According to one description of Fontane's *Nachlass*, the author used "some twenty quarto-sized boxes bound in dark green calico"[59] to store his correspondence. The same source reports that "40 manuscript folders, stuffed to capacity"[60] (*prallgefüllte Handschriftenmappen*) were found in Fontane's desk after his death, each containing paper sleeves filled with the manuscripts of novels and all sorts of draft materials. The catalog *Vermißte Bestände* (*Lost Holdings*), which reconstructs the holdings of the *Theodor-Fontane-Archiv* prior to the comprehensive damage caused by World War II, accounts for some of these folders and mentions several dozens of additional folders and sleeves, across most genres of Fontane's output.[61] Moreover, Fontane left hundreds of loose folio sheets with draft materials for all kinds of literary projects.[62] The repository he maintained for the *Wanderungen* and beyond, then, constituted a sea of mobile textual units, stored in numerous individual receptacles that encouraged versatile processing.

At the same time, Fontane's material repository lacked the typical archival features that could have assigned his stored items a permanent place and made the contents reliably searchable. His attempts at ordering and comprehensively indexing his archive remained haphazard at best. The notebook labels, for example, do not provide complete inventories of the contents; on the contrary, only a few of the covered topics or locales are typically mentioned.[63] In the notebooks, reading notes are mixed with field notes; entries for the same Brandenburgian village surface multiple times across different booklets; the tables with which the author attempted to systematize his research on "carved altarpieces"

---

59 Hermann Fricke, "Das Theodor-Fontane-Archiv. Einst und jetzt," *Jahrbuch für Brandenburgische Landesgeschichte* 15 (1964): 167.
60 Ibid.
61 The catalog lists twenty-nine paper sleeves for the novel project *Allerlei Glück* and another fourteen sleeves for the *Wanderungen* sequel, *Das Ländchen Friesack und die Bredows*, in addition to sleeves mentioned in the context of all sorts of other literary, political, and historical writings. The shifting terminology makes it very difficult to reconstruct with precision how many folders and paper sleeves there were—the catalog of missing items speaks at times of "Zeitungsumschlägen", "[Konvolut-]Umschlägen", "Streifband", and "Kreuzband", as well as "Mappen" and "blauen Aktendeckeln". See Manfred Horlitz, ed., *Vermißte Bestände des Theodor Fontane Archivs. Eine Dokumentation im Auftrag des Theodor-Fontane-Archivs* (Theodor-Fontane-Archiv, Potsdam, 1999), 35; 39–45; 52; 58; 89–93. References to paper sleeves can also found across Fontane's correspondence.
62 Horlitz, *Vermißte Bestände*, 39. A large number of Fontane's extant textual building blocks and unpublished fragmentary drafts, belonging to 133 different fictional literary projects, have recently been made available in F1.
63 Gabriele Radecke, "Schneiden, Kleben und Skizzieren. Theodor Fontanes Notizbücher," in *'Gedanken Reisen, Einfälle kommen an.' Die Welt der Notiz*, ed. Marcel Atze and Volker Kaukoreit (Vienna: Praesens, 2017), 204.

(*Schnitzaltäre*) and other surveys have evidently been abandoned prematurely; empty headings crop up everywhere; and there is no central register or other such search aid. The paper sleeves show a similar lack of systematization and do not distinguish between current and past projects. Fontane routinely stuffed source materials into the same sleeve with manuscript drafts, galleys, and published writings; he used the two sides of a manuscript sheet for notes on completely different projects; and he even stored items in the sleeves that he knew were of no use to him. Rather than throwing out the obsolete material and giving relevant notes their own space in his repository, the author simply let the pile grow. For example, he wrote on one bundle's label:

> Miscellaneous. *Not* to be considered for inclusion in new editions of vols. I to IV of the *Wanderungen*. (Everything to be considered on such an occasion has been placed in a blue folder.)— This package contains only a few new materials [added: for Wanderungen etc.], which are unlikely to be of any use. [In a different pen:] The notes on the Luther sites and on Lucas Cranach are to be found in this bundle.[64]

> *Allerlei. Bei den neuen Auflagen von Band I. bis IV. der Wanderungen nicht durchzusehen. (Alles was bei der Gelegenheit durchzusehen ist, liegt in einer blauen Mappe.) – Dies Paket enthält nur ein paar neue Stoffe* [added: *für Wanderungen etc.*], *von denen aber schwerlich etwas zu brauchen ist.* [In a different pen:] *Auch die Notizen über die Luther⸗Plätze und Lucas Cranach liegen in diesem Convolut.*

His storage media, then, created only moments of order against a backdrop of ongoing accumulation.

Fontane certainly had other options. As a pharmacist, he had received training in a profession that relied on the systematization and exact ordering of the natural world, not to mention the specific techniques of administrative note-taking and accounting that he undoubtedly learned as a pharmaceutical apprentice. The notational method of double-entry bookkeeping, a three-step process in which the messy notes of day-to-day transactions were copied into increasingly ordered account books and thus put into a final form, had long been standard for large-scale research projects in all sorts of disciplines.[65]

---

64 Stiftung Stadtmuseum Berlin, Nachlass Fontane, Archival Signature 48_522.
65 On the emergence of double-entry bookkeeping as a scholarly notational practice, see Anke te Heesen, "Die doppelte Verzeichnung. Schriftliche und räumliche Aneignungsweisen von Natur im 18. Jahrhundert," in *Gehäuse der Mnemosyne. Architektur als Schriftform der Erinnerung*, ed. Harald Tausch (Göttingen: Vandenhoek & Ruprecht, 2003), 263–86.

Fontane's archive, however, was evidently driven by different priorities. He chose a repository that prioritized not permanence and order, but increased productivity in the here and now.

In her theory of cultural memory, the cultural historian Aleida Assmann introduces a distinction useful for describing this dichotomy. She distinguishes two interacting modes of recollection (*Erinnerung*): functional memory (*Funktionsgedächtnis*) and storage memory (*Speichergedächtnis*).[66] In Assmann's model, storage memory operates in the background—one might say as the "memory drop box"—of a given individual or culture. It is unselective and cumulative, and it gradually amasses a growing stock of heterogeneous elements, which are partly inert, unproductive, and latent. Functional memory, in contrast, operates in the foreground. It is selective and future-oriented, and its task is to choose elements from the "amorphous mass" (124–5) and to configure them into meaningful stories with which an individual or culture might make sense of itself. Assmann stresses that both dimensions are separated by a "flexible and hence productive boundary" and must be in constant exchange. Without internal traffic between foreground and background, there would be no revitalization in the stories a culture or individual tells about itself, and the contents of the storage memory would ultimately become meaningless.

It is easy to see how Fontane's paper sleeves function as a "memory drop box," or media of storage memory, and provide an "amorphous mass" of latent elements to be tapped. But Fontane also used them as media of functional memory, and he literally configured stories with the help of his paper sleeves. Friedrich Fontane's account of his father's work routine (in the context of the project *Geschichte und Geschichten aus Mark Brandenburg*) tells us as much:

> The material, gathered from far and wide, melded with preexisting material, shapes itself, takes on a form. Viewed, examined, selected, and structured, it is divided in chapters, which—partly sketched in brief, partly written out straight away—now receive their names and are placed in the envelopes destined for them.[67]
>
> *Der Stoff, von überallher zusammengetragen, mit schon Vorhandenem verschmolzen, formt sich, nimmt Gestalt an. Gesichtet, geprüft, ausgewählt, gegliedert wird er in Kapitel eingeteilt, die – teils kurz*

---

66 Aleida Assmann, *Cultural Memory and Western Civilization: Functions, Media Archives* (Cambridge: Cambridge University Press, 2011), 119–34.
67 Friedrich Fontane, "Geschichten aus Mark Brandenburg," *Ruppiner Kreiskalender* (1933): 40.

skizziert, teils gleich hintereinanderweg geschrieben – jetzt ihre Namen erhalten und in die für sie bestimmten Umschläge gelegt werden.

Further describing his father's work process, Friedrich Fontane points out that a layman would have no clue what to make of such a "mountain of paper" (*Papierberg*) and the myriad sheets that were covered, some in full, others in part, with writing in ink, pencil, and crayon. The "trained eye," however, would admire "the painstaking industry evident in the preparations for what we shall call an 'anthology of prose pieces' (*Anthologie von Prosastücken*)". The account reveals that Fontane used the sleeves to segment and allocate material to episodes and chapters, a crucial step in his creative process. At the same time, as we know from the many revisions to the labels on the sleeves, these allocations were a work in progress. The arrangements of material were only temporary and could quickly change. Fontane thus used the paper sleeves as media at once of storage and of *ad-hoc* production. New elements from the storage memory could be transferred to the functional memory and added to a developing story; old elements could be pushed out; and new configurations could easily be created. The internal traffic between background and foreground, or between storage and functional memory, was particularly intense in Fontane's material repository, because it realized both dimensions in one and the same medium.

The tight interweaving of both sorts of memory in Fontane's archive had poetic consequences that deeply affected his authorship, from the production of individual texts to his capacity for authorial self-administration. On the one hand, he enjoyed increased flexibility when it came to generating texts. Because the content of chapters and volumes was configured only for a period of time, he was able to manipulate the structure of the whole (e.g., the *Wanderungen* book volumes) while still working on the parts (the episodes). This flexibility permitted him to cope with hard deadlines. Pressed to get the still unfinished manuscript for the second edition of the first *Wanderungen* volume to the printers, he sent out batches of text from one end of the project while he continued to patch together bits for additional episodes on the other end, writing to Hertz: "I shall send you the essay 'The Hill Country of Ruppin' (*Ruppiner Schweiz*) tomorrow. Should you, however, already be short of manuscripts tomorrow, Bernstein [the printer, PM] is free to print the essay 'Villages and Hamlets' (*Dörfer und Flecken*) *first* and *conclude* with this essay ('The Hill Country of R.')" (BaH 117). Moreover, the fluid boundary between storage and production in the archive enabled Fontane to treat the distinction between material (*Stoff*) and text as flexible, ensuring that he rarely ran out. Because the paper sleeves did not distinguish between the notes, drafts, and "finished" (i.e., printed) texts that Fontane had authored and those written by others, the sleeves invited him to become creative again with his own earlier writings—and the writings of others. What had already been turned into "text" could be creatively recycled into "material" as Fontane saw fit. He thus established a work process that could feed partially on itself. Indeed, he reused materials initially generated for the *Wanderungen* in every one of his later novels and novellas.

On the other hand, the qualities of Fontane's archive that proved beneficial in the day-to-day interaction with the literary marketplace also limited its long-term usability. Without reliable sorting mechanisms and indices, it was difficult to do with Fontane's storage media what Cornelia Vismann, in her media theory of archives, describes as "establishing feedback"[68] with one's own actions and, by extension, the archive's content. Fontane simply could not know for sure or easily look up what his archive contained. He often searched in vain for individual items. For example, when *Grete Minde* went into a second printing in 1887, Fontane asked Hertz whether there would be room to add a brief preface. Fontane had received word about new findings pertaining to the historical Grete Minde and her trial, which he hoped to incorporate. The lack of order in his archive, however, impeded this project—unable to find his old notes on Grete Minde's case ("and who ever retrieved a note once it had been stored away"), he eventually had to write again to Hertz: "It is embarrassed of countenance that I appear before you today with the request to publish dear 'Grete Minde' *without* a foreword after all. All my efforts have been in vain" (BaH 292–3). It is little wonder, then, that Fontane frequently worked on the brink of "nervous ruin" (*Nervenpleite*).[69]

Perhaps even more importantly, the nature of his archive made it difficult for Fontane to take full control of his authorship and thus to shape his legacy. As the case of Goethe had demonstrated decades earlier, shaping one's legacy required a clear awareness of one's historicity and a sense of closure; at the least, it required that the author draw a line between his current production and his archive, so that whatever had entered the latter could be put into its final, desired form.[70] At the age of seventy-three, Goethe began this process of legacy

---

68 Cornelia Vismann, *Files: Law and Media Technology*, trans. Geoffrey Winthrop-Young (Stanford, CA: Stanford University Press, 2008), 112.
69 See the letter to his wife from September 16, 1862, in GBA XII.2: 252 and the entry "Nervenpleite," in Helmuth Nürnberger and Dietmar Storch, *Fontane-Lexikon: Namen – Stoffe – Zeitgeschichte* (Munich: Hanser, 2007), 323.
70 See Vismann, *Files*, 114. On Goethe's role and the historical emergence of modern authorial practices of legacy formation, see Kai Sina and Carlos Spoerhase, "Nachlassbewusstsein. Zur literarischen Erforschung seiner Entstehung und Entwicklung," *Zeitschrift für Germanistik* 23, no. 3 (2013): 607–23.

formation and authorial image-fashioning by meticulously ordering his *Nachlass*, an undertaking for which he hired a secretary, the young Friedrich Theodor Kräuter, a "sprightly young man well-versed in library matters."[71] According to Vismann's famous analysis of Goethe's case, the author's "ultimate goal" was "a literary estate that [would] arrange the patchwork of life in such orderly and coherent fashion that it [could] assume its rightful place in the Elysium of world literature."[72] Purposeful self-administration and the establishment of the authorial function thus went hand in hand.[73] Goethe's model was highly influential in the nineteenth century; Wilhelm Raabe essentially adopted it (minus the hired help) when, right after his seventieth birthday, he decided to put down his pen, retire from his existence as a freelance writer, and subject his entire *Nachlass* to a "strict scrutiny" (*strengen Durchsicht*).[74] After Raabe had carefully gone through every manuscript and every note he had written—and after he had destroyed a considerable number of them—he had his estate sealed by a notary. The retired writer then handed it over to his wife and daughter, anxious to ensure not only that they would benefit from the royalties after his death, but also that the image of himself that he envisioned would be passed down to posterity.[75]

Fontane, however, did not follow this model, nor would he have been able to. A material repository that fundamentally blurred the line between current production and archive encouraged recursive continuity, not closure. Moreover, Fontane's serial publishing in the periodical press scattered his output so thoroughly across various media that he could not easily file away full sets of his manuscripts. In the pre-typewriter era, authors often made only one fair copy of a given project to send out, and many journals kept the manuscripts of the

---

71 Goethe, qtd. in Vismann, *Files*, 115.
72 Vismann, *Files*, 114.
73 Assmann maintains a similar view in her theory of memory and points out that pure storage memory is unable to provide foundations for identity and subjectivity. See Assmann, *Cultural Memory and Western Civilization*, 127.
74 Horst Denkler, *Wilhelm Raabe. Legende – Leben – Literatur* (Tübingen: Niemeyer, 1989), 17. Ironically, however, Raabe's publisher Otto Janke, with whom he signed a contract for an edition of *Sämtliche Werke in Einzelausgaben* in November 1889, did not display the same degree of eagerness and care. Rather than following through, Janke continually delayed the preparation of Raabe's complete works and ended up selling the rights to the publishing company of Hermann Klemm shortly after the author's death. The first edition of Raabe's complete works thus appeared posthumously after all. See Hans-Jürgen Schrader, "Editionsgeschichte und Nachlass," in *Raabe-Handbuch. Leben – Werk – Wirkung*, ed. Dirk Göttsche, Florian Krobb, and Rolf Parr (Stuttgart: Metzler, 2016), 12–15.
75 Denkler, *Wilhelm Raabe*, 17.

writings they received, which were therefore lost to the author's personal archive.[76] This was the case for Fontane, who had to make efforts to keep track of his manuscripts and include the journal prints in his archive in order to piece together at least one complete copy of a given project. A paper sleeve from the autobiographical book project *Von Zwanzig bis Dreißig* demonstrates this situation particularly well. According to its label, the sleeve had been set up to store three chapters that belonged to the book's third major section, "Bei 'Kaiser Franz.'" Yet additional comments on the label imply that Fontane no longer had the manuscripts for these chapters. He wrote:

> Third section. "At 'Kaiser Franz.'" Consists of three chapters, the essence of which has been published in number 3 of *Pan*. Missing, however, in *Pan* are the introduction, i.e., the transition from the stay in Leipzig (with Dresden in between) to Letzthin and Berlin. A copy of that transitional piece is to be found in this bundle.
>
> *Dritter Abschnitt. Bei 'Kaiser Franz'. Besteht aus drei Kapiteln die im wesentlichen im Pan Heft III abgedruckt sind. Im Pan fehlt aber die Einleitung, d. h. der Uebergang von dem Leipziger Aufenthalt (Dresden dazwischen) nach Letschin und Berlin. Dies Uebergangsstück liegt in der Abschrift in diesem Convolut.*[77]

In other words, the paper sleeve and the *Pan* prints were supposed to supplement one another in their archiving function. Only together would they provide a full copy of Fontane's text. This made the task of comprehensive legacy formation all the harder. With each successful journal publication essentially tearing a hole in Fontane's archive, even such a crucial step as the production of a complete edition of his works became difficult.

It is therefore small wonder that Fontane's practices of legacy formation stand in stark contrast to Raabe's and Goethe's. These two writers consciously decided to stop writing, or at least pause, to dedicate themselves full-time to sorting their *Nachlässe*. Fontane never retired; in fact, when he turned seventy, his most important novels were still to come. To be sure, from 1890 to 1891, he attempted a "complete edition" of the novels and novellas that had appeared up to that point,

---

76 Writers' unions and their organs therefore rallied for "best practices" that they wanted publishers to adopt, including the return of manuscripts. See the editorial, "An die Herren Collegen!" in the opening issue of *Die Feder* (1, no. 1, April 1898), which articulates many of these best practices.
77 Stiftung Stadtmuseum Berlin, Nachlass Fontane, Archival Signature V 67_864_B, Kaiser.

but this effort ended in disaster.[78] He would not try again. Instead of ordering his archive, at age seventy-two he drew up his will, which charged his wife Emilie and a *Nachlasskommission* with that task. Apparently, the whole business of legacy formation annoyed Fontane. If it had been entirely up to him, he would have had all of his unpublished manuscripts burned after his death.[79] Only after his lawyer had convinced him that this option was not in his family's best interests did he work carefully through the draft of the will that the lawyer provided. The wording of the one extant note from this process strongly suggests that Fontane was happy to leave the details to others: "§4. Can be omitted, I think, since I delegated this business [this reference is unclear, but §4 referred to the right to the inheritance of money and stocks; PM] once and for all to Theo. It's for him to deal with all that bother (*Brast*) now, not me."[80] "All that bother" leaves little doubt about how Fontane felt about legacy formation. What is more, he scribbled this note on the back of an *Effi Briest* manuscript page. Even as Fontane worked on his will, he did not separate the legacy-related business from his current literary production.

Despite all this, however, Fontane did in fact bring the decades-long *Wanderungen* project to a close. In the preface to the second edition of the third *Wanderungen* volume, he informed his readers that he would no longer incorporate updates or make other revisions based on new materials but would now offer a picture of the region "as it presented itself to the eye around the year [18]70 (*wie sich's etwa*

---

78 *Theodor Fontanes Gesammelte Romane und Novellen*, 12 vols. (Berlin: Dominik, 1890) (vols. 1–7); Deutsches Verlagshaus (vols. 8–9); [Friedrich] Fontane (1890/1891, vols. 10–12). According to Gotthard Erler, the edition was hampered from the start by a "copyright dilemma": individually, Fontane's novels and novellas had appeared with so many different publishing houses that the copyright situation for a complete edition was extremely complicated. Dominik, the publisher who began the project, had been able to obtain the rights only for a part-issue edition and was therefore forced to distribute novels that would have fit into one volume over two or more books. Moreover, the publisher did not bother to include the author in the constitution of the text, which was ridden with errors. See Erler, "Druck- und Editionsgeschichte, Nachlaß, Forschungsstätten," in *Fontane-Handbuch*, ed. Christian Grawe and Helmuth Nürnberger (Stuttgart: Kröner, 2000), 894–5.
79 See Christel Laufer, "Der handschriftliche Nachlaß Theodor Fontanes," *Fontane Blätter*, 20 (1974): 264. The fact that Emilie Fontane did carry out her husband's wishes, and burned a considerable amount of material that struck her as "unsuitable" to be preserved for posterity, has not received much attention in the Fontane scholarship. How comprehensive Fontane's *Nachlass* really was, then, is unknown. For an up-to-date account of the fate of the *Nachlass*, see the editors' introduction to F1, xxii–xxxiv.
80 Qtd. in Laufer, "Der handschriftliche Nachlaß Theodor Fontanes," 265.

ums Jahr [18]70 dem Auge präsentirte)."[81] His *Wanderungen* episodes thus received a time stamp, turning his dynamically functioning collection itself into a collectible, a historical artifact:[82] the final four-volume set and its reprint in the *Wohlfeile Ausgabe* came into being only because Fontane had decoupled it from the circulation of materials in his archive.

This did not mean, however, that the material-generating apparatus ceased to operate. From 1881 to 1888, Fontane produced episodes for the thematically connected volume *Fünf Schlösser. Altes und Neues aus Mark Brandenburg (Five Castles. Old and New in Mark Brandenburg)*, began planning a four-volume work with the accumulated materials to supplement the *Wanderungen*, and started working on another volume with the title *Das Ländchen Friesack und die Bredows (The Little Country of Friesack and the Bredow Family)*. Just three days before his death, Fontane asked one of his informants about sources for this volume (HFA IV.4: 755). In short, there was never a scarcity of material in Fontane's archive.

Bridging Social Distance: The Effects of a Postal Library Network

The case study of the *Wanderungen* has shown how Fontane installed a living archive at the heart of his authorship. In it, material accumulated yet was not filed away for good; rather, it circulated between the author's personal storage media and the journals in which he published. The same basic principle of accumulation and circulation characterizes Fontane's procurement of material beyond the *Wanderungen*. He derived textual sources on all kinds of topics through an interpersonal correspondence network, built on his social connections, which stretched across a vast number of individuals and text-producing institutions within Germany and even beyond. In this network, which Fontane labeled his "library connections"[83] (*Bibliotheks-Konnexionen*), temporary access to reading materials was far more important than permanent possession; in effect, the network was a gigantic lending library. He sent letters to people he knew requesting bibliographical references, expert knowledge, literature, or historical documents, and

---

81 Theodor Fontane, *Havelland. Die Landschaft um Spandau, Potsdam, Brandenburg* (Berlin 1880), v–vi.
82 I owe this observation to Crane's *Collecting and Historical Consciousness*, 119–20, in which she describes how collectors' journals from the 1840s, which were designed to display historical objects, eventually turned into historical objects themselves.
83 BaHey 114; see also *Theodor Fontane und Bernhard von Lepel. Der Briefwechsel*, 2 vols., ed. Gabriele Radecke (Berlin: De Gruyter, 2006), I:111.

returned the items he received—such as book volumes and maps—when he was finished with them.[84]

This was not the only use Fontane made of his contacts, however. He also used his "library connections" to pick up or verify societal news. As a journalist, he had an intrinsic interest in titillating stories, rumors, and social gossip, especially gossip about the upper crust: "It's always the same old story," Fontane wrote to his informant Friedlaender, "the *high life* is interesting not on account of being interesting in and of itself, but because it is *high life*" (BaF 324). Fontane was fascinated by "people who have 5000 miners in their employ, found factory cities, and dispatch expeditions to colonize central America," by "ship-owners," "press barons" (*Zeitungsfürsten*), and "railway kings" (HFA IV.3: 314), not to mention the numerous barons, baronesses, and other members of the nobility who resided all over Germany and reliably caused entertaining scandals. The author reworked such societal news into literary narratives (one well-known example is the "Ardenne" case, which Fontane rendered in literary form in *Effi Briest*) that purposefully stretched the limits of the acceptable in the periodical press and were therefore all the more appealing to his readership.[85] The *chronique scandaleuse* thus provided an important element in Fontane's material repository. At the same time, he was well aware that some regions had juicier stories to offer than others, and that confining his research to the Mark Brandenburg would not get him the most scandalous news. Yet again corresponding with Friedlaender, Fontane wrote:

> Of course, each region has its murder, its great bankruptcy, its case of adultery with a child burned in the oven, its duel and its mad eccentric, no region is quite empty of such material, but their measure varies greatly. In seaboard towns, in regions whose beauty attracts a great many people, in border and moonshining districts, and also in regions where great riches and great poverty exist side by side—there is more going on in such regions than in

---

84 Rasch argues convincingly that from the outset, "borrowing" determined Fontane's relationship with his reading materials, the early sources of such borrowing being reader circles, lending libraries, and the personal libraries of wealthier friends. See Wolfgang Rasch, "Zeitungstiger, Bücherfresser. Die Bibliothek Theodor Fontanes als Fragment und Aufgabe betrachtet," *Imprimatur* 19 (2005): 107.

85 Fontane's treatment of risqué topics at times led to problems with publishers. For example, *Stine*, purportedly termed a "gräßliche Hurengeschichte" by one of the co-owners of the *Vossische Zeitung*, was rejected by three journals before the newly founded weekly *Deutschland* finally published it. See Christian Grawe, "'Die wahre hohe Schule der Zweideutigkeit': Frivolität und ihre autobiographische Komponente in Fontanes Erzählwerk," *Fontane Blätter* 65/66 (1998): 139.

humdrum regions, where a solid, industrious, prosaic population lives alongside one another in passable circumstances.

> *Natürlich hat jede Gegend ihren Mord, ihren großen Bankrutt, ihren Ehebruch mit im Ofen verbranntem Kind, ihr Duell und ihr verrücktes Original, ganz leer an solchem pikantem Stoff ist keine Gegend, aber im Maß sind sie sehr verschieden. In Seestädten, in Gegenden, deren Reichthum und Schönheit viele Personen anlockt, in Grenz- und Schnapsdistrikten, auch in Gegenden, wo großer Reichthum und große Armuth nebeneinander leben, – in solchen Gegenden ist mehr los, als in Mittelgutsgegenden, wo eine solide, fleißige, prosaische Bevölkerung in auskömmlichen Verhältnissen nebeneinander herlebt.*
>
> (BaF 165)

The Mark Brandenburg, according to Fontane, was one of those "humdrum regions." In Friedlaender's area, the Jelenia Gorá Valley (*Hirschberger Thal*) at the foot of the Giant Mountains, however, there were people more to the journalist's liking, such as a compulsive arsonist, a spectacularly indebted prince, and a "felon taking leave of his wife in bridal dress." The structure of Fontane's network, which included direct and indirect contacts from distant social milieus and geographical locales, enabled him to reach into these "happening regions" to obtain the gossip he wanted, as we shall see later.

In light of this library network, it is no surprise that the remnants of Fontane's physical personal library are unimpressive: at the end of his life, one large and one small bookcase plus two open shelves sufficed to store the few hundred volumes that the author owned, a fraction of which can be found on display at the *Theodor-Fontane-Archiv* in Potsdam.[86] Fontane's real "library" differed from the personal libraries of other nineteenth-century writers: it was not bound to one physical place; it was not constrained to defined subject areas but rather was constantly developing; and it was stocked not with a countable number of items but with varying sources, gossip emphatically included.

Generally speaking, networks consist of "relations that have achieved a certain degree of regularity or permanence"; they can be understood as "traceable configurations of *repetitive* relations or interactions."[87] From the very beginning of his activities as a letter writer, Fontane worked hard to cultivate his communicative relationships so that a reliable network could emerge. In the quotidian routines of note-taking

---

86 Rasch, "Zeitungstiger, Bücherfresser," 103–4.
87 Jürgen Osterhammel, *The Transformation of the World: A Global History of the Nineteenth Century*, trans. Patrick Camiller (Princeton, NJ: Princeton University Press, 2014), 710.

in his diaries, notebooks, and correspondence with his wife (in which he often reported the events of his day), the author gave an overview of his epistolary conversations and accounted for requests he had sent and materials he had received.[88] These logistical notes provide the sound empirical basis from which the infrastructure and the patterns of his interactions with his postal library network can be abstracted. The pattern that best describes his library use, to borrow a phrase from the philosopher Manfred Sommer, is "collecting like an octopus" (*sammeln wie ein Krake*):[89] Fontane was the moving center from which long arms reached out in several directions at once. Over time, these many grasping arms grew in size and number, so that the author's inquiries covered a territory whose physical and thematic boundaries were pushed out further and further.

Three factors were decisive in the quick growth of Fontane's library network and its efficiency. First, the Prussian postal service implemented a new media standard for communication by mail over the course of the nineteenth century, from which Fontane's network benefited directly. Several innovations defined this new standard. These included the delivery of letters through professional mailmen (introduced in Berlin in 1827); the installation of mailboxes, first across neighborhoods for the purpose of collecting letters and then at the doors of official buildings and private homes for receiving them (starting in 1849); the transformation of the old payment model, in which postage was collected from the recipient, into the British model of standardized prepayment with stamps (starting in 1850); the gradual expansion of express stagecoach routes, steamship lines, and railroad connections for faster passage between cities and states; and a number of laws and contracts through which the postal network first extended across Germany and then, after the founding of the Universal Postal Union in 1874, connected destinations across the globe.[90] As a result, the Prussian postal service turned from a local, traditional system that had relied heavily on physical presence into a comprehensive, modern machinery of anonymous interfaces and relays in which collection and delivery were mechanized and physical presence had been rendered superfluous. While previously one had to send letters from a postal counter, one

---

88 For examples, see Notebook D2, 11R–39R, GBA XI.2: 55, and GBA XII.3: 424–6. Fontane's notational practices resembled those of bookkeeping, a similarity that the author himself acknowledged in coinages such as *tagebuchen*. See GBA II.2: 364.

89 Sommer, *Sammeln*, 209–10.

90 For a more detailed discussion of these innovations and a compelling ontological interpretation of their effects, see Bernhard Siegert, *Relays: Literature as an Epoch of the Postal System*, trans. Kevin Repp (Stanford, CA: Stanford University Press, 1999), 95–145.

could now write them from anywhere, affix prepurchased stamps, and drop them into a mailbox. Conversely, the private letter box or slit in the door enabled the delivery of letters even during the recipient's absence.[91] In the new system, an address, a stamp, and access to a mailbox sufficed to allow letters to travel through the channels of the Prussian post.

As a "collecting octopus," Fontane exploited these features of the Prussian postal service to the fullest when he disseminated letters in many directions at once, often to distant places, and when he temporarily borrowed the address of a hotel or a friend to receive mail while away from home. He even responded to the progressive modernization of the postal system with increased rationalization on his part. By the mid-1890s, he had developed a method of writing letters "factory style" (*fabrikmäßig*); that is, he first prepared a number of envelopes and stamped them before he wrote the letters, hoping to get through "days of solid letter-writing" (*stramme Briefschreibetage*, BaF 291) more easily in this way. (Fontane's "letter factory" did have occasional glitches, however, which illustrate the new media standard rather wonderfully: his friend Friedlaender once received nothing but an empty envelope because Fontane had forgotten to put the letter inside.) The author's library network thus co-evolved with and benefited from the momentous changes that turned the Prussian postal system into a modern machine with dehumanized interfaces, efficient relays, and an enormous territorial scope.

The second factor that allowed the library network and its thematic range to proliferate quickly consisted of an emphasis on compendious textual genres—genres that conveniently summarized information—that Fontane maintained from the very beginning. The author tried to keep abreast of an enormous variety of topics by making a habit of evaluating newspaper reports, popular-scientific journal articles, review essays, bulletins of regional historical societies, and encyclopedia entries.[92] In short, the compiler systematically scoured other compilations. He then took brief notes on what he had encountered or pasted the decisive parts of a given textual source directly into his filing system so that he could follow up on them later. Recurring entries in Fontane's diaries and notebooks document the extent to which looking through papers and other compendious sources had become a daily

---

91 Ibid., 109.
92 In addition, Fontane frequently attended the weekly meetings of cultural and literary clubs featuring academic guest speakers from a broad range of disciplines. See Roland Berbig and Bettina Hartz, eds., *Theodor Fontane im literarischen Leben: Zeitungen und Zeitschriften, Verlage und Vereine* (Berlin: De Gruyter, 2000), 410–64.

routine: "Read German papers" (*Deutsche Blätter gelesen*) or some variant of this formulation is a familiar refrain in his diaries.[93] As a result of these plural readings, the author's growing library network became just as thematically inclusive as the differentiated press system on which it drew. This quality, in turn, provided an important prerequisite for Fontane's successful compilation of literary texts that were well suited to publication in periodicals: if periodical literature integrates the "themes, styles, and manners of addressing the readers"[94] of its own publication context, Fontane's library network, with its emphasis on varied materials from the mass press, enabled him to do the same, as he adapted selected content from the periodical press for his own literary output.

The third factor that increased the reach and effectiveness of Fontane's network was the variable density of its structure. His network was made of a number of "strong" ties and an even greater number of "weak" ones, to use the now classic terms coined by the sociologist Mark S. Granovetter in 1973. Granovetter distinguishes between these two types of interpersonal connections, demonstrating that weak ties— those based on superficial acquaintance, as opposed to friendship— play a surprisingly important role in diffusing information (or influence, favors, rumors, etc.) quickly through a network. In fact, Granovetter argues that "whatever is to be diffused can reach a larger number of people, and traverse greater social distance . . ., when passed through weak ties rather than strong."[95] The reason is that people connected by strong ties tend to have many mutual friends, and whatever is passed through them is therefore "much more likely to be limited to a few cliques than that going via weak ones." Of course, strong ties are valuable because one can typically make greater demands on people with whom one is close. Only weak ties, however, can serve as so-called "bridges" (the *only* paths between two individuals) and thus extend into the marginal sectors of a given social territory. We can gather from Granovetter's study that a network of variable density—composed of strong or close-knit ties in some areas, and of weak or loosely knit ties in others—is particularly effective for anyone with an interest in diffusing requests and asking favors.

This dual quality describes precisely the structure of the postal library network that Fontane maintained. The network had several central nodes to which Fontane was linked through strong ties and with

---

93 For examples, see GBA XI.1: 164; 190; 192; 245.
94 On this characteristic of periodical literature, see Kaminski, Ramtke, and Zelle, *Zeitschriftenliteratur/Fortsetzungsliteratur*, 8.
95 Mark S. Granovetter, "The Strength of Weak Ties," *American Journal of Sociology* 78, no. 6 (April 1973): 1366.

whom he had numerous friends in common. The most important node, at least initially, was Fontane's long-term friend Bernhard von Lepel, a member of the Northern German nobility and the owner of a well-stocked library from which Fontane borrowed numerous sources. Lepel in turn introduced him to Mathilde von Rohr and the Countess of Schwerin, both of whom provided him with considerable material for a number of projects and contacts to other members of the nobility.[96] Through Lepel, Fontane was also accepted in 1844 into the literary society *Tunnel über der Spree*, in which he would meet several of his most important lifelong friends, such as Franz Kugler, Paul Heyse, George Hesekiel, and Wilhelm von Merckel, who gave him publishing opportunities.[97] In addition to maintaining this close-knit network, Fontane actively increased the number of weak ties, which amounted to his extended network, through strategic data-mining and a practice perhaps best described as social tagging.[98] He accumulated a personal stock of addresses by mining sources such as municipal address directories, the guest lists of towns he visited, bibliographical dictionaries such as the *Moniteur des Dates*, and the Who's Who of the Prussian nobility.[99] Moreover, he recorded in his diaries with whom he had communicated in spoken or written form, in which context or through which intermediaries he had made a new acquaintance, and whom the new acquaintance in turn knew. Whenever possible, the author tagged new people with additional pieces of information, such as their social status, professional profile, or area of expertise. The resulting sets of data, which often began with a dateline, typically read as follows:

> At half-past four to a little dinner with Mr. W. Hertz, Bendler-Strasse 13. Present: Mr. Booth of Hamburg, an authority on forestry and particularly versed in North American silviculture;

---

96 See Fürstenau, *Fontane und die märksiche Heimat*, 64.
97 See Berbig and Hartz, *Fontane im literarischen Leben*, 418.
98 It would be a fascinating project to map the development of this network over time to obtain a clear sense of its geographical and social scope. Given, however, that Fontane authored more than 5,800 letters (according to the figures in the *Briefverzeichnis*) over the course of his life, and that one would also have to consider the vast number of letters that he received, I will leave this project to someone properly equipped for big-data analysis.
99 Among the small number of book volumes that Fontane owned were the five-volume *Neues preussisches Adels-Lexicon oder genealogische und diplomatische Nachrichten* and the *Hand- und Adreßbuch für die Gesellschaft von Berlin*. See Rasch, "Zeitungstiger, Bücherfresser," 140–2. For examples of active data-mining, see Fontane's letter to his wife, August 18, 1877, in GBA XII.3: 80, and his letter to Friedlaender, September 7, 1886, in BaF 53.

furthermore: Mrs. von Olfers and Miss Marie von Olfers, Mr. & Mrs. Hans Hertz, Mr. von Putlitz, a candidate for the Civil Service (son of Gustav zu Putlitz) and one young Mr. von Arnim. Very pleasantly lively company. Mr. Booth, who often visits Friedrichsruh, told all manner of things about Bismarck.

> Um 4 ½ zum kl. Diner bei Herrn W. Hertz, Bendler-Straße 13. Zugegen: Herr Booth aus Hamburg, eine Autorität in der Forstwissenschaft und speziell mit nordamerikanischen Forstculturen vertraut; ferner: Frau v. Olfers und Frl. Marie v. Olfers, Herr Hans Hertz und Frau, Herr Referendar v. Putlitz (Sohn von Gustav zu Putlitz) und ein junger Herr v. Arnim. Sehr angenehm animirte Gesellschaft. Herr Booth, der oft in Friedrichsruh ist, erzählte allerlei von Bismarck.
>
> (GBA XI.2: 96)

The example demonstrates how several of the new acquaintances Fontane made during this particular dinner party are associated with information specific to their gender, age, family, profession, and knowledge domain, while the entry itself, through its block format, remains individually selectable as a discrete data set. Such entries abounded in Fontane's diaries and amounted to a stock of direct and indirect contacts that were ready to be exploited.

The strength of these "weak" ties becomes particularly apparent when Fontane is compared to fellow writers whose interpersonal library networks were predominantly composed of strong connections. Heinrich Heine provides an instructive case. An itinerant intellectual and émigré, Heine was similar to Fontane in that he borrowed, rather than purchased, the vast majority of the books that passed through his hands over the course of his writerly life.[100] The sources for Heine's borrowing included public and university libraries, the libraries of wealthy friends, and above all lending libraries. Like Fontane, Heine read "greedily" yet did not bother to collect books.[101] His relationship to books was strictly utilitarian, and when he was done with a volume, he saw no reason to keep it. Later in his life, this preference for borrowing reading materials turned into a biographical necessity—living in

---

100 Joseph Kruse speaks of approximately 2,000 titles that Heine mentions (or that are referenced) in his works, letters, and conversations. This information and the other insights about Heine as a reader are taken from Kruse's essay "Heines Leihpraxis und Lektürebeschaffung," in *Die Leihbibliothek als Institution des literarischen Lebens im 18. und 19. Jahrhundert: Organisationsformen, Bestände und Publikum*, ed. Georg Jäger and Jörg Schönert (Stuttgart: Hauswedell, 1980), 199.
101 Ibid.

Parisian exile and eventually in his "mattress crypt" (*Matratzengruft*), Heine had access to German books and journals only through a postal network of German family members, his publisher, and selected friends. He would send book orders to his relatives in Hamburg, who would then obtain the desired titles from a local lending library and send them to Heine in Paris, whence he would eventually organize their return via the same channels. Compared to Fontane's postal network, however, the number of Heine's "library connections" was very small. He usually passed his requests on through three people: his sister Charlotte Embden, his mother, and Julius Campe; occasionally, he involved his nephew and the young publisher Michael Schloß.[102] His contacts accessed the lending libraries Jowien, Bernhardt, and Laeiß in Hamburg and at times also Schloß in Cologne, but when an item was not available through any of these libraries, he could rarely get hold of it. As Joseph Kruse has shown, Heine perceived this mode of accessing books as extremely laborious and frustrating (in his letters, he spoke of "much bother," or *große Quälerey*, and enervating "fuss and fidgeting")—not just because it was comparatively slow, but also because his requests were subject to frequent mix-ups. Rather than branching out to other intermediaries, however, Heine continued to make his requests through the few people to whom he had strong ties. During the final decades of Heine's life, his postal library network thus had significant limitations.

When we consider the number of people through whom Fontane passed his requests for source materials, the difference between his network's capacities for effective diffusion and Heine's becomes evident. The instructions that Fontane gave to his friend Paul Heyse for postal research on Heyse's current project provide a localized example, shedding light on Fontane's skill at exploiting contacts. Heyse, one of Fontane's strong ties, had asked him for literature about tales, sayings, customs, and everyday life in historic Pomerania and Lusatia, with which he intended to flesh out his drama *Hans Lange*. Fontane responded with the following elaborate strategy:

> For my part, I have nothing of the kind . . ., but I shall get in touch first with Otto Roquette, then with one Mr. von Behr near Greifswald, and what one will be unable to accomplish, the other will do. [Otto Roquette] himself, I believe, doesn't think much of Wendish and Pomeranian culture and is little versed in these matters, but he is close friends with all the local Friedländers in that term's most venturesome sense and can obtain whatever he

---

102 Ibid., 204–5.

wants from the Friedländers, who, like the Schwerins and Winterfeldts in the Army, traditionally and in large numbers serve in libraries and archives. . . . Mr. von Behr, who is a friend of mine, is a member of a Pomeranian archeological society and would, should the pump that is Otto Wald [Otto Roquette; PM] or Friedländer dry up, surely be willing to obtain this and that from Greifswald.

Ich selbst habe nichts von der Art . . ., aber ich werde mich zunächst mit Otto Roquette, dann mit einem Herrn v. Behr in der Nähe von Greifswald in Verbindung setzen, und was der eine nicht schaffen kann, wird der andre tun. [Otto Roquette] *selbst, glaub ich, denkt nicht hoch von Wenden- und Pommerntum und ist schwerlich in diesen Dingen bewandert, er ist aber mit der ganzen hiesigen Friedländerei in der verwogensten Bedeutung des Worts nah befreundet und kann von den Friedländers, die, wie die Schwerins und Winterfeldts in der Armee, traditionell und massenhaft in Bibliothek und Archiv dienen, alles erhalten, was er will. . . . Herr v. Behr, mit dem ich befreundet bin, ist Mitglied einer pommerscharchäologischen Gesellschaft und würde, wenn die Pumpe Otto Wald* [Otto Roquette; PM] *resp. Friedländer kein Wasser mehr geben sollte, gewiß bereit sein, das eine oder andre aus Greifswald herbeizuschaffen.*

(BaHey 113–14)

In case neither the first nor the second contact yielded the desired results, Fontane pointed Heyse to a mutual friend, the publisher Wilhelm Hertz, whose brother Martin was a classical philologist in Greifswald. "If Professor Hertz should not come through," Fontane continued, "there also lives in Greifswald Professor Schaeffer or Schaefer, to whom our Hertz is quite an intimate friend. Schaeffer is a historian and much respected and would have no trouble obtaining anything." This research strategy of using direct and indirect contacts, or strong and weak ties, enabled Fontane's request to "snowball" through the network, allowing the search to grow rapidly in scope. Furthermore, Fontane used his own social capital to initiate the request and then to make it pass through several other contacts. The request was thereby loaded with the accumulated social capital until it became sufficiently weighty to break through the barriers between the author and the desired material. In the example cited earlier, the long arm of the "octopus" Fontane thus reached, via Otto Roquette and the Friedlaender family, into several libraries and archives, among them the Königliche Bibliothek, the Preußisches Geheimes Staatsarchiv, the library of the Preußische Kriegsakademie, and the Greifswald

University library.[103] As the example shows, the weak ties (here: one Professor Schaef[f]er) were especially relevant, because they helped the author to build "bridges" into geographical and social realms that would otherwise have been out of reach. Owing to his weak ties, Fontane was thus able to—and in fact did—communicate with interlocutors from a wide social spectrum, including professors, ministers, industrial executives, dukes and countesses, nuns, middle-school teachers, preachers, police officers, innkeepers, second-rate actors, and various mistresses.

Fontane's daily practice of corresponding across social strata is reflected in his fiction, which is "home to a large family of epistolary ghosts."[104] The protagonists of virtually all of his novels and novellas are woven into "giant informational networks" but are "unaware of their magnitude"; they trade love messages, send telegrams and postcards, hide fateful letters, and become the subjects of gossip or pass on gossip themselves, as Ilinca Iurascu has recently shown. In the fictional narratives, Fontane exploits the moments of friction and the risks that attempts to bridge social distance entail. One of the strongest examples is *On Tangled Paths* (*Irrungen, Wirrungen*), a novella about the impossible love affair between a seamstress, Lene, and a baron, Botho. Their correspondence by mail does not close the social rift between them, but rather exposes it. When Botho receives a bundle of mail in the morning, he sorts through it according to what Iurascu calls a telling hierarchical model—he opens the formal-looking letter from his uncle first and saves Lene's love letter for last, an "epistolary order" that "prefaces the main turn of events, the decision that he should wed the rich Käthe von Sellenthin and thus solve the financial problems of his family."[105] Lene's letter, with its incorrect spelling and simple, "faithful" (*treu*) language, delights the liberal-minded Botho, yet it ultimately reminds him of the marital and social order to which he is bound.[106]

---

103 The Königliche Bibliothek, the Preußische Geheime Staatsarchiv, and the library of the Preußische Kriegsakademie are institutions to which the Friedlaenders' connections can be established with certainty; presumably, these represent only a part of their network. See Ernst Friedlaender, "Emil Gottlieb Friedlaender (1805–78)," *Allgemeine Deutsche Biographie* (henceforth *ADB*) (Leipzig: Duncker & Humblot, 1904), 48:778–80. "Schaefer" refers to Arnold Dietrich Schaefer, professor of ancient history at Greifswald and, from 1865, Bonn. See Julius Asbach, "Schaefer, Arnold Dietrich," in *ADB* (Leipzig: Duncker & Humblot, 1890), 30: 521–4.
104 Ilinca Iurascu, "'Annoncenliteratur': Kleist, Fontane and the Rustle of Paper," *Oxford German Studies* 43, no. 3 (2014): 253.
105 Ibid., 258.
106 Theodor Fontane, *On Tangled Paths*, trans. Peter James Bowman (London: Penguin, 2013), 37; GBA I.10: 39.

In this and Fontane's other narratives, "media channels ... come together to shatter the air of tranquility to which protagonists cling and reveal the economic and social tensions underneath."[107] The mastery with which Fontane stages these clashes and creates unlikely contact between "the various material and textual categories that make up the vast communicative network" (ibid.) gives us a sense of the sophistication with which he exploited the media channels of late nineteenth-century Berlin in his own life, for his own library and social network.

In its rapid proliferation, Fontane's library network functioned without firm internal principles of organization. Like the *Wanderungen* archive, Fontane's virtual library had no fixed classification systems. Rather, it collected its heterogeneous sources according to an accretive logic and fluctuating selection criteria. Epistemologically, the unsteady selection criteria and the implicit impossibility of systematic classification were the library's greatest assets, for they enabled potentially limitless growth. Had Fontane plotted out a master plan, a table of contents for his library, he would have predetermined the points at which material could be added; he would have brought the expansion of the library into an orderly, fixed, and limited sequence. Yet without this systematization, Fontane's library could grow like Niklas Luhmann's famous card catalog: anything could be added anywhere, and nothing was *per se* excluded.[108]

A compact example of this additive logic and its consequences can be found on two double pages from Notebook E 2 (Figures 3.3 and 3.4), on which Fontane listed the sources he intended to consult for his first novel, *Before the Storm* (*Vor dem Sturm*). The set of entries demonstrates two of the library network's most important aspects. First, it shows how closely social connections and library contacts are intertwined. In columns on directly facing pages, the author enumerated the "books" that he hoped to borrow and the intermediaries he planned to involve in this process. Second, the list of "books" demonstrates how the inclusive logic of the postal library network leads to the radical juxtaposition of items from a wide generic spectrum, extending from light, popular literary sources to philosophical writings. This juxtaposition, in turn, radicalized the notion of intertextuality with which Fontane worked as a compiler:

---

107 Iurascu, "Annoncenliteratur," 254.
108 This is modeled closely on Niklas Luhmann's 1981 essay "Kommunikation mit Zettelkästen." The image of the table of contents is also taken from Luhmann's essay. See "Kommunikation mit Zettelkästen. Ein Erfahrungsbericht," *Universität als Milieu. Kleine Schriften*, ed. Niklas Luhmann and André Kieserling (Bielefeld: Haux, 1992), 53–61.

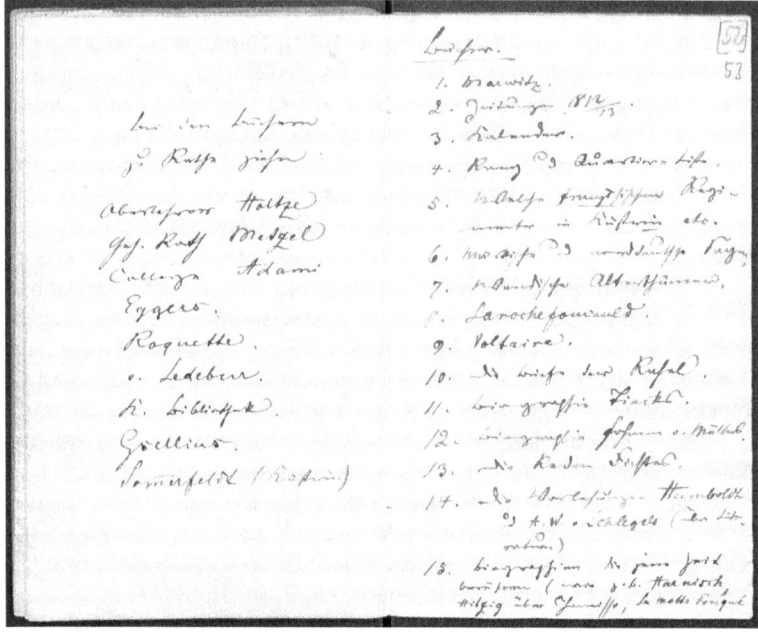

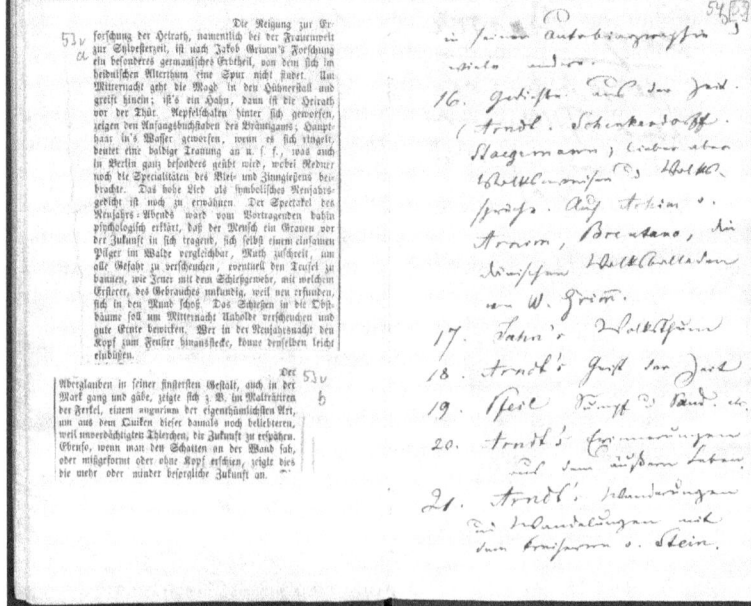

Figures 3.3 and 3.4 Two consecutive double-pages from Fontane's Notebook E 2, listing sources for research on the project *Before the Storm*.

Bei den Büchern zu Rathe ziehen: Oberlehrer Holtze Geh. Rath Metzel College Adami Eggers Roquette. v. Ledebur. K. Bibliothek. Gsellius. Sommerfeldt (Küstrin)	<u>Bücher.</u> 53 1. Marwitz. 2. Zeitungen 1812/13. 3. Kalender. 4. Rang und Quartir≠Liste. 5. Welche <u>französischen</u> Regimenter in <u>Küstrin</u> etc. 6. Märkische und norddeutsche Sagen. 7. Wendische Alterthümer. 8. Larochefoucauld. 9. Voltaire. 10. Die Briefe der Rahel. 11. Biographie Tiecks. 12. Biographie Johann v. Müllers. 13. Die Reden Fichtes. 14. Die Vorlesungen Humboldts und A. W. v. Schlegels (über Literatur.) 15. Biographien die jene Zeit berühren (wie z. B. Harnisch, Hitzig über Chamisso, La Motte Fouqué
In the matter of the books consult: Schoolmaster Holtze Privy Councilor Metzel Colleague Adami Eggers Roquette. von Ledebur. Royal Library. Gsellius. Sommerfeldt (Küstrin)	<u>Books.</u> 53 1. Marwitz. 2. Newspapers 1812/13. 3. Calendars. 4. Army registers. 5. Which French regiments in <u>Küstrin</u> etc. 6. Tales of the Marches and northern Germany. 7. Wendish antiquities. 8. Larochefoucauld. 9. Voltaire. 10. The letters of Rahel. 11. Biography of Tieck. 12. Biography of Johann von Müller. 13. Fichte's speeches. 14. Lectures of Humboldt and A. W. von Schlegel (on literature.) 15. Biographies touching upon that time (like e.g., Harnisch, Hitzig on Chamisso, La Motte Fouqué

164   The Fontane Workshop

	54
[*Clippings from a newspaper article on folklore, customs, and superstition in Brandenburg; with markings in red crayon, most likely by Fontane.*]	in seiner Autobiographie und viele andre. 16. Gedichte aus der Zeit (Arndt. Schenkendorff. Staegemann, lieber aber Volksweisen und Volkssprüche. Auch Achim v. Arnim, Brentano, die dänischen Volksballaden von W. Grimm. 17. Jahn's Volksthum 18. Arndt's Geist der Zeit 19. Pfeil Sumpf und Sand. etc. 20. Arndt's Erinnerungen aus dem äußern Leben. 21. Arndt's Wanderungen und Wandelungen mit dem Freiherrn v. Stein.

	54
[*Clippings from a newspaper article on folklore, customs, and superstition in Brandenburg; with markings in red crayon, most likely by Fontane.*]	in his autobiography and many others. 16. Poems of the time (Arndt. Schenkendorff. Staegemann, but preferably folk tales and folk sayings. Also Achim von Arnim, Brentano, the Danish popular ballads of W. Grimm. 17. Jahn's *Volksthum* 18. Arndt's *Geist der Zeit* 19. Pfeil Sumpf und Sand. etc. 20. Arndt's *Erinnerungen aus dem äußern Leben*. 21. Arndt's *Wanderungen und Wandelungen mit dem Freiherrn v. Stein*.

While the themes of the items on this list are not surprising—after all, the author planned to produce a popular historical novel, and several of the items can be understood as historical sources—their generic diversity is. Under the shared heading "Books," the list mixes metonymies standing for the writings of certain authors ("Marwitz," "Voltaire") with specific references ("Jahn's *Volksthum*," "Fichte's

Speeches") and then again specific references with entire textual genres ("Newspapers 1812/13"), including calendars, statistical sources such as army lists and billets, local tales, biographies, and poems. Even an open question ("Which French Regiments in Küstrin etc.") and a topic ("Wendish antiquities") figure as "Books" and are given the same status on this list as, for example, the Danish folktales by Wilhelm Grimm. The list thus underscores that the channels of Fontane's library network were semantically neutral, so that all kinds of items could pass through them under the label of "book." The generic spectrum is further enriched by the newspaper clippings on 53V, which add a sensationalist element to the accumulated material. Describing in graphic detail superstitions that, to quote from the smaller of the two clippings, were "very much alive in the Brandenburg Marches"—such as "maltreating piglets . . . so as to foretell the future from the squeals of these harmless animals"—the clippings stand in stark contrast to canonical references like Voltaire or Fichte on the list of "Books." The inclusiveness of the library, however, catalogued all of the sources under the same heading and prepared them for unconstrained recombination in further processing efforts. This breadth stretched the notion of intertextuality with which the library (and its user) operated to the extreme. By default, texts not only could be found together with other texts, but were also fundamentally connectable and intermixable.

Just as in the case of the *Wanderungen* archive, the modes of notation with which Fontane managed his library ensured that its classifications would never be restrictive. The author either used his notebooks to record sources in the form of open lists (as in the example earlier) or attached keywords and logistical references to the running chronology of his daily life and social calendar in his diaries. These methods did little to sort the content, but they were easy to expand and open to additions; even the newspaper sheet in which book deliveries were wrapped, the *Einpackebogen* (BaHey 170), could become an item in this constantly growing library.

Sampling the Archive: From Antiquarianism to Sensationalism

As we have seen, Fontane's accumulation of material through the *Wanderungen* project and the library network followed particular priorities, principles, and rules that help to explain why certain topics and types of material prevail in his storage media. In other words, the internal logic of the material-generating apparatus that was the *Wanderungen* project and the composition of the library network provide a key to reading Fontane's archive as a corpus. What would otherwise look like a mass of disconnected entries about all kinds of topics can now be surveyed and characterized as a repertoire of stable elements, albeit appearing in various permutations, that Fontane used to produce his works. Because of the significant losses that Fontane's *Nachlass* suffered, we cannot make a definitive list of all of the types of material in his repository, but a survey of the extant notebooks related to literary prose projects provides a credible basis for some general claims.[109]

The research parameters set by the *Wanderungen* project led to an abundance of materials in the notebooks that revolve around the objects and localities of domestic life and death. They provide the thematically and numerically most significant group of entries. We have seen that the reader-contributors of the *Wanderungen* were supposed to find their histories, their ways of life, and indeed themselves represented in the project. This priority is reflected in the emphasis on antiquarian objects in the notebooks. The booklets abound in descriptions of material remains that are representative of the everyday life of local individuals and dynasties, both past and present, with which text-based historiographies of the Mark could be supplemented. To name the most frequently recurring objects and localities, there are descriptions of local churches, graveyards, tombstones, memorial plates, and family monuments, often including epitaphs and inscriptions on church bells, baptismal fonts, or church registers;[110] palaces, mansions, parks, statues,

---

109 As noted previously, Emilie Fontane burned a considerable number of letters, drafts, and other materials after Fontane's death; moreover, 75 percent of the Fontane *Nachlass* that the *Schriftenarchiv* (now the *Theodor-Fontane-Archiv*) once held were destroyed during and soon after the Second World War. The *Theodor-Fontane-Archiv* is in the process of producing a current inventory of the remaining holdings. However, a couple of catalogs—the catalog for the auction in 1933 through which the *Schriftenarchiv* obtained its pre-War holdings and Manfred Horlitz's overview of *Vermißte Bestände*—provide descriptions of many of the lost items. Additionally, some of Fontane's draft materials have been published in the appendices to various editions of his works and, most recently, in F1. From all of these sources, one can conclude that in his other storage media, Fontane gathered together contents that resembled those in the notebooks. To be clear, though, I am not attempting a complete inventory of Fontane's notebooks here. I have focused on notebooks in the groups A and E, which are the groups with the greatest relevance to literary prose projects. Nor am I saying that Fontane's notebooks are confined to the topics that I identify as prominent. Rather, my aim is to provide an initial typology of the notes that were particularly relevant to Fontane's literary production, to be further refined by other scholars. A detailed description of the content of *all* of the preserved booklets is underway for the genetic-critical edition of the notebooks. See https://fontane-nb.dariah.eu/test/index.html.
110 Here and in what follows, I will give only a spectrum of examples for each group of objects and localities, not complete listings of all the notebook pages on which they occur: churches, tombstones, church bells, etc., e.g., A 1, 3R, 4R, 5R, 6R; A 2, 14R–15V, 47R–49R; A 3, 10R–10V, 40R, 59R, 74R, 88R; A 4, 10V–11R; A 5, 47R–50R; A 6, 27V, 30R–31R; A 7, 82R; A 18, 1R–2R; B1, 39R–40R.

gardens, ponds, and notable trees;[111] inventories of interiors consisting of bridal chambers, bedrooms, libraries and studies, tea rooms, garden pavilions, stucco ceilings and friezes, fireplaces, mirrors, staircases, coffee tables, and chairs;[112] items of food and clothing (hats, coats, shirts, vests, pants, skirts, and belts);[113] and elements of visual décor, particularly descriptions and titles of paintings.[114]

Fontane's predilection for legends, Romantic folklore, anecdotes, and popular literary storytelling in the *Wanderungen* project and beyond becomes visible in an altogether different set of entries, which encompasses elements from popular literary culture and the realm of secondary orality. He recorded samples from popular discourses in his notebooks, including stanzas of folksongs, pious *sententiae*, truisms, idioms, aperçus, and jokes, some of which were witty, and some of which were remarkably banal.[115] Fontane also noted down anecdotes and rumors recounted by his contributors, which often served as sources for his fictional narratives—indeed, at least eight of Fontane's works of prose fiction took rumors and other orally transmitted material as their starting point.[116] This type of material, too, was a mainstay of the mass press. Newspapers competed from the very beginning with oral forms of communication (public announcements, *fama*, tales of wonder, personal memories, etc.); situated at the intersection of print and orality, they presented verifiable, "bookish" information in conjunction with older and less secure types of oral knowledge.[117] Anecdotes, rumors, proverbs, and jokes have no clear origin or single source—they are just

---

111 Palaces, gardens, trees, etc., e.g., A 2, 16R; A 3, 9V; A 7, 29R, 57R; A 14, 8R–11R.
112 Interiors, e.g., A 2, 27R-28V; A 3, 1R, 56V–58R, 87V–88R; A 5, 16R–18V, 29R–31V; 45V–46R; A 7, 15V–17R; A 13, 4V–7V, 20V; A 15, 34R–39R; A 17, 18R, 19R.
113 Food and clothing, e.g., A 5, 78R–78V; E5, 14R–15R, 16V–18R, 38V–48R.
114 Paintings, e.g., A 1, 50R; A 3, 30R; A 7, 17R–18V; A 9, 50R–52R, 63V–65V, 78V; A 17, 25R–28R; B1, 9R–10V; B 9, 57R–60R; E 2, 1R–28R.
115 For example, see A 2, 73V–74V; A 9, 51R; A 12, 25R; A 17, 28R–29V; B 1, 5V–6R; E 3, 24R. The following entry illustrates the typical level of banality: "Ein Professor begann seinen Vortrag folgendermaßen: 'Meine Herrn es hat zu allen Zeiten Menschen gegeben die an einen Gott glaubten und es hat solche gegeben, die nicht an einen Gott glaubten; – meine Herrn, es wird hier wie überall, die Wahrheit in der Mitte liegen'" (E 6, 12R).
116 Norbert Mecklenburg points out that *Schach von Wuthenow, Ellernklipp, L'Adultera, Cécile, Quitt, Unterm Birnbaum, Frau Jenny Treibel*, and *Effi Briest* were demonstrably based on "oral sources," and he assumes that the same holds true for works whose source base is unknown. See Norbert Mecklenburg, *Theodor Fontane. Romankunst der Vielstimmigkeit* (Frankfurt a. M.: Suhrkamp, 1998), 126.
117 On the tension between orality and print in the periodical press, see Hedwig Pompe, "Botenstoffe. Zeitung – Archiv – Umlauf," in *Archivprozesse. Die Kommunikation der Aufbewahrung*, ed. Hedwig Pompe and Leander Scholz (Cologne: DuMont, 2002), 129–30.

168   The Fontane Workshop

"around," verified simply by circulation, and they are therefore associated with vernacular knowledge and "the mouth of the people" (*Volksmund*). It was precisely in this function that Fontane collected them and exploited them in his literary writings.[118] He drew on such elements to capture the *zeitgeist* and characterize societal phenomena. It is only apt, then, that he collected many of the entries of this type in a separate notebook titled "Tages≠Notizen" (E 6), which reads in part like a library of sound samples, stocked with recordings of popular quotations and jokes of the day. That Fontane used these samples for proto-sociological purposes, as illustrations of the *Zeitgeist*, becomes evident from the way he edited them, enhancing and overdrawing the features that were socially significant. For example, Fontane added a clipping from the *Kölnische Zeitung* to his archive that illustrated the sassy wit for which Berliners were famous, yet he immediately improved it through an added remark. The clipping, revolving around a pun that is based on a rhyme and very difficult to translate into English, reads as follows:

> The gravity of the situation has done nothing to curb the Berlin sense of humor. It is said that when somebody in a position of authority was asked what Berliners made of the new ministry, he answered frankly: "For all their satisfaction at it being a high office, they would rather it were not a Heydt Office." (Von der Heydt, the soul of the present Prussian ministry, is known to be most unpopular in Prussia.)
>
> *Der Ernst der Lage hat dem Berliner Witz keinen Einhalt gethan. Es wird erzählt, als an hoher Stelle Jemand gefragt wurde, was die Berliner zu dem neuen Ministerium sagten, die freimühtige Antwort gelautet habe: „Man ist zufrieden, daß es ein Einheitsministerium ist, möchte aber lieber, daß es kein Heydts Ministerium wäre. (V. d. Heydt, die Seele des jetzigen preußischen Ministeriums, ist bekanntlich sehr wenig beliebt in Preußen.)*

(E 6, 64R)

Below this clipping, Fontane added: "To put it better: It is already a high office, no Heydt Office would be better" (*Besser ausgedrückt: Einheits≠Ministerium ist es nun, Kein Heydts≠Ministerium wäre besser*). This addition rephrases the key elements of the pun, *Einheit* and *Keinheit* or *Kein-Heydt*, in a way that makes it pithier, more effective, and thus even

---

118 My analysis of the anecdotes and jokes in Fontane's notebooks is indebted to Mecklenburg's observations about the function of oral knowledge in the *Wanderungen*. See Mecklenburg, *Theodor Fontane. Romankunst der Vielstimmigkeit*, 120–43.

better at rendering the Berliners' peculiar sense of humor. As in the case of his library network and methods of interclass epistolary communication, Fontane reflected this aspect of his practice of collecting and mobilizing material in his fiction. In *Effi Briest,* Effi's cousin Dagobert collects circulating jokes. When Effi asks him to entertain her with a sample (*Probe*) of jokes that are in vogue, Dagobert promises her "something really exquisite" and presents her with the latest, a "Bible joke," quizzing her: "Who was the first house-guest?" When Effi cannot figure it out, Dagobert reveals the answer: "The first house-guest was sorrow. It says in the Book of Job, 'No longer shalt thou be visited by sorrow.'"[119] But Effi does not get it; as the narrator comments, she was "one of those fortunate people who have no appreciation of that play on words" (*die für derlei Dinge durchaus kein Organ haben*), and Dagobert gets into "more and more of a tangle" as he tries to explain the joke. When she finally understands it, Effi expresses her dissatisfaction: "Oh, I see. I'm sorry, Dagobert, but I think that really is *too* stupid." Her disapproval, however, does not stop her from treating the joke as a "good omen" that she will be spared future sorrow. The scene, then, precisely stages Fontane's functionalization of the jokes, anecdotes, and discursive samples that he collected. Both trivialities and significant social symptoms, they characterize the protagonists, their differing tastes, and their mentalities.

A third set of entries that emerges across different booklets deepens the popular cultural dimension of Fontane's notes and concerns itself with the sensational, the erotic, and the occult. These entries must be understood in conjunction with his fascination with societal news, especially news that would instigate communication among his readers and turn his writings into news items themselves. These materials occur in edited and in unedited form, presumably depending on Fontane's experience with the moral standards of the periodical press. Family magazines essentially banned open descriptions of sex of any kind and also discouraged authors from making overt reference to prenuptial love affairs, adultery, and divorce. Fontane's notes show that he edited his materials only as much as he had to, depending on the

---

119 Theodor Fontane, *Effi Briest,* trans. Mike Mitchell (Oxford: Oxford University Press, 2015), 156. It is worth pointing out how much the English translation differs from the German here. In German, this part of the dialogue reads as follows: „Wer war der erste Kutscher?" . . . „Nun vielleicht Apollo." „Sehr gut. Du bist doch ein Daus, Effi. Ich wäre nicht darauf gekommen. Aber trotzdem, Du triffst damit nicht ins Schwarze." „Nun, wer war es denn?" „Der erste Kutscher war ‚Leid.' Denn schon im Buche Hiob heißt es: ‚Leid soll mir nicht widerfahren' oder auch ‚wieder fahren' in zwei Wörtern und mit einem e" (GBA I.15: 229). The wordplay, then, is a good bit more subtle because it is based on a homonym; moreover, Effi's knowledge of Greek mythology is lost in translation.

topic. His summary of the life of "Countess (*Gräfin*) Schw . . . . n" in Notebook A 12, for example, illustrates how Fontane prepared material about a member of the nobility to create a piquant yet still acceptable story. Having heard about the life of the Countess of Sophie von Schwerin (1785–1863) from Mathilde von Rohr, Fontane, in his notes, turns the proper names of the two most important figures into ciphers, thus casting the material in the style of a rumor or a fictional tale while organizing the plot around popular literary elements such as unrequited love, misfortune, a duel, and adoption:

> Countess Schw . . . . n (after communications from Ms. v. R.)
> She was very beautiful (by birth a Countess D . . . . ff) and married in 1807. Two brothers loved her; on the wedding day, on which she married the elder, the younger shot himself. . . . Eight years later her husband (the elder brother) fell at the head of his regiment of Cuirassiers at Ligny or Waterloo. The following year her only brother, Count D . . . . ff, who had returned from the war unhurt, in Göttingen where he studied, was by his closest friend, Count Saldern, shot in a duel. (What occasion?) The marriage of the young Count S. (one of her nephews if I'm not mistaken) with a suspicious personage, caused her worry. – Then later the adoptive daughter and the foster daughter.

> *Gräfin Schw. . .n (Nach Mittheilungen von Frl. v. Rohr)*
> *Sie war sehr schön (eine geb: Gräfin D . . . . ff) und vermählte sich 1807. Zwei Brüder liebten sie; am Hochzeitstage, an dem sie sich dem ältren vermählte, erschoß sich der jüngre. . . . Acht Jahre später fiel ihr Mann (der ältre Bruder) an der Spitze seines Kürassier*⸗*Regiments bei Ligny oder Belle*⸗*Alliance. Das Jahr drauf wurde ihr einziger Bruder, Graf D . . . . ff, der aus dem Kriege glücklich heimgekehrt war, in Göttingen wo er studirte, von seinem intimsten Freunde, dem Grafen Saldern im Duell erschossen. (Welche Veranlassung?) Die Vermählung des jungen Grafen S. (eines ihrer Neffen wenn ich nicht irre) mit einer bedenklichen Personage, machte ihr Gram. – Dann später die Adoptiv*⸗*Tochter und die Pflege*⸗*Tochter.*
> (A 12, 87R–88R)

In this form, the material was fit not only for family magazines, but also for further processing in Fontane's textual machinery. Broken down into semantically open narrative formulas ("The adoptive daughter and the foster daughter"), the material could easily be expanded or woven into other textual patches.

The notebook entries on the occult make it clear that Fontane exploited the leeway that family magazines granted contributors on this particular topic. His notes on occult phenomena provide much more evocative and precise detail than do his notes on other topics. This detail accorded fully with the standards of the magazines, in which articles on supernatural events, spiritualist practices, and superstitious beliefs appeared frequently. In the *Gartenlaube* and the *Deutsche Roman-Zeitung*, to mention but two examples, numerous articles delve into great descriptive detail, at times presented in the guise of folkloristic or scientific accounts, such as "The Possessed Boys of Illfurth,"[120] "Pigment Rot and Bleeding Hosts (*Hostien*),"[121] or "An Electric Girl."[122] A set of glossed newspaper clippings that Fontane pasted into Notebook E 2 operates along precisely these lines. The clippings give some folkloristic background, though their emphasis—heightened through Fontane's markings in red crayon—is on the recounting of the superstitious fears and practices of soothsaying, such as "Those born on a holy day, Sunday children in particular, can see the funeral processions of those who will die in their neighborhood long in advance" and "Also, when one saw the shadow on the wall, or appeared misshapen or headless (*mißgeformt oder ohne Kopf*), this foretold a more or less worrisome future" (50VA–51VA). How prominent a place occult stories occupy in Fontane's filing system becomes clear from a list of "Ghost stories" (*Spukgeschichten*) that Fontane assembled and tagged with references to the locations where each story could be found (A 15, 8R, 9R).

Across these three larger groups, Fontane's materials share a striking property: they are remarkably well-suited to his general project of producing *Zeitschriftenliteratur*, literary writings whose primary publication context was the periodical press. To recall, family magazines and other mass media attempted to speak to a heterogeneous readership that extended from adolescents to adults and from members of the lower-middle class to the social and intellectual elite (see Chapter 1). A contributor's first task was therefore to produce writings that were "popular and understandable to all,"[123] yet which the more educated readers would still find entertaining. The materials that Fontane gathered in his repository allowed him to meet this challenge. Many of them, as has become evident, were directly culled from the mass press

---

120 *Die Gartenlaube* 52 (1872): 854–56.
121 *Die Gartenlaube* 14 (1873): 227–30.
122 *Deutsche Roman-Zeitung* 33 (1880): 719.
123 Ernst Keil, the founder of the *Gartenlaube*, qtd. in Andreas Graf, "Die Ursprünge der modernen Medienindustrie: Familien- und Unterhaltungszeitschriften der Kaiserzeit (1870–1918)," in *Geschichte des deutschen Buchhandels im 19. und 20. Jahrhundert*, ed. Georg Jäger, Dieter Langewiesche, and Wolfram Siemann (Frankfurt a. M.: MVB, 2003), 1.2:424.

or treated topics that were frequently covered therein.[124] With these materials, Fontane could create an easy sense of familiarity with his output. The sensationalist and light items constituted the desired access points at which less-educated consumers of journals could enter a given narrative. At the same time, these items could be deployed for aesthetic effects that appealed to more sophisticated readers. In abundance, then, they opened up creative possibilities for Fontane.

For example, Fontane's "antiquarian" notes could be used for the straightforward description of literary settings with a high degree of verisimilitude, yet they could also be deployed for ironic exaggeration as an aesthetic effect. Richard Brinkmann has remarked that Fontane's production, especially his fiction, abounds in what he calls "set pieces (*Versatzstücke*) of genre imagery," a reference to the very items of furniture, tableware, food, clothing, and images mentioned earlier.[125] Brinkmann argues that through the ostentatious deployment of these set pieces, Fontane renders the procedure of realistic description ironic. The strongest example is a scene in *Mathilde Möhring* in which the working-class protagonist's mother contentedly gazes at a genre painting of a flute-playing shepherd boy by the contemporary French traditionalist William Bouguereau, while the protagonist Mathilde, fixing her hair, watches this entire scene in the mirror (GBA I.20: 14–15). A study of Fontane's notebooks reveals the abundance of domestic and everyday objects that made such ironic doubling possible in the first place.

In sum, Fontane's notes map to a striking extent onto the topics, discursive modes, and moral standards that prevailed in the contemporary periodical press. His material repository must thus be seen as the fluid contact zone between the mass media and his own output. It was an archive with porous walls, programmatically open to

---

124 Reviewing a bibliography of articles that appeared in family magazines between the 1850s and 1880s shows the extent of the thematic overlap between Fontane's notes and these periodicals. It was not only topics on occult phenomena that figured prominently in the mass press, but also myriad contributions on what I have termed "antiquarian" topics, i.e., church bells, mansions, old trees, etc., the titles of which are almost interchangeable with Fontane's notebook entries, not to mention the anecdotes, folktales, portraits of notable people, and sensational news items that occurred regularly in the periodical press. See Alfred Estermann, ed., *Inhaltsanalytische Bibliographie deutscher Kulturzeitschriften des 19. Jahrhunderts* (Munich: Saur, 1995). For this study, the *Gartenlaube* (IBDK vol. 3.1 and 3.2), *Deutsche Roman-Zeitung* (vol. 6), and *Westermanns Monatshefte* (vol. 8) have been evaluated. They represent the spectrum of themes and topics between liberal-popular and more intellectual periodicals.
125 Richard Brinkmann, "Der angehaltene Moment: Requisiten, Genre, Tableau bei Fontane," *Deutsche Vierteljahrsschrift für Literaturwissenschaft und Geistesgeschichte* 53, no. 3 (1979): 436.

the exoteric themes and images that circulated through the mass media or that were fit for this mode of publication. Reception and production were closely connected in this archive. The antiquarian details, communicative commonplaces, popular literary types, and societal news that piled up in it allowed Fontane to produce writings that combined elements from the full spectrum of popular culture, from the yellow press to sophisticated magazines. At the same time, the contents of Fontane's storage media made possible some of the most-discussed hallmarks of his literary prose. The question then arises as to which reading techniques Fontane used to traverse his archive and interact creatively with the accumulated material.

Material Reading Feats
As a reader, Fontane approached the massive quantities of material produced by the *Wanderungen* project and the library network with a technique that scholars of the history of reading call "brutal"[126] or "discontinuous"[127] reading. Driven solely by affect and unconcerned with impropriety, "brutal" readers ruthlessly break up the texts they encounter into passages that catch their interest, while ignoring everything else.[128] Brutal reading was especially widespread in the nineteenth century, because it was essentially the mode of journal readers. Freely crisscrossing the texts, journal readers constellated the different articles, sections, and images presented on a given page or within a given journal issue into their personal reading sequences, skipping around the offered contents as they saw fit.[129] Fontane, who received his early socialization as a reader through newspapers and journals, provides a textbook case of brutal reading.[130] Indeed, it was this technique that enabled him to work creatively with the excess of material generated by his library network. This skill turned reading from a predominantly receptive act into a productive one, encouraging a recombinant poetics that would become increasingly inventive, as Fontane had more and more material at his disposal.

The prerequisite of brutal reading is a stance toward the text that is at once emphatic and conjectural, for it is a reading that at one moment engrosses itself in the text completely only to let go of it at the next, shuttling between full immersion and taking liberties. Fontane realized

---

126 See Georg Stanitzek, "Brutale Lektüre um 1800/heute," in *Poetologien des Wissens*, ed. Joseph Vogl (Munich: Fink, 1999), 250; 253–4.
127 Stallybrass, "Books and Scrolls: Navigating the Bible," 46–7.
128 Stanitzek, "Brutale Lektüre um 1800/heute," 254.
129 Kaminski et al., "Zeitschriftenliteratur/Fortsetzungsliteratur," 27.
130 On Fontane's early reading socialization, see Rasch, "Zeitungstiger, Bücherfresser," 107–8.

this stance to the fullest through a repertoire of virtuosic reading skills. He shuttled between reading rapidly and slowly, with focused and hovering attentiveness, high and low intensity, selectively on the hunt for something specific and just on the off chance, from beginning to end and in sections.[131] He could become immersed in a text to the point of frenzy, regardless of whether he was dealing with a set of poems, a book review, or a historical document. Numerous diary entries and letters indicate that he experienced strong affective reactions while reading, including tears of joy, fever, dizziness, and surges of emotion. Then again, when a text failed to arouse an "effect" (*Wirkung*), the ultimate yardstick by which Fontane gauged its quality, he passed a drastic value judgment on it—"Kretzer's book is a piece of filth" (*eine Schweinerei*, GBA XI.2: 233)—and abruptly turned to something else.

The author attributed strong poetic implications to his practice of brutal reading, which he dubbed "my method proceeding in leaps and bounds" (*meine sprungweise Methode*; HA IV.4: 616). In fact, as a highly instructive metaphorical comparison in his personal reading notes indicates, Fontane viewed the brutal reading of passages as an apparatus of creativity. Commenting on the correspondence between Goethe and Schiller and on Schopenhauer's *Parerga and Paralipomena*, he stated:

> I just read 30 pages in the Schiller-Goethe correspondence. All very fine, noble, and for all the reserve there is a nice candor to it. Nonetheless, compared to Schopenhauer's mode of writing it seems insipid, nearly dull. I should like to compare Goethe / Schiller to a voltaic pile, Schopenhauer to a charged Leyden jar or a running electrostatic generator. The former's galvanic current is powerful indeed, but it does not flash and glow like the flying spark does.

> *Eben habe ich 30 Seiten im Schiller-Goethe-Briefwechsel gelesen. Alles sehr fein, vornehm und bei vieler Reserviertheit doch eine schöne Offenheit. Nichtsdestoweniger wirkt es im Vergleich zu Schopenhauers Schreibweise insipide, beinah langweilig. Ich möchte Goethe/Schiller mit einer Voltaschen Säule, Schopenhauer mit einer geladenen Leydener Flasche oder mit einer in Tätigkeit begriffenen Elektrisiermaschine*

---

131 Fontane's numerous descriptions of his reading reflect the depth of this repertoire, ranging from "durchstöbern" (GBA XI.1: 256) to "schmökern" (GBA XII.2: 244), "überfliegen" (GBA XII.3: 23), "von a bis z durchlesen" (GBA XII.2: 397), "extrahieren" (GBA XI.2: 148), "zerlesen" (GBA II.1: 54), "den Text langsam trinkend zu sich nehmen" (BaHey 19), and "sich wie blind und toll darauf stürzen" (GBA XII.3: 177).

vergleichen. Der galvanische Strom jener ist von großer Kraft, aber er blitzt und leuchtet nicht wie der überspringende Funke.

(NFA XXI.2: 101)

Note that Fontane's comment does not concern itself with the content of the writings of Schiller, Goethe, and Schopenhauer. Rather, it focuses on their modes of writing (*Schreibweisen*), considering them the actual sources of the texts' energy. What distinguishes the two modes is that the exchange of letters between Schiller and Goethe is an unfolding yet thematically cohesive dialogue, whereas Schopenhauer's text is aphoristic; as the title says, it contains "disconnected thoughts" (*vereinzelte Gedanken*) and thus ought to be processed *qua* genre in an ongoing reading of passages. It is precisely to this reading of discrete passages, a reading for which there is no context and that proceeds in leaps, that Fontane attributes the stronger electrifying qualities: whereas the effect of Schiller and Goethe's mode of writing is like a "voltaic pile," which produces a continuous current, Schopenhauer's writing is like an electrostatic generator, giving off short-lived but heavy discharges of energy at high voltages. This latter mode sets free the spark that jumps over to the reader. Consistent with the technology of his age, Fontane underpins the traditional metaphor for creativity, the spark, with a machine that performs a repeatable task. If we take this image to be a description of Fontane's "method proceeding in leaps and bounds," its poetological function becomes clear: through his brutal reading technique, he is able to set the "electrostatic generator" into motion and derive electrifying digressive energy[132] even from texts that were in themselves neither aphoristic nor electrifying. Applying his whole virtuosic repertoire, he jumps back and forth in texts, rips passages out of their contexts, brings them into contact with one another, and causes "sparks" to fly.

Fontane's notes on Goethe and Schiller provide an example of how the "electrostatic generator" works. The machine begins with a leap from Schopenhauer's philosophical reflections in *Parerga und Paralipomena* to Jean Paul's *Grönländische Prozesse* (*The Greenland Lawsuits*) and another of his volumes, which "happen to treat the same matters as the *Parergas*." After briefly mocking Jean Paul's style, he concludes: "compared to this Schopenhauer is a demigod indeed. The independence, clarity, and concision of his mode of writing exerts a considerable appeal, which becomes fully apparent only when reading something else alongside it" (*wenn man anderes daneben liest,*

---

[132] This term is taken from Roland Barthes, "Writing Reading," in *The Rustle of Language*, trans. Richard Howard (Oxford: Blackwell, 1986), 30.

NFA XXI.2: 101). Fontane's commentators noted with some irritation that this remark about Jean Paul and Schopenhauer "in form and content seems like a foreign body" in Fontane's reading notes and "temporarily loses sight of the actual topic" (NFA XXI.2: 802). What these commentaries miss, however, is the point of Fontane's reading technique. Through the intensifying *Stellenlektüre*, or "reading of passages," Fontane took the liberty of leaving the subject of the text behind, thus opening up his reading to a multiplicity of associative and otherwise productive forms.

Fontane's diaries and separate reading notes document both the frequency and the artistry with which he used this mode of reading; time and again, he described himself as reading *in* a text. Typical diary entries say "Read in Storm and [in] Heine's *Romanzero*" or "Read in Gneist's book."[133] Characteristically, this entry does not bother to specify which of Theodor Storm's writings he read. Proceeding in irregular stretches, the brutal reader Fontane leaped from text to text and book to book, unconstrained in his combinations of authors and genres. In this fashion, he shuttled repeatedly between Scott's *Waverley* and *Tales of a Grandfather* (BaH 135–6), read Turgenev and Lessing "alternately" (GBA XII.3: 247–8), and switched "in 30-minute intervals"[134] (*halbstündig wechselnd*) between the essays of two historians.

Two technological devices assisted the brutal reader in the performance of this mode of reading, underlining its importance in Fontane's productive process and helping him to make passages "spark." The first, a ball-in-a-cup or *Fangeballspiel*, resided on the author's desk and proved useful when Fontane read continuously for hours, as it exercised some of the skills essential to brutal reading: rhythmical movement and the momentary concentration needed to catch the ball (i.e., a passage) at the right moment (GBA XI.1: 201).[135] The other device was a particular bookbinding that facilitated thumbing through and jumping around a large number of pages at high speed. Every now and then, Fontane requested that one of his Berlin bookbinders bundle up the piles of newspapers, magazines, and loose

---

133 GBA XI.1: 82, 237. In the diary entries for the year 1856 alone, this technique occurs explicitly on January 22, February 10, July 19 and 28, August 7 and 18, October 28, and November 27. This list does not include the countless instances in which his formulations strongly suggest reading in passages but are not explicit enough to be treated as more than suggestive evidence.
134 Richard Sternfeld, "Fontane als Historiker," in '*Erschrecken Sie nicht, ich bin es selbst,' Erinnerungen an Theodor Fontane,* ed. Wolfgang Rasch and Christine Hehle (Berlin: Aufbau, 2003), 165.
135 There is also anecdotal evidence of Fontane's usage of the ball-in-a-cup, as told by the lawyer of the Fontane family, Paul Meyer, in "Theodor Fontanes Fangeball," in "*Erschrecken Sie nicht, ich bin es selbst,"* 228–9.

sheets that were scattered all over his home into volumes with strong covers.[136] These bindings were cheap, with the bound pages trimmed only roughly by the bookbinder. They were presumably meant to increase not the durability of the material, rather its usability. They transformed the loose sheets into a book-like medium that the "brutal" reader could access more easily.[137]

Fontane's central reading method had forceful poetic implications that exceeded the effect that he described as the "flying spark." His method actualized and accelerated an old rhetorical technique, the *percursio*, which was also based on daring leaps from passage to passage. This technique becomes explicit in a letter in which Fontane, describing what he finds "highly poetic" (*hochpoetisch*) about reading newspapers, rapidly strings together keyword-like references gathered on a fast-paced run through the *Vossische Zeitung*:

> I read the newspaper with a philistine's devotion, but with an attitude that is the very opposite of philistinism. Not a day passes without something highly poetic speaking to me from that miserable blotting paper: the emperor and Bismarck, the silent and then again the noisy battling between the two, the court preacher's party, Kögel, Stoecker, Dryander, [Robert] Koch and the [tuberculosis] bacillus, Goßler, 2000 foreign physicians, the celebration of the Great Elector, Wißmann, and the steamers on Lake Victoria—all this quickens my heart....
>
> *Ich lese die Zeitung mit der Andacht eines Philisters, aber mit einer Gesinnung, die das Gegenteil von Philisterium ist. Es vergeht kein Tag, wo nicht aus diesem elenden Löschpapier etwas Hochpoetisches zu mir spräche: der Kaiser und Bismarck, die stille und dann auch wieder laute Kriegführung zwischen beiden, die Hofpredigerpartei, Kögel, Stoecker, Dryander, Bazillus-Koch, Goßler, 2000 fremde Ärzte, Große Kurfürsten-Feier, Wißmann und Dampfschiffe auf dem Victoriasee – das alles macht mir das Herz höher schlagen....*
>
> (BaHey 211–12)

Leaping from the German emperor to a conference on medicine to steamboats on Lake Victoria, the rapid string of references represents a

---

136 See Rasch, "Zeitungstiger, Bücherfresser," 114.
137 Eckhard Schumacher explains why books are exceptionally amenable to browsing and assesses the potential of browsing to function as a productive technique in his "Aufschlagesysteme 1800/2000," in *Literatur als Blätterwerk. Perspektiven nichtlinearer Lektüre*, ed. Jürgen Gunia and Iris Hermann (St. Ingbert: Röhrig, 2002), 23–45.

percursio, the rhetorical term for a "brief enumeration of objects"[138] or headlines without a main body. According to traditional rhetoric, each object deserves further elaboration and yet is simply enumerated in a list and separated abruptly from the others by commas. In this manner, the rhetorician or compiler can traverse a vast thematic territory with high velocity.[139] Fontane's "objects" are topics of contemporary newspaper discourse, each marking the location of an argument in current debates and conversations. The entire procedure thus turns out to be a high-speed version of a classical technique of rhetorical invention (*inventio*). As always in rhetoric, the topics function as a means of finding formulations and assisting the writer in producing text. Yet their rapid and unregulated combination in Fontane's fast-paced run, the *percursio*, allows him to leave behind the standard ways of connecting them. Deviation from standard use, the forging of new connections, is indeed "highly poetic."

It is worth pointing out that Fontane's recourse to an associative technique of invention with a longstanding tradition in rhetoric was not unprecedented in the nineteenth century. On the century's cusp, Jean Paul—one of Fontane's preferred sources—had developed a similar technique for literary production as part of his "encyclopedic"[140] poetics. In *Vorschule der Ästhetik* (*Introduction to Aesthetics*, 1804) and *Leben Fibels* (*The Life of Fibel*, 1812), Jean Paul spelled out a method of *Ideen-Assoziazion* that was based on the decomposition of textual matter and its recombination into new constellations, an act of ongoing dissociation and association.[141] According to Andreas Kilcher's assessment of Jean Paul's combinatorial poetics, its "most salient feature is . . . how arbitrarily it proceeds,"[142] which brings it into close proximity with Fontane's method. In Jean Paul's model, however, the creation of new combinations was a game (*Spiel*) in which chance played a major role.[143] Fontane's procedure, despite being clearly indebted to this Romantic model, was less probabilistic and more concretely bound to a material

---

138 Heinrich Lausberg, *Handbook of Literary Rhetoric. A Foundation for Literary Study*, trans. Matthew T. Bliss, Annemiek Jansen and David E. Orton; ed. David E. Orton and R. Dean Anderson (Leiden: Brill, 1998), §881.
139 My observations draw on Wegmann and Bickenbach's analysis of *percursio* in Herder's *Reisejournal*: Nikolaus Wegmann and Matthias Bickenbach, "Herders Reisejournal. Ein Datenbankreport," *Deutsche Vierteljahrsschrift für Literaturwissenschaft und Geistesgeschichte* 73, no. 1 (1997): 406–12.
140 For a detailed historicization and analysis of associative recombination as an "encyclopedic" mode of writing, see Andreas Kilcher's fundamental study *mathesis und poiesis. Die Enzyklopädik der Literatur 1600 bis 2000* (Munich: Fink, 2003), 383–415.
141 See ibid., 391.
142 Ibid.
143 Ibid., 392.

basis. It was not a game, but *a reading technique*, one that the author frequently applied to mass media. He used it, in other words, in a fragmented and thematically diverse textual environment in which plenty of material was available for making associative connections.

How much stock Fontane put in this method as a creativity-enhancing technique becomes evident from his response to a survey on "Die Technik des künstlerischen Schaffens" ("The Technique of Artistic Production"), which the magazine *Der Zuschauer* sent to a number of established writers in 1893. The magazine's editor, Constantin Brunner, intended to put together a "practical manual" that would inform readers about the most important techniques of successful authors.[144] While not every respondent agreed that there were techniques of artistic production—Hermann Bahr, for example, insisted on "love," "art," and "the inscrutable" in his response—Fontane's answer *was* his technique. Again, he used a *percursio* to emphasize the method underlying his creativity:

> I take a walk in the Tiergarten and think about Bismarck or a Berlin bun or the splash on my boot and then something comes to mind that I might relate equally well to the emperor of China or to la Lucca or to Nante Strump, loitering on the street corner. If and when, from a dreamlike state, I become conscious that my idea possesses a reasonable claim of being shared with the world, I begin to wonder what form it might take, which varies from day to day. As a rule, nothing at all comes of it; it gets lost, it evaporates. If, however, it stays in mind, something ultimately results. *C'est tout.*[145]

> *Ich gehe im Thiergarten spazieren und denke an Bismarck oder an eine Berliner Schrippe oder an einen Spritzfleck auf meinem Stiefel und da fällt mir was ein, was ich ebenso gut auf den Kaiser von China wie auf die Lucca oder den Ecksteher Nante Strump beziehen kann. Kommt es mir aus einem traumhaften Zustande heraus zum Bewußtsein, daß das, was mir einfiel, einen passablen Anspruch darauf haben dürfte, der Welt mitgeteilt zu werden, so beginne ich mich mit der Form dafür zu beschäftigen, die heute so ist und morgen so. In der Regel wird überhaupt nichts draus; es verthut sich, es verfliegt wieder. Geht der Beschäftigungsprozeß aber weiter, so ist schließlich was da.* C'est tout.

Though Fontane does not explicitly reflect here on an act of reading, the principle is the same as in the account of the "highly poetic" dimension of discontinuous newspaper readings. Fontane describes the beginning of

---

144 Constantin Brunner, "Die Technik des künstlerischen Schaffens. Vorläufige Mitteilung!" *Der Zuschauer* 1, no. 1 (February 15, 1893): 34.
145 *Der Zuschauer* 1, no. 10 (1893): 305.

his artistic production as driven by associative connections—as the phrase "something comes to mind" (*da fällt mir was ein*) suggests—that are based on the free and ongoing recombination of topics from the mass media: Bismarck, the Chinese emperor, [Pauline] Lucca, an Austrian opera diva, and Nante Strump, a hired hand and (in)famous local character who appeared in a number of fictional texts, including Fontane's political satire, *Nante Strump als Erzieher*. All of these figures were popular in the late nineteenth-century mass press. The process is open; the connections are so ephemeral and shifting that they frequently lead to nothing. Yet if the process continues, "something" eventually comes up. Fontane's interaction with his library network made this moment more likely. It enabled precisely this kind of radically associative recombinant poetics, transforming reading into a site for technically supported creativity.

A couple of notebook entries document the creative application of this technique in Fontane's production. Particularly when he drafted dialogues between fictional interlocutors, Fontane noted down cascades of topics from a wide thematic territory. At times, these topics are thematically so distant from one another, and yet follow each other so immediately, that one cannot but identify the *percursio* as the underlying technique, as in this example from his notes for "Dialogues" in *Before the Storm* (Figure 3.5)

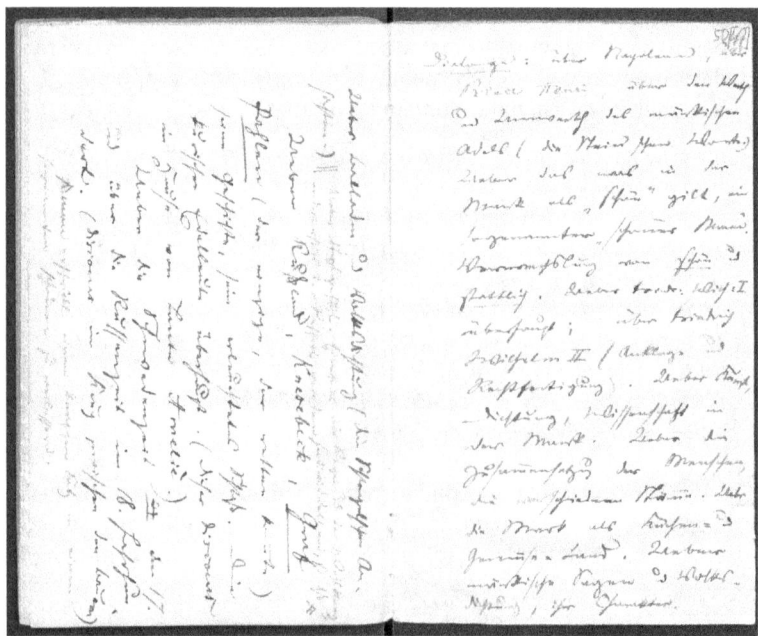

Figure 3.5 Double-page from Fontane's Notebook E 2, containing a cascade of topics for dialogues in *Before the Storm*.

50[49]

Dialoge: über Napoleon, über Prince Henri, über den Werth und Unwerth des märkischen Adels (die Stein'schen Worte.) Ueber das was in der Mark als „schön" gilt, ein sogenannter „schöner Mann". Verwechslung von schön und stattlich. Ueber Friedr: Wlh: I überhaupt; über Friedrich Wilhelm II (Anklage und Rechtfertigung). Ueber Kunst, Dichtung, Wissenschaft in der Mark. Ueber die Zusammensetzung der Menschen, die verschiednen Stämme. Ueber die Mark als Kuchen= und Gemüse=Land. Ueber märkische Sagen und Volksdichtung, ihr Charakter.

Ueber Balladen und Volksdichtung (die Schlegelschen Ansichten) //Ueber Stylgefühl. Einerseits die Regel und der Wohlklang, andrerseits der Respekt vor dem Individuellen, so daß F

Ueber Rußland, Knesebeck, Graf Pahlen (der einzige, der retten konnte) seine Geschichte, sein erleuchtetes Schloß. Die kurischen Edelleute überhaupt. (Dieser discours im Hause von Tante Amelie.)

Ueber die Schwedenzeit ↯ im 17. und über die Russenzeit im 18. Jahrhundert. (Discours im Krug zwischen den Bauern) F man erschrickt einen knappen Satz in einen sogenannten schönen zu verbessern.

50[49]

Dialogues: on Napoleon, on Prince Henri, on the value or otherwise of the Brandenburg nobility (what Stein said about it.) On that which is called beautiful in the Marches, a so-called "beautiful man." Confusion of beautiful and handsome. On Friedr: Wlh: I in general; on Friedrich Wilhelm II (indictment and defense). On art, literature, science in the Marches. On the composition of the people, the various tribes. On the Marches as the land of cake and vegetables. On the legends and folktales of the Marches, their character.

On ballads and folktales (Schlegel's opinions) //On the sense of style. On the one hand rules and sonorousness, on the other respect for individuality, so that F

On Russia, Knesebeck, Count Pahlen (the only one, who might have saved) his history, his resplendent castle. The Curonian nobility in general . (This discourse in the house of Aunt Amelie.)

On the Swedish occupation a in the 17th and on the Russian in the 18th century (Discours in the tavern between the peasants) F one is startled to improve a concise sentence to a so-called beautiful one.

Running from Napoleon via reflections on beauty and handsomeness to the Mark Brandenburg as a garden state, Schlegel's remarks on style, and the historical period of the Russian occupation, Fontane's cascade indicates the huge scope that the *percursio* can cover. The orderly yet cursively angled handwriting, paired with large amounts of space between punctuation marks and words, suggests that Fontane wrote this entry quickly and in one sitting. The speed of the *percursio*, it seems, carried him across the thematic gaps between topics. One can easily read this technique as part of Fontane's "art of chatter" (*Plauderkunst*), one of the characteristics of his realist prose, and relate it to the seemingly natural and free-flowing dialogue for which the author's literary production is famous. But this entry does not yet represent a real set of dialogues; it is no more and no less than a chain of topics. The decisive point, however, is that this highly stimulating rhetorical technique made possible additional creative procedures and literary effects. Fontane indeed returned to the entry, added more topics and remarks in pencil, and re-engaged with the accumulation of distant keywords that he, through the technique of the *percursio*, had at his fingertips. The entry thus documents the creative potential of his principal reading method.

To summarize, Fontane's "method proceeding in leaps and bounds" radicalized his stance toward written material and turned reading from an act of productive reception into an act of receptive production. It was not just a means to scour and evaluate written sources; it was a genuinely creative practice, one that allowed him to constellate and mix, in new and exciting ways, the multitude of sources that the mass-media marketplace provided. The story of Fontane-the-reader completes the reconstruction of the material-generating apparatus with which this chapter has been concerned. It is clear that the individual components of this apparatus—the principle of the "living" archive, Fontane's storage media, the network structure of the postal library, and the technique of "brutal" reading—interacted with one another. This interaction produced much more than a mere accumulation of materials. Through this interaction, Fontane put intertextual remix at the core of his poetics and practiced it successfully under the conditions of early mass media. That his material was in excess did not hinder him, but rather increased his creative output. The media apparatus with which Fontane filled his archives had a built-in means to foster creativity.

Four The Manufacture of Literature: Generating Output

The Agency of the Market: Keller vs. the *Rundschau*

When Gottfried Keller set out to write what would be his final novel, *Martin Salander*, he hoped to break new ground in multiple ways.[1] He was eager to try his hand at a short work that would treat contemporary societal conditions, and, inspired by Spielhagen's theory of the novel, he wanted to experiment with new narrative perspectives. Above all, however, he was determined to finally get his collaboration with the periodical press right. All too frequently, Keller had found himself finishing chapters in haste while struggling with the deadlines that serialized publication in periodicals imposed. *Martin Salander*, he vowed, would be written at his own pace. As an established novelist no longer dependent on the periodical press for his income, Keller repeatedly put off his long-time publisher, Julius Rodenberg of the *Deutsche Rundschau*, who had begun to inquire which issue could feature the first portion of *Martin Salander*. For once, Keller explained, he wanted to avoid "hasty endings and their unfinished state (*die übereilten Schlüsse und deren Unfertigkeit*)"[2] and have the entire manuscript in front of him before publication started.

Alas, Keller had underestimated the agency of the market. The *Rundschau* was about to enter its second decade in the fall of 1884, and it seemed the perfect moment to publish Keller's new work. Zurich booksellers, having gotten wind of the novel in the making, jumped the gun with an advertisement in the *Neue Zürcher Zeitung* that claimed that the *Rundschau* would open its eleventh year of publication

---

1 See the editorial commentary in *Martin Salander: Apparat zu Band 8*, ed. Thomas Binder et al., vol. 24, *Gottfried Keller: Sämtliche Werke. Historisch-Kritische Ausgabe*, ed. Walter Morgenthaler (Basel: Stroemfeld/Verlag Neue Zürcher Zeitung, 2004), 15–19.
2 Letters to Julius Rodenberg, July 8, 1883; July 5, 1884, printed in *Martin Salander: Apparat*, 460; 468.

with the "new novel by Gottfried Keller."[3] The news spread quickly. Colleagues and admirers wrote to Keller to express their excitement about the prospect of reading his new novel soon. In the face of these "accursed subscription advertisements," Keller yet again found himself under "duress"[4] (*Zwang*) and rushed into serial publication after all, even though he had enough manuscript only for the first installment. It did not go well. Publication began in January 1886, and after just a few months, a combination of writer's block, illness, and general malaise caused Keller to fall behind. Even though Rodenberg accommodated him in all possible ways, accepting shorter installments than had been agreed upon and inserting "stop-gaps" (*Lückenbüßer*) by other writers to buy Keller time, disaster ensued, and the author did not deliver. The serialization had to be interrupted twice; neither the March nor the August issue contained installments. Readers complained, and Rodenberg finally forced Keller to bring the novel to an abrupt close for the September issue, with which the run (*Jahrgang*) of 1886 concluded. Ironically, *Martin Salander* became the novel that was most drastically shaped by the mechanisms of the periodical press. Yet again, the literary market had insinuated itself into Keller's creative process, demanding significant aesthetic concessions in the interest of deadlines. He would never again pick up his pen to write another novel.

Keller's story represents a clear, if extreme, example of the way numerous nineteenth-century writers experienced the market: as a constraining force with which they had to cope, and indeed wrestle, if they wanted to push through their own ideas. To this familiar story, Fontane added a new twist. He developed working methods that allowed him not only to cope with the literary market, but also to include it deliberately as an agent in his creative process.[5] In the previous chapter, we saw how this inclusion came about in Fontane's storage media. Amounting to an archive with porous walls, his storage media—notebooks, "paper sleeves," cardboard boxes, and other receptacles—provided a fluid contact zone between the literary market and his output, a zone in which reception could easily tip over into production. Indeed, Fontane used his storage media not only in their archiving function, but also as writing surfaces for the projection of

---

3   The advertisement is reprinted in *Martin Salander: Apparat*, 470.
4   Ibid., 475.
5   For an early attempt at analyzing the relationship between Fontane's production and the literary market, see Manfred Windfuhr, "Fontanes Erzählkunst unter den Marktbedingungen ihrer Zeit," in *Formen realistischer Erzählkunst*, ed. Jörg Thunecke (Nottingham: Sherwood Press, 1979), 335–46.

ideas, sketches, dispositions, and formulated drafts. The notebooks in particular, a unique and mostly unexplored body of evidence, document the transition from "input" to "output" with great clarity. In conjunction with other surviving evidence, they demonstrate how Fontane's creative process interacted with the forces of the market at every major stage.

This chapter analyzes Fontane's market-driven modes of text production, from the mechanical compilation of bread-and-butter articles for daily papers to the virtuosic mixing together of complex reality effects in his novellas and novels. Inquiries into Fontane's working methods have until now attempted to reconstruct the development of single novels from start to finish, but here the goal is different: this chapter analyzes the interplay of Fontane's technologies of writing and his aesthetic strategies on a broad plane, drawing together examples from several well-documented projects.[6] It describes Fontane's assemblage of storage and writing media as an *interface* (a theoretical concept I will discuss in more detail later) on which his aesthetic deliberations, creativity, and the literary marketplace met. Analyzing draft materials from a number of novels and novellas, the chapter focuses on the notational techniques and creative practices that Fontane used repeatedly and that gave rise to some of the most celebrated hallmarks of his art, such as his credible, all-too-human characters and the "real-life" sound of their conversations—two

---

6   Many of the examples are taken from the production processes of *Vor dem Sturm, Schach von Wuthenow,* and *Der Stechlin.* These works encompass the roughly three decades during which Fontane published his prose fiction. The production of *Vor dem Sturm* and of *Schach von Wuthenow* has left plenty of traces in Fontane's notebooks; moreover, there are 2,700 folio sheets of manuscript materials that Walter Hettche has analyzed in an enormous undertaking. My inquiry gratefully incorporates his findings. See Walter Hettche, "Die Handschriften zu Theodor Fontanes *Vor dem Sturm.* Erste Ergebnisse ihrer Auswertung," *Fontane Blätter* 58 (1994): 193–212. I also draw on Roland Berbig's study of the production history of *Vor dem Sturm,* "'aber zuletzt – [. . .] schreibt man doch sich selbst zu Liebe.' Mediale Textprozesse. Theodor Fontanes Romanerstling *Vor dem Sturm,*" in *Theodorus Victor: Theodor Fontane, der Schriftsteller des 19. am Ende des 20. Jahrhunderts. Eine Sammlung von Beiträgen,* ed. Roland Berbig (Frankfurt/Main: Lang, 1999), 99–120. As for *Der Stechlin,* I am building on Julius Petersen's study, "Fontanes Altersroman," *Euphorion* 29 (1928): 1–74, which describes the production history of the novel and makes numerous pages of draft materials available. When I quote from the drafts of *Der Stechlin,* I rely on Petersen's transcriptions. Gabriele Radecke's comprehensive genetic study of Fontane's working methods in *L'Adultera* is also an important source for this chapter. See Gabriele Radecke, *Vom Schreiben zum Erzählen. Eine textgenetische Studie zu Theodor Fontanes 'L'Adultera'* (Würzburg: Königshausen & Neumann, 2002).

hallmarks that were crucial to the "ruse"[7] of Fontane's realism. Through his practices of notation and composition, he seized control of the conditions of the market that typically put pressure on literary authors, ranging from the formal requirements of periodicity and serialization to the demand to provide a mass readership with fascinating forms of literary entertainment, and made them a conscious part of his working methods.

Perhaps the biggest surprise offered by this chapter is the extent to which Fontane reversed what might strike many as the normal writing process and approached the design of his novels "backwards." Just how deliberate, inorganic, and technique-driven his compositional methods were becomes apparent if we compare them to one of the most radical technical poetics of the nineteenth century, Edgar Allan Poe's "Philosophy of Composition" (1846). Fontane, as far as I know, was not aware of this text, but it nonetheless serves as an illuminating point of comparison. According to Poe's provocative advice, an author should start *not* with a "thesis" or a central plot idea to be developed "from page to page" and through whatever means would "render themselves apparent."[8] This, Poe insisted, was the "radical error" in the "usual mode of constructing a story." Rather, the author should begin with a preconceived aesthetic or epistemological *effect*. According to Poe, this deliberately chosen effect—in his case, an intense feeling to be evoked in the reader—ought to determine how the writer combines his or her poetic means. The desired effect has to guide the creative process on all levels: the choice of topic, setting, and stylistic register, the creation of pretexts that make the effect plausible, and the "cautious selections and rejections" of formulations and ideas, as Poe put it. In short, the effect ought to guide the countless decisions that together make up the hard work of writing, and push the writer to a level at which all the details of a chosen design interlock.

As we shall see, this is more or less how Fontane proceeded—he too put the effect first. In his case, the desired effect was the illusion of a social reality. The poetic means that he deliberately combined consisted mainly of elements of the "popular style"[9] of his age that he culled from several media realms—theatrical stock characters, narrative scenes

---

7   Robert C. Holub deploys this notion in his analysis of realist poetics in *Reflections of Realism: Paradox, Norm, and Ideology in Nineteenth-Century German Prose* (Detroit: Wayne State University Press, 1991), 35.
8   Edgar Allan Poe, "The Philosophy of Composition," in *Literary Criticism of Edgar Allan Poe*, ed. Robert L. Hough (Lincoln: University of Nebraska Press, 1965), 20–1.
9   Martin Meisel, *Realizations: Narrative, Pictorial, and Theatrical Arts in Nineteenth-Century England* (Princeton, NJ: Princeton University Press, 1983).

inspired by domestic genre imagery, historical anecdotes, idioms, gossip, and human interest stories, to name but a few key ingredients of his drafts. He blended these elements, superimposing the aesthetics and communicative modes of different source media upon one another, and produced complex aesthetic effects through which his novels could compete with the periodical press, their primary publishing environment. Because literature now typically appeared first in outlets in which it had to seek the readers' attention while vying with large-format images, news stories from around the world, scandals, puzzles, and other kinds of stimulation and divertissement (see Chapter 1), Fontane developed aesthetic strategies that produced sophisticated and entertaining reality effects. These strategies ensured that his novellas and novels would counter the lure of the periodical with a refined and even more alluring mixed media aesthetic of their own.

The analysis of Fontane's writing media and draft materials warrants the revision of long-held beliefs about his creative process and about the power of writing in general as a recording medium (*Aufzeichnungsmedium*) and cultural practice. Fontane himself promulgated the Romantic myth that he wrote each first draft in a sort of frenzy, in an "eruptive flow of narration,"[10] only to spend weeks tinkering with the style, as expressed in his often-quoted maxim, "Style is painted on [later]" (*der Stil wird angeputzt*, BaF 38). Through her extensive textual-genetic analysis of the drafts for *L'Adultera*, Gabriele Radecke has already provided important corrections to this picture. Debunking the myth of the frenzy, she characterizes Fontane's working methods as consistently purposeful and deliberate and distinguishes four consecutive stages in his creative process: the "productive phase of gathering ideas and material," the "productive phase of planning and preparation" (*Dispositions- und Entwurfsphase*), the "productive and reproductive first draft," and the "reproductive and receptive phase of revision,"[11] with the last stage being extremely laborious. Her analysis, however, envisions literary texts as developing in a linear fashion—the text gradually gravitates away from its sources and becomes increasingly autonomous and artistic with every new stage. But further analysis shows that one can neither separate the four stages quite so sharply nor fully map them onto the logic of linear development. Fontane's writing process was much more inorganic. In his drafts, text sections and components in varying stages of refinement were brought together—Figure 4.1, for example, shows how Fontane has pasted

---

10 Berbig, "Mediale Textprozesse," 104.
11 Radecke, *Vom Schreiben zum Erzählen*, 73–90.

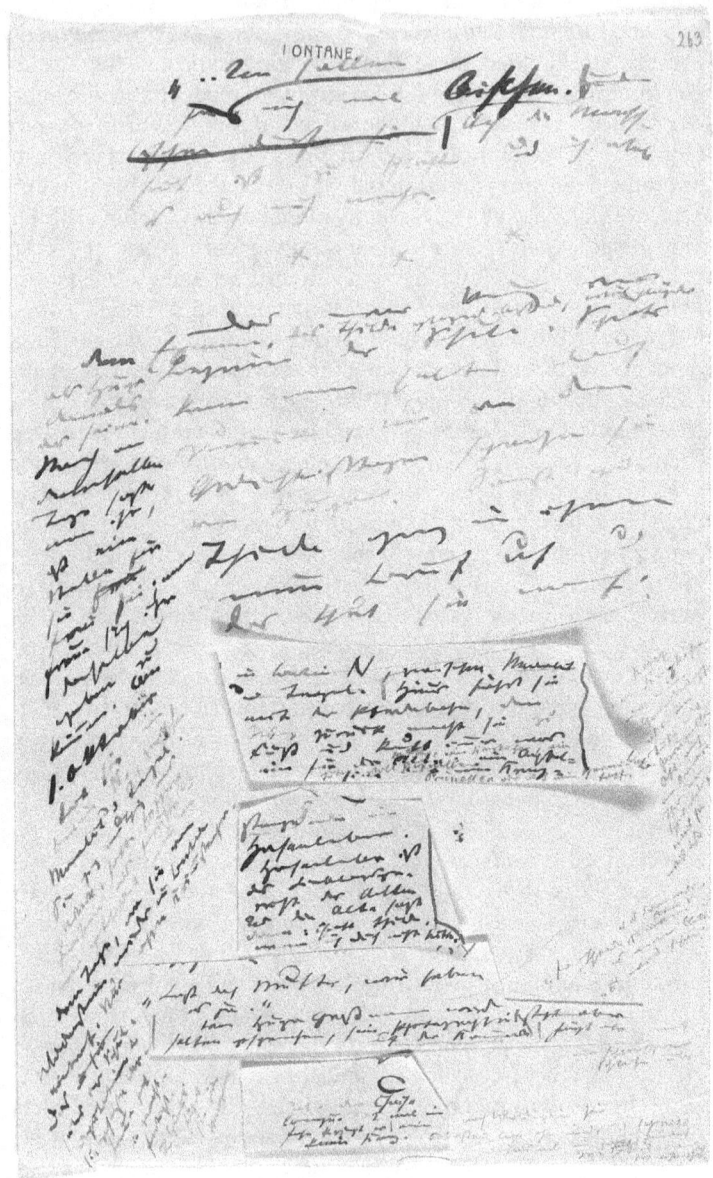

Figure 4.1 Manuscript page from Fontane's unfinished novel *Mathilde Möhring*, showing his practice of pasting notes directly into advanced drafts.

pieces of a notebook page containing snippets and keywords into developed prose on a manuscript sheet. Even his advanced drafts participated in an ongoing exchange with the archive and, through the archive, with the surrounding media scene.

Rather than thinking of Fontane's writing process as a self-contained procedure moving forward in distinct steps, one ought to envision it as an ongoing process of mediation and material remixing that took place in recursive loops. Fontane continued to oscillate between his archive and market forces on the one hand and his dispositions and drafts on the other, all the while making momentous changes and swapping in components from his archive or removing them as he saw fit.

Fontane's creative process, then, treated writing as an inscription practice geared toward recombination and reordering. His notes suggest a rich notion of writing that is not characterized by linearity. Such a notion provides an important corrective to what has become a default view of writing in media and literary studies. Ever since Walter Ong and Marshall McLuhan analyzed alphabetic script, the impact of writing as a cultural practice has been assessed in terms of the consequences that linearity—the "arrangement of signs into rows that must be grasped ordinally"[12]—had on the human faculties of perception and the cultural, political, and economic organization of societies. But more recent theories of writing, such as that of J. D. Peters in *The Marvelous Clouds*, argue that McLuhan's pronounced emphasis on linearity is historically shortsighted, because writing always has been more about storing and reordering data than about linear progression, and that this manipulation of data is where its true cultural impact lies. After all, the earliest forms of writing in ancient Mesopotamia were essentially databases: they were lists of goods to be inventoried, divided, and distributed. Thinking about writing predominantly in terms of linearity, then, misses "what's most important about writing as a medium: the temporal reversibility that spatialization makes possible," as Peters puts it. Fontane's working notes provide powerful evidence for this revised understanding of writing as a nonlinear recording medium. An analysis of these notes can not only offer a better understanding of his personal creative process, but also exorcise one of the most obstinate notions that Romanticism has bestowed upon posterity—the notion that "to write" as a literary author is to dip the pen in ink and let thoughts and narratives "flow" from page to page.

---

12   John Durham Peters, *The Marvelous Clouds: Towards a Philosophy of Elemental Media* (Chicago: University of Chicago Press, 2015), 304.

Paper Tools as Interface and the Formatting of Fontane's Notes

The market was a capricious patron, and what it would favor was hard to predict. "The market prescribes neither a particular semantics nor a particular form. It demands them if they are available—or not, as the case may be—and the motives underlying this demand are complex," as Gustav Frank explains.[13] Although several decades before Fontane, writers such as Ludwig Tieck had still been able to take occasional refuge from the market and live on patronage, this model of financing one's writerly existence was no longer an option. By the mid-1860s, the market ruled, and with its rule came all kinds of vagaries. Publishing opportunities arose spontaneously and across all sorts of genres. Periodicals and other print products established a confounding multitude of publishing rhythms and complex temporalities—for example, the journal *Ueber Land und Meer* came out in six simultaneous editions in 1884: in four differently priced variations of a weekly folio edition, in a biweekly folio edition, and in a biweekly "salon edition" in a smaller format and altogether different layout.[14] Most significantly, however, the market offered absolutely no guarantees that a writer's efforts would be rewarded, or that the time and work invested in a project would have any bearing on the price the author could ask for it.[15]

Fontane's writing media, methods of notation, and techniques of composition proved an effective fit for these challenging conditions. The particular capacities of his writing media become visible when they are viewed in light of a concept derived from software studies: *interfaces*. Generally speaking, an interface is a contact surface at the boundary between different realms. In computing, interfaces are "the point of juncture between different bodies, hardware, users, and what they connect to and are part of," as Florian Cramer and Matthew Fuller put it.[16] They articulate the "asymmetries of power" between the elements conjoined and can help to condition and alleviate these asymmetries and structure workflows. To cite one of Cramer and Fuller's examples,

---

13 Gustav Frank, "Tiecks Epochalität," in *Ludwig Tieck: Leben – Werk – Wirkung*, ed. Claudia Stockinger and Stefan Scherer (Berlin: De Gruyter, 2011), 142.
14 Andreas Graf, "Die Ursprünge der modernen Medienindustrie: Familien- und Unterhaltungszeitschriften der Kaiserzeit (1870–1918)," in *Geschichte des deutschen Buchhandels im 19. und 20. Jahrhundert*, ed. Georg Jäger, Dieter Langewiesche, and Wolfram Siemann (Frankfurt a. M.: MVB, 2003), 1.2:412.
15 See Rolf Parr, *Autorschaft. Eine kurze Sozialgeschichte der literarischen Intelligenz in Deutschland zwischen 1860 und 1930* (Heidelberg: Synchron, 2008), 35.
16 Florian Cramer and Matthew Fuller, "Interface," in *Software Studies: A Lexicon*, ed. Matthew Fuller. (Cambridge, MA: MIT Press, 2008), 150.

when a software program interfaces with the hardware of a personal computer, it limits the options of the computer as a universal machine in such a way that the computer acts like a specialized machine, such as a word processor. One might also think of a search engine as an interface that mediates "between the user and the data being sought."[17] Fontane's notebooks and other paper tools acted as interfaces both in the general sense and in the sense related to computing. Containing materials culled from mass media and literary drafts, calculations of a novella's length and its expected fees, the addresses of correspondence partners and the names of publishers, these paper tools constituted a contact surface that mediated between different realms: his working methods, his material repository, his publishing goals, and the literary marketplace. Moreover, the notebooks and paper tools interfaced with the materials that Fontane stored in his archive (his "data") by way of a particular spatial and visual formatting of the notes. What would otherwise have been a mass of entries thus amounted to a *versatile* and *convertible stock of textual building blocks* that made it easier to respond to the quickly changing demands of the market. The formatting of the entries helped Fontane attenuate the asymmetries of power between the literary marketplace and his own creative process; it facilitated a workflow through which he reconciled the formal constraints and unpredictable temporalities of the publishing industry with the heavy materiality and at times sluggish nature of his writing.

We have already seen that the materials in Fontane's storage media were not tied to a binding order; rather, they were mobile units to be individually selected and retrieved. Surveying the abundance of entries in terms of their formal features, it becomes possible to nuance this description: Fontane's preferred techniques of notation kept the contents of his storage media in a noncommittal yet lightly patterned state that increased his writerly versatility. Mere notebook entries and materials stored on folio sheets turned into *copia*, a multitude of available elements with a "capacity for elaboration and variation,"[18] which enabled him to use the same items for different tasks and purposes. In other words, when Fontane noted down material for later use, he achieved a simultaneity of structure and openness. The fact that materials were lightly structured (as opposed to entirely raw) sped up text production, for it meant that Fontane did not have to start from

---

17 Ibid., 151.
18 John Guillory, "The Memo and Modernity," *Critical Inquiry* 31 (Autumn 2004): 123.

scratch when a publishing opportunity arose. Rather, he could convert and combine existing materials from his archive. The noncommittal nature of his stored entries, moreover, ensured that he could mobilize them for more than one opportunity. For example, notes on the city of Copenhagen in the Notebook D 2, taken on a trip in September 1864, could be used for the travelogue "Kopenhagen" in Cotta's *Morgenblatt* (March 12, 1865), yet they could just as well be used to color the setting of the 1891 novel *Irretrievable* (*Unwiederbringlich*). Similar patterns run through Fontane's creative process across all genres. The materials first generated for the *Wanderungen* frequently did double duty in providing historical figures, descriptions of localities and buildings, legends, anecdotes, and general historical background that were recycled in novels and novellas. The working titles of several of his draft materials for explicitly fictional projects indicate their generic nature. Titles such as "Novella (Brother, Sister, Man)," "Novel or Novella. An Amusing Character," and "Dialogue Materials in Good Berlin Society"[19] (*Dialogstoffe in guter Berliner Gesellschaft*) document how frequently Fontane refrained from allocating ideas to specific projects and opted instead to note them down as uncommitted elements in the interest of increased versatility. This characteristic of his note-taking technique became particularly important in the build-up to the year 1878 and afterward, when Fontane finally published his first novel, *Before the Storm* (*Vor dem Sturm*) and found the courage to make the leap into becoming a freelance novelist. The materials that would allow him to open up "a small novelist's shop" (HFA IV.2: 572) now became increasingly important.

Three notational forms in particular helped Fontane to keep his materials in the desired state of convertibility: lists, discrete bounded entries, and compact drawings. Operating between text and image, all three forms of notation break up the discursive order of writing and divide the material into individual portions that are visually comprehensible, easily movable, convertible, and expandable. They facilitated the "pharmaceutical" core operations—"separation," "breaking down," "mixing," and "transplantation" (*zertrennen, zersetzen, vermischen und versetzen*)—that Fontane learned and internalized during his first professional training (see Chapter 2) and that were at the heart of his creative practice. At the same time, the lists, bounded entries, and compact drawings strengthened the recombinatorial potential and database function of writing, providing the material conditions for textual creation as remix. In practice, these forms cannot be separated so strictly. They usually appear in combination, such as in a sequence of numbered

---

19 These draft materials are reprinted in F1: 267, 394–5.

modular entries that constitute a list. The specifics of their functionality for Fontane's creative process and their poetic implications, however, become clearer when they are analyzed separately.

Lists constitute the most pervasive form of notation in Fontane's storage media. Their formal features have poetic implications that are best understood by analyzing what makes lists into special kinds of scripts. As a "response to the stupefaction of so many things to know,"[20] the list stands like no other type of entry for the abundance of data that the nineteenth century, with its emphasis on historical collecting, statistics, archival documentation, and cataloguing, made available in unprecedented quantities. By definition abstract and reductive forms, lists bring together contents that may share no properties other than being listed together.[21] What is in a list has been excised from its original context and can thus easily be reordered, moved around, cut out, or expanded. Lists therefore lay out new potential combinations and connections among the accumulated items, and they also invite associative continuation.[22] Several entries in Fontane's notebooks document that his lists inspired him to expand on them; for example, in Notebook A 5, the brief items on a list documenting the interior of "Freienwalde Palace" (*Schloß Freienwalde*) grow in size as the list keeps going, while Fontane switches from terse keywords to a narrative description in coherent prose (16R–19V).[23] Vertical lists, moreover, lend a graphic dimension to the listed items and put them in proportional relations, such as top and bottom; first, second, third; left and right; or layers of indentation.[24] They therefore insert graphic features—or, in Sibylle Krämer's words, "notational iconicity"[25]—into the script on a notebook page, break up the predominantly discursive order of written text, and assist in organizing content graphically (Figure 4.2).

The many different lists in Fontane's notebooks show the pervasiveness of the form. They appear as stand-alone entries with

---

20 Peters, *The Marvelous Clouds*, 9.
21 Sabine Mainberger, *Die Kunst des Aufzählens. Elemente zu einer Poetik des Enumerativen* (Berlin: De Gruyter, 2003), 19–20.
22 Ibid., 7.
23 Hettche analyzes this phenomenon in light of Fontane's novel project *Before the Storm* and sees in it the basis for Fontane's literary technique of letting the characters, dialogues, and plots describe "themselves," without the palpable mediating instance of a narrator. See "Handschriften zu *Vor dem Sturm*," 201–2.
24 Jack Goody, *The Domestication of the Savage Mind* (Cambridge, MA: Cambridge University Press, 1977), 81.
25 Sybille Krämer, "Writing, Notational Iconicity, Calculus: On Writing as a Cultural Technique," *MLN* 118, no. 3 (April 2003): 519.

Figure 4.2 A typical Fontanean list, in Fontane's Notebook C 1.

their own headings (A 2, 40V–41V) or as parts of other entries (A 10, 25R–29R); their length varies from one (A 6, 2R) to seventy items (E 2, 29R–40R); they come in vertical and horizontal orientations, with numbers, letters, or a combination thereof marking individual items (A 5, 58R); they have indentations that can be several layers deep (A 6, 16R–20R); they grow as legends around drawings; and they provide structure for longer entries (A 3, 36R–40V). The items in a list can be simple keywords, phrases, complete sentences, or entire paragraphs (A 9, 47R–54V). Fontane deployed lists indiscriminately, regardless of whether he was composing the proverbial shopping list (A 10, 2V–3R), noting down the names of seasonal plants (E 4, 8R–9R), or describing the character traits of a protagonist (E 3, 14V).

There is no indication that Fontane's lists belong to the realm of deskwork, nor can they simply be attributed to fieldwork. Some appear neatly stylized, others hastily written; some are in ink, others in pencil, documenting both spontaneity and careful revision. In fact, it is often impossible for an outside reader to tell without elaborate gumshoe work whether a list records Fontane's personal impressions or contains knowledge gleaned from others. While he was lax about documenting his sources anyway, the reductive form of the list cut off even more contextual clues, so that the culled materials and Fontane's own thoughts at times become indistinguishable. The list, then, acted as an equalizer on the recorded materials, eradicating differences in provenance. They thus fostered a central aspect of Fontane's notion of originality, namely, the liberality with which he blended what was and was not his own invention.

The strength of the form cannot be sufficiently explained through the dynamic features of Fontane's archive alone, although the list, in its malleability, is highly suitable to unstable systems of order.[26] The list's pervasive presence is due to a fundamental influence that Lorraine Daston has called "the template function of reading."[27] Note-taking binds together the practices of observing and reading, Daston writes, and in the key analogy of her contribution, she likens the excerpting of quotations from a running text to the practice of cropping "short, pithy facts from the continuum of experience." From this perspective, Fontane's enumerations and lists are the writerly correlate of his practice of "brutal" reading (see Chapter 3): just as he traversed newspapers on the hunt for passages to be strung together, he riveted his attention on the pieces of interior design in a Brandenburg palace, which he accommodated under a shared heading. Considering the foundational importance of reading in Fontane's creative process, it becomes quite clear that reading determined how and what he noted. The notebooks, in other words, extended the textual practices of Fontane-the-reader beyond the desk.

One of the most salient examples of the formative influence of Fontane's textual practices on his perception can be found in Notebook C 1, which he used during a trip through the Rhine Valley in 1865 (Figure 4.2). His description of Cologne is the result of a hybrid between deskwork and fieldwork. While his observations are rigorously cast in list form, with the lists running over multiple alphabetical bullet points and eventually branching out into two layers of indentation, they are still written diary-style, as a glance at the beginning (C 1, 12R) indicates:

---

26 One of the best examples is yet again contained in Fontane's Notebook A 5. The complex of notes around the towns of "Freienwalde" and "Cunersdorff" repeatedly uses lists to lay down preliminary configurations of the accumulated material, yet as Fontane absorbed more and more, the lists shifted and changed. See 5V–6R, 29R, 51V, 57V, 82R.
27 Lorraine Daston, "Taking Note(s)," *Isis* 95, no. 3 (September 2004): 444.

	Koeln. Hôtel Disch. Montag d. 28. [12] a. <u>Minoriten</u>-Kirche. Gottesdienst. Blick hinein. Der betende Blaukittel am Eingang. b. Museum <u>Wallraf-Richartz</u>. Entrée 7 ½. Die römischen (meist in Cologne gefundenen) Alterthümer: Votivsteine, Grabdenkmäler, Büsten, Münzen, Mosaikfußboden, Steinsärge etc. Auch die permanente Bilder⸗Ausstellung gesehn. c. „Groß-<u>Martin</u> Kirche" von außen gesehn. d. Zur Table d'hôte. Der ^{anekdoten⸗erzählende} Direktor des Wallraf⸗Mu
	Cologne. Hotel Disch. Monday 28th. [12] a. <u>Friars Minor</u> Conventual Church. Service. Glanced inside. The bluejacket praying by the entrance. b. <u>Wallraf-Richartz</u>-Museum. Entrance 7 ½. The Roman (found mostly in Cologne) antiquities: votive tablets, tombstones, busts, coins, mosaic floors, stone sarcophagi etc. Also saw the permanent collection of paintings. c. "Great St. <u>Martin</u> Church" seen from outside. d. To the table d'hôte. The ^{anecdote-telling} Director of the Wallraf⸗Mu

Generating Output 197

The subsequent entries on this list, moreover, contain remarks on his personal impressions of certain paintings and show other signs of spontaneity, such as clumsy formulations, erroneous punctuation, and inconsistencies in verb tenses. Regardless of the specific textual sources to which the structure of his Cologne notes may be attributed, the point stands that reading practices left their imprint on Fontane's techniques of notation, molding his impressions—even the personal ones—into the highly artificial list form. Fontane's reading practices, manifest in his notational techniques, thus contributed to the formal flexibility of the material underside of his text production.

Discrete bounded entries, the second important form of notation in Fontane's paper cosmos, also introduce iconicity into the order of script, presenting comprehensible portions of material and thus inviting the recombinant patching-together of text. Yet in contrast to lists, they do not suggest any modifiable preliminary internal order. Rather, they are stand-alone entries in modular form that frequently bear their own headings and are clearly distinguishable from other entries through horizontal or vertical lines, circles, empty space, or changed text direction (Figure 4.3).

While this formatting is not unusual—one finds a very similar use of horizontal lines as dividers between compact entries in, for

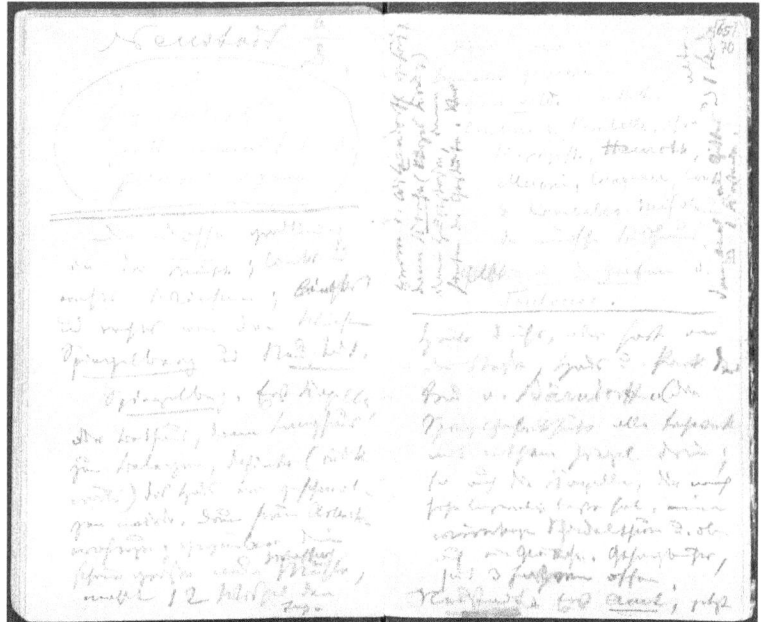

Figure 4.3 Modular entries, delineated with thick pen strokes, in Fontane's Notebook A 2.

example, Keller's literary notebooks,[28] Nietzsche's miscellaneous jottings,[29] and Kafka's *Oktavhefte*[30]—the extent to which Fontane reflected on and encouraged these formal features is unique. In a note to himself, he called such entries "elements" (*Elemente*, A 12, 140R), highlighting with this technical term their propensity to be put together or integrated into a larger project-in-the-making. In addition to personal handwritten entries in this modular form, the notebooks hold plenty of text portions that Fontane either copied or clipped directly from books, letters, catalogs, and newspapers (e.g., A 8, 30V; E 6, 6R, 10R–10V, 52R, 68R–68V). Clippings and handwritten modular entries follow essentially the same logic. Through sharp cuts, realized either with a pair of scissors or through horizontal dividing lines, they homogenize the material. The sharp cuts, in turn, at once separate entries from one another and enable new connections, thus making it possible for the compiler to put entries together like tiles.[31] On the level of the content, the beginnings and endings of the modular entries correspond to the sharp cuts. Rather than establishing thematic or logical cohesion, they are frequently confined to content-free adverbs of time that can form a rough sequence, such as "first," "then," "now" (*erst, dann, nun*). Logical connectors or moments of thematic cohesion occur much more rarely and at times even receive separate entries (A 5, 51V, 82V). Through these homogenizing features, the modular entries and clippings contribute to the convertibility and instability of the material repository on which Fontane's production is based.

Finally, *drawings* provided Fontane with a fully visual means of recording and organizing data in his notebooks. There are two main kinds of drawings: sketches—mostly elevation views and sectional views of buildings and smaller objects (e.g., a chalice in a church or the coat of arms of a noble family)—and diagrams. In these drawings,

---

28 For example, see Gottfried Keller, Notizbuch Ms. GK 70, *Sämtliche Werke. Historisch-Kritische Ausgabe*, ed. Walter Morgenthaler (Zurich: Stroemfeld/Verlag Neue Zürcher Zeitung, 2001), 16.2:221–58.

29 For example, see Friedrich Nietzsche, Notizbuch N-VI-2, *Digitale Faksimile-Gesamtausgabe* (DFGA), ed. Paolo D'Iorio, Klassik Stiftung Weimar, 2009—, online at http://www.nietzschesource.org/DFGA/N-VI-2.

30 Franz Kafka, Oxforder Oktavhefte 1&2, *Historisch-kritische Ausgabe sämtlicher Handschriften, Drucke und Typoskripte*, ed. Roland Reuß and Peter Staengle (Basel/Frankfurt a.M.: Stroemfeld, 2006–11).

31 My observations on horizontal lines in Fontane's notebooks draw on Malte Kleinwort's essay "Kafkas Querstrich. Der Schreibstrom und sein Ende," in *Schrift und Zeit in Franz Kafkas Oktavheften*, ed. Caspar Battegay et al. (Göttingen: Wallstein, 2010), 37–66.

Fontane's "ways of seeing and knowing"[32] are preserved. They invite us to trace what Fontane, pen in hand, found worth noticing and fixing on paper as he surveyed a landscape, looked at a historical dress, or studied a map. They show that Fontane applied list-driven thinking to the world even when he was drawing; time and again, one notes his impulse to itemize and divide up what he saw into sections or, in Wolfgang Rost's terminology, into "pieces" (*Teile*) and "strips" (*Streifen*). Hence the prominence that is given in the drawings to naturally occurring borders, such as rivers, and to lines and other divisional markers, such as train tracks and bridges.[33] His "ways of seeing and knowing" were driven by divisional gestures, or by the attempt to single out and capture what interested him in ways that made the captured material both usable and manageable.[34]

Each kind of drawing facilitated Fontane's text production in a different way. First, the sketches assisted in producing more finished descriptions by allowing him to record the most basic and characteristic details. As a particularly quick mode of notation, sketches temporarily relieve the mind of having to find words for things that are easy to represent visually but hard to verbalize on the spot. Miniature versions of such sketches even appear as logographic elements in the middle of Fontane's sentences, providing visual clues for verbalization to be carried out later (A 5, 49V; A 6, 30R). Second, the numerous diagrams that accompany descriptions of buildings, parks, towns, and landscapes provide orientation. For this purpose, the self-proclaimed "map aficionado"[35] (*Kartenmensch*) Fontane produced diagrams with floor plans, site plans, maps, and topographical top views of places he read about, visited, or invented (e.g., A 13, 3R; 5R, 10R). Furnished with captions, the diagrams displayed the relative positions of

---

32 Omar Nasim, *Observing by Hand. Sketching the Nebulae in the Nineteenth Century* (Chicago/London: University of Chicago Press, 2013), 14–15.
33 See Wolfgang E. Rost, *Örtlichkeit und Schauplatz in Fontanes Werken* (Berlin: De Gruyter, 1931), 38.
34 Svetlana Efimova suggests a different approach to Fontane's drawings. In a recent essay, she explores them through the lens of Arnheim's theory of perception, arguing that Fontane used text–image hybrids in his note-taking to increase the level of abstraction and order his materials. While this is an interesting perspective, her essay leaves out the established secondary literature on this topic (Rost, Hettche, von Graevenitz) and attributes a static function to the notes. Their poetological impact, however, lies in their contribution to the flexibilization of Fontane's materials. See Svetlana Efimova, "'Man hat hier alles in Bild und Schrift beisammen': Wissenserzeugung in Theodor Fontanes Notizbüchern und Werk," *Zeitschrift für deutsche Philologie* 4 (2017): 501–32.
35 Gerhart von Graevenitz, *Theodor Fontane: ängstliche Moderne. Über das Imaginäre* (Konstanz: Konstanz University Press, 2014), 351.

buildings, roads, hills, and other landmarks, regardless of whether the subject of the description was factual or fictional.[36] They provided the basis for what Graevenitz has called one of Fontane's most important narrative strategies, the translation of maps into vivid, three-dimensional images, and allowed him to describe places from changing perspectives.

Notes from the context of the novella *Grete Minde. Nach einer altmärkischen Chronik* (*Grete Minde: After an Altmark Chronicle*; 1879/1880) provide a compelling example of the transformation of a flat map into a multi-perspectival landscape. It is assumed that Fontane took these notes on an 1878 research trip to the town of Tangermünde, which served as the main setting for his historical novella with its seventeenth-century plot. Exploring the ruins of Tangermünde castle, he drew three diagrams and recorded multiple detailed descriptions of the historic structures and the surrounding landscape (E 5, 7V–13R; figs. 4.4 and 4.5; the third diagram is not reproduced here).

His notes include remarks about the panoramic view that opened up from a particular vantage point, the so-called "sharp corner" (*scharfe Ecke*), a corner of a low drystone wall running between two towers on the rampart. Having marked the spot in one of his diagrams (Figure 4.4), he noted down the following account of the view:

> From this sharp corner, a wonderful vista opens up. Ahead of one directly and almost at one's feet the Elbe, into which "the Tanger" flows from the right-hand side. On the far side broad meadows, on the horizons lines of forest, from which project tall church spires; to the extreme right <u>Buch</u>, then <u>Jerichow</u> with its double towers then <u>Fischbeck</u>, deeper behind <u>Kablitz</u> etc. and then <u>Schönhausen</u>. One cannot possibly see more.

> *Von dieser scharfen Ecke aus erschließt sich einem ein wundervolles Bild. Vor einem unmittelbar und fast zu Füßen die Elbe, von der rechten Seite her mündet 'der Tanger' ein. Drüben weite Wiesenflächen, am Horizonte Waldlinien, aus denen Kirchthurmspitzen hoch hervorragen; am weitesten rechts <u>Buch</u>, dann <u>Jerichow</u> mit Doppelthurm dann <u>Fischbeck</u>, tiefer dahinter <u>Kablitz</u>, etc. und dann <u>Schönhausen</u>. Mehr kann man nicht sehen.*

(E 5, 8V–9R)

Precisely this view has a central function in two key scenes of the published novella. It first appears in the ninth chapter, "Auf der Burg"

---

36 On Fontane's sketches of fictional localities for the novel project *Before the Storm*, see Hettche, "Die Handschriften zu *Vor dem Sturm*," 196.

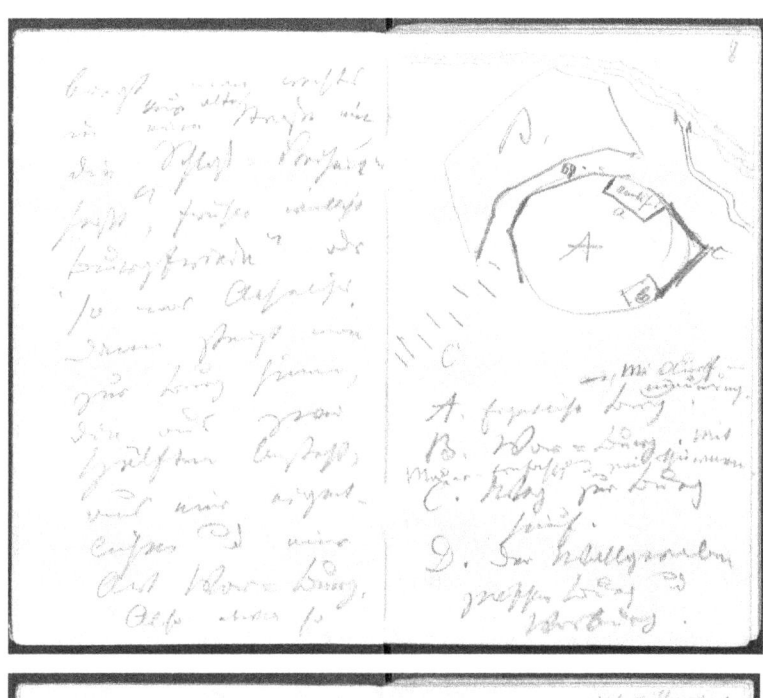

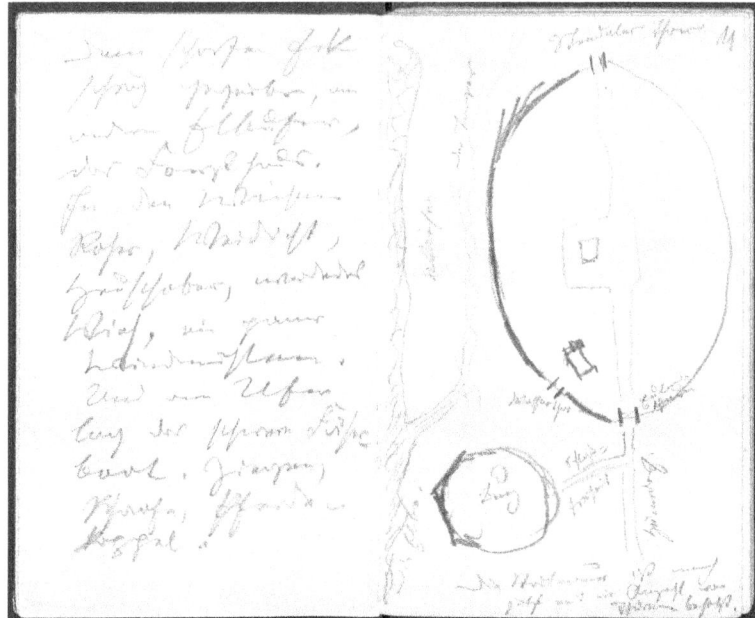

Figures 4.4 and 4.5 Double-pages from Fontane's Notebook E 5 with topographical site plans of Tangermünde castle and Tangermünde.

("On the Castle"), where it causes the heroine, a half-orphan named Grete, to realize that she feels oppressed at home and wants nothing more than to run away. Grete walks up to the castle with her childhood friend and later lover, Valtin, and they sit down on the "sharp corner":

> [U]pon this wall they sat and gazed out into the landscape. At their feet they had the broad river and the narrow Tanger, which joined the river at an acute angle, across however, on the far bank, extended the meadows, behind which lay a line of shadow, from the clearings of which a church spire emerged now and again, gilded by the red gloaming. The sky was blue, the air was fresh; gossamer floated in the wind, and the tinkling of the first homeward bound herds blended with the peals of the evening bell. "Oh, how lovely," said Grete. "It's ages since last I was up here."

> [A]*uf diese Mauer setzten sie sich und sahen in die Landschaft hinaus. Zu Füßen hatten sie den breiten Strom und die schmale Tanger, die spitzwinklig in den Strom einmündete, drüben aber, am andern Ufer, dehnten sich die Wiesen, und dahinter lag ein Schattenstrich, aus dessen Lichtungen hier und dort eine vom Abendroth übergoldete Kirchthurmspitze hervorblickte. Der Himmel blau, die Luft frisch; Sommerfäden zogen, und in das Geläut der ersten heimwärts ziehenden Heerden mischte sich von weit her das Anschlagen der Abendglocke. „Ach, wie schön", sagte Grete. „Jahr und Tag, daß ich nicht hier oben war."*

(GBA I.3: 49)

Stunned by the beauty of this wide and open landscape, Grete realizes that atop the castle, everything is "so fresh and so wide," whereas at home, everything feels "so dull and so close." Fontane amplifies the effect of open space and depth perception by verbalizing what is only implicit in his drawing (Figure 4.4) and his notes. He spells out the contrast between the "broad" river Elbe and the "narrow" Tanger; he finds an evocative adverb, "at an acute angle; cuspidately" (*spitzwinklig*), to describe how the latter flows into the former; he enhances the description of the "meadows" (Figure 4.5) with a verb, "extended" (*dehnten sich*), which lends them agency and underscores their expansiveness; and he staggers the different visual impressions through adverbial phrases such as "on the far bank" (*am andern Ufer*) and "behind which" (*dahinter*). Add heightened contrast between the "line of shadows" and the "clearings," striking colors ("red gloaming"; "gilded spires"), and sounds, both nearby and distant, and the transformation of a flat map into a vivid three-dimensional scene is complete.

This scenic view reappears, yet again with a key function, in the twelfth chapter, "Am Wendenstein," the turning point of the novella. This time, though, the angle has changed. Grete and Valtin go on a walk in the meadows that formed part of their panorama from their vista on the rampart and look from a slightly elevated vantage point—a boulder—back at the castle. The narrator explicitly points out that they encounter "the same image (*dasselbe Bild*) that was before their eyes last fall from the castle and its ramparts" (GBA I.3: 61); the only difference is that the villages, which in the initial image were merely suggested by the church towers showing through the shadowy silhouette of the forest, are clearly identifiable this time. As Valtin and Grete start to name the villages—they get as far as Buch und Fischbeck—they also trade local anecdotes associated with them. One of the anecdotes, revolving around a Fischbeck farmer's son who ran away to follow his true calling to be a pastor, becomes an important justification for Grete's own desire to escape, which she is ever more determined to do. The new/old image—the narrator describes the same scenery from a different direction—indicates, then, that Grete has quite literally changed her perspective. The (modified) repetition of the panoramic view expresses her newly strengthened resolve to run away, and she indeed embarks on her escape with Valtin after a fight with her stepmother in the following chapter. The ease with which Fontane changed the angle from which he presented the panoramic view has its root in the precise diagrams that he used to orient himself during the writing process. They provided the pivot points around which factual and fictional descriptions rotated freely, enabling evocative images, mirror perspectives, and meaningful repetition.

In sum, the formal features of Fontane's various notational techniques—the numbered lists, modular entries, and drawings—helped him maintain his materials in a state of measured convertibility. All three forms break up the discursive order of script, yet they do so without entirely abandoning organization. Rather, the introduction of visual structuring devices, running from iconographic to logographic and purely graphic elements, opens up the material to many more methods of recombination, elaboration, and refinement than an exclusively discursive mode of notation could possibly provide.

Methods of Flexible Textual Production

Fontane's convertible notes facilitated working methods that were well suited to address the particular challenges of the market. For one thing, they enabled him to proceed in the manner of a polygraph and apply consistent rules to the production of texts. With a stock of eminently usable ingredients at hand, the author could follow "recipes" when he transformed the input in his archive into an outflow. Wilhelm Hauff's satire "Die Bücher und die Lesewelt" ("Books and the World of Reading") ridicules such recipes, and Fontane himself had reservations about formula-driven mass production (see Chapter 1). Nevertheless, recipes came into play in straightforward fashion when he compiled low-stakes contributions to the periodical press. Across his letter exchanges, one finds several of these recipes, all demonstrating his process of breaking down the production of standard texts into a clearly defined course of action that generated text from preproduced elements. For example, in a letter to Friedlaender, Fontane spells out and even itemizes the steps that his friend should take to efficiently produce a lecture on theater history: "I propose, having always done accordingly in the same situation, a. Introduction / b. Disposition. Skeleton. / c. Draping that skeleton with material from the encyclopedia (*Behängung dieses Skeletts mit Conversationslexikonmaterial*) and / d. Adorning the drapery with anecdotes from the lives of famous artists (*Ornamentierung dieses Behangmaterials mit Anekdoten aus dem Leben berühmter Künstler und Künstlerinnen*)" (HFA IV.3: 514). Fontane's archive kept everything that he needed for steps "c" and "d" at hand. Such text-generating programs also existed for the production of *Wanderungen* episodes.[37] This mechanized practice left its mark on the quality of some of Fontane's feuilletonistic writings. At times, the reader encounters the patchwork's obvious seams, for example in the "typically Fontanean" transitional sentences with which he moves from one topic or subsection of an article to the next.[38] Phrases such as "Let us dispose of a few remarks on . . . in advance" (*Wir schicken einige Bemerkungen über . . . voraus*), "Just a few words on this" (*Hierüber nur ein paar Worte*), and "So much for the description of . . ." (*Damit wäre . . . beschrieben*) at the beginning or the end of subsections put the structure of the articles on display[39] and make a virtue out of a necessity, though they are sometimes quite clumsy. Moreover, large parts of the *Wanderungen* are very repetitive in content and textual design, following the same contrastive pattern that Jens Bisky has described as an "on the one hand/on the other hand structure."[40] At the same time, the mechanized practice

---

37 For example, see Fontane's letter to Mathilde von Rohr from July 4, 1864, in which he explicitly speaks of the "Rezept" according to which he plans to put a new episode together. BaR, 45.
38 Clarissa Blomqvist points out that this "explizite Überleiten" is one of the most striking features of Fontane's unique prose style and "tone." See Clarissa Blomqvist, "Der Fontane-Ton. Typische Merkmale der Sprache Theodor Fontanes," *Sprachkunst. Beiträge zur Literaturwissenschaft* 35, no. 1 (2004): 23–34.
39 Ibid., 29.
40 Jens Bisky, "Zur Verlagsgeschichte der 'Wanderungen durch die Mark Brandenburg' 1860–1945. Mit einer kommentierten Bibliographie," *Berliner Hefte zur Geschichte des literarischen Lebens* 1 (1996): 114.

based on convertible notes helped Fontane make a living by sustaining productivity across several genres. When it came to longer, more complex writings, the convertible notes proved helpful because they facilitated uneven, inorganic project development, which in turn permitted Fontane to accommodate the vagaries and irregular temporalities of the market. On the one hand, he was able to move multiple projects at once to the front burner and pursue them simultaneously; for example, while he worked on *Before the Storm*, he also compiled his three massive *Kriegsbücher*, continued to produce episodes for the *Wanderungen*, and regularly published theater reviews.[41] Symptomatically, it is often impossible to pinpoint the definite beginnings of individual projects; it is unclear when exactly he began the production for the novel *L'Adultera* and the novella *Ellernklipp*, to cite but two examples.[42] On the other hand, Fontane was able to wait out longer interruptions. The drafts for *Stine*, for example, lay dormant for a long time, until he found a publishing opportunity.[43]

Possibly the most important feature of his convertible notes, however, is that they allowed Fontane to maintain control of the cost-benefit relationship of his work on novels. Fontane generated rough drafts with the help of a built-in stop mechanism that prevented him from investing too much effort in the laborious procedure of polishing his loosely coupled projects if reliable revenue was not in sight: He reserved a special receptacle, one of his *Kasten*, for storing drafts that were sufficiently advanced to be pitched to publishers. Here his higher-stakes projects awaited decision; the *Kasten* marked the limit of the time and labor Fontane would invest in a project without knowing about its success. One can infer as much from his letter to Julius Grosser, the editor of the magazine *Nord und Süd*, to whom he offered the novella project *A Man of Honor* (*Schach von Wuthenow*):

> I have six or seven novellas completed as drafts and must first set about straightening out and cleaning up these things lying in my drawer [*Kasten*] before turning to new business. Might I propose one of these novellas to you? It is called "*Schach von Wuthenow*," is set in the years 1805 to 6 and describes the *handsomest* officer in the Berlin garrison at that time, who, in a fit of high spirits and whimsy, courts the most charming, but also the ugliest lady in Court circles at that time. . . . All true, as it happens.

---

41 See the editorial commentary on *Vor dem Sturm*, GBA I.2: 393–408.
42 Radecke, *Vom Schreiben zum Erzählen*, 51n160.
43 See Helmuth Nürnberger and Dietmar Storch, "Brouillon," in *Fontane-Lexikon: Namen – Stoffe – Zeitgeschichte*, ed. Helmuth Nürnberger and Dietmar Storch (Munich: Hanser, 2007), 76.

> *Ich habe sechs oder sieben Novellen im Brouillon fertig und muß nun erst an das Glatt- und Saubermachen dieser im Kasten liegenden Dinge gehn, bevor ich mich Neuem zuwende. Darf ich Ihnen eine dieser Novellen proponieren? Sie heißt* "Schach von Wuthenow", *spielt in der Zeit von 1805 auf 6 und schildert den schönsten Offizier der damaligen Berliner Garnison, der, in einem Anfall von Uebermuth und Laune, die liebenswürdigste, aber häßlichste Dame der damaligen Hofgesellschaft becourt. . . . Uebrigens alles Thatsache.*
>
> (HFA IV.3: 175–6)

Thanks to its integrated stop mechanism, this particular *Kasten* gave Fontane room to accommodate a publisher's wishes without great losses on his part, as he did, for example, with *Grete Minde*. While the rough version contained drafts for a chapter that was supposed to depict the heroine's life among "unsteady people," Fontane left this chapter out of the later version for the sake of "condensing" (*Comprimirung*, BaH 190), for he knew that Rudolf Lindau, the prospective publisher, was a "sworn enemy of the 'to be continued'"[44] (*geschworener Feind des "Fortsetzung folgt"*) and had a strong preference for compact novellas. In this case, the *Kasten* allowed Fontane to polish only as much material as he could reliably sell. What is more, when Fontane did not manage to sell off a project at all, it could go back into the convertible stock and become integrated into other projects. This feature was crucial to Fontane's working methods, for it protected him against the waste of precious resources. Rather than discarding the text sections he had already produced and roughly patched together, Fontane could unravel and recycle them. The fate of the novel project "Allerlei Glück", Fontane's first attempt at a social novel (*Gesellschaftsroman*), provides a clear example of this economical practice. When Fontane could not sell it, he eventually removed it from the *Kasten*, threw it back into the repository, and used its components for a whole range of other projects, from *A Man of Honor* to *The Stechlin* (*Der Stechlin*).[45]

---

44 The publication history of *Grete Minde* is fully explained in the editorial commentary to the *Große Brandenburger Ausgabe*, which also includes a printing of the disposition for the chapter that Fontane never realized. See GBA I.3: 135–43, 162.

45 In fact, Fontane recycled so much of the prepared material that when a publishing opportunity for "Allerlei Glück" presented itself at long last, Fontane had to decline. See Petra McGillen, "Poetische Mobilmachung im Textbaukasten. Fontanes Listen und die Kunst der Weiterverwendung – der Fall 'Allerlei Glück,'" in *Formen ins Offene. Zur Produktivität des Unvollendeten*, ed. Hanna Delf von Wolzogen and Christine Hehle (Berlin: De Gruyter, 2018), 97–119.

Fontane's writing media and his convertible notes thus enabled him to plan and draft entire novels before he took them to market and had them published in installments. This practice spared him, with one minor exception, the "Keller problem" of having to produce in serial, finishing narratives under mounting time pressure and at the expense of aesthetic perfection. To be sure, writing in serial was not without advantages. Authors who had embraced this mode of production, such as Fontane's English contemporary, Charles Dickens, enjoyed a "more intimate relationship"[46] with readers, who participated in the stories that unfolded from month to month and voiced their opinions about how they should develop. Authors writing in serial, moreover, were in better control of the design of individual installments, whereas Fontane had to live with the consequences when a journal editor cut his novels for publication in ways he did not condone. Yet the well-documented example of Dickens also demonstrates how many compromises writing in serial required. He had to work with two foci, keeping the "design and purpose of the novel ... constantly in view" while also thinking in terms of "the identity of the serial number, which would have to make its own impact and be judged as a unit."[47] Balancing these two requirements did not come easily. In the midst of working on *Nicholas Nickleby*, Dickens admitted: "The devil of it is, that I am afraid I must spoil a number now and then, for the sake of the book. It's a hard case, but I *ought* to be hard as iron to my own inclinations and do so."[48] Over the years, Dickens developed complex modes of self-administration that helped him reconcile the production of individual numbers with the grand design of the book. He began devising "number plans" (Figure 4.7, p. 227) that listed the key points of the plot and main characters for each installment, serving simultaneously as outlines for what he still had to produce and records of what he had already done.[49] The number plans thus helped him maintain an overview of the unfolding story and tie together the many loose ends of a given narrative to "work the story round"[50] as it neared its close.

---

46 John Butt and Kathleen Tillotson, *Dickens at Work* (London: Methuen, 1957), 15–16.
47 Ibid., 15.
48 Dickens to Thomas Mitton, April 7, 1839, *The Letters of Charles Dickens*, ed. Madeline House and Graham Storey, vol. 1, 1820–1839 (Oxford: Oxford University Press, 1965), 540.
49 Dickens started to design his novels more systematically with *Martin Chuzzlewit*, and by the time of *Dombey and Son*, his method of working with "number plans" had fully evolved. The plans are reprinted, with illuminating commentary, in Harry Stone, ed., *Dickens' Working Notes for his Novels* (Chicago: University of Chicago Press, 1987).
50 Stone, introduction to *Dickens' Working Notes*, xvii.

Fontane, however, still preferred writing whole books, for he was convinced that writing in serial yielded aesthetically unsatisfactory results. His characterization of Dickens's method reveals as much. In a review, Fontane pronounced that writers like Dickens and Thackeray "'spin their yarn,' as the characteristic phrase goes, and thread any number of pearls as well as glass beads (*echte und unechte Perlen*) onto it. The thread having reached a given length, it occurs either to the readers and publishers or, ideally, to the author that it might be time to bring matters to a close" (HFA III.1: 296). According to Fontane's characterization, the serial novelist then tied both ends of the thread quickly together and called this a "rounding-off and conclusion" (*Abrundung und Abschluß*). Fontane's own standards for a "round" conclusion were higher, however. He insisted on developing whole books because he intended to design powerful aesthetic effects that involved the *entire* novel. Creating a comprehensive effect, or *Wirkung*, was the ultimate goal of his poetics, but doing so required that he be able to manipulate all of the parts—beginning, middle, end, setting, figures, dialogue, leitmotif, etc.—of a given novel freely at all times; otherwise, the countless details would simply not add up. As we shall see in a moment, his method of composition allowed him to do just that—he kept the grand design of the book and the creation of comprehensive realist effects in view from the outset.

In the Engine Room of Realism: Media Crossings in Fontane's Drafts

If Fontane had clear-cut recipes for the production of low-stakes feuilleton articles, it is important to note that he also had a recipe or basic formula—albeit a much less mechanical one—for the composition of novels. This formula, a poetological memo with the title "Die Kunst des Erzählens" ("The Art of Storytelling"), puts the creation of an aesthetic effect front and center, and it also spells out how this effect ought to be achieved: through an interplay among different media. In this memo, written for his eyes only, Fontane noted:

> For all that laws or a standard recipe are sought, the matter really is altogether simple. Essentially, it comes down to much the same as writing a play, and if somebody is able to create people and to make these created people relate to each other naturally, let him write, he knows his business. Just like a play: characters and situations. . . . We must be able to *follow* that which plays itself out before our eyes with glad approval in every moment. It is this ability to follow that counts. One finds oneself drifting down the river in a barge, always stimulated, always satisfied by the images on the shore. Should the cruise stay, should the barge run aground

on a sandbank, then this incident must not last too long; if it lasts only a short time, it may indeed add to the cruise's charm.

Es wird so viel nach Gesetzen, nach einem Normal-Rezept gesucht und doch ist die Sache grundeinfach. Im Wesentlichen läuft es auf dasselbe hinaus wie beim Drama und wer Menschen zu schaffen und diese geschaffenen Menschen in natürliche Beziehungen zu einander zu bringen weiß, der schreibe, der versteht sein Metier. Ganz wie beim Drama: Charaktere und Situationen. . . . Wir müssen dem, was sich da vor uns vollzieht, in jedem Augenblick unter freudiger Zustimmung folgen können. *Auf dies Folgen=können, kommt es an. Man gleitet in einem Kahn den Fluß hinunter, immer angeregt, immer befriedigt durch die Bilder am Ufer. Stockt die Fahrt, geräth der Kahn auf eine Sand-Bank, so darf dieser Zwischenfall nicht zu lange währen; währt er nur kurze Zeit, so kann er den Reiz der Fahrt erhöhen.*

(F1: 429)

Here Fontane envisions the successful novel in terms of its effect on the reader. It is supposed to induce a stream of images that unroll before the reader's inner eye, to invite her to follow along, and to evoke her "glad approval." To create this effect, the novelist ought to enlist the capacities of another medium, the theater, and start with the creation of plausible human characters and "situations." The ideal novel, then, is a hybrid form, half play and half prose narrative, and gently carries the reader away into a credible and agreeable fictional world.

With the help of classical media theory, we can unpack Fontane's condensed formula and fill in what it leaves blank, which is the connection between the interplay among media and the creation of powerful aesthetic effects. As every reader of Marshall McLuhan's *Understanding Media* knows, "the 'content' of any medium is always another medium." "The content of writing," McLuhan explains, "is speech, just as the written word is the content of print, and print is the content of the telegraph."[51] Media, then, "come in pairs, with one acting as the content of the other" and—this is the key point for the creation of effects—concealing the operation of both: "For the 'content' of a medium is like the juicy piece of meat carried by the burglar to distract the watchdog of the mind." In brief, when one medium is given another medium as "content," the effect is made "strong and intense." While most people never penetrate this *modus operandi* of media and simply remain spellbound by what they see, read, or hear, artists, according to

---

51 Marshall McLuhan (1964), *Understanding Media: The Extensions of Man*, critical edition, ed. W. Terrence Gordon (Corte Madeira: Ginko Press, 2003), 19.

McLuhan, are uniquely able to take advantage of this mechanism and "hybridize" different media deliberately to produce powerful aesthetic effects. He then presents an array of innovative artists who understood how to use one medium "to release the power of another," from Frédéric Chopin's adaptation of the pianoforte "to the style of the ballet" to T. S. Eliot's "careful use of jazz and film form" in modernist poetry. Some of his most emphatic praise, however, goes to Charles Dickens and George Bernard Shaw:

> When the press opened up the "human interest" keyboard after the telegraph had restructured the press medium, the newspaper killed the theater, just as TV hit the movies . . . very hard. George Bernard Shaw had the wit and imagination to fight back. He put the press into the theater, taking over the controversies and the human interest world of the press for the stage, as Dickens had done for the novel.
>
> (77)

Fontane's poetological memo indicates that he too should be included in this pantheon of innovative artists who skillfully combined the possibilities of media. Indeed, his drafts show that he blended far more than theater and the novel. The forms he enlisted for his creative purposes and put into his novels were drawn from several overlapping realms of mass media and popular culture. From the stage, Fontane took the compositional unit of the dramatic situation or scene, direct dialogue, stock characters, and the comic device of the "tag" (a frequently repeated quotation that identifies a character); from the realm of mass-produced images, he adopted the domestic genre painting and its conventionalized iconography; from the world of the newspaper, he integrated current events, quotations, indirect speech, political commentary, human interest stories, and gossip; from the twin domains of popular historiography and proto-sociology, he adopted typologies of people, localities, and milieus, along with anecdotes, idioms, and jokes.

An analysis of Fontane's working notes and drafts shows that in the creative process, these elements constituted the key ingredients of his novellas and novels, which thus turned into elaborate and highly effective media hybrids. Three elements in particular typically enjoyed "genetic priority"[52] in Fontane's fiction projects, which is to say that he

---

52 I have adopted this term from Klaus Hurlebusch, "Den Autor besser verstehen: aus seiner Arbeitsweise. Prolegomenon zu einer Hermeneutik textgenetischen Schreibens," in *Textgenetische Edition*, ed. Hans Zeller and Gunter Martens (Tübingen: Niemeyer, 1998), 39.

put them down first when he began to work on a new novella or novel: narrative genre scenes, socially legible types, and what I will term "discursive sound bites," or direct quotations and other striking utterances. These core elements provided not only the initial building blocks of his projects, but also the foundation for the various realist effects he designed. In observing his compositional process, we can thus see that he began not with an overarching idea or plot line (as one might have expected), but with the aesthetic effects that he hoped to realize through deliberate media crossings. Three in-depth examples show concretely how Fontane compounded media forms to assemble novels with genre scenes, typified characters, and discursive sound bites as starting points; why his preferred formats of notation—especially modular entries and lists—mattered for this process; and which realist effects he configured with them.

Example I: Narrative Genre Scenes

Fontane's use of narrative genre scenes at the heart of his drafts is nowhere more apparent than in the working notes for his first novel, *Before the Storm* (1878). This lengthy story describes the mood in Prussia before the Liberation Wars of 1813 through a plot that revolves around two noble families from the Oderbruch region, the von Vitzewitzes and the Ladalinskis, both of which participate in guerilla action against the Napoleonic oppressors. Fontane began his drawn-out creative process, which stretched over more than fifteen years and left its marks in several notebooks, by amassing lists of highly pictorial narrative scenes.[53] These scenes reproduce the aesthetics of mass-produced contemporary genre imagery, exploiting genre painting's capacity to mediate atmospheres and emotions in immediately accessible ways. Genre painting, the "particular trove of imagery from the illustrated family magazines,"[54] offered an iconography and expressive conventions for the representation of "typical" everyday life that was comprehensible to everybody. The "sentimental 'realism'" of domestic genre painting, epitomized by sought-after *Gartenlaube* artists such as Franz Defregger, concerned itself with "descriptions of simple, purely human conditions (*Schilderungen der einfachen rein menschlichen Verhältnisse*), such as are to be found repeated across the world and hence may be understood everywhere".[55]

---

53 For an instructive overview of the genesis of *Before the Storm*, see the editorial commentary by Christine Hehle in GBA I.1: 390–411; Berbig, "Mediale Textprozesse"; and Hettche, "Die Handschriften zu Theodor Fontanes *Vor dem Sturm*."
54 Graevenitz, *Theodor Fontane: ängstliche Moderne*, 361.
55 *Die Gartenlaube* (1885): 284; qtd. in Graevenitz, *Theodor Fontane: ängstliche Moderne*, 402.

It highlighted emotions, atmospheres, and relationships through a visual and affective vocabulary that the beholder easily recognized. By referencing genre imagery, Fontane could tap into this vocabulary to express the emotions and atmospheres that received priority in the early drafts of *Before the Storm*.

He then increased the aesthetic effectiveness of genre imagery even further by combining it with a compositional and perceptual device derived from the stage: the theatrical scene. In his drafts, he worked not just with simple (and static) genre imagery, but with deliberately composed dynamic genre scenes, arranging figures, objects, plot elements, and ambiance into legible and even clichéd configurations that stood on their own and communicated meaning. He thus exploited the dramatic scene's usefulness as both a compositional tool and an effective mode of organizing perception.[56] For Fontane as an author, the scenes generated atmospheric effects and provided units that could easily be moved without destroying their inner composition. At the same time, for the reader of the finished novel, the scenes invited a mode of reading that worked well with (and even increased the attractiveness of) serialized storytelling. The narrative of a serialized novel "was not an endless ribbon to pull . . ., but a series of packets to be opened individually," and "[p]art of their attractiveness was the variety that lay within."[57] A scene thus offered the opportunity to visualize the narrative in bounded segments that could be absorbed and explored, with the reader temporarily slipping into the role of spectator.[58] The scenes' capacity to turn the reader into a spectator afforded opportunities to realize even more complex aesthetic effects, as we shall see in a moment.

One can study the genetic priority and aesthetic functioning of narrative genre scenes in the earliest extant notebook entries on *Before the Storm*, a set of working notes presumably dating to 1862. Under the general heading of "material," Fontane accumulates what he calls "scenes" (*Szenen*) as the basic ingredients of his project. These scenes provide the compositional aesthetic nuclei of the novel. In just a few keywords, they integrate objects, accessories, typified figures, and their characteristic surroundings—the ingredients that were crucial to Fontane's "realist" narratives—into units that help organize the story.

---

56 For an excellent study of the scene as a material and aesthetic technology, see Heiko Christians, *Crux Scenica. Eine Kulturgeschichte der Szene von Aischylos bis YouTube* (Bielefeld: Transcript 2016).
57 Meisel, *Realizations*, 53.
58 See Christians, *Crux Scenica*, 80.

The scenes do not order the narrative in linear or chronological terms, however. Even though the notes begin with a rough timeline, they do not fully sequence the elements of the story, nor do they provide an arc to the plot. Fontane simply amasses a number of atmospheric stills frozen in time, as both the content and the stylistic features (nominal formulations, the sparing use of verbs, and a preference for the present and present perfect tense over the simple past) indicate. The beginning of the entry reads:

Material.
The period between Christmas Eve 1812, and the eve of Easter 1813. Winter landscape, snow. Parsonage.
Half a mile away (locality: mixed aspect, Wuthenow, Kränzlin, etc.) another village with an old nobleman's castle. Something like Friedersdorff and Marwitz. A bit like Marwitz in character, but less severe, many features of Knesebeck. . . .
In Klosterstraße [Abbey Road], a furnished room rented by the 2 friends from the countryside (preacher's son and nobleman's son) and a meeting place for the literary club. (half the Dresden locality, half Jüdenstraße.) . . .
Village characters: the mad joiner who searches the old churchyard for the crock of money. – The man who sees the corpse or sees the parked hearse. –The ghostly reapers. – The Pukerstock [a poem in low German; PM] in Claus Groth, – The black woman (perhaps a better character).
The scenes in the upper class of the grey abbey. Old Bellermann or whatever his name was.
Something of the life of the colony. Their defense [of] why they were so French.
A scene on the ice. A light. People drowning. Rescue.
Three months later: flooded marshland in the Oderbruch area, previously covered by ice.

Material.
Die Zeit vom Weihnachtsheilig ⸗Abend 1812 bis Osterheiligabend 1813. Winter⸗ und Schnee⸗Landschaft. Predigerhaus.
Eine halbe Meile entfernt (Lokalität: gemischte Züge, Wuthenow, Kränzlin etc.) ein andres Dorf mit dem Schloß eines alten Adligen. Etwa Friedersdorff und Marwitz. Charakter Marwitz, aber gemäßigter, viel Züge von Knesebeck. . . .
*In der Klosterstraße eine Chambre garnie für die 2 Freunde vom Lande (Predigersohn und Adelssohn) und Zusammenkunftsort für den literarischen Club. (halb die Lokalität aus Dresden, halb Jüdenstraße.)
. . .*

> *Dorffiguren: der wahnsinnige Tischler, der den Geldtopf auf dem alten Kirchhof sucht. – Der Leichenseher oder der, der den Leichenwagen stehen sieht. – Die gespenstischen Mäher. – Der Pukerstock in Claus Groth. – Die schwarze Frau (vielleicht eine beßre Figur).*
> *Die Scenen in der Prima des grauen Klosters. Der alte Bellermann oder wie sonst er hieß.*
> *Etwas Colonie⹀Leben; ihre Vertheidigung warum sie so französisch waren.*
> *Eine Scene auf dem Eise. Eine Lume. Ertrinkende. Rettung.*
> *Drei Monate später: überschwemmtes Sumpfland in der Oderbruchgegend, vorher durch Eis gedeckt.*
>
> (Notebook A 12, 136R–137R)

Clearly, the scenic elements take priority in this first set of notes, profiling the paradigmatic axis, not the structural or syntagmatic axis, of the story. They structure clusters of types and localities, absorb references to popular literary sources, and arrange them into atmospheric units. (Notice that the "man who sees the corpse" among the "village characters" and the "black woman" relate directly to Fontane's notes on superstition, analyzed in the previous chapter).

In the subsequent entries (A 12, 138R–140V), the pivotal function of genre scenes as devices for the expression of atmospheric effects becomes even more pronounced. Moving through his materials, Fontane modifies almost all of the central components of his project—he divides it up anew, changes the time frame of the story, rewrites the constellation of figures originally centered on two friends with a new emphasis on two pairs of siblings, and notes two different endings. The genre scenes, however, remain undisturbed by these large conceptual shifts. In fact, with a more detailed disposition for the first volume, Fontane even expands the genre scenes, assigning ever more importance to atmospheric elements such as time of day, locality, and mood, while relegating the plot to a comparatively minor position:

> <u>Volume one.</u>
> I. Christmas Eve. Snow. Stars. Lewin. Reveries. Landscape. Arrival. Locality. Nocturnal silence. All quiet in the house. The room. Meta's greeting and little courtesies. He unwraps his gifts and lays them on the table. Sleeps.
>
> II. Morning. The old servant cleaning boots. Stoking the fire from outside in the old tiled oven; the cracking of the big logs and peat cuts. The old servant awakens him. . . . Christmas tree. The old man on the sofa. . . . Coffee by the fireplace. The old man smokes his short pipe. Chit-chat.

Erster Band.
I. Weihnachtsnacht. Schnee. Sterne. Schlitten. Lewin. Träumereien. Landschaftliches. Ankunft. Lokalität. Nachtstille. Alles still im Haus. Das Zimmer. Meta's Grüße und kleine Aufmerksamkeiten. Er packt seine Geschenke aus und legt sie auf den Tisch. Schläft.
II. Der Morgen. Der alte Diener, der die Stiefel putzt. Das Einheitzen von außen in den alten Kachelofen; das Bummsen der großen Scheite und Torfstücke. Der alte Diener weckt ihn. . . . Weihnachtsbaum. Der Alte auf dem Sopha. . . . Der Kaffee am Kamin. Der Alte dampft seine kurze Pfeife. Plaudereien.

(A12, 138V–139R)

It would exceed the limits of this study to reproduce Fontane's entire disposition for the first volume. Suffice it to say that he fleshed out more of the previously accumulated scenes in the same manner and inserted a plethora of additional scenes. Formulations such as "V. The peasant wedding or some other such festivity with as much local color (*Lokalton*) as possible" underline yet again that Fontane did not employ these genre scenes randomly but clearly reflected on their use, mobilizing them as vehicles for the desired effects of "local color" and familiarity. In this function, a set of unchanging atmospheric genre scenes recurs across Fontane's production. Christmas and New Year's Eves, outings, sleigh rides, church visits, weddings, funerals, and dinner parties are staples of Fontane's narratives; they belong to the "vertical" threads, to adopt Renate Böschenstein's felicitous coinage, that run through his various literary projects and that have given rise to a number of *Motivstudien* in Fontane criticism.[59] The prominence of these scenes, as an analysis of the notebooks reveals, is derived from Fontane's textual strategy of organizing his compositional process around them.

If we now turn to a refined genre scene from the published version of *Before the Storm*, we can specify the enhanced aesthetic effects that resulted from Fontane's fusion of genre imagery with the theatricality of the scene. Consider the following example from the opening pages of the novel. The protagonist, young Lewin von Vitzewitz, is traveling in

---

59 Böschenstein speaks of "vertikalen Geschichten" to characterize the basic narrative constellations that occur repeatedly in Fontane's different novels. See Renate Böschenstein, "Namen als Schlüssel bei Hoffmann und Fontane," *Colloquium Helveticum* 23 (1996): 67–91 and "Caecilia Hexel und Adam Krippenstapel. Beobachtungen zu Fontanes Namensgebung," *Fontane Blätter* 62 (1996): 31–57. An example of a "Motivstudie" is Walter Salmen, "'Am Sylvester war Ressourcenball. . .': Tänze und Bälle bei Theodor Fontane," *Fontane Blätter* 88 (2009): 104–26.

a horse-drawn sleigh from Berlin to his family's estate in the countryside. It is Christmas Eve. The scene begins with the coachman and Lewin getting out of the sleigh for a break at a local inn. The scene first and foremost creates an illusion of reality based on the simple principles of repetition and recognition—through Lewin's eyes, the reader encounters an idyllic image of Christmas. Having literally seen this image before, in illustrations of Christmas Eve that circulated in the mass press and constituted one of its visual stock topics, the reader easily acknowledges it as familiar:

> Lewin too had dismounted. He stamped once or twice in the snow as though to set his blood circulating, and then went into the guest-room to warm himself and find something to eat. Inside all was dark and empty; but behind the counter, where three steps led to an alcove higher up, a Christmas tree glittered with lights and golden chains. In a Christmas tableau contained in the narrow space of the room there stood the innkeeper's wife in a bodice and flannel skirt with a little blonde-headed child on her arm reaching out for the lights on the tree; the innkeeper himself stood beside her and gazed upon the happiness that life and this day had bestowed upon him. Lewin was deeply moved at the sight of this tableau: it was almost as though the scene were an apparition. He retreated again more quietly than he had come in....[60]

> *Auch Lewin war abgestiegen. Er stampfte ein paarmal in den Schnee, wie um das Blut wieder in Umlauf zu bringen und trat dann in die Gaststube, um sich zu wärmen und einen Imbiss zu nehmen. Drinnen war alles leer und dunkel; hinter dem Schenktisch aber, wo drei Stufen zu einem höher gelegenen Alkoven führten, blitzte der Christbaum von Lichtern und goldenen Ketten. In diesem Weihnachtsbilde, das der enge Thürrahmen einfaßte, stand die Krügersfrau in Mieder und rothem Friesrock und hatte einen Blondkopf auf dem Arm, der nach den Lichtern des Baumes langte. Der Krüger selbst stand neben ihr und sah auf das Glück, das ihm das Leben und dieser Tag bescheert hatten. Lewin war ergriffen von dem Bilde, das fast wie eine Erscheinung auf ihn wirkte. Leiser als er eingetreten war, zog er sich wieder zurück...*

(GBA I.1: 11–12)

---

[60] Theodor Fontane, *Before the Storm. A Novel of the Winter of 1812–13*. Trans. R. J. Hollingdale (Oxford: Oxford University Press, 1985), 6.

The reader of conservative family magazines is right at home in this image, for it is replete with familiar visual codes, from the lights on the Christmas tree to the representation of the archetypical "German" family in a traditional regional costume. The textually composed image, however, realizes more complex effects that exceed those of simple repetition. As a carefully staged and theatrical scene, it brings the narrative to a halt, inviting the reader to linger and experience a perceptual realism on multiple sensory registers. The scene provides visual stimuli that are enhanced through the dramatic contrast between the dark main room and the sparkling lights in the alcove; in addition, there are acoustic stimuli (an intense sense of quiet) and even visceral ones (Lewin is cold and hungry, and his limbs have gone numb). To the conscious reader, moreover, the entire staging is rendered obvious through frames within frames: through the doorway, Lewin watches the innkeeper look at his wife and child.[61] Finally, the narrator's comment that the whole tableau had almost the effect of "an apparition" (*Erscheinung*) upon Lewin prompts us to read this scene in allegorical terms, as Gerhart von Graevenitz has recently argued. It is an allegory of the "great promise of salvation held out by the Christian family" and anticipates Lewin's own marriage. The emotive, perceptual realism of this generic moment frozen in time is superimposed, then, with a second layer of meaning, in which the beholder's visual curiosity and desire to interpret the ostentatiously familiar image are thematized. Fontane's compounding of genre imagery with the theatrical device of the scene results in a reality effect that toggles between an unmitigated appeal to the reader's sense of familiarity and the self-conscious doubling of this process.

This comprehensive effect is possible because of the plethora of connections to mass-produced genre paintings that appear all throughout Fontane's working notes. The exchange between his creative process and popular visual culture, then, happened much more directly than the recent scholarship has recognized. Graevenitz, who knows Fontane's image worlds like no other but does not include the working notes in his study, cautions against setting up "simple correlations" between Fontane's literary imagination and circulating genre imagery: "A schematic and deterministic 'media realism,' which would sweepingly declare all texts and their imagery to be products and feeble imitations of the press and its images, would be misguided."[62] He insists that Fontane's imagination remained altogether distinct

---

61 See Graevenitz, *Theodor Fontane: ängstliche Moderne*, 358.
62 Ibid., 397.

from the world of mass media, even though he also concedes that the images produced by both gravitated toward one another "increasingly frequently." Evidence from the notebooks and other working notes suggests that Graevenitz's insistence on the difference between Fontane's images and mass-produced genre paintings misses the point. The connections between his literary drafts and genre paintings were direct and deliberate—in fact, Fontane at times even referred to specific popular genre painters and their work in his notes. In the drafts for the opening scene of the novella project "Großmutter Schach" ("Grandmother Schach"), to name but one example from the *Nachlass*, Fontane jotted down: "The village. The peculiar garden. Pear tree. The wooden shed (*Latten-Laube*) à la [Theodor] Hosemann. The old woman joins with a grandchild, a little girl in her arms" (F1: 295). Theodor Hosemann, dubbed "the painter of the common people,"[63] was a well-known Berlin genre painter and caricaturist of the day whose images were found everywhere, from restaurant menus to home décor, and Fontane instructed himself to model the setting for his story explicitly upon his style. To grasp Fontane's innovations as a mass media artist, one needs to recognize this direct overlapping between his production and the media forms that surrounded him.

Example II: Typified Characters

As indicated earlier, atmospheric genre scenes were not the only elements with which Fontane usually initiated the drafting process. He also started new projects with notes on typified characters, frequently developing their social legibility before he knew which specific function in the narrative a given character would assume and how it would relate to the plot as a whole. In the development of his characters, Fontane integrated the representational modes and expressive potential of multiple media forms. He had recourse to the stock figures of popular theater, the descriptive conventions of the *roman à clef*, and the emergent iconography of the sociological type, layering these different templates upon one another according to the principles of serial variation of the periodical press. This compounding of media forms resulted in figures with increased degrees of verisimilitude, figures that seemed both so "typical" and so "real" that they prodded readers to play games of decoding and invited them to guess which "actual" people were hidden in the fiction.

Again, working notes for *Before the Storm* provide one of the best-documented examples of Fontane's methods of character construction

---

63 Lothar Brieger, *Theodor Hosemann. Der Maler des Berliner Volkes* (Munich: Delphin, 1920).

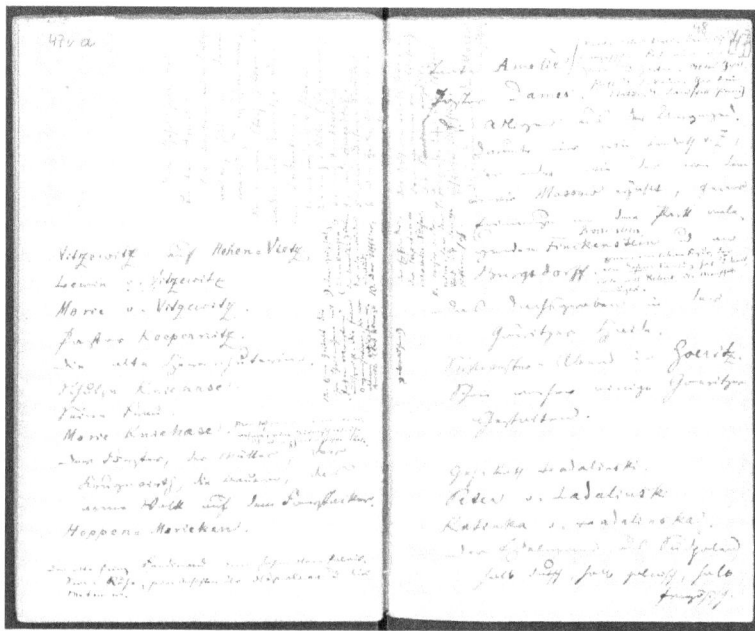

Figure 4.6 Double-page from Fontane's Notebook E 2, showing the interaction of modular entries and lists for the development of literary characters in the context of *Before the Storm*.

and cumulative building of verisimilitude (Figure 4.6). The notes—a set of entries in Notebook E 2—show that this process was list-driven. If the list, with its capacity for formal flexibility and expansion, had already mattered for Fontane's accumulation of atmospheric genre scenes, it had even more significance for his method of character construction, for it allowed him to shuttle repeatedly between his archive and his drafts as he layered more and more materials upon one another. Contrary to what previous investigations into Fontane's manuscripts posit, then, the lists with which he began his novel projects were devices not of static structure, but of motion. They were not used to "organize" the "glut of material"[64] (*Materialfülle*), but rather to mediate a process of ongoing supplementation, superimposition, and increasing complexity.

---

64 Hettche, "Die Handschriften zu *Vor dem Sturm*," 203.

Die Gesellschaft bei Tante Ameliè.
Sie liebte nur Originale, solche von denen was zu erzählen war, die einen Stich hatten, entweder ins Komische oder ins Bedenkliche.
1. nach Landrath v. Zieten.
2. nach v. Rohr (Kapernaum)
3. nach Finkenstein.
4. nach Burgsdorf.
5. Der Dosen-Sammler.
6. Der Herbe, Trübsinnige, der die Geschichte erlebt hat mit den verbrannten Briefen, die Sander [?] erzählt.
7. Jürgaß, der die Stiefelgeschichte ausführte.
8. Die Figur von der Massow erzählte.
9. Der Geizhals (Blankensee und der Bresl=Zieten der nie wieder einlud.
10. Der Tifftler, der Erfinder, der Perpetuum mobile-Sucher.
11. Major v. Arnim, der den Tod auf den Gesichtern sah.
12. Eine Gestalt die ihre Theilnahme mit „John Morton" ausspricht. Die feine Organisation, die vor allem Häßlichen erschrickt. (Erst später zu gebrauchen.)

Vitzewitz auf Hohen=Vietz
Lewin v. Vitzewitz
Marie v. Vitzewitz.
Pastor Koepernitz.
Die alte Herrenhuterin.
Schulze Kniehase.
Seine Frau.
Marie Kniehase Man sah sie war eine vornehme, eine leidenschaftliche und eine phantastische Seele.
Der Förster, der Müller, der Krugwirth, die Bauern, das arme Volk auf dem Forstacker.
Hoppen=Marieken.
Der alte Prinz <u>Ferdinand</u> im Johanniter-Palais.
Seine Ruhe, seine Ansichten über Napoleon und dies Meteor.

Tante Ameliè. Reich. Prince Henri. Preußisch und französisch. Fast nur im Zimmer und Garten. Alles Gesellschaft und Lektüre. Gar kein Natur= und Landschaftssinn.]
Pastor Dames.
Die Adligen aus der Umgegend. Darunter einer wie Landrath v. Z, der andre wie der von dem wie Massow erzählt, ferner Erinnerungen an den Park anlegenden ^{Drosselstein} Finckenstein und an Burgsdorff. Einer, eine lederne Figur, der eine <u>Dosen</u>=Sammlung hat und damit, wie mit Rebus, die Menschen ennuyirt.

Das Dachsgraben in der Göritzer Haide.
Sylvester=Abend in Goeritz. Schon vorher einige Goeritzer Gestalten.

Geh. Rath Ladalinski
Peter v. Ladalinski.
Katinka v. Ladalinska.
Der Edelmann aus Südpolen, halb deutsch, halb polnisch, halb französisch.

Vitzewitz of Hohen-Vietz
Lewin von Vitzewitz
Marie von Vitzewitz.
Pastor Koepernitz.
The old Herrnhut woman.
Mayor Kniehase.
His wife.
Marie Kniehase She evidently was a noble, a passionate, and an imaginative soul.
The forester, the miller, the innkeeper, the peasants, the poor people on the woodland acre.
Hoppenmarieken.

Old Prince <u>Ferdinand</u> at the Johanniter Palace. His silence, his opinions on Napoleon and this [?] meteor.

Gathering at Aunt Ameliè's. She cared only for originals, specimens about which there was a story to tell, who were imbued with a little spice, be it comical or troubling.
1. after prefect von Zieten.
2. after von Rohr (Kapernaum)
3. after Finkenstein.
4. after Burgsdorf.
5. The tin-can collector
6. The sullen, down-hearted man, who witnessed the story about the burned letters that Sander [?] told.
7. Jürgaß, who recounted the boot story.
8. The character of which Massow told.
9. The miser (Blankensee and the Bresl=Zieten who never again invited.
10. The tinkerer, the inventor, the searcher after the perpetual motion machine.
11. Major von Armin, who saw death in faces.
12. A figure announcing his sympathy for "John Morton." The fine organization which recoils from all ugliness. (To be used later.)

Aunt Ameliè. Rich. Prince Henri. Prussian and French. Nearly always indoors or in the garden. All company and reading. No sense whatsoever of nature or landscape.]
Pastor Dames.
Aristocrats from the surrounding area. Among them one like prefect von Z, the other like the one of whom Massow tells, also reminiscences of ^Drosselstein Finckenstein laying out the park and of Burgsdorff. One, a leathern character, who has a collection of <u>tin-cans</u> and, like with Rebus, goes around bothering people with it.

Digging for badgers on Göritz heath. New year's eve at Goeritz. Already [introduce] some Goeritz characters earlier.

Privy councillor Ladalinski Peter von Ladalinski.
Katinka von Ladalinska.
The nobleman from southern Poland, half Polish, half German, half French.

This process becomes clear from the interacting lists with which Fontane realized and expanded the initial *dramatis personae* of *Before the Storm* (Figure 4.6). The cast of characters begins with a list of easily recognizable stock figures: on the first layer of notation, identifiable by the larger script in ink and the regular text direction, characters are clustered by their social strata, which are clearly signaled by noble names, collective designations such as "Aristocrats from the surrounding area," or professions (as in "mayor Kniehase"). The two opposite ends of the social ladder are marked by Brandenburgian petty nobility and "the poor people on the woodland acre," with representatives of the upper middle class in between. The characters, moreover, appear narratively interpreted—that is, most of them are not "invented," or *erfunden*, but "found," *gefunden*—according to straightforward roles reminiscent of popular theater ("The innkeeper") or according to recognizable social types ("The old Herrnhut woman"). The worn-out tab on the top of the left page indicates that Fontane kept returning to this budding *dramatis personae* to add to it. Indeed, he expanded the initial list on the right in a different sitting—the differences in text direction, writing utensil, and shade of ink suggest as much—and supplemented it with twelve figures through which the cast of characters evolves into an entire "Gathering (*Gesellschaft*) at Aunt Ameliè's." Some of the added figures are evidently derived from materials that Fontane had initially researched for the *Wanderungen* and that he could now conveniently pull up in his archive, such as figure no. 2, which he planned to model on "v. Rohr (Kapernaum)." This is shorthand for Georg Moritz von Rohr, a philandering eighteenth-century nobleman with the nickname "Hauptmann von Kapernaum," on whom Fontane had already received material for a *Wanderungen* episode.[65]

The circle of narratively pre-encoded social types on double-page 47V–48R becomes wider still on the following notebook pages, growing from a small number of figures into an entire society. Fontane assembled people in various clusters (e.g., "The different officers"). With entries in other notebooks and glued-in paper slips, he gradually complemented the outlined array of types, systematically amassing figures in six numbered groups—"The military group," "The finance group" (*Die kameralistische Gruppe*), "The teachers' group," "The merchants' group," "The artists' group," and "The theologians' group"—all of which

---

65 Fontane had requested details about Georg Moritz von Rohr's turbulent life from one of his informants, Mathilde von Rohr, in a letter dated July 4, 1864, while he was researching a *Wanderungen* episode on the family history of the von Rohrs. See the editorial commentary in GBA V.1: 730–1.

culminate in his summarizing phrase "This is the very stock of society" (*Dies ist der Stock der Gesellschaft*; E3, 6V). The above example thus makes very clear that the protagonists are placeholders for social strata, the milieus associated therewith, and ultimately a typifying description of society as a whole.[66]

Over the course of the different rearticulations, the main characters receive additional personal features that create a heightened effect of verisimilitude. Fontane relied on the representational and epistemological principles of the periodical to achieve this effect. Periodicals operate according to the serial logic of repetition and variation in their presentation of content. There is a tendency in the periodical form, Margaret Beetham writes, "to keep reproducing elements which have been successful" to ensure that readers continue to buy each number.[67] Moreover, to make new knowledge communicable, periodicals mediate it with familiar schemata, for example by sorting it into standing rubrics and connecting it to topics that readers have already encountered. "Periodicals prepare the new as something familiar or present variations of the familiar as novelties," as Stefan Scherer and Claudia Stockinger explain.[68] Over time, the accumulating content might gradually transform the schemata—a rubric might become obsolete and be replaced by a new one, or a topic might sink to the bottom of the news cycle and be overlaid by more current topics— yet the overall communicative mechanism operating in periodicals, "variation of schemata as repetition" (267), ensures the basic legibility of the new material. Fontane applied a very similar logic to his construction of characters, realizing a paradoxical "individualization" of the constructed types. Note that Aunt Ameliè and Marie Kniehase receive additional attributes on double-page 47V and 48R, which lend them more personal profiles. The new characteristics that Fontane attached to Aunt Ameliè are these: "Rich. Prince Henri. Prussian and French. Nearly always indoors or in the garden. All company and reading (*Alles Gesellschaft und Lektüre*). No sense whatsoever of nature or landscape." With these additions, Fontane exceeded the narrative

---

66 This social panorama does not appear in full in the published novel; Fontane pruned it back in the further processes of text production. See GBA I.2: 387–9.
67 Margaret Beetham, "Towards a Theory of the Periodical as a Publishing Genre," in *Investigating Victorian Journalism*, ed. Laurel Brake et al. (Basingstoke: Palgrave Macmillan, 1990), 24.
68 Stefan Scherer and Claudia Stockinger, "Archive in Serie. Kulturzeitschriften des 19. Jahrhunderts," in *Archiv/Fiktionen: Verfahren des Archivierens in Literatur und Kultur des langen 19. Jahrhunderts,* ed. Daniela Gretz and Nicolas Pethes (Freiburg i. Br.: Rombach, 2016), 266–7.

device of the popular literary type and furnished his figures with peculiarities, quirks, and antics that invite readers to see the figures as individuals. One sketch of Lewin von Vitzewitz (which Fontane ultimately did not use) describes him as "An elderly gentleman of nearly 70, refined, elegant, can subsist only at a temperature of 17° C, servant with coat and topcoat, always a little pot of hot water at his side during dinner to regulate the temperature" (*beim Diner immer ein Töpfchen heißes Wasser neben sich zur Regulirung der Temperatur*; E 3, 25R). To be sure, even the supposed peculiarities still *signify*; they tie in with current discourses and commonplaces that the reader could recognize, opening up the seemingly individual character traits to interpretation within wider frameworks of social iconography and meaning. Lewin von Vitzewitz's quirk, for example, is readable in light of contemporary newspaper discourse; at the time, the *Gartenlaube* and other family magazines dedicated numerous articles to the regulation of body temperature and the merits of hot water.[69] Fontane, adding more and more such double-coded attributes to his figures, perfected this paradoxical "individualization" of his types to the point that even present-day readers perceive them as realistic *individuals* representative of Wilhelminian values and middle-class life in late nineteenth-century Prussia, rather than as carefully constructed types.[70] Differently put, Fontane superimposed socially legible, typifying patterns until an altogether new pattern emerged, a pattern that made his figures look like original individuals.

For many of his fictional characters, Fontane livened up the epistemological principle of serial variation by including telling details that encouraged readers not only to map fictional figures onto social types, but also to decode which historical or living persons in particular were being described. Such hints were often given in the names of the figures, and sometimes in their character traits and relationships. The names of Berndt and Lewin *von* Vitze*witz*, the fictional father and son at the center of *Before the Storm*, resonated noticeably with the names of the historical brothers Friedrich August Ludwig and Alexander *von* der Mar*witz*, two Prussian officers and noblemen who garnered fame in the war against Napoleon. Hints such as these encouraged a mode of

---

69 See Alfred Estermann, ed., *Inhaltsanalytische Bibliographien deutscher Kulturzeitschriften des 19. Jahrhunderts* (Munich: Saur, 1995), 3.2:15; 6:505; 8:258. I am indebted to Alice Christensen for pointing me to the widespread discourse on body temperature, the thermometer, and the role of the thermometer in the later nineteenth-century bourgeois household.
70 For example, see Edith Krause, "Domesticity, Eccentricity, and the Problems of Self-Making: The Suffering Protagonists in Theodor Fontane's *Effi Briest* and Leopoldo Alas's *La Regenta*," *Seminar* 44, no. 4 (2008): 414–32.

reading that was "referentializing"[71] and constantly looked for points of reference in the "real" world outside the text. Fontane, then, mixed yet another media form into his construction of characters, having recourse not only to the popular stage and the serial logic of the periodical, but also to the entertaining principle at the heart of the *roman à clef*. The *roman à clef*, or "novel with a key," is a literary genre based on the decoding of secret messages and identification of disguised persons, triggered by unmistakable "real-world" details in the fictional text. In the modern German tradition, decoding turned into a way of reading social novels, especially after Goethe's *Werther* (1774), and over the course of the nineteenth century, it became firmly established in the popular realm as an entertaining practice of reception. The unmistakable detail—such as the open copy of *Emilia Galotti* that was found on the desk of the historical "Werther," Carl Wilhelm Jerusalem, after he had committed suicide—provides a "verifiable trace of reality,"[72] which then prompts the reader to connect all of the narrated details to historically verifiable events and facts, regardless of whether they were fictional. Compelling the reader to "decode" a given novel, then, was the most effective way to ensure that the reader would map the reality of the text onto his or her own reality and interweave the two. It was the perfect mechanism to generate maximum verisimilitude.

To be sure, decoding as a mode of reading also carried an air of impropriety in the nineteenth century. Fontane's colleague Friedrich Spielhagen frowned upon the reading public's "passion" to figure out "what 'truth' there actually was 'to the story'; not in the aesthetic sense, but in the altogether philistine one of the homespun truth" (*im banausischen Sinne der hausbackenen Wahrheit*), and he called it a "quite baffling desire (*ganz absonderliches Gelüst*) to know who was 'meant' by this or that person."[73] Because decoding violated the notion of autonomous art for the sake of a simplistic, voyeuristic "realism," many writers looked down on it. Fontane, however, was quite taken with its potential for intrigue. In the context of *Before the Storm*, he wrote with noticeable satisfaction to his publisher, Hertz, that readers at home in the *Oderbruch* region would "agonize" (*sich abquälen*) over "who was actually meant by Vitzewitz, Pudagla, Drosselstein etc." and added: "*This* always forms the center of interest. Solving puzzles (*Räthsel lösen*). Everything else is inconsequential" (BaH 192). Shuttling back and forth

---

71 Gertrud Maria Rösch, *Clavis Scientiae. Studien zum Verhältnis von Faktizität und Fiktionalität am Fall der Schlüsselliteratur* (Tübingen: Niemeyer, 2004), 113. She mistakenly describes Berndt and Lewin as "brothers" (165).
72 Ibid., 173–4.
73 Friedrich Spielhagen, "Finder oder Erfinder," 4–5; qtd. in Rösch, *Clavis Scientiae*, 167–8.

between his dispositions and his archive, Fontane ensured that the puzzles would not be too easy to solve and that critics would not be able to reproach him for vulgar modes of mimetic mirroring. He superimposed so many "individualizing," "real-world" details upon one another that his figures and settings became both highly suggestive and ambiguous. In a note on the figure that would later turn into "Berndt von Vitzewitz," Fontane remarked: "A bit like Marwitz in character, but less severe, many features of Knesebeck. Particularly the strategic element, too" (A 12, 136R). To play the game of concealing and revealing with his audience effectively, Fontane relied on what he elsewhere called "mixed traits" (*gemischte Züge*) and "mixed locales" (*gemischte Lokalitäten*; A 12, 136R), providing an undercurrent of ambiguity that protected him against simplifying modes of reception.

Fontane extended this ambiguous game well beyond the text of his novels. When he talked about his writings after publication, he was careful to circulate rumors that people were reading his novels as real-world stories, even citing examples of readers who had taken their identification with the fictional characters too far. In a letter to the literary critic Paul Schlenther, sent after the publication of *On Tangled Paths* (*Irrungen, Wirrungen*), Fontane described an encounter with a female reader who claimed to be the protagonist of his most recent work: "Just now ... I was visited by a lady of forty-six who told me 'she was *Lene*; I had written her story.' It was a terrible scene with much weeping (*Massenheulerei*). I still don't know whether she was mad, sad, or a swindler" (HFA IV.3: 566). Even post-publication, then, Fontane tried to set the terms for the "referentializing" mode of reception, yet expressed reservations about one-to-one connections between his writings and the "real" world. The question of how "real" his texts were remained mysterious and was thus a source of ongoing entertainment and communication—*Unterhaltung* in the literal sense—among his readers.

Fontane's practice of drafting characters with the help of running lists left him with significant creative leeway. A brief comparison with Dickens's preferred media of drafting, the "number plans" (Figure 4.7) mentioned earlier, throws into relief just how unconstrained by formal concerns Fontane's method allowed him to be. Like Fontane, Dickens drove the development of his novels by shuttling back and forth between dispositions in keywords and a repository of material, which in his case encompassed a special notebook, the so-called *Book of Memoranda*, a "series of small paper bags, filled with scraps of paper containing various memoranda" on his desk (as one source reports),[74]

---

[74] Butt and Tillotson mention the paper bags filled with scraps in *Dickens at Work*, 29n1.

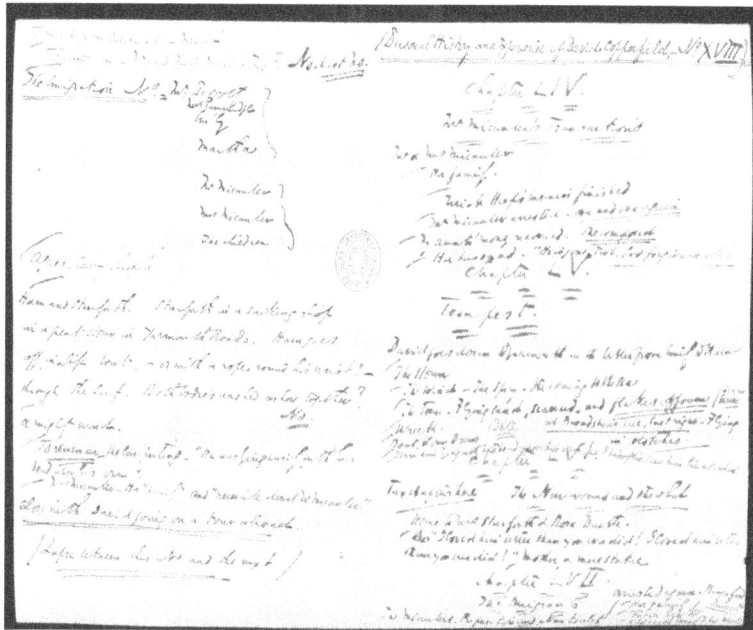

Figure 4.7 Charles Dickens's Number Plan for number XVIII of *David Copperfield*.

To finish from last Nº – Uriah	(Personal History and Experience of David Copperfield. – Nº XVIII.
To bring up – Mr and Miss Murdstone? No – <u>Last No.</u>	Chapter LIV.
<u>The Emigration</u>	Mr Micawber's Transactions
Nº = Mr Pegotty	Mr & Mrs Micawber.
Mrs Gummidge	Her family.
Em'ly	Uriah Heep's business finished.
Martha	Mr Micawber arrested – <u>over and over again.</u>
Mr Micawber	My Aunt's money recovered. <u>She composed.</u>
Mrs Micawber	
The children	Her husband. "He's gone, Trot. <u>God forgive us all!</u>
<u>Agnes.</u> Carry through.	Chapter LV.
Ham and Steerforth. Steerforth in a sinking ship in a great storm in Yarmouth Roads. Ham goes off, in a life boat, – or with a rope	<u>Tempest.</u> David goes down to Yarmouth with letter from Emily to Ham The Storm

round his waist? – through the Surf. Both bodies washed ashore together? <u>A mighty</u> wind. To <u>remember</u>—the last parting. – "He was lying easily, with his head upon his arm". Mrs Micawber—Her "family" and "never will desert Mr Micawber". Close with David going on a tour boat. (<u>Lapse between this N^o and the</u> next)	The Wind – The Spray – the coming to the Sea The Town – Flying sand, seaweed, – and <u>flakes of foam</u> / seen at Broadstairs here, last night – Flying in blotches. Wreck. <u>Bell</u>. Boat, blown down I saw him lying with his head upon his arm, as I had often seen him lie at school. <center>Chapter LVI.</center> Two chapters here. <u>The</u> New <u>wound and the old</u>. Home to Mrs Steerforth & Rosa Dartle. xx "I loved him better than you ever did! I loved him better than you ever did! Mother, a mere statue. <center>chapter LVII.</center>

	The Emigrants. arrested again.
	 The Micawbers. Hungerford.
	 Preparation and Sunset Her
	 Nauticality family
	                           Tween Decks
	                           close with Emily
	                           & her uncle

and, of course, whatever ideas he carried in his mind. Yet if Fontane's dispositions in list form could grow in any way he wanted, Dickens's number plans were formatted in such a way that whatever material Dickens retrieved from the repository had to be committed very quickly to "numbers," chapters, or specific moments in the narrative.

Dickens always set up the plans in more or less the same way. He "took a sheet of approximately 7" × 9" ... paper ... and folded it, long side horizontal, in half."[75] He then opened the folded sheet, and on the left-hand side, he noted down the general "mems," including tags, motifs, names of characters, possible developments, and brief queries

---

75 Stone, introduction to *Dickens' Working Notes*, xiv–xvi.

to himself, which mostly concerned narrative timing and the calibration of effects ("To bring up—Mr. and Miss Murdstone? No—Last Number"). On the right-hand side, he plotted a basic grid, consisting of the name of the novel, the number of the monthly part, and, with space after each entry, the title of each chapter in the plan. In the space under each chapter, he jotted down the central events and motifs of that chapter. Sometimes he wrote the chapter notes before he wrote the corresponding chapter, sometimes after; the notes on the right-hand side served both as rough plans of what Dickens still needed to write and records of what he had already written.[76] If one surveys the plans and traces the interaction between the notes on the left and the notes on the right, one can see Dickens "in the process of mediating what ingredients shall go into the number to be written";[77] moreover, one can see him committing material from the left to key points in the narrative on the right. Indeed, one can trace how Dickens imposed structure upon his ideas and reined them in, so as to reconcile them with the formal considerations that he always kept in mind—the number plans were also the media with which he calculated how many more pages he had to fill. Whereas Dickens, then, had to make immediate decisions about the development of his characters and stories, check off ideas, and fit them into a grid, Fontane enjoyed the increased flexibility of the running list: he added material wherever he wished, allowing his project to unfold any way he wanted and layering into his narratives more and more references to the media world in which his fiction was embedded.

Fontane's compounding of media forms for the purpose of character construction resulted in characters who waver between "originals" and socially representative types. They emerge from the superimposition of social specimens, patterns, or models (*Mustern*), and in the published texts, Fontane explicitly renders the relationship of his characters with social models. In *Frau Jenny Treibel*, Wilibald calls Jenny "a model (*Musterstück*) of a bourgeois woman" (GBA I.14: 15); in *Unterm Birnbaum*, the reader learns that Line, for once at a loss for proper deportment, is normally "a model of unflappability" (*ein Muster von Nichtverlegenwerden*; GBA I.8: 76); Hugo Großmann, a middle-class character and the ticket to a better life for Mathilde Möhring in the eponymous novel, is designated a "model (*Muster*) of solidity" (GBA I.20: 27); Major von Schach, in *A Man of Honor*, shudders at the prospect of marrying Victoire, for "the ridicule of an oh-so-happy country marriage" appears before his inner eye "in a truly exemplary model" (*in einem wahren Musterexemplare*; GBA I.6: 100)—and so on. Explicitly relating his characters to the social

---

76 Ibid., xvi.
77 Butt and Tillotson, *Dickens at Work*, 27–8.

patterns and typologies that gave rise to them in the first place, Fontane stages minute social gradations; for every character and narrative situation, the reader has to determine the relationship between individuality and social norm, original and pattern. According to Norbert Mecklenburg's analysis of Fontane's novels, this play with "socio-cultural patterns"[78] (*soziokulturellen Mustern*) is what makes the novels "realist." Their capacity to incorporate "socio-culturally predetermined systems of signs" and work through the "patterns of language, thought, and imagery according to which the life of the individual, its contradictions, and the cultural and social distinctions that contribute to shaping it are interpreted" creates a reality effect in which modern society, with its propensity for minute class distinctions, recognizes itself. The basis for this effect, as we have seen, is the fusion of several popular media forms and the list-driven expansion of characters.

Example III: Discursive Sound Bites

The third element with which Fontane often started the composition of a new novella or novel was discursive sound bites, short snippets of discourse that exemplify particular speaking styles and the social type, segment of society, or worldview associated with this style.[79] Brief entries that depict figures through distinctive utterances, or capture nothing but an utterance, can be found across Fontane's *Nachlass*, as in Notebook E 3: "Characters in a novel: a lady or gentleman, gentleman likely to be better, who always says: 'if you didn't see *that*, you didn't see anything'" (50V). In this manner, Fontane put down characteristic "principal stock phrases" (*Hauptredensarten*), "favorite quotations" (*Lieblingscitate*), and "dialogue material" (*Dialogstoffe*) that he planned to use, at times describing speaking styles abstractly—as in the note on a "real Berliner of an average education (*Durchschnittsbildung*) . . ., age 50, former merchant," who talks too much and cannot keep any secrets (F1: 393)—and at other times working with direct quotes, as in this note: "A person (*either* bumptious young gold-bespectacled scholar *or* eccentric self-important amateur) who keeps saying: '*it is a scientific certainty*' (*Es steht wissenschaftlich fest*). This he applies to matters great

---

78 Norbert Mecklenburg, *Theodor Fontane. Romankunst der Vielstimmigkeit* (Frankfurt a. M.: Suhrkamp, 1998), 31.
79 Mecklenburg and Vellusig broach the foundational role of utterances in Fontane's working notes, but neither extends that study to an analysis of the notes or to Fontane's creative process. See Mecklenburg, *Theodor Fontane. Romankunst der Vielstimmigkeit*, 174–5; Robert Vellusig, "'Ein Widerspiel *des* Lebens, das wir führen.' Fontane und die Authentizität des poetischen Realismus," *Zeitschrift für deutsche Philologie* 125, no. 1 (2006): 212.

and small alike, to Nero, Tiberius, the earth's rotation, bran bread etc." (F1: 393). These discursive samples provide the basis for the "dialogism" of the Fontanean novel, a notion that Mecklenburg, drawing on the theories of Mikhail Bakhtin, has fruitfully developed for the analysis of Fontane's fiction and by which he means "the novel's responses to the many-voiced social diversity of speech." The working notes demonstrate, though, that Fontane's novels do not merely "respond" to the polyphony of social discourse, nor do they "soak it up," as Mecklenburg suggests.[80] Rather, they are purposefully *built on* and *around* these discursive snippets, which are one of Fontane's most effective tools for the staging of social distinctions.

Fontane's discursive sound bite fuses the possibilities of two media. For one thing, it exploits the liveliness of the stage. In particular, Fontane adopted in Dickensian fashion the theatrical device of the "tag," a repeated utterance that identifies a figure (think of Ebenezer Scrooge's signature "Bah! Humbug!"). From the stage, Fontane also borrowed the strategy of engaging figures in direct dialogue, without the mediation of a narrator, and letting them characterize one another in the course of the dialogue through their ways of speaking and responding to one another—the classic Fontanean *Figurenrede*.[81] Yet he blended this theatrical use of speech with the nuanced treatment that speech received in the nineteenth-century newsroom. Newspapers mediated an extraordinarily rich social and political polyphony; one need only browse a randomly chosen issue of a paper with which Fontane regularly interacted—for example, the *Neue Preußische (Kreuz-) Zeitung*—to perceive the multitude of voices that papers contained. On the first two pages of issue no. 208 (from September 7, 1859) alone, the reader encounters almost thirty different voices that are quoted directly or indirectly, an array that includes passages from royal speeches, official memoranda, verses from the Bible and from Christian Friedrich Scherenberg's epic *Waterloo,* anecdotes told by soldiers, excerpts from the Welsh General Code of Law, passages from reports by Napoleon Bonaparte, and the personal voices of foreign correspondents, not to mention quotations from rival papers in Germany, England, France, Belgium, and Spain. Considering that these were just two pages of a distinctly conservative paper, it is easy to imagine how diverse and intense this daily buzz must have been across the full spectrum of publications available in Berlin. With his discursive sound bites, Fontane put this polyphony into his novels—or rather, he built his novels on top of this polyphony. In so doing, he adopted the fine

---

80 Mecklenburg, *Theodor Fontane. Romankunst der Vielstimmigkeit*, 80.
81 Ibid., 71.

distinctions between different ways of reporting utterances that newspaper editors had developed.

Newspapers distinguished carefully between their own voice(s) and those of others, and to this end, they used direct and indirect discourse in their reporting, following conventions that are still in place today. Direct discourse typically appeared in quotation marks and the indicative mood and was reserved for instances in which the exact wording of an utterance mattered. When the wording was less relevant, papers defaulted to indirect discourse in the special subjunctive mood, which emphasized the reported nature of the utterance and signaled critical distance. From today's perspective, there was just one oddity: at times, one finds combinations of indirect discourse and quotation marks in nineteenth-century papers, as if to double-flag the reported nature of a quoted passage. The opening article of the *NP(K)Z* issue from September 7, 1859, a historical piece on the "Cispadane Republic," describes Bonaparte's support for the formation of a republic of Italian provinces after the battle of Lodi, citing a statement made by Bonaparte in indirect discourse *and* quotations marks:

> And indeed it suited the *bon plaisir* of the potentate of the day, "because after all—as [Bonaparte's] report to the Directory went—...there *was* no compulsion to ... act likewise with regard to the states of the duke of Modena. They *could* after all persist united as a free state and become the germ from which ... *might* develop the independence of all Italy." (Emphasis added)

> *Und es entsprach in der Tat dem* bon plaisir *des augenblicklichen Gewalthabers, "weil man ja – so lautete* [Bonapartes] *Bericht an das Directorium –* ... *doch nicht gezwungen* sei, es mit den ... Staaten des Herzogs von Modena eben so zu halten. Sie *könnten ja als ein freier Staat vereint fortdauern und zu einem Keime werden, aus welchem sich* ... *die Unabhängigkeit von ganz Italien* entwickele."

From today's perspective, the dependent clause starting with "because" and the following sentence should have been rendered either in direct quotation marks and the indicative mood, or without quotation marks and in the subjunctive mood. Yet in this passage, both features occur together.

Fontane adopted the full set of journalistic instruments for the reporting of speech, including this curious combination of quotation marks and indirect discourse. He drafted direct dialogues over multiple pages in classical *Figurenrede*, for which the narrator typically provides context; he cited figures in the indicative or subjunctive mood with isolated statements, that is, without embedding these citations in narrative contexts (what Mecklenburg calls a *Figurenzitat* and what English-language scholarship calls a sonic signature or a tag, as noted earlier); and at times, he flagged particularly prominent passages *within* a sonic signature that is given in the subjunctive mood in quotation marks. Among Mecklenburg's most salient examples is the narrator's characterization of Kommerzienrat van der Straaten at the beginning of *L'Adultera*, which reads: "He was, to introduce him by one of his favorite sayings, not in the habit of 'making his heart a den of thieves' . . ." (*Er pflegte, um ihn selber mit einer seiner Lieblingswendungen einzuführen, "aus seinem Herzen keine Mördergrube zu machen"*, GBA I.4: 5). Mecklenburg is the first scholar to devote sustained attention to this phenomenon in Fontane's prose, and he argues rightly that through this peculiar practice, Fontane nudges the reader to focus on the exact wording, syntactical form, register, and style of the quoted passage, which thus communicates more than just the verbal content: "The fragment of speech set in quotations marks is thus marked out as a symptom, a characteristic element of a whole *way* of speaking and with it an individual or collective form of consciousness."[82] In the case of van der Straaten, moreover, the passage in indirect discourse *and* quotation marks emerges as the banal version of a Bible verse (Matthew 21:13); it must be recognized as unoriginal and trite. The narrator's treatment of this passage exposes its unoriginality, casting a "critical light on the figure of van der Straaten and its problematic 'proverbiality'"[83] (*Redensartlichkeit*). To Mecklenburg's observation, however, we need to add that this mode of flagging and exposing speech is not a Fontanean invention, but the clever repurposing of a journalistic practice, one that Fontane blended with theatrical modes of dialogue.

Fontane's fusion of the directness of dramatic dialogue with the nuanced forms of reporting speech in the press turns the discursive sound bite into a particularly versatile tool for the effective representation of social polyphony. Fontane was able to make fine distinctions in the speaking styles of his fictional figures to represent their consciousness and worldviews; he mixed discursive samples together, pitted them against one another, and split political or ideological positions into different interacting voices, creating resonances, tensions, echoes, and effects of depth. As a sonic device, the discursive sound bite functioned as the counterpart to the pictorial device of the genre scene, complementing the visual dimension of the Fontanean novel with a different media mode.

---

82 Mecklenburg, *Theodor Fontane. Romankunst der Vielstimmigkeit*, 70.
83 Ibid., 88.

Fontane's work with discursive sound bites can be studied particularly well in notebook entries for *A Man of Honor* (1882). The *Tale* (*Erzählung*) *from the Days of the Gensdarmes Regiment*, as the subtitle describes it, picks up on a societal scandal that had actually happened in 1815. Fontane transposes it into the spring of the calamitous year 1806, in the fall of which Prussia would lose the battles of Jena and Auerstedt to the French. In the novella, the handsome Major von Schach, a member of the elite "Gensdarmes Regiment" and a frequent visitor to the Berlin home of one beautiful Madame von Carayon, begins an affair with Victoire, Madame von Carayon's charming but disfigured daughter. Pressured by Madame von Carayon, the Prussian king, and his own notion of honor, Schach marries Victoire but shoots himself right after the ceremony, for he is unable to bear his comrades' mockery of his ugly bride and the prospect of a secluded life as a married man.[84] The novella presents a critical portrait of contemporary Prussia and its decadence through a historical lens. It treats Schach as a stand-in for a hollow notion of honor and skillfully ties his personal misery and misconduct to political debates about Prussia's status, strained relationship with France, and social and military decline. In the first chapter of the novel, set in Madame von Carayon's salon, the personal and the political immediately intersect, and the protagonists hash out their different views of Prussian politics and society in conversation. Fontane composed this chapter from extensive working notes in Notebook E 1 that demonstrate concretely how he approached the creative process through the discursive positions and striking utterances that he intended to include.

There are two sets of interacting entries. The first set runs mostly on the rectos of Notebook E 1 and captures a very brief *dramatis personae*—"Frau v. Carayon, Victoire v. Carayon, Bookseller Sander, Lieutenant v. Alvensleben, Heinrich v. Bülow"—along with a general description of the dynamics of the conversation, the political positions of the participants, and their speaking styles:

> Herr von Bülow is speaking, namely to Sander, from time to time also to Alvensleben, who is his countryman from the Altmark. Schackh [*sic*] is the last to arrive. Presently the conversation takes a different turn. Schach speaks in a very Prussian manner, very loyally, royalist and princely [in attitude] always in time-honored, conventional terms. Bülow hears him out, occasionally

---

84 Fontane had heard about this scandal from Mathilde von Rohr and put down an abbreviated account of it in Notebook A 12. See Chapter 3 of this study.

contradicting him, but ultimately holds his tongue. Then they go their separate ways.

> H. v. Bülow führt das Wort, namentlich gegen Sander gerichtet, dann und wann auch gegen Alvensleben, der sein altmärkischer Landsmann ist. Zuletzt kommt Schackh [sic!]. Das Gespräch nimmt momentan eine andre Wendung. Schach spricht sehr preußisch, sehr loyal, sehr königlich und prinzlich immer in hergebrachten, conventionellen Formen. Bülow hört es an und fährt ihn über den Mund, thut sich aber doch noch Zwang an. Dann trennen sie sich.
>
> (E 1, 12R; 13R)

In the same set of entries, Fontane also jotted down notes about the figure Heinrich von Bülow, listing details that he had culled from press reports and from the book *Der Feldzug von 1805 militärisch politisch betrachtet* (The Campaign of 1805 from a Military and Political Perspective, Leipzig, 1806), a controversial account of the Austro-Russian tactics during the War of the Third Coalition authored by the historical Dietrich Heinrich von Bülow, a military writer and intellectual. The notes spell out Bülow's political views ("1. He is a supporter of the alliance with France, a supporter of Haugwitz and Lombard.... 2. Hatred of Russia and Austria. Despises Czar Alexander," 3R) and refer to a historical incident of violent political protest—in 1806, the Prussian king instructed one of his ministers, Christian Graf von Haugwitz, to negotiate a deal with France to keep the peace, which angered Prussian war hawks and Prussia's English allies to such an extent that they smashed Haugwitz's windows ("On April 14, the *Morning Chronicle* reports that minister Haugwitz's windows have been smashed.... If I set... the whole scene in late April or early May, this Haugwitz-business will be easy to introduce as news," 4R). The notes also contain two sound bites, at least one of which was gleaned from *Der Feldzug von 1805*: "One of the others [i.e., of the other fictional protagonists] speaks the passage (*sagt die Stelle*): 'he corrects everybody, fights battles on paper, and cannot so much as lead a company across a ditch.' 4. 'Hanover, which is a seat of all prejudice and the most trifling conceit.' S. LII" (5R). The second set of entries runs mainly over the versos (1V–9V; 12V–15V) and fleshes out the working notes into a fairly advanced draft of the novella's first chapter up to Schach's appearance. The narrator depicts the communicative situation at the salon and introduces the topics of conversation before the characters take over and engage in a direct dialogue with one another:

> This conversation... seemed to revolve around matters of the day, for these were the days of May 1806 and there was still much ado about Haugwitz's mission, which had led to an accord over

the annexation of Hanover. Frau von Carayon, an attractive lady of 36, appeared to disapprove of this accord and specifically the present made of Hanover. "I mean, one cannot give away what is not one's own," she remarked, and the officer of the Gensdarms seated beside her kissed her hand . . . .

> Dieses Gespräch . . . schien sich um Tagesfragen zu drehn, denn es waren die Maitage 1806 und die Aufregung war noch groß über die Haugwitzsche Mission, die zu einem Einvernehmen zur Besitzergreifung von Hannover geführt hatte. Frau v. Carayon eine schöne Frau von wenig über 36 schien diese Abmachung für misslich anzusehn und namentlich das Geschenk Hannovers als misslich zu betrachten. „Ich meine, man kann nicht verschenken, was man nicht hat", bemerkte sie und der neben ihr sitzende Offizir vom Regiment Gensdarms küßte ihr die Hand . . . .
>
> (E 1, 2R–2V, 3V)

If one now compares these notebook entries to the published version of the first chapter, it becomes apparent that Fontane develops the abstract description of speaking styles, political positions, and sound bites in the first set of notes, and the dialogue draft in the second set of notes, into a complex, polyphonic system of relationships and communicative interactions in which discursive positions are not only effectively staged, but also call one another into question repeatedly. Whereas the notebook version of the first chapter renders the initial conversation of the protagonists predominantly as a direct exchange, the published version of the chapter delays the onset of the direct exchange through indirect discourse:

> The conversation in which they were engaged seemed to concern the Haugwitz delegation, which had just completed its mission and which in Bülow's view had not only led to a desirable restoration of harmonious relations between Prussia and France but had, in addition, secured Hanover [for us] by way of a "postnuptial gift." Frau von Carayon, however, took exception to this "postnuptial gift," since one could not very well dispose of or make a present of something one did not possess, a remark that prompted her daughter Victoire, who had been busying herself unnoticed at the tea table until then, to fling her mother an affectionate glance, and Alvensleben to kiss the charming lady's hand.[85]

---

85 Theodor Fontane, *A Man of Honor*, trans. E. M. Valk, in *Theodor Fontane: Short Novels and Other Writings*, ed. Peter Demetz (New York: Continuum, 1982), 4. The following quotations are also taken from this translation.

> Das Gespräch, das eben geführt wurde, schien sich um die kurz vorher beendete Haugwitzsche Mission zu drehen, die, nach Bülows Ansicht, nicht nur ein wünschenswertes Einvernehmen zwischen Preußen und Frankreich wieder hergestellt, sondern uns auch den Besitz von Hannover noch als „Morgengabe" mit eingetragen habe. Frau v. Carayon aber bemängelte diese „Morgengabe", weil man nicht gut geben oder verschenken könne, was man nicht habe, bei welchem Worte die bis dahin unbemerkt am Theetisch beschäftigt gewesene Tochter Victoire der Mutter einen zärtlichen Blick zuwarf, während Alvensleben der schönen Frau die Hand küßte.
>
> (GBA I.6: 6)

The use of indirect discourse makes possible multiple effects. It enables the narrator, who initially occupies a fairly detached position ("The conversation *seemed* . . . to concern"; "in Bülow's view") to slip into the figure of Bülow and briefly discard all distance by identifying with his (Bülow's) perspective, as the telling use of the collective dative pronoun *uns*, "[for] us," indicates. This perspective is not sustained, however, because the narrator continues to use the distancing subjunctive mood in the remainder of the sentence ("had secured [for us]"; *uns mit eingetragen habe*). At the same time, the indirect discourse provides the backdrop against which the word *Morgengabe*, postnuptial gift, can be flagged particularly effectively through direct quotation marks. The *Morgengabe*, a term from feudal German law, is a groom's gift to his bride, given after the wedding night to reward the bride for her virginity. Compared to *Geschenk*, the word for "present" used in the working notes, it is the much more polemical choice, aptly expressing Bülow's personality and cynical view of Prussia's weakness and dependence on France. Precisely this term sets off Madame v. Carayon's objection, thus illustrating her ability to engage in provocative conversation and counter Bülow's polemics with a pointed remark of her own. Her rejoinder, in turn, triggers her daughter's admiration, who is introduced as a calm and thoughtful observer. Victoire's admiring glance turns her into a relay in the network of relations between her mother and the male representatives of Prussian society, a function that she continues to fulfill throughout the novella. Only after all of these characteristic details, political views, and interpersonal relationships have been established does the narrator hand the situation over to the interlocutors, and the scene shifts to direct dialogue.

In the unfolding dialogue, all of the protagonists continue to characterize themselves and one another through their word choices and speaking styles. Frau von Carayon gently mocks Bülow for his polemics and temper ("Victoire, do pass Herr von Bülow the Carlsbad wafers. It's the only thing Austrian, I expect, he'll tolerate"), and Bülow explains his sharply critical attitude to Prussia and Austria. In Bülow's speech, the sound bite from *Der Feldzug von 1805* about Hanover reappears, albeit in edited form: Bülow calls Hanover "the seat of stagnation, a hotbed (*Brutstätte*) of prejudice" (7), a change that yet again shows his divisive mode of speech, even more than the original formulation. When Schach enters the salon and shares the news about the violent protest in front of Haugwitz's house, he indeed speaks "in a very Prussian manner," "loyally," and "in conventional terms," just as Fontane planned in the working notes. His condemnation of the protest ("And that in the state of Prussia, under His Majesty's very eyes") and his vouching for a self-sufficient Prussia ("It's time that the state of Frederick the Great remembered what it owes to itself"; "the ultimate goal: . . . a strong and independent Prussia") is an accumulation of conservative stock phrases.

Discursive echoes of this initial conversation reverberate throughout the novella and lead to a constant re-evaluation and critique of every political and moral position taken by the protagonists. Bülow's sharp-tongued toughness becomes the subject of the narrator's mild mockery at the end of the second chapter, with the narrator calling out Bülow's soft spot: "Like most *frondeurs* occupied with the decline and fall of the state, [Bülow] had his soft spots, too, and one of them had been affected by the song [a sentimental song performed by Victoire]" (14). As Bülow, usually the epitome of sarcasm, gazes at the stars and loses himself completely in a line from the song, the narrator's comment— "Willy-nilly and without being aware of it, he was a child of his age and yielding to a sentimental mood (*und romantisierte*)"—instructs the reader not to take Bülow's overall attitude too seriously, but to look at it in the context of its time. Schach, in turn, receives his share of criticism in the third chapter when Bülow, Alvensleben, and Sander talk about him behind his back and dissect his narrow-mindedness, which, for Bülow, is condensed in the mantra-like stock phrases by which Schach allegedly lives:

> And . . . this man *Schach*! . . . to me he's just a pompous prig and at the same time the embodiment of that Prussian parochialism that operates with exactly three articles of faith: article one, 'the world rests no more securely on the shoulders of Atlas than the state of Prussia rests on the shoulders of the Prussian army'; article two, 'a Prussian infantry offensive defies resistance'; thirdly and lastly, 'no battle is ever lost so long as the Garde du Corps Regiment hasn't gone over to the attack.' Or also, of course, the Gensdarmes Regiment. . . . I loathe this kind of rhetoric, and

the day isn't far off when the world will see through the sham of rodomontades like these.[86]

> Und ... dieser Schach! ... *mir ist er nichts als ein Pedant und Wichtigthuer, und zugleich die Verkörperung jener preußischen Beschränktheit, die nur drei Glaubensartikel hat: erstes Hauptstück „die Welt ruht nicht sichrer auf den Schultern des Atlas, als der preußische Staat auf den Schultern der preußischen Armee", zweites Hauptstück „der preußische Infanterieangriff ist unwiderstehlich", und drittens und letztens „eine Schlacht ist nie verloren, so lange das Regiment Garde du Corps nicht angegriffen hat". Oder natürlich auch das Regiment Gensdarmes. . . . Ich verabscheue solche Redensarten, und der Tag ist nahe, wo die Welt die Hohlheit solcher Rodomontaden erkennen wird.*
>
> (GBA I.6: 25)

The long-distance battle of the phrases continues in the fourth chapter, in which Schach pits his position against Bülow's, using one of the mantras that Bülow so strongly detests, and posits it as the better alternative to Bülow's "morbid conceit:" "I find this odious. I loathe such braggadocio (*Fanfaronaden*). He speaks of Brunswick and Hohenlohe as though they were ludicrous figures (*Größen*), but *I* stand by the Frederickian [sic] axiom that the world rests no more securely on the shoulders of Atlas than does Prussia on those of her army" (39). Throughout the novella, discursive sound bites, along with the opinions and values they communicate, call one another into question in this way. What begins in the notebooks as a simple accumulation of quotes, speaking styles, and discursive positions thus becomes the foundation of an increasingly polyphonic interplay of societal and political voices.

In the analysis of these and other sound bites, it is crucial to make one qualification. The sound bites should *not* be understood as authentically captured from the public squares, bourgeois sitting rooms, officers' messes, and noble mansions of late-nineteenth century Berlin and the surrounding countryside. There is no doubt that Fontane, the professional journalist, listened to the conversations around him with open ears. But as Mecklenburg rightly points out, we have no tapes from this period that would enable us to measure the feigned orality (*fingierte Mündlichkeit*) in his novels against the ways people *actually* spoke.[87] The notebooks make this important point abundantly clear, for

---

86 Fontane, *A Man of Honor*, 20.
87 Mecklenburg, *Theodor Fontane: Romankunst der Vielstimmigkeit*, 122.

they demonstrate that Fontane's sound bites consisted mainly of *past media content*, not transcriptions of what he had heard in the streets. They also show that when he did transcribe a live conversation, he applied selective mechanisms and filters to enhance the representative potential of the material (see Chapter 3). His concern was not scientific; it was aesthetic and critical. The sound bites, then, are really *samples* in the pop-cultural sense of the term: as "recognizable portions of existing recordings,"[88] they represent entire genres, artistic styles, or simply the most characteristic aesthetic features of a single work for the creation of a new song. They are not faithful citations. Rather, they are subject to fluid transformations and might be repeated in loops, split onto different tracks, mashed up, blended, or played back at different speeds in the medium of the Fontanean novel.[89]

One last glance at *Schach von Wuthenow* shows the filters that Fontane applied to edit and enhance the signifying potential of his samples. In the sixth chapter, the fictional Bülow disparages Czar Alexander I in a cold exchange with Schach, sarcastically labeling the Russian monarch "the 'good Czar'" (*der gute Kaiser*). To develop Bülow's rant, Fontane sampled the acerbic reflection "The good Czar" from the historical Bülow's *Der Feldzug von 1805*, but he tweaked it. The direct comparison, assisted by highlighting, reveals the nature of Fontane's editorial interventions. Passages in dark gray mark verbatim adoptions; passages in light gray show adoption of the general sense but with changes in wording; and unmarked passages indicate Fontane's additions. Through his tweaks, Fontane adapted the socio-political and cultural messages implicit in the source and strengthened its rhetorical punch:

D. H. von Bülow, The Campaign of 1805, "The good Czar," vol. II, 78–9:	Theodor Fontane, *A Man of Honor*, trans. E. M. Valk (emended), 47:
The good emperor [Czar]. This byname is not flattering for a ruler. A genuinely honest and virtuous man—for the two are not identical—will not be called a good man by a generation such as ours. He is apt to be the object	"He's the 'good Czar'" and that's enough. . . . A *truly* great man is not lauded to the skies for his goodness, much less so referred to by name. On the contrary, he's apt to be a constant object of slander. For the rank and file,

---

88 Dan Hosken, *An Introduction to Music Technology* (New York: Routledge, 2014), 73.
89 On the basic operations of sampling in pop music, see Felix Stalder, "Neun Thesen zur Remix-Kultur," *Der Autor am Ende der Gutenberg Galaxis* (Zurich: Buch & Netz, 2014), 37.

of their calumnies and vilification. Vice fears virtue; caring only for its own kind. Brenkenhof in his paradoxes, which are now forgotten, quite rightly says that in our day and age the worthiest people are bound to enjoy the worst reputation. Frederick would have been vexed if he had been called the good Frederick, nothing being good but the only "God." Good kings are such as lead their kingdom to its grave. The last king of Poland was also a so-called good man. Usually, these good men are inveterate whoremongers of feeble character.	who everywhere predominate, care only for their own kind. Brenkenhof, who for all his paradoxes ought to be more widely read than he is, goes so far as to maintain that 'in our day and age the worthiest people are bound to enjoy the worst reputation.' The good Czar! Come now, imagine how Frederick the Great would have rolled up his eyes if he'd been called the 'good Frederick.' . . . All kings nicknamed the 'good,' . . . are the kind that have led the kingdom entrusted to them to its grave or at any rate to the verge of revolution. The last king of Poland was also a so-called 'good' man. Such royal personages are usually equipped with large harems and small brains. And when they're off to war, some Cleopatra must always tag along, whether with or without an asp."
D. H. v. Bülow, *Der Feldzug von 1805,* "Der gute Kaiser," vol. II, 78–9:	Theodor Fontane, *Schach von Wuthenow*, GBA I.6: (58–9):
Der gute Kaiser. Dieser Name ist nicht schmeichelhaft für einen Regenten. Ein wahrhaft ehrlicher und tugendhafter Mann – denn beides ist nicht einerlei – wird von einer Generation wie die unsrige nicht ein guter Mann genannt werden. Er wird der Gegenstand ihrer Colomnien und ihres Abscheus seyn. Das Laster fürchtet die Tugend; es liebt nur das was ihm gleicht.	„Er ist der ‚gute Kaiser' und damit Basta. . . . Ein *wirklich* großer Mann wird nicht um seiner Güte willen gefeiert und noch weniger danach benannt. Er wird umgekehrt ein Gegenstand beständiger Verleumdungen sein. Denn das Gemeine, was überall vorherrscht, liebt nur das, was ihm gleicht. Brenkenhof, der, trotz seiner Paradoxien, mehr

Brenkenhof in seinen Paradoxen, die nun vergessen sind, sagt ganz recht, daß in unserm Zeitalter die besten Menschen die schlechteste Reputation haben müssen. Bei Friedrich würde man schlecht gefahren seyn, wenn man ihn den guten Friedrich genannt hätte, nichts ist gut als der einige ‚Gott.' Gute Regenten sind solche, die ihr Reich zu Grabe bringen. Der letzte König von Pohlen war auch ein sogenannter guter Mann. Gewöhnlich sind diese guten Männer Erz⸗Hurer von schwachem Charakter.	gelesen werden sollte, als er gelesen wird, behauptet geradezu, ‚daß in unserm Zeitalter die besten Menschen die schlechteste Reputation haben müßten'. Der gute Kaiser! Ich bitte Sie. Welche Augen wohl König Friedrich gemacht haben würde, wenn man ihn den ‚guten Friedrich' genannt hätte. . . . Alle Könige . . . die den Beinamen des 'guten' führen, sind solche, die das ihnen anvertraute Reich zu Grabe getragen oder doch bis an den Rand der Revolution gebracht haben. Der letzte König von Polen war auch ein sogenannter ‚guter'. In der Regel haben solche Fürstlichkeiten einen großen Harem und einen kleinen Verstand. Und geht es in den Krieg, so muß irgend eine Kleopatra mit ihnen, gleichviel mit oder ohne Schlange."

Fontane's interventions fall into two categories. Some of them bolster the rhetorical effectiveness of the historical Bülow's text, for example through increased contrast and adverbial amplifiers ("on the contrary"; "constant"; "go so far as"; "large harems / small brains") and the emotionalization of the kings' responsibilities ("the kingdom entrusted to them"). Others modify the cultural-critical impetus of the passage, making it both more general and more contemporary, as in the transformation of "Vice fears virtue and cares only for its own kind" into "For the rank and file, which everywhere predominate, care only for their own kind." Ultimately, Fontane's edits prove a general point that Mecklenburg makes about Fontane's relationship to language: he drew on the voices of others in an attempt to tease out and amplify their "implicit socio-cultural meanings."[90] His transformations of the source materials were thus not intended to create an "autonomous poetic

---

90 Mecklenburg, *Theodor Fontane: Romankunst der Vielstimmigkeit*, 80.

counter-language" as an esoteric alternative to the contaminated, corrupted, and impure societal babble that reverberated through the media landscape. On the contrary, Fontane's aim was to exaggerate and caricature the "practice of societal speech" (*gesellschaftliche Sprachpraxis*) and, by playing it back, put it on display. Hence the enormous spectrum of samples, extending from absurdly general and outright stupid statements to commonplace observations, fashionable opinions, and pointed insights, such as "the pistol ends where cowardice begins" (Adam Petöfy in *Graf Petöfy*); "what does it mean to pour out [one's heart]? After all, the essence (*das Eigentliche*) stays behind" (Luise von Briest in *Effi Briest*); "whimprin's uneducated" (Mathilde in *Mathilde Möhring*); and "all handsome men are weak" (Lene in *On Tangled Paths*). Hence also the frequent gestures of comparing and ranking societal phenomena, as in Leo's calculation of the worth of different kinds of rich relatives in *The Poggenpuhl Family* (*Die Poggenpuhls*): "Anyone not having an uncle will surely have a grandfather or a godfather or a maiden aunt (*Stiftsdame*). Maiden aunts are the best. They'll believe anything, any story to tell them . . ., and though they may not have much themselves, they will give everything, their last." These kinds of utterances function as "condensates of everyday knowledge and 'knowledge of human nature' (*Menschenkenntnis*)," as Mecklenburg has observed; they reduce complexity, throw stereotypes into relief, and express socio-cultural taxonomies.[91]

As a result, the individual speaking styles of Fontane's fictional protagonists acquire a larger meaning and turn into shorthand for social phenomena, ideologies, and values. When protagonists clash over seemingly trivial issues, or when the narrator calls a protagonist's position into question and nudges the reader to re-evaluate it, it is not just utterances that are at stake. Rather, the protagonists stand in for the ceaseless and ostentatious negotiation of worldviews, a negotiation in which discursive positions relativize one another and are always subject to change. One of the most characteristic hallmarks of Fontane's style is the manifestation of this ongoing negotiation even on the level of the syntax, from paratactic sentences "with neither commas nor periods" to the characteristic abundance of concessive and contrastive conjunctions such as *obwohl* (although) and *aber* (but; however).[92] The reader, tracing the many twists and turns in the conversations, is thus led to believe that the novel provides access to a communicative and social reality.

---

91 Mecklenburg, *Theodor Fontane: Romankunst der Vielstimmigkeit*, 146–7.
92 On these and other syntactical features of Fontane's prose, see Blomqvist, "Der Fontane-Ton," 30.

Remixing the *Genus Medium*: Nonlinear Editing and the Realism of the Middle

Having just seen, on a scale both panoramic and granular, how many different media elements Fontane blended in his dispositions and drafts, one wonders whether there was an aesthetic master program that regulated the processes of selection and fusion. In other words, if the crossing of media is "a moment of truth and revelation from which new form is born,"[93] as McLuhan puts it, one might ask what overall form Fontane's creative process generated. Yet again, the domain of rhetoric, one of the recurring subtexts in the methodological background of this study, offers instruments through which Fontane's creative practice can be assessed. Specifically, a category from the theory of the three styles—the *genus medium*, or middle style—emerges as an illuminating description of the aesthetic master program operant in Fontane's realism.[94] The applicability of the *genus medium* becomes visible if we sum up what rhetoric knows about this stylistic register and map it onto Fontane's poetics, triangulating between rhetorical theory, his programmatic remarks about the realist novel, and his creative practice.

The system of the three styles is one of the basic elements of rhetoric. It regulates the relationship between things/ideas (*res*) and words (*verba*) according to the yardstick of aptness; it systematizes which stylistic register and associated elocutional devices are appropriate for which rhetorical purpose.[95] According to this theory, the *genus humile*, or plain style, is appropriate for supplying information and providing proof. Its unadorned and simple sentences align it with "everyday speech." On the other end of the spectrum, there is the *genus grande*, or grand style, which is the appropriate choice for swaying an audience and arousing forceful emotions through ornate, passionate, and opulent language. The *genus medium*, or middle style, is located between these two registers. Participating in both plain and grand style, it must be neither too simple nor too opulent; it is the appropriate register for the rhetorical objectives of edification and pleasure (Horace's *prodesse* and *delectare*). The *genus medium* takes aim at the audience's affect, yet

---

93 McLuhan, *Understanding Media*, 80.
94 Here, I am picking up a cue provided by Manuela Günter in "Realismus in Medien. Zu Fontanes Frauenromanen," in *Medialer Realismus*, ed. Daniela Gretz (Freiburg i. Br.: Rombach, 2011), 172. Günter associates Fontane's prose with the *genus medium*, but she does not explore this association in detail or consider it in the context of Fontane's compositional process.
95 Heinrich Lausberg (1973), *Handbook of Literary Rhetoric: A Foundation for Literary Study*, ed. David E. Orton and R. Dean Anderson, trans. Matthew T. Bliss, Annemiek Jansen, and David E. Orton (Leiden: Brill, 1998), §1078.

without attempting to overwhelm *ratio*.⁹⁶ Rather, according to Cicero, it should convey "a minimum of vigour and a maximum of charm."⁹⁷ To this end, the oratory should proceed in a calm and peaceful flow. The orator may resort to "all figures of language, and many of thought," deploy commonplaces in the development of arguments, lighten up the speech with metaphors and allegories, and produce "brilliant and florid, highly coloured and polished" prose in which "all the charms of language and thought are intertwined."⁹⁸ Likewise, Quintilian defines the *genus medium* in *The Orator's Education* as a "speech sweeter than honey"⁹⁹ and characterizes it with this striking simile: "With the prettiness of digressions, its well-structured Composition, and its seductive *Sententiae*, it is like a gentle river, clear but shaded by green banks on either side."¹⁰⁰ In 1790, J. J. Eschenburg's *Allgemeine Theorie der prosaischen Schreibart* (General Theory of the Prosaic Manner of Writing) carried the theory of the three styles into the late eighteenth century and further specified some of its features. Closely following Quintilian, Eschenburg allocates the middle style to the double purpose of "instruction" and "agreeable entertainment of the mind,"¹⁰¹ which is fully in line with Enlightenment poetics. Moreover, Eschenburg details the "oratorical ornament" (*Redeschmuck*) and in particular the imagery appropriate to the middle register: "The middling style of writing can tolerate a certain measure of oratorical ornament, but of an agreeable rather than a sparkling kind, charming images (*reizende Bilder*) rather than great and wondrous ones."¹⁰² By the nineteenth century, the middle style was no longer actively theorized, yet it had become the unspoken norm for prose in journals and magazines. This is hardly surprising, given that these media were designed to provide information and pleasure for a wide spectrum of readers. A style that was neither so plain as to bore an educated middle-class reader nor so opulent as to get in the way of imparting information proved fitting for this purpose.

---

96 Karl Spang, "Dreistillehre," in *Historisches Wörterbuch der Rhetorik*, ed. Gert Ueding (Tübingen: Niemeyer, 1996), 3:923.
97 Marcus Tullius Cicero, *Brutus. Orator*, trans. G. L. Hendrickson, H. M. Hubbell, Loeb Classical Library 342 (Cambridge, MA: Harvard University Press, 1939), 371.
98 Ibid., 375.
99 Quintilian, *The Orator's Education*, vol. 5, Books 11–12, ed. and trans. Donald A. Russell, Loeb Classical Library 494 (Cambridge, MA: Harvard University Press, 2002), 317.
100 Ibid., 315.
101 J. J. Eschenburg, *Entwurf einer Theorie und Literatur der schönen Wissenschaften; zur Grundlage bey Vorlesungen* (Frankfurt; Leipzig, 1790), 308.
102 Ibid., 309.

Fontane's poetics of the novel overlaps extensively with the *genus medium*, both in theory and in practice. His famous statement about the principal task of the realist novel, embedded in a review of Gustav Freytag's *Die Ahnen*, converges with the rhetorical criteria for the middle style and its associated twofold objective of *prodesse* and *delectare*. In this review, Fontane wrote:

> [A novel] is supposed to tell us, while avoiding all that is exaggerated and ugly, a story in which we *believe*. It is supposed to speak to our imagination and our heart, to provide stimulation without causing upset; it is supposed to make a world of fiction seem real to us for a few moments, make us cry and laugh, hope and fear, but ultimately feel that we have lived partly among dear and pleasant people, partly among distinctive and interesting people, whose company gave us a few enjoyable hours and provided us with support, clarity, and instruction.
>
> [*Ein Roman*] *soll uns, unter Vermeidung alles Übertriebenen und Häßlichen, eine Geschichte erzählen, an die wir* glauben. *Er soll zu unserer Phantasie und unserem Herzen sprechen, Anregung geben, ohne aufzuregen; er soll uns eine Welt der Fiktion auf Augenblicke als eine Welt der Wirklichkeit erscheinen, soll uns weinen und lachen, hoffen und fürchten, am Schluß aber empfinden lassen, teils unter lieben und angenehmen, teils unter charaktervollen und interessanten Menschen gelebt zu haben, deren Umgang uns schöne Stunden bereitete, uns förderte, klärte und belehrte.*
>
> (HFA III.1: 316–17)

The decisive terms in this passage—the avoidance of extremes, the appeal to "imagination" (*Phantasie*) and "heart" (*Herz*), "cry and laugh," the emphasis on "a story in which we *believe*," "dear and pleasant people," "support" and "instruction"—closely align with the rhetorical purposes of edification and delight and the measured affect of the *genus medium*.[103] And if the *genus medium* calls for emotive and smooth language, the use of accessible commonplaces, colorful descriptions, well-structured sentences, and pleasant digressions, Fontane's creative practice strives to meet precisely these criteria, as we have seen earlier. His drafts abound in "agreeable" and "charming little images," namely the numerous genre scenes, which convey atmospheres that one might indeed term charming, inviting, and vivid. His characters emerge as mixtures of commonplace types layered with colorful, individualizing

---

103 See Günter, "Realismus in Medien," 172.

details; his discursive sound bites set into motion pleasantly digressive and (seemingly) free-flowing conversations. Last but not least, the central metaphor from Fontane's poetological memo, "Die Kunst des Erzählens" ("The Art of Storytelling"), corroborates the overlap between his conception of the realist novel and the rhetoric of the middle style. The memo uses an idyllic image of the novel as a gently flowing river that echoes Quintilian's central simile.

Evidently, the *genus medium* is a strong conceptual fit for the description of the master program tacitly organizing Fontane's compositional process. It provides a vantage point from which his creative practice can be evaluated and his achievements as a media artist can be gauged. One of these achievements is the production of sophisticated literary entertainment for journal readers. Fontane's media crossings led to novels that fulfill the double objective of *prodesse* and *delectare*, that is, "benevolent identification, amusing entertainment" and "moral instruction,"[104] but that add the crucial dimension of empathetic involvement. Fontane's characters, as we have seen, make claims to being real; over and over again, the reader is invited to map them onto "real" people or "real" social types and empathize with them. The characters, moreover, act out societal incidents and scandals that circulated as human-interest stories through the mass press and that the readers also recognized as real. In Fontane's novels, this "confusion of fiction and reality," a danger in the eyes of Enlightenment theorists, is "no longer a danger, but is desired"[105]—and is a key source of entertainment. Fontane's variant of *genus medium*, with its blending of several media modes, thus updated the Enlightenment model of the novel in such a way that it could compete with the nineteenth-century mass press, beating the mass press at its own human-interest-driven game and in its own stylistic register.

If sophisticated entertainment is one of the products of Fontane's creative practice, the grand achievement is the emulation of an overarching reality effect, a sustained "realism of the middle." Unlike reality effects based merely on peculiar yet narratively unmotivated details (the barometer on the wall in Flaubert's *A Simple Heart*, to cite Barthes' canonical example), it extends over multiple aspects of Fontane's poetics. His characters arise from the middle of life, bundling typifying attributes and embodying social types that always stop short of representing social extremes—on Fontane's social ladder, the lowest rungs are occupied by figures such as "die Runtschen," the one-eyed and slightly eerie household help in *Mathilde Möhring*, while on the top rungs, one finds country gentry or city aristocrats. No beggars; no

---

104 Ibid.
105 Ibid.

kings; and in the rare event that a king makes an appearance, he speaks not as a statesman, but as a human being.[106] Moreover, Fontane's narrator, as we saw in *A Man of Honor*, at times blends in with these fictional characters and at times comments on them ironically or sympathetically from a distance. The narrator speaks neither from a naïvely auctorial position nor as a fully decentered postmodern subject, as Mecklenburg puts it. Rather, the narrator, with his or her own personality, flaws, and inconsistencies, tells the story from the position of being "all-too-human"[107]—a middle position. Likewise, the interplay of discursive samples evokes the impression that life itself is speaking. Conversations seem to continue on their own, replicating a middle ground of commonsensical knowledge and values and pitting discursive positions against one another. Fontane's preferred imagery and his lexical and syntagmatic means realize this middle position linguistically and reinforce it. Each moral, political, or ideological position posited by one voice may be called into question by another voice. Throughout Fontane's narratives, value judgments, social concepts, and worldviews thus become unstable, and the reader is called upon either to observe or to enter the polyphonic sound- and image-scape of the novel—fictional, yet utterly familiar—and to discern his or her own position in it. As soon as the unsuspecting reader takes part in this game, the medium works its magic, pushing the content into the foreground. The effect closes the gap between *res* and *verba*, and the central questions that trouble the protagonists—the question of honor in *A Man of Honor*, art (*Kunst*) vs. kitsch in *Frau Jenny Treibel*, and guilt and gender roles in *Effi Briest*, to name but a few—acquire the status of real-life problems.[108] But Fontane's realism of the middle also

---

106 These characters extend the tradition of the bourgeois "middle hero," as defined by Lessing in his poetics of bourgeois tragedy. For an incisive discussion of the middle hero, see Paul Fleming, *Exemplarity and Mediocrity: The Art of the Average from Bourgeois Tragedy to Realism* (Stanford, CA: Stanford University Press, 2009), 48–62.
107 Mecklenburg, *Theodor Fontane: Romankunst der Vielstimmigkeit*, 119.
108 That Fontane's novels still have this effect on some critics becomes clear from Kathryn Ambrose, *The Woman Question in Nineteenth-Century English, German, and Russian Literature: (En)Gendering Barriers* (Leiden: Brill, 2016), 117–51. Ambrose reads selected Fontane novels, from *Ellernklipp* to *Mathilde Möhring*, at face value, as a mirror of both the author's and the era's changing attitude toward women, while it would seem more useful to trace how the novels themselves observe and process the contemporary gender discourse. For a treatment of this topic that takes into consideration how Fontane's novels *stage* the "Geburt sozialer Wirklichkeit aus ... Diskurselementen," see Gabriele Brandstetter and Gerhard Neumann, "'Le laid c'est le beau.' Liebesdiskurs und Geschlechterrolle in Fontanes Roman *Schach von Wuthenow*," *Deutsche Vierteljahrsschrift für Literaturwissenschaft und Geistesgeschichte* 72, no. 2 (1998): 246.

has something to offer the suspicious reader. Such a reader watches the process of world-making from a distance, enjoying the cunning and the cleverness with which Fontane not only constructs a fictional world through media effects, but lets the reader observe the construction.

Fontane's comprehensive *genus medium*, then, emulates a linguistic, aesthetic, and epistemological middle, a world that replicates and then deliberately goes beyond the mass-mediated source materials on which it is based. That it *emulates* rather than mimetically describes this middle is more than a terminological nuance. Mimesis takes "nature" as its source, striving to imitate and represent it. Emulation (*aemulatio*) also defines a process of imitation, but in contrast to mimesis, it is based on existing textual sources, not nature: *aemulatio* is a rhetorical exercise in which the orator takes up subject matter that has already been treated by another author and gives it a new treatment, transposing it into a new genre or putting it through a catalog of possible modifications.[109] It is performed in a conscious mode of competition in which the orator seeks to "rival and vie with the original in expressing the same thoughts"[110] and may even take the liberty "to go beyond the original." As a competitive practice based on pre-mediated sources, it describes with precision how Fontane proceeds. He may have claimed to be working on the basis of "real life," yet by now it should be clear that the substance of his realism was media content that he transformed, enhanced, and eventually reissued in the medium of the novel.

The *genus medium* that Fontane employed, however, was not a static given nor a ready-made object from a rhetorical catalog. Rather, he had to blend it together, going up and down the spectrum between naturalism at the bottom and aestheticism at the top, between platitudes and witty aperçus, colloquialisms and high-profile literary quotes, simple genre images and artfully arranged scenes. It also required that he dynamically mix voices together, turn up their volume (even when they were a bit jarring) or fade them out, for the sake of effective polyphony. "Of course it is possible to have too much of a good thing, and if Bülow were to speak throughout all 21 chapters, it would be simply insufferable," Fontane concedes, only to justify in the next breath why he gave Bülow so much air time: "from chapter 8 onwards, these witticisms (*Geistreichigkeiten*) cease altogether or recur only sporadically. And thus, I think, they can be tolerated, all the more so because it was my intention truly to convey . . . an image of the times (*Zeitbild*)" (HFA IV.3: 206). His statement underscores that it is the

---

109 Lausberg, *Handbook of Literary Rhetoric*, §1100–2.
110 Quintilian, *The Orator's Education*, vol. 4, Books 9–10, 357–8.

overall effect that counts, and that he deliberately calibrated this effect by adjusting the quantities of the ingredients that went into the mixture.

The process of comprehensive effect calibration in the *genus medium* was challenging because details on so many different levels had to be tweaked, and heterogeneous materials in so many different versions and stages of refinement had to be intercut with one another. In the words of McLuhan, "effect involves the total situation, and not a single level of information or movement."[111] Fontane's creative practices in the post-disposition stage can be understood as a (tacit) response to precisely this challenge. When he transitioned from the running lists, tentative dispositions, and initial building blocks of his compiling to coherent drafts and revision, he applied a procedure perhaps best described as "nonlinear editing." A concept derived from digital sound and video production, nonlinear editing refers to a practice in which segments of recorded material are rearranged freely on the recording surface, "thus breaking the linear flow of time."[112] The editor does not have to proceed in a set order but may modify any segment of a project, regardless of what comes before and after it. A "pre-digital" version of nonlinear editing is what we observe in Fontane's writing and revision process, which differed quite a bit from the processes of other nineteenth-century authors. Many of his colleagues wrote a first draft and then went through it page by page, editing it by scribbling changes directly into the manuscript. Annette von Droste-Hülshoff, for example, revised her manuscripts with interlinear edits so relentlessly that they became notoriously difficult to read, with entire sections appearing plain black.[113] While Fontane also made interlinear edits, he followed a method that deviated from Droste-Hülshoff's in two ways. He proceeded in small batches—usually chapters or individual scenes, which he wrapped up and stored together with working notes and alternate versions in paper envelopes—that did not necessarily follow the order of the narrative. He also put himself in a position in which he could read and evaluate his own dispositions and advanced drafts from a distant perspective. He often used extra sheets of paper to record his reading impressions of whatever he had in the making and to note down instructions for revision, as in the following example from *The Stechlin* (*Der Stechlin*). On a sheet of paper that he kept with drafts for the chapters on the election in Rheinsberg-Wutz, he commented: "The

---

111 McLuhan, *Understanding Media*, 43.
112 Peters, *The Marvelous Clouds*, 308.
113 A selection of Droste-Hülshoff's working manuscripts has been reprinted in Walter Gödden and Jochen Grywatsch, eds., *'Ich, Feder, Tinte und Papier.' Ein Blick in die Schreibwerkstatt der Annette von Droste-Hülshoff* (Paderborn: Schöningh, 1996).

preceding pages fail to tackle the matter properly. It must be about elections not to the [Prussian] *House of Representatives*, but to the *Reichstag*.... Katzenstein is there, too. Herr von Buch, however, is not, and in his stead speaks old Stechlin, who sends Herr von Buch's (take a better, more lumbering name) warmest compliments."[114] Fontane physically separated the processes of drafting, fleshing out, and blending together his projects from the processes of reading and evaluating them, and he realized both sets of operations with the help of various media of notation.

John Durham Peters rightly points out that writing has always functioned as a nonlinear recording medium, for as soon as words are fixed in writing, they can be moved around, replaced, and deleted: "writing, by spatializing data, makes it possible to play with time."[115] Any author's manuscript thus allows for "time-axis manipulation," to use the Kittlerian term. In theory, then, there is no reason Annette von Droste-Hülshoff could not have performed nonlinear editing with her manuscripts, too, and revised a section in the middle before turning to a section elsewhere. But Fontane's case differs in that his forms and media of notation maximized the potential for time-axis manipulation. The modules, lists, loose sheets, and batches of advanced material wrapped in paper sleeves facilitated nonlinear editing because they kept the material in all stages so eminently mobile and disconnected. Fontane's "writing" therefore consisted of much more than turning dispositions and notes into coherent drafts and polishing them. It prominently included activities such as "inserting" (*einschieben*), "interjecting" (*einschalten*), "besprinkling" (*einstreuen*), "interpolating" (*einrangiren*), "utilizing" (*verwenden*), "incorporating" (*unterbringen*), "implementing" (*erledigen*), "using" (*benutzen*), and "connecting" (*anknüpfen*), as he put it in his notes.[116]

Fontane's allocation of the processes of drafting and evaluating his drafts to different media of notation made it possible for him to move forward in recursive loops when mixing everything together. Commenting on his drafts from a distance, as his own first reader, Fontane turned revision into a communicative process in which two of his author personae—Fontane-the-compiler and

---

114 Cited according to the transcription provided in Julius Petersen, "Fontanes Altersroman," *Euphorion* 29 (1928): 25.
115 Peters, *The Marvelous Clouds*, 306.
116 These and similar verbs appear frequently in Fontane's notes as quoted in Petersen, "Fontanes Altersroman," 16; 22; 28; 39; 55; and Radecke, *Vom Schreiben zum Erzählen*, 246; they also appear, among other places, in E 3, 1V, 7R, and 22R.

Fontane-the-reader—conversed with one another.[117] Through such conversations with himself, he defamiliarized his drafts and subjected revision to the recursive logic of communication.[118] Externalizing his reading impressions, he could easily observe and assess them, reread them, and relate them anew to the sections of the project to which they referred. This process allowed him to observe his own readings of his drafts. He thus entered into a movement that Christoph Hoffmann, analyzing the notebooks of the physicist Ernst Mach, calls "loops of reading and revising" (*Schreib-Lese-Schleifen*).[119] Through these loops, Fontane continuously manipulated and reworked his heterogeneous drafts.

Fontane applied this procedure to all kinds of materials that were part of his projects, from unmodified source texts and dispositions in the form of keywords to drafts that had already been rewritten multiple times. The externalized stance of the reader, then, provided some crucial homogeneity in the challenging process of developing his projects and perfecting the *genus medium*. Whether a text section was in the first draft or the fifth, it became subject to the distinct observations of Fontane-the-reader, and these observations set in motion the recursive operative chains with which the author worked through his projects, one batch at a time. In this manner, Fontane-the-compiler and Fontane-the-reader were in a constant exchange, and the reader instructed the compiler on all creative core operations. For example, on drafts of the twenty-seventh chapter of *The Stechlin*, and specifically the figure of Adelheid, Fontane-the-reader commented: "The things Adelheid says are all very well, but it all ought to sound a little more aristocratic and—by inserting some good, sensible phrases—smack a little more of a good family (*ein bißchen mehr nach guter Familie schmecken*)."[120] In addition to such evaluative statements, the reader also told the compiler the order in which he should arrange certain components, which parts he should treat as central, and which parts he should shorten, delete, rewrite, or expand.

---

117 Previous inquiries into Fontane's working methods have already noted the peculiar *Selbstgespräche* that the author had with himself. None of them, however, analyzes what this really means for his poetics: that it subjects revision to the recursive logic of communication. See Petersen, "Fontanes Altersroman," 16; Berbig, "Mediale Textprozesse," 105; Hettche, "Die Handschriften zu *Vor dem Sturm*," 201; Radecke, *Vom Schreiben zum Erzählen*, 74–90, 121–6.
118 Sullivan suggests that it is easier for writers to take a removed, revisionary stance toward their own creations if they see them in a new form or medium. See Sullivan, *The Work of Revision* (Cambridge, MA.: Harvard University Press, 2013), 39.
119 Christoph Hoffmann, "Umgebungen. Über Ort und Materialität von Ernst Machs Notizbüchern," in *Portable Media. Schreibszenen in Bewegung zwischen Peripatetik und Mobiltelefon*, ed. Martin Stingelin et al. (Munich: Fink, 2010), 90.
120 Quoted according to Petersen's transcription in "Fontanes Altersroman," 57.

The specificity of Fontane's comments and instructions reveals that when he slipped into the role of the reader, he acted from a perspective that was not informed merely by his personal taste or intuition. Rather, he embodied his primary target audience, the readers of illustrated family journals, and—evaluating his drafts through their imagined eyes—to some degree *customized* his projects-in-the-making for them. Including the audience in his creative process was not an easy undertaking, considering how diverse this audience was (see Chapter 1). Here, Fontane benefited from his exhaustive sociological knowledge of his readers. Possessing such knowledge was not the norm in the German media landscape, where legal peculiarities erected barriers between writers and their readers. Journals were not sold in the street, but predominantly through subscription, and were then delivered by mail or through local booksellers.[121] Journal publishers thus often knew how many subscribers they had, but not who these subscribers were. This situation made "publisher's knowledge"[122] (*Verlegerwissen*) of the social composition, geographical differentiation, and preferences for topics or genres of the readership in a given region all the more valuable. Fontane spent a significant portion of his waking hours on acquiring such knowledge, as we have already seen (Chapter 3). With his *Wanderungen* network, he acquainted himself personally with many of the patriotically inclined readers for whom he wrote *Before the Storm*. Beyond this initial circle of readers, the practicing journalist Fontane observed the larger media scene with a degree of professionalism that fellow writers rarely mustered. In the course of his career, he published his novels in an astonishingly wide variety of newspapers and journals, for each of which he could precisely describe the "house sound," political leanings, preferred topics, moral limitations, and predominant types of readers.[123] "Every exertion of the mind takes on . . . a particular odor (*Geruch*) from the place where it reposes,"[124] Fontane wrote to the

---

121 Graf, "Die Ursprünge der modernen Medienindustrie," 416–20. See Chapter 1.
122 Ibid., 419.
123 See Roland Berbig and Bettina Hartz, eds., *Theodor Fontane im literarischen Leben: Zeitungen und Zeitschriften, Verlage und Vereine* (Berlin: De Gruyter, 2000). The spectrum extended from the highly conservative *Daheim* and *Gartenlaube* to the much more liberal *Vossische Zeitung*, the modern *Nord and Süd*, and the intellectual *Deutsche Rundschau*.
124 Letter to Julius Rodenberg, March 1, 1885, qtd. in Berbig and Hartz, *Fontane im literarischen Leben*, 101. This is not to say, however, that Fontane was *always* right in his assessment of outlets. For example, he assumed that *On Tangled Paths* (1887) would be a perfect fit for the readers of the *Vossische Zeitung*, whereas the risqué subject matter actually outraged the readers. See Berbig and Hartz, *Fontane im literarischen Leben*, 76.

publisher Julius Rodenberg, emphasizing how much a good fit between a literary project, a publishing house, and its audience mattered. Fontane became increasingly specific in the customization of his projects, trying to place his writings where they would be read by a suitable readership. For example, he strove to design "Berlin novels" for Berlin newspapers, to publish his detective stories in the *Gartenlaube*, and to publish the novel *Graf Petöfy* (set in Vienna and Hungary) in a Southern German journal, Hallberger's *Ueber Land und Meer*.[125] Once a novel-in-the-making had been accepted by a journal, Fontane referred to it as "the *Gartenlaube* novella" or "my novella for the *Vossin*," and when a deal with a periodical threatened to fall through, he nervously looked for other periodicals with a similar profile.[126] The readerships of these different media, imagined and embodied by Fontane, entered directly into the revision process. Fontane anticipated their expectations and catered to them while his novels were still in progress.

Regardless of Fontane's intended audience, his edits were designed to maximize the total aesthetic effect that a given customized project would have on the reader. It is indicative of Fontane's commitment to maximizing the effect that he approached this process through constant, tentative, and painstaking adjustments. The dialogue between Fontane-the-reader and Fontane-the-compiler is frequently driven by modal verbs, unfolds in the subjunctive mood, and is interspersed with adverbs that cast their referents in terms of provisionality and probability rather than definiteness: "I ought" (*ich müsste*), "I may" (*ich darf*), "probably," "perhaps," "for the time being" (*vorläufig*). As we have seen, the dialogue included numerous definite instructions, yet they often became considerably less certain in the next recursive loop and were thus not so binding as it might seem. Again, a comparison with Dickens, who also consciously calibrated literary effects with his number plans, brings the careful nature of Fontane's late-stage revision practice fully to light. Dickens ticked off brief questions one after another in a matter-of-fact style—the left side of the number plan for the fourth number of *Little Dorrit* reads: "[C]harging everything on providence? No. . . . Clenman's old sweetheart? Yes. Flora. . . . More of his character? Yes. How he stands toward Dorrit? Hardly" etc.[127] By contrast, Fontane weighed options, pondered alternatives, and

---

125 See Hans-Joachim Koniezcny, "Theodor Fontane und Westermann's illustrierte deutsche Monats-Hefte," *Fontane Blätter* 24 (1976): 574.
126 For example, see the letter that Fontane, anxiously waiting to hear from the editor of the *Vossische Zeitung* about the fate of *On Tangled Paths*, wrote to Emil Dominik, the editor of the journal *Zur guten Stunde*. HFA IV.3: 550–51.
127 Stone, *Dickens' Working Notes for his Novels*, 277.

tinkered—up until the very last minute. For example, on the envelope containing the well-developed draft of the fifth chapter of *L'Adultera*, Fontane remarked that while the chapter was "largely fine in pace and content," two changes had to be made: "1. Van der Straaten must already sprinkle in a few Berlinisms (*ein paar Berolinismen einstreuen*) when things are still going well," and listed a few options, including *wenn schon, denn schon* ("In for a penny, in for a pound"), and *na ob* ("Have I ever"). He went on: "2. A few more interruptions. Duquede must once again say: "He is overrated" (*Er wird überschätzt*) and the police councilor has to get in his two cents again, as well (*und der Polizeirath muß auch noch 'mal hineinreden*)."[128] Fontane's drafts, then, remained open to modification until the very end, regardless of whether they had already undergone multiple rewrites. These modifications often entailed strengthening textual features that would increase the journal readers' fascination with a given novel and help carry them across the interruptions between installments—they included the multiplication of allusions, increased ambiguity in the descriptions, symbolic threading, the refinement of the narrative perspective, and a growing emphasis on acoustic effects.[129] They also entailed dialing back. In a note, added to lists of idioms and quotations intended for the project *Allerlei Glück*, Fontane cautioned himself against the overuse of acoustic features, reminding himself: "I must be particularly wary of over-using certain peculiarities for mere effect (*durch zu viele kleine Eigenheiten wirken zu wollen*), like quotations, adages, Berlinisms, foreign expressions etc. It ends up just sounding too affected and overwrought (*gesucht und überladen*)."[130] The "effect" or *Wirkung*, in short, had to be carefully calibrated on a case-by-case basis, in accordance with what the audience of journal readers expected and with what Fontane expected of himself as a media artist. *This* was the "labor of whittling and shucking," the *Feil- und Pularbeit*, to which Fontane so often referred and that made the final stages of his creative process so time-consuming and laborious.

In sum, the reconstruction of the most salient parts of Fontane's creative process reveals its starkly inorganic nature. Nothing in this manufacture of literature was left to coincidence or chance. From the very first dispositions, through the stitching together and refinement of drafts, to the final, homogenizing rounds of revision, Fontane proceeded

---

128 I owe this example to Radecke, *Vom Schreiben zum Erzählen*, 247.
129 This general characterization of the direction that Fontane's revision often took follows Radecke's succinct summary of the research on Fontane's manuscripts in *Vom Schreiben zum Erzählen*, 17–32.
130 Quoted according to Petersen's transcription in "Fontanes Altersroman," 68.

purposefully and in direct exchange with what he assumed to be the demands of the market and his different audiences. Perfecting his "realism of the middle," in its straightforward entertainment and its self-reflexive, artful qualities, was his first priority, both in his poetics of the novel and in his compositional practice. The notational forms that enabled the inorganic creative process, the constant adjustments to the media scene in which Fontane published, and the calibration of a comprehensive reality effect were Fontane's textual building blocks and lists. Until the very end, these remarkably mobile and flexible forms kept open the possibility of modification. They helped Fontane to carry out a creative program that is perhaps best expressed in a marginal note, added to a disposition for the project "Allerlei Glück": "it must all be thoroughly blended"—*alles muß sich sehr mischen* (F1: 169).

Coda

The "Uncreative" Writing of *Mathilde Möhring*

The terms with which Fontane's creative process has been described in this study—mechanical, inorganic, derivative, calculating—raise questions about the nature of his authorship and the aesthetic status of the texts he produced. Can compiling, the intentional use of secondhand sources, actually be a form of art? Or might the deliberate nature of Fontane's textual practices—what Flaubert, in a different context, derisively called "the stratagems of the plan, the combinations of effects, all the underhanded calculations"[1]—preclude the creation of genuine works of art? Fontane confronts this question in one of the last—if not *the* last—of his book-length prose projects, the unfinished novel *Mathilde Möhring* (1891/1896), which was published only after his death.[2] The

---

1   Letter to Louise Colet, June 26, 1853, qtd. in Roland Barthes, *The Preparation of the Novel: Lecture Courses and Seminars at the Collège de France (1978–1979 and 1979–1980)* (New York: Columbia University Press, 2010), 129.
2   Fontane left the project in a very advanced draft that was nevertheless incomplete and unpolished. Among other things, the closing section of the final chapter ends abruptly; Chapters 9–11 are numbered provisionally; figures appear with alternative names; a couple of "continuity errors" occur; and there are numerous unfinished sentences, as well as alternative phrasings (*Mehrfachformulierungen*), throughout the manuscript, according to Radecke's textual-genetic analysis. Fontane's notes indicate that he was in the middle of making revisions when he set the project aside and planned to revise it at least one more time. The reasons he abandoned it are unclear; Radecke assumes that his inability to secure a publishing contract for the project kept him from finishing it. The text appeared for the first time in 1906 in the *Gartenlaube* in a heavily modified edition supplied by Josef Ettlinger and then again in 1969 in an edition provided by Gotthard Erler that was much closer to Fontane's manuscripts. Both of these editions, however, glossed over the textual-genetic marks of incompletion and "fixed" inconsistencies. Finally, Radecke's historical-critical edition, published as part of the *Große Brandenburger Ausgabe* in 2008, offers a more accurate impression of the actual *Textgestalt*, representing marginal

novel reflects several of the textual practices and technological conditions to which Fontane's literary production owes its material foundations and aesthetic profile, and provides an ironic commentary on compiling as a creative mode of authorship.

On the surface, *Mathilde Möhring* is a sometimes cynical tale about social mobility, interclass marriage, gender dynamics, and money. Set in the Berlin of the *Gründerzeit* era, it charts 23-year-old Mathilde Möhring's temporary foray into the upper middle class. The early death of her father, the family's breadwinner, hits her and her mother hard. They are forced to share a modest apartment, "three or four floors up" (*3 oder 4 Treppen hoch*, GBA I.20: 5), which they rent from a *nouveau riche* speculator. To make ends meet, they sublet the better of their two bedrooms to lodgers, an operation that the unprepossessing and very pragmatic "Thilde" controls. She is determined not to let herself or her mother slip into poverty; in fact, this ambitious working-class woman wants not just financial security, but also "standing" (*Ansehen*) and "a title" (67). Mathilde recognizes her opportunity when a handsome but apathetic law student and prospective civil servant (*Rechtskandidat*) with the promising name of Hugo Großmann moves in. According to Thilde's instantaneous and cold assessment, he is a "shiftless slugabed" (*bequemer Schlappier*) without "spunk" (*Muck*) but "as good as gold" in terms of his solidity and prospects (12; 16). Despite her mother's criticism—"O Thilde, you will insist on calculating everything" (*du rechnest immer alles aus*, 40), her mother exclaims—Thilde gradually inserts herself into Hugo's life and takes the reins. Their different social positions effectively create a mésalliance, but she manages to coach the lackadaisical student through his final exam, find him a job as mayor of the provincial town of Woldenstein in western Prussia, and engineer their joint rise to Woldenstein's upper crust through clever political scheming. The couple does not get to enjoy its success, however. Exhausted by the social functions that they now have to attend, Hugo falls ill with pulmonary tuberculosis. Upon his death, Thilde returns to Berlin. She moves back in with her ailing mother and makes a living as a schoolteacher, only somewhat better off than before her brief marriage. As one of Fontane's last notes to himself about the project indicates, Thilde and her mother's "financial circumstances" remain "insecure" (*unsicher*, 286) to the very end.

---

comments made by Fontane, incomplete sentences, and alternative formulations through a simple linear apparatus in the text (most importantly, alternatives appear between double slashes and backslashes // \\). The following analysis of *Mathilde Möhring* is based on this edition. For a detailed account of the genesis of the text, its history, and the principles behind the edition, see Radecke's editorial commentary in GBA I.20: 151–209.

Yet matters of money, marriage, and class constitute only the novel's surface. Wrapped in this "novel of calculation"[3] (*Roman des Rechnens*), we find yet another tale—one that skillfully brings opposing creative principles and aesthetic modes into interaction. The text drops several hints that it ought also to be read as a self-reflective novel about textual production methods, material poetics, and the aesthetic status of compiled texts. Thilde's eyes, as the reader learns at the very beginning, have an "altogether prosaic gleam" (*ganz prosaischen Glanz*), a phrase that, as Elisabeth Strowick points out, evokes Hegel's notion of the prosaic condition of the world.[4] Indeed, Thilde embodies "the prosaic" from head to toe. With the exception of her "sharply cut profile," her appearance is entirely plain, as the unusually unforgiving narrator emphasizes:

> the thin lips the ashen hair sparsely stuck on, the ear remaining too small from which all manner seemed to be missing[,] deprived the whole of any sensuous magic and the most sober seemed the water-blue eyes.... if once people spoke of a silver gaze here it would have been fit to speak of a tin gaze.
>
> *die dünnen Lippen das spärlich angeklebte aschgraue Haar, das zu klein gebliebne Ohr daran allerhand zu fehlen schien alles nahm dem Ganzen jeden sinnlichen Zauber und am nüchternsten wirkten die wasserblauen Augen.... wenn man früher von einem Silberblick sprach so konnte man hier von einem Blechblick sprechen.*
>
> (8)

With her utilitarian nature and pronounced lack of emotional depth, she clearly epitomizes *Prosa*. Hugo stands for the opposite—for *Poesie* and a traditional, if somewhat tired, notion of aesthetic beauty. A handsome man, he is an enthusiastic reader of Calderon, Schiller, English novels, Lenau, and Zola. Occasionally, Hugo, possessed of "aesthetic feeling" and endowed with a "latent poetic force" (*latenter Dichterkraft*, 45), allows himself to daydream about life as an actor, but he is altogether too lethargic—"definitely more of a dormouse" than a "country postman" (*entschieden mehr Siebenschläfer als . . . Landbriefträger*, 21), as his decadent friend Rybinski mockingly puts it—to break out of

---

[3] I am borrowing this formulation from Hugo Aust, "*Mathilde Möhring*. Die Kunst des Rechnens," *Interpretationen. Fontanes Novellen und Romane*, ed. Christian Grawe (Stuttgart: Reclam, 1991), 275–95.

[4] Elisabeth Strowick, "'Mit dem Bazillus is nicht zu spaßen.' Fontanes 'Finessen' im Zeichen der Infektion," *Der Deutschunterricht* 55 (2003): 43–50.

his predetermined path to an administrative position. Convinced of his uselessness, and fully aware that times have become tough even for the upper middle class, he too is troubled by status anxiety: "They won't accept just anyone these days, and being a candidate (*Referendar*) is the minimum" (24). The "poetic" mode associated with him is insecure and characterized by resignation. Thilde and Hugo thus embody the two sides of the cultural debate with which this study began: they represent the alleged "ill-matched marriage of literature to industry," as Hermann Hauff termed it, the consequences of which Fontane and his concerned contemporaries attempted to gauge.

If the outward appearances and personalities of the two main characters already provide important clues to the poetological dimension of the novel, Thilde's name corroborates this idea still further. "Mathilde," as readers of Fontane know from one of his other works, *Cécile*, is a name with a special significance, one "that [evokes] the sound of the keyring" (*bei dem man das Schlüsselbund hört*, GBA I.9: 95). She provides hermeneutic access, then, to the narrative's coded layer of meaning. Her actions leave no doubt that the knowledge she "unlocks" has to do with Fontane's creative process: Thilde performs textual practices that echo several of the methods that this study has shown to be central to Fontane's authorship. In fact, her means of reading, researching, and patchwriting are crucial for the novel as a whole, insofar as they shape every major turning point of the plot.

This intertwining of textual practices and plot development begins at the story's outset. The first practice that proves formative is Thilde's measured reading of erotically charged literature, which leads directly to Hugo's marriage proposal. Just a few weeks after Hugo has moved in with the Möhrings, he contracts measles. Thilde cares for and reads to him during his convalescence. When Hugo shyly asks whether she might be willing to read "that story of Zola's in which paradise appears" (43), that is, the rather explicit *La faute de L'Abbé Mouret* (1875), she realizes that this is an opportunity to make herself attractive to him and show that she is not "priggish" (*spießbürgerlich*, 44). Usually careful to retain an overall semblance of "virtue," she agrees to purposefully overstep what is considered proper by reading the risqué story. Her tactic of walking the line between "propriety" (*Sittlichkeit*) and eroticism stages Fontane's own tactic of stretching the limits of the acceptable with sexually charged topics and allusions to appeal to a wide audience, but without fully transgressing the moral codes of the family magazines in which he usually published. Even though we have reason to assume that Thilde's reading is rather awkward—she tells Hugo that she will pronounce every word "perfectly loud and clear and with full emphasis," "like Luther" (44)—her strategy works; Hugo is puzzled but intrigued by her "enlightened opinions" in conjunction with her solid character and decides to propose to her.

Next, we encounter Thilde rapidly combining newspaper topics, which she strings together associatively for the sake of lighthearted and witty conversation, or causerie, another key Fontanean method. She accepts Hugo's marriage proposal under the condition that he first pass his final law exam (47). Convinced that Hugo is not motivated enough to get through the exam on his own, she quizzes him every night for three months, sweetening the bitter pill of exam preparation with entertaining study breaks or "entrefilets" (75): Thilde distracts Hugo by reading newspaper passages to him, creating all sorts of interesting connections between topics until he is sufficiently refreshed to continue studying. (This and other of Thilde's textual practices are discussed in more detail later.) Again, Thilde succeeds—Hugo scrapes through the exam, and they can get married.

As the novel advances into its final section, Thilde's textual practices continue to shape the couple's fate. After Hugo has passed the exam, Thilde ventures out every day to the *Lesehalle für Frauen*, the women's reading hall, with a pencil and a piece of scrap paper (*Conceptbogen*) in her pocket to scour the papers, looking for a position for him. Just like Fontane in his authorship, she goes through a variety of papers—"one [newspaper] is not enough; I need many" (83). When she spots a promising advertisement for the position of mayor of Woldenstein, she immediately copies it, takes it home, puts Hugo on the night train to the province, and tells him to present himself to the "city council" the next day. He follows through and lands the position. In Woldenstein, Thilde deploys a local informer to learn what is on the Woldensteiners' mind, and she teaches Hugo how to exploit knowledge about current topics to gain publicity:

> "And see, Hugo, that's how you have to go about it . . . always on the *qui vive*, always keep an eye on what benefits the whole, that's how you make it happen and that's what I called the 'ideas.' Not everybody is able to take the world to a higher place but to take Woldenstein far enough to appear in the papers every week and for the people to learn 'there's a place called Woldenstein,' yes, Hugo, *that* is possible and in your hand . . ." "Or in yours," smiled Hugo.

> „Und sieh, Hugo, so mußt Dus anfangen . . . immer auf der Auskiek, immer sehen, was so dem Ganzen zu gute kommt, damit zwingst Du's u. das is [sic], was ich die „Ideen" genannt habe. Die Welt kann nicht jeder auf einen höhren Fleck bringen, aber Woldenstein so weit zu bringen, daß es alle Woche mal in der Zeitung steht und daß die

Menschen erfahren „es giebt einen Ort, der heißt Woldenstein", ja, Hugo, das ist möglich und das ist in Deine Hand gegeben . . . " „Oder in Deine" lächelte Hugo.

(94)

Again, one cannot fail to see the pronounced thematization of Fontane's own methods of working with local informers and mobilizing current topics in his prose projects.

The parallels between Thilde's textual practices and those constituting Fontane's authorship extend further still and become increasingly ostentatious. Managed by his well-informed wife, Hugo quickly becomes popular with the Woldensteiners. Only the most powerful local politician, Prefect (*Landrath*) von Dunajewski/ Schmuckern, remains reserved. But Thilde manages to turn him around by cleverly patching together a false newspaper article that praises the Prefect's personality and treats his victory in the upcoming local elections as a foregone conclusion. The anonymous article is attributed to Hugo, who now becomes the object of the Prefect's enthusiastic support. The textual practices staged on the level of the narrative conclude with Thilde's use of sound samples to convey her position in a particular social and political class. Dancing with the Prefect on New Year's Eve, she repeats a statement that he made on the *Simultanschulfrage*, the question of interdenominational schools. Impressed, the Landrath inquires about Thilde's political interests, to which she responds with Bismarckian tropes: "I may say that only the prince's speeches made me what I am. There has been so much talk of blood and iron. But I should beg leave to say this of his speeches: to me they are a wellspring of iron, a bath of steel. (*Aber von seinen Reden möchte ich für mich persönlich sagen dürfen: Eisenquelle Stahlbad.*) I always came away feeling refreshed" (102). Thilde, then, profiles herself sociologically with the help of discursive sound samples, performing an aesthetic strategy that was also the key to Fontane's construction of fictional characters.

Thus, as a whole, *Mathilde Möhring* is as much about reading and text production as it is about money, gender, and class. Its complex staging of figures, their actions, and the ensuing consequences begs to be read poetologically. Against a backdrop of status anxiety and financial insecurity, Fontane's late prose project reflects on key characteristics of his freelance authorship, which was shaped by his desire to rise to the literary upper crust and distinguish himself from mere "novelistic tin," *Romanblech* (a term that resonates metaphorically with Thilde's "tin gaze", BaH 198), but which was also determined by material considerations, opportunistic decisions, careful aesthetic calculations, and mechanical working methods. Precisely because Fontane opened his authorship up to such "prosaic" textual practices as formulaic writing and compiling, he placed a great deal of emphasis on his "laying out his evidence, in his capacity as author, before *others*" (*Dichterbeweisführung vor anderen*, BaH 291), that is, on his ability to produce great literature with these practices. In describing Mathilde's and Hugo's interaction, the novel thus takes up the uncomfortable question of whether compiling, the deliberate designing of effects, and related textual practices can be reconciled with the idea of creating works of art.[5]

Upon first sight, the novel appears to underwrite the cultural-critical idea of the "ill-matched marriage" and convey the incompatibility of *Poesie* and *Prosa*. After all, Thilde's textual practices seem to leave no room for art. In fact, she actively stifles whatever artistic potential they might contain. The opposite of an aesthetic soul, Thilde has utilitarian motives for everything she does with written material. Her textual practices have lethal consequences for Hugo—tellingly, he dies from *Schwindsucht*[6] (pulmonary tuberculosis; the German name of the disease resonates with *schwinden*, to waste away, gradually disappear), providing what seems to be the perfect metaphor for the fate of "the poetic" when it comes under the unmitigated authority of "the prosaic." Upon closer scrutiny, however, the novel lays out the dynamics of a relationship that is much more complex, turning what initially appears to be a simple instance of mésalliance into a multifaceted story of mutual dependency and changing perspectives. Hugo is not merely the victim in this narrative; he too exploits his partner, realizing that Thilde "had just what he was lacking, being lively, resourceful, practical" (45). Conversely, without him, she is unable to maintain her upper middle-class lifestyle and slips back into her "small" ways (*das ganz Kleine*), a working-class existence determined by financial constraints, which is to say that she depends on him as much as he depends on her. What is more, Hugo and two other figures from his social sphere discover the artistic potential in Thilde's textual practices and attribute aesthetic value to them. A complex interactional pattern thus unfolds in the narrative, in the course of which compiling's aesthetic status changes several times. Trying to take advantage of Hugo, Thilde performs textual practices that she herself pronounces uncreative. But Hugo and

---

5   To be clear, I am not arguing for a straightforward autobiographical reading with one-to-one correlations. Scholars have already explored this interpretative possibility, drawing parallels between Hugo and Fontane and mapping Thilde interchangeably onto Fontane's mother, wife, daughter Methe, or friend Mathilde von Rohr. The present reading maintains that rather than writing directly about himself in *Mathilde Möhring,* Fontane comments on the material media and discursive system that made his writing possible.

6   I owe this observation about the telling name of Hugo's disease to Stefan Greif, "'Neid macht glücklich.' Fontanes 'Mathilde Möhring' als wilhelminische Satire," *Der Deutschunterricht* 50, no. 4 (1998): 54.

his acquaintances then undercut Thilde's judgment and elevate her methods of reading and text production above the merely utilitarian level. Through the constellation Thilde/Hugo, the narrative of *Mathilde Möhring* thus demonstrates in a sophisticated and very entertaining manner that *Prosa* and *Poesie*, "calculation" and "art," "industry" and "literature," far from being mutually exclusive, are constitutively connected. It also shows how much is at stake in the evaluation of Thilde's textual practices and the "artwork" question, an evaluation that is fundamentally a matter of perspective.

A detailed analysis of two examples suffices to establish this pattern. The examples reveal the stunning extent to which Thilde's textual practices coincide with Fontane's, and they demonstrate how dramatically the value of compiling and the other textual operations changes depending on who assesses them. The first can be found in Thilde's assembling of a false newspaper article for the most popular local newspaper, the *Königsberger Hartungsche Zeitung*. Her practice closely resembles Fontane's own methods of patching together false foreign correspondence from printed sources (Chapter 2). Driven by a societal and political agenda, Thilde systematically looks through the "electoral matters" in the *Vossische Zeitung* every day and finally finds what she needs "in a little correspondence from Myslowitz." Describing the process, she explains to Hugo: "And according to this model I dressed it [her own article; PM] up. Once the frame is in place, it's quite easy to make a doll" (*Und danach hab ich es zurecht gemacht. Wenn man erst das Gestell hat, ist es ganz leicht eine Puppe zu machen*, 99). Like Fontane in his writings for the *Kreuzzeitung*, Thilde follows a template, a familiar schema, and uses preproduced elements that she needs only to adapt.[7] The resulting article mimics Fontane's own false foreign correspondence in tone (note the collective plural *wir*, "us," the subjunctive voice, and the impersonal constructions with *man*, "one," and *es*, "it") and content, as the beginning indicates:

> Woldenstein December 14th. Much activity is already being undertaken in our county for the elections, without there being much of a pressing need for it. For the election of our Prefect von // [1] Dunajewski [2] Schmuckern \\ may be considered a foregone conclusion, since, so far as we have hitherto been able to learn, his political opponents have foregone putting up a candidate against him. Both the Polish-Catholic and the progressive party // [1] are, their contradictory political opinions notwithstanding, to so high a degree persuaded of / [1a] the [1b] the outstanding \ [2] unite in

---

7   Aust also notes that Thilde juggles with "standardisierten Textfunktionen," but he does not connect this observation to Fontane's own practices of assembling texts. See Aust, "*Mathilde Möhring*. Die Kunst des Rechnens," 281.

paying tribute to the outstanding \\ character and administrative abilities of Prefect v. Z. that they consider it their duty, even at the cost of their other political convictions, to express their trust in him. It seems fit to speak here of a triumph of personality which is all the more impressive for the prefect's household exerting such an attraction upon the Poles.

<u>Woldenstein 14. September.</u> *In unsrem Kreise rührt man sich bereits für die Wahlen, ohne daß eine besonders pressante Benöthigung dafür vorläge. Denn die Wahl unsres Landraths v.* // [1] *Dunajewski* [2] *Schmuckern* \\ *darf wohl als gesichert angesehn werden, da, seine politischen Gegner so viel wir bisher erfahren konnten, seine politischen Gegner auf Aufstellung eines Gegenkandidaten verzichtet haben. Sowohl die polnisch-katholische sowie die fortschrittliche Partei* // [1] *sind, trotz entgegenstehender politischer Anschauungen, in so hohem Grade von* / [1a] *den*[1b] *den hervorragenden* \ [2] *vereinigen sich in Würdigung der hervorragenden* \\ *Charakter- und Verwaltungseigenschaften des Landraths v. Z. überzeugt, daß sie's für ihre Pflicht halten, selbst auf Kosten ihrer sonstigen politischen Ueberzeugungen, ihrem Vertrauen gegen ihn Ausdruck zu geben. Es läßt sich hier von einem Siege der Persönlichkeit sprechen der umso glänzender ausfällt als das landräthliche Hauswesen eine Anziehung auf das Polenthum äußert.*

(97)

Even Thilde's strategies for "authenticating" her "news" echo Fontane's exactly. The article cites vague sources; later, it deploys local knowledge ("Mrs. von Schm. has founded a nursery association, to which the third denomination has also contributed"), uses commonplace tropes, and closes with a platitude that corroborates the worldview of the conservative circles it targets: "Nobility, if it reads the signs of the times and foregoes exclusivity, is always the locality's best representative" (*Adel, wenn er die Zeit begreift und auf Exclusivität verzichtet, ist immer die beste Lokalvertretung*, 98). The article is so well written that Hugo initially doubts his wife's authorship: "But no that could not be, it was all too adroit (*zu gewandt*), too practiced (*zu routinirt*)." Another voice—one of Hugo's Woldenstein acquaintances—confirms the article's aesthetic value, calling it "// [1] a fine little article. [2]" "Very well written; fine, I should say . . . ." \\"[8] Thilde herself firmly negates these aesthetic

---

8   Here, it is particularly interesting that Fontane revised his preliminary formulation, "feins Artikelchen," with a phrase that emphasizes the evidence that the article has been *authored*, i.e., its stylistic and tonal qualities ("Sehr gut *geschrieben*"), thus setting the stage for Thilde to negate these qualities ("geschrieben nicht eigentlich").

qualities and denies that the text has any originality. In response to Hugo's "now really—you wrote it?" she explains: "No, not exactly wrote" (*geschrieben nicht eigentlich*, 98), attributing the authorship to "a stranger, whom I now owe a debt of gratitude," that is, the author of the correspondence from Myslowitz. While Thilde sees herself as a "mere" compiler and craftswoman, it is the Prefect—a voice of authority—who insists that her textual practices are more than a craft. After he has danced and conversed with Thilde on New Year's Eve, he congratulates Hugo on his formidable wife, definitively raising the status of her textual practices above the level of the "merely journalistic" and mechanical:

> "Mayor, my friend, that's a top-notch wife you've got yourself there. Stupendously crafty. In the know like a reporter or better, actually; reporters are machines and only follow with their hands and ears. But your wife, my word, she's got something, spunk, breeding, chic. Tell me, what's she by birth? colonists perhaps or a family that dropped out the nobility."
>
> *„Burgemeister, Freund, Sie haben eine famose Frau. Kolossal beschlagen. Weiß ja Bescheid wie'n Reporter oder eigentlich besser; die Reporter sind Maschinen und folgen blos mit Ohr und Hand. Aber, Ihre Frau, Donnerwetter, da merkt man was, Muck, Race* [sic]*, Schick. Sagen Sie, was is es für eine geborne? vielleicht Colonie oder Familie, die den Adel hat fallen lassen."*
>
> (102)

The Prefect's enthusiastic remark indicates that Thilde is superior to reporters, who are described as recording media without agency. She, by contrast, mediates information and texts actively (*da merkt man was*; "she's got something"), even artistically—the reference to the "colonists" suggests as much. With this reference, the Prefect associates Thilde with the French refugee families who, having migrated to Brandenburg and Berlin after the Edict of Potsdam of 1685, made significant contributions to the intellectual and cultural life of this region (Fontane's own ancestors were among these French refugees).[9] In brief, whereas Thilde interprets her own practice as unoriginal and uncreative, Hugo, his Woldenstein acquaintance, and the Prefect adduce evidence that calls her self-assessment into question. In this scene, it is Thilde's understanding of her past, of her origin, that is at stake in the evaluation

---

9 For historical background on the colonists, see Radecke's editorial commentary, GBA I.20: 383.

of her working methods. Depending on the perspective, Thilde's textual practices corroborate either her "modest origins" (102) or her association with an established intellectual and aesthetic tradition.

The second example, Thilde's cross-reading of newspapers during the review sessions with Hugo, strengthens the idea that the question of the aesthetic value of her textual practices is both momentous and fundamentally a matter of perspective. Here, Thilde's method mirrors Fontane's practice of "reading in leaps and bounds." Recall that for Fontane, associative chains of topics, inspired by the rapid combination of reading materials, were at the heart of the creative process (Chapter 3). He used this technique liberally, as the analysis of his working notes on the "dialogues" for *Before the Storm* (Notebook E 2) evinced. In *Mathilde Möhring*, Thilde applies this technique with great precision to rally Hugo's "weak energy" (*schwache Kraft*) during study breaks:

> When examining, which [Thilde] tried where possible to turn into a lively game of question and answer, began to wear and signs of fatigue began to appear in Hugo's features, she would bring a glass of tea or red wine or a ginger nut and while she presented him with it ... and spoke of the Moluccas where they pickled ginger the best and where they had (or perhaps they just copied them) the great porcelain jugs from China, she passed on to matters of the day and read to him about the persecution of Christians in China or about the French in Annam and Tonkin or about the war the Dutch were forced to fight with the natives or about the French in Tonkin or the great persecution of Christians in China. Weren't the Japanese far ahead of the Chinese and a people that had such observation of nature and was able to make such flowers and such birds, did it not represent a culture of the highest sort, as you could see in every tea tray. And that was not to speak of the lacquer, which was unsurpassed too. And Thilde was great at transitions and if with the help of the ginger nut she had begun with the Moluccas and Japan and China, she had no trouble in finding her way back to Kroll and la Sembrich and even to Rybinski, and if she then offered up a spicy morsel that she collected specifically for Hugo's benefit and it had refreshed him, she said now then does a sale break a lease or not?
>
> (75–6)

Wenn das Examiniren, das [Thilde] nach Möglichkeit in ein quickes Frage- und Antwortspiel verwandelte, bedrücklich zu werden anfing und sich in Hugo[s] Zügen etwas von Ermüdung zeigte, so brachte sie ein Glas Thee oder Rothwein oder eine Ingwertüte und während sie ihm daraus präsentirte ... und von den Molucken sprach wo der Ingwer am

> *besten eingemacht würde und wo sie von China her (oder vielleicht würden sie auch nachgemacht) auch die großen blaugeblümten Porzellankrüge hätten, glitt sie zu Tagesfragen über und las ihm von Christenverfolgungen in China vor oder von den Franzosen in Anam und Tonkin oder von dem Kriege den die Holländer mit den Eingebornen führen müßten oder von den Franzosen in Tonkin oder von den großen Christenverfolgungen in China. Die Japaner seien den Chinesen doch weit voraus und ein Volk daß* [sic!] *solche Naturbeobachtung habe und solche Blumen und solche Vögel machen könne, das repräsentire doch eine allerhöchste Cultur, was man jedem Theebrett absehen könne. Dabei wolle sie noch nicht einmal von dem Lack sprechen, der doch auch unerreicht dastehe. Dabei war Thilde groß in Uebergängen und wenn sie so mit Hülfe der Ingwertüte bei den Molucken und Japan und China begonnen hatte, war es ihr ein Leichtes sich bis zu Kroll und der Sembrich und sogar bis zu Rybinski zurückzufinden und wenn sie dann noch was Pikantes das sie eigens für Hugo sammelte zum Besten gegeben und ihn erfrischt hatte, sagte sie nun aber bricht Verkauf Miethe oder nicht.*

Thilde performs exactly the kind of fast-paced run (or *percursio*) through newspaper articles that, according to Fontane, turns reading into a generative act. Even the categories of topics that Thilde connects map onto those that Fontane put down in his response to the survey "The Technique of Artistic Production" and his working notes: news from exotic places appears right next to stories about national celebrities and anecdotes about locals (here: "Moluccas" – "Kroll and la Sembrich" – "Rybinski"; in Fontane's survey response: "the emperor of China" – "la Lucca" – "Nante Strump, loitering on the street corner"); and grand generalizations about culture give way to everyday objects (here: "observation of nature" – "tea tray"; in the survey response: "Bismarck" – "Berlin bun"; in his notes on *Before the Storm*: "the various tribes" – "On the Marches as the land of cake and vegetables").

In such chains of topics, the "big world" enters into the "small world,"[10] which, as the Fontane scholarship has thoroughly established, is a process with great aesthetic merit. The narrating voice in *Mathilde Möhring* even hints at this aesthetic dimension when it states that Thilde was "great at transitions" and emphasizes her ability to make the

---

10 As Strowick puts it, in these combinations of topics, "Heterogenes wird zusammengebracht, das Große metonymisch mit dem Kleinen/Alltäglichen verbunden". See "'Mit dem Bazillus ist nicht zu spaßen,'" 45. The entry "Kleine und Große (das)" in the *Fontane Lexikon* provides more background on this connective narrative principle in the context of Fontane's poetics. See *Fontane-Lexikon. Namen – Stoffe – Zeitgeschichte*, ed. Helmuth Nürnberger and Dietmar Storch (Munich: Hanser, 2007), 244–5.

thematic leaps from Indonesia's production of ginger back to the theaters of Berlin with ease. But whatever aesthetic potential the process contains, Thilde's utilitarian nature squashes it—the lighthearted and witty train of topics culminates in her asking Hugo a legal question, gunpoint style, which abruptly stops the associative play. Hugo, by contrast, fully recognizes the aesthetic potential inherent in Thilde's practice. Equipped with an "aesthetic sense capable of appreciating finesse" (*aesthetischen Sinn, der sich an Finessen erfreuen konnte*), he is also able to appreciate "the method by which Thilde proceeded" and observes it "with a certain artistic pleasure" (*künstlerischen Behagen*, 75). Using the term *Finessen*, "finesse" or "subtleties," a key word in Fontane's poetics, Hugo attributes creativity and artistry to her practice, clearly elevating it above the utilitarian level. Hugo shows us what to watch for and what to cherish in Thilde's technique, which thus ceases to be a merely prosaic exercise. For Hugo, this is a decisive discovery because it helps him to overcome the "occasional disgruntlement" (75) that strikes him when he analyzes "the un-heroic aspect (*das Unheldische*) of his situation." Nothing less than Hugo's happiness thus hinges on the evaluation of Thilde's technique and performance.

The two examples demonstrate how much is at stake in the assessment of Thilde's textual practices. At the same time, they show that on the level of the narrative, the novel refuses to give a conclusive answer to the question of whether these practices might result in original works of art. This overarching question is ultimately answered not through narrative developments, but through literary form: the novel *performs* the *Finessen* that Thilde is unable to appreciate, but which, according to Hugo's remark, turn her method into art. Fontane, as we have seen, understands *Finessen* as "the art of association, establishing relations, building bridges"[11] (*Kunst des Anknüpfens, des Inbeziehungbringens, des Brückenschlagens*). In other words, he treats the concept as a narrative technique that creates connections among textual elements—allusions, moments of prefiguration, cross-references, quotations, recurring symbols, and other forms of repetition—and thus generates a surplus of meaning. *Mathilde Möhring* is replete with these *Finessen*. Many of them occur intratextually. For instance, after Hugo has recovered from the measles, he is described with the words "he does still look a bit scraggy" (*ein bißchen spack sieht er noch aus*, 58) during

---

11 NFA XXI/2: 109. On the understanding of *Finessen* as a fundamental Fontanean narrative technique, see Strowick, "'Mit dem Bazillus is nich zu spaßen,'" 43–5; Renate Böschenstein (1985), "Fontanes 'Finessen.' Zu einem Methodenproblem der Analyse 'realistischer' Texte," in *Renate Böschenstein: Verborgene Facetten. Studien zu Fontane*, ed. Hanna Delf von Wolzogen and Hubertus Fischer (Würzburg: Königshausen & Neumann, 2006), 85–90.

his and Thilde's engagement celebration. This formulation, as Strowick has noted, returns in the scene in which Thilde, now widowed, eagerly prepares for her teaching exam and her mother expresses concern for her health: "I'm just so terribly worried by all your learning. You look so scraggy and have such a sheen about you (*Du siehst so spack aus und hast solchen Glanz*). He had the consumption, after all. And in the end . . ." (120). The repetition of the phrase *spack aussehen* creates a connection between Hugo's illness and Thilde's eagerness to study, indicating that he has "infected" her—not in the medical sense, but affectively, with a passion for reading, which the surprised Thilde recognizes ("and now I find that he had more of an influence on me than I on him", 118).[12] This *Finesse* calls for the re-evaluation of Thilde and Hugo's relationship. This new perspective invites the reader to go back to the beginning and read Thilde and Hugo's interaction differently, which might lead to the discovery of new *Finessen*, setting in motion the interpretive spiral for which Fontane's novels are famous.

However, such intratextual subtleties provide only the base layer on which the novel proves its artistry. *Mathilde Möhring* also contains *Finessen* that branch out, in self-aware fashion, to a number of Fontanean works as intertexts. What makes *Mathilde Möhring* such an important text in the debate about the aesthetic status of compiling is that it adds a layer of self-reflexive irony to Fontane's work with *Finessen*. The novel plays with entire constellations of figures, plot elements, phrases, narrative symbols, and ethical values that are fixtures in the genre that Fontane helped to shape—the Berlin social novel (*Berliner Gesellschaftsroman*)—only to subvert them. In other words, Fontane showcases his artistry in *Mathilde Möhring* by sampling his own authorship. In reusing key elements of his textual production in new and entertaining ways, he generated a work that was "derivative" (derived from materials and ideas that he typically used) but that nonetheless emerged as one of his most original compositions. It would exceed the scope of this coda to analyze all of the ways Fontane subverts the patterns of his own authorship; it suffices to track how *Mathilde Möhring* ironically inflects three key elements of *Effi Briest*, the novel with which he developed the genre of the Berlin social novel to perfection and which he completed before and while he worked on *Mathilde Möhring*. These elements are traditional gender roles, the honeymoon as a classical plot device, and the narrative symbol of the "pink lamp hanging by three chains" (*rosafarbne Ampel an drei Ketten*). In

---

12 See Strowick, "'Mit dem Bazillus is nicht zu spaßen,'" 46–7. As Strowick shows, many more such intratextual connections are established through recurring formulations like "mit Masern/Thilde war nicht zu spaßen"; "wie am Schnürchen", "ohne [mit] Muck"; "der kommt [nicht] wieder".

all three instances, Fontane's reuse of these elements yields comic and original results.

In *Effi Briest*, clearly recognizable "feminine" and "masculine" gender roles, and their associated expectations and norms, provide the foundation for the narrative and motivate the conflict that drives the novel forward: a coldly calculating career bureaucrat, Innstetten, marries an emotionally intense young woman, Effi. Both parties enter this marriage due to social ambitions, but Effi ultimately does not survive it. *Mathilde Möhring* repeats this basic constellation but satirically inverts the distribution of "typically masculine" and "typically feminine" personality traits. Here, the female protagonist, Thilde, plays the part of the calculating and emotionally deprived character. The parallels between Thilde and Innstetten are striking indeed. Like Innstetten, she dislikes extravagant pleasures, is initially described as frigid ("kissing is not her strong suit," *küssen ist nicht ihre Force*, Hugo remarks with noticeable regret), and is manipulative. She instrumentalizes the "creeps" (*Grusel*) that the Möhrings' disfigured household help gives Hugo in ways that invert Innstetten's deployment of the "haunting Chinaman." Thilde attempts to decrease Hugo's fear, while Innstetten's *Angstapparat aus Kalkül*, his "device deliberately calculated to create fear,"[13] is designed to frighten Effi and keep her under control. Hugo, in turn, exhibits some of the personality traits that in *Effi Briest* are attributed to the woman. Like Effi, he yearns for emotional warmth, affection, and entertainment, is easily bored, and has a soft spot for *Phantastisches* and adventures that are tinged with a bit of danger: "I should after all have become something of that kind, performing artist or // [1] aeronaut or [2] balloonist (*Luftschiffer*) [. . .]. Or \\ animal tamer (*Thierbändiger*), from childhood, that's always had an appeal to me" (70). Furthermore, he resembles Effi in that he possesses an impressionable imagination, and he is drawn to a show by an artist called "the Daughter of the Air" (*die Tochter der Luft*), which is, of course, Effi's epithet. Add that like Effi, Hugo dies from tuberculosis, and that a sleigh ride proves fateful in both narratives, and one cannot but read Mathilde/Hugo as the comic inversion of Innstetten/Effi, an inversion that spoofs not only the gender conventions of Wilhelmine society but also the narrative motor of Fontane's own masterpiece.

The honeymoon, an established plot device in *Effi Briest* and in Fontane's Berlin social novels in general, also becomes the subject of narrative mockery in *Mathilde Möhring*. Conventionally, the honeymoon presents an opportunity to prefigure the development of the newlyweds

---

13 Theodor Fontane, *Effi Briest*, trans. Mike Mitchell (Oxford: Oxford University Press, 2015), 106; GBA I.15: 157.

and emphasize certain dynamics in the relationship. In *Effi Briest*, it is an affair of splendor and leads the couple to Italy, a classical destination and site of cultural-historical significance that prompts Innstetten to introduce his wife to the principal artistic treasures (*Hauptkunstschätze*)[14] of the world. *Mathilde Möhring* picks up this plot device but transforms it. Hugo explicitly rejects the traditional model of the Fontanean honeymoon, stating "I don't think it right that it must always be Dresden and Brühl's Terrace, let alone the Zwinger" (80). Instead, his and Thilde's "honeymoon" is a brief stop in Küstrin on the way to Woldenstein, where Hugo suggests they see "Crown Prince Frederick's prison . . . and the site where Katte was executed."[15] This is a deeply ironic use of the honeymoon as a narrative device, as it replaces a destination known for its beauty with a local historical site known for a tale of insubordination and execution that prefigures Hugo's own "captivity" and death in the province.

Finally, the "pink lamp [hanging] by three chains" (*rosafarbne Ampel an drei Ketten*), a symbol of sexual desire, anxieties, and violence that occurs with striking prominence in both novels, corroborates the idea that *Mathilde Möhring* consciously samples and inverts central symbols of *Effi Briest*. In *Effi Briest*, the lamp is a wish: the not-yet-married Effi hopes to receive one as a wedding present, imagining how poetic it would be to see everything in her bedroom bathed "in a red glow."[16] The wish remains unfulfilled, however, because her mother worries about Effi's reputation in the province, where people might "laugh" at the lamp or talk about her "being badly brought up, and perhaps even worse"[17] Besides, married life is easier to bear, Effi's mother indicates, when there is "darkness instead of light and a soft glow" (*statt Licht und Schimmer ein Dunkel*, ibid; GBA I.15: 33). In *Mathilde Möhring*, the red lamp returns with opposite connotations. Thilde receives it as an unsolicited wedding present from her neighbor, a coarse woman named Schmaedicke/Schmädicke, who gives it to encourage Thilde and Hugo's erotic activity:

> I took a long time thinking what was best. And then I remembered how gloomy it was when Mr. Schmaedicke came. I don't mind saying it was a dreadful moment and a bit like a thief creeping in the night. And yet Mr. Schmaedicke was as harmless a man as

---

14 Fontane, *Effi Briest*, trans. M. Mitchell, 27; GBA I.15: 41.
15 GBA I.20: 80. Greif, who analyzes this passage in terms of its narrative irony, attributes this statement to Thilde, but in Radecke's edition, it is clear that it must be ascribed to Hugo. See Greif, "'Neid macht glücklich,'" 51.
16 Fontane, *Effi Briest*, trans. M. Mitchell, 22.
17 Ibid.

you might wish for. And ever since, whenever there's a wedding, this is what I give. Too much light ain't good neither, but a bit muted, that's all right.

(88)

Ich hab es mir lange überlegt, was wohl das Beste wäre. Da mußt ich dran denken, wie duster es war, als Schmaedicke kam. Ich kann wohl sagen, es war ein furchtbarer Augenblick und hat so was wie wenn ein Verbrecher schleicht. Und Schmaedicke war doch so unbescholten wie einer nur sein kann. Und seitdem, wenn eine Hochzeit is, schenke ich so was. Zu viel Licht is auch nich gut, aber so gedämpft, da geht es.

As if to further mock the use of the lamp in *Effi Briest* and Frau von Briest's concern about the vulnerability of young women's reputations in small towns, Thilde first hangs the lamp not in the bedroom, where nobody would see it, but in the hallway of her and Hugo's house in Woldenstein (90). It shines "so wonderfully" that it kindles the Woldensteiners' curiosity and convinces them that "surely that sort of thing is in vogue among Berliners" (*Berliner haben doch einen Schick für so was*, 94). Indeed, the red lamp becomes fashionable and an object of envy in Woldenstein, to the point that one of the other villagers, Rebbeca Silberstein, inveigles her father "that he might likewise acquire such an object." Again, we are invited not merely to relish this "satirical deconstruction"[18] of Wilhelmine social codes, but also to enjoy Fontane's cynical inversion of one of his own key narrative symbols. Through these inversions, the novel becomes a satirical and sophisticated mirror image of *Effi Briest* that demonstrates the artistry of its underlying compositional method.

In the final analysis, *Mathilde Möhring* treats the question of art in a fitting way: in true Fontanean fashion, it lays out complex reasons for and against the aesthetic value of compiling and the related textual practices, remaining ambivalent on the level of the narrative. As a whole, however, it provides an answer that is as performative as it is ironic. The novel takes Fontane's mode of creativity a step further and *remixes* key patterns of his previous literary production, resulting in a "derivative" work that is both entertaining and aesthetically effective *because* it constellates familiar materials anew. With one of his last prose works, Fontane arguably delivered the best evidence of the art, creativity, and originality of his authorship. Assembling a novel that mixes key elements of his poetics together in an ironic way, he departed from the pattern of the Berlin social novel to break genuinely new ground.

* * *

---

18 Ibid.

This study began with a close examination of Fontane's official portrait and authorial image (Figure 0.1). Over the course of four chapters, the image has been taken off the wall, removed from its old frame, put under a magnifying glass, and turned around a few times. Its central elements have been closely scrutinized: the posturing author supposedly writing in solitude, of course, but also his desk, tools, sources, and media of writing. This investigation has made clear to what extent the material realities of Fontane's text production deviated from the scripted fantasy of creativity that the staged photograph conveys. In the age of digital image editing, it would be easy to produce a new version of Fontane's portrait, one that comes closer to the material dimension of his creativity.

The new version would show a bustling writer's workshop, a working environment conducive to a form of authorship that was to some extent collective, to some extent rationalized, economically smart, and highly productive. The photograph would be quite crowded—we would certainly add in Fontane's wife, along with his other helpers, and we would also include many more stacks of newspapers, piles of journal issues, draft materials in all forms and sizes, letters, and paper slips than are visible in the original photo. We would push the desk away from the window and into the middle of the room to show its design peculiarity, the numerous drawers at the front and at the back. We would pull the drawers open and make sure the notebooks, paper sleeves, and cardboard boxes were in the picture, because these "writing tools," to borrow a well-known coinage by Nietzsche, "took part in the forming" of Fontane's output. We would expose the lists that were so crucial to Fontane's compiling and show the special *Kasten* in which his novels in progress awaited decision. The workshop activity would still center on Fontane, but he would be shown in interaction with his network of co-contributors and technologies of production.

This modified image could hardly go back in the old frame. Differently put, the Fontane workshop adds to the criticism of narratives that treat German realism as "provincial," isolated, and backward-looking. The Fontane workshop was a site of literary innovation: it embraced the new technological conditions and derived both a business model and a new form of art from the abundance of sources that defined the media-historical moment. As we have seen, Fontane's workshop poetics led to innovations on the level of form, to a "remixed" middle style and a brand of realism that hybridized mass media for the sake of heightened aesthetic effectiveness. What is more, it led to innovations on the level of actual creative practice. With the help of his workshop, Fontane *sampled* late nineteenth-century culture on a new scale, applying his "pharmaceutical" core operations—"separation," "breaking down," "mixing," and "transplantation"—to the mass media of his time. His realism emerged from an unruly database of cultural elements that were available for creative recombination. This mode of creativity was far from parochial. On the contrary: the case of Fontane's workshop shows that if we look underneath the smooth textual surfaces and behind the sentimental plots of the second half of the nineteenth century, creative procedures and textual strategies come into view that turn the supposed "valley between two peaks" into a period keenly relevant to understanding literary creativity in our own time.

Bibliography

Archival Materials

Deutsches Literaturarchiv Marbach, Marbach am Neckar, Germany:
MPF: A: Fontane, Theodor. Prosa. Materialien. "Figur in einer Berliner Novelle." Folio sheet. Accession Number 59.1196.

Staatsarchiv Coburg, Coburg, Germany:
Nachlass (NL) Hesekiel 3.4, manuscript sheet "Frankreich," in George Hesekiel's hand. Includes three newspaper clippings.

Staatsbibliothek zu Berlin – Preußischer Kulturbesitz, Berlin, Germany:
Handschriftenabteilung, Nachlass Theodor Fontane. *Notizbücher*. Archival Signatures A 1–21; B 1–15; C 1–14; D 1–11; E 1–6. Currently held at the *Theodor Fontane-Arbeitsstelle*, Georg-August-Universität Göttingen, Germany.
Handschriftenabteilung, Nachlass Theodor Fontane. *Mathilde Möhring*. Manuscript draft, page 263R.

Stiftung Stadtmuseum Berlin, Berlin, Germany:
Literatursammlung, Nachlass Theodor Fontane.
Paper Sleeves (*Banderolen*) with Labels (*Etiketten* or *Zettel*). "Hoppenrade." Folded Newspaper sheet, with label. Archival Signature V 67_863_B,Hoppenrade.
"Pichelsdorf." Folded Newspaper sheet, with label. Archival Signature 48_522 R_B,Pichelsdorf.
"Marquardt." Folded Newspaper sheet, with label. Archival Signature V 67_869_B,Marquardt.
"Havelland." Folded Newspaper sheet, with two labels. Archival Signature V 67_869_B,Havelland.
"Mein Leipzig lob ich mir." Folded Newspaper sheet, with label. Archival Signature V 67_864_B,Leipzig.

The British Library, London, United Kingdom:
German Newspaper Collection, Max Schlesinger's "Englische Correspondenz." Shelf Mark LOU.LON 2 [1861].

German Newspaper Collection, Max Schlesinger. "Englische Correspondenz." June 22, 1861. Lithographed sheet.
German Newspaper Collection, Max Schlesinger. "Englische Correspondenz." June 24, 1861. Lithographed sheet.
German Newspaper Collection, Max Schlesinger. "Englische Correspondenz." June 25, 1861. Two lithographed sheets.
German Newspaper Collection, Max Schlesinger. "Englische Correspondenz." June 26, 1861. Lithographed sheet.
German Newspaper Collection, Max Schlesinger. "Englische Correspondenz." June 27, 1861. Lithographed sheet.
German Newspaper Collection, Max Schlesinger. "Englische Correspondenz." June 28, 1861. Two lithographed sheets.

Theodor-Fontane-Archiv, Potsdam, Germany:
Nachlass Theodor Fontane.
"Mappe für die 'Wanderungen', alle 4 Teile. (Bei jeder neuen Auflage durchzusehn.)" Blue folder with label, containing manuscript materials, newspaper clippings, and letters. 29 sheets. Archival Signature Kf.
"Schreibtischfoto." Theodor Fontane at his desk. 17.5 cm x 23 cm. Studio Zander & Labisch, Berlin, 1896. Archival Signature TFA_AI 96_33853.
Wanderungen durch die Mark Brandenburg. Erster Theil. Die Grafschaft Ruppin. Barnim=Teltow. Berlin: Hertz, 1865. [Interleaved and annotated copy.] Archival Signature Q10.
Wanderungen durch die Mark Brandenburg. Zweiter Theil. Das Oderland. Barnim. Lebus. Berlin: Hertz, 1863. [Interleaved and annotated copy.] Archival Signature Q11.

Victoria and Albert Museum, London, United Kingdom:
National Art Library, Forster Collection. Charles Dickens's "Number Plan" for number XVIII of *The Personal History of David Copperfield*. Manuscript, Archival Material 1850.

Printed Sources
Note to the reader: Fontane's works appear in alphabetical order, rather than date order, for clarity.

"An die Herren Collegen!" [Editorial.] *Die Feder* 1, no. 1, April 15, 1898.
"Das genesende Kind. Nach dem eignen Oelgemälde auf Holz gezeichnet von Ernst Fischer." *Die Gartenlaube* 15 (1865): 229.
"Der Gang zur Mitternachtschristmesse in den Tiroler Alpen. Nach der Natur aufgenommen von Stauber." *Die Gartenlaube* 3 (1865): 37.
"Fontane, Theodor." In *The Oxford Companion to German Literature*, 3rd ed. Edited by Henry Garland and Mary Garland. Online edition. Oxford: Oxford University Press, 2005, no pag.
"Pressen der HHrn. Bauer und König in Oberzell bei Würzburg." *Polytechnisches Journal* 21, no. 114 (1826): 474–6.
"Vor der Hundehütte. Originalzeichnung von L. Beckmann." *Die Gartenlaube* 20 (1865): 309.

Bibliography 279

"Wie die Illustrirte Zeitung entsteht." *Leipziger Illustrirte Zeitung* no. 1000, August 30, 1862.

Ambrose, Kathryn. *The Woman Question in Nineteenth-Century English, German, and Russian Literature: (En)Gendering Barriers*. Textxet: Studies in Comparative Literature 80. Leiden: Brill, 2016.

Asbach, Julius. "Schaefer, Arnold Dietrich." In *Allgemeine Deutsche Biographie (ADB)*. Vol. 30. Leipzig: Duncker & Humblot, 1890, 521–4.

Assmann, Aleida. *Cultural Memory and Western Civilization: Functions, Media, Archives*. Translated by Aleida Assmann with David Henry Wilson. Cambridge: Cambridge University Press, 2011.

Assouline, Pierre. *Simenon: A Biography*. Translated by Jon Rothschild. New York: Knopf, 1997.

Aust, Hugo. "Mathilde Möhring. Die Kunst des Rechnens." In *Interpretationen. Fontanes Novellen und Romane*, edited by Christian Grawe, 275–95. Stuttgart: Reclam, 1991.

Banham, Rob. "The Industrialization of the Book 1800–1970." In *Companion to the History of the Book*, edited by Simon Eliot and Jonathan Rose, 273–90. Malden, MA: Blackwell, 2007.

Barthes, Roland. "Inaugural Lecture." In *A Barthes Reader*, edited by Susan Sontag, 461–7. New York: Hill and Wang, 1982.

Barthes, Roland. "The Reality Effect" (1968). In *The Rustle of Language*. Translated by Richard Howard, 141–8. Oxford: Blackwell, 1986.

Barthes, Roland. "Writing Reading." In *The Rustle of Language*. Translated by Richard Howard, 29–32. Oxford: Blackwell, 1986.

Barthes, Roland. *The Preparation of the Novel: Lecture Courses and Seminars at the Collège de France (1978–1979 and 1979–1980)*. Translated by Kate Briggs. European Perspectives: A Series in Social Thought and Cultural Criticism. New York: Columbia University Press, 2010.

Becker, Eva D. "Literaturverbreitung 1850 bis 1890." In *Literarisches Leben: Umschreibungen der Literaturgeschichte*, 109–41. St. Ingeberg: Röhrig, 1994.

Beetham, Margaret. "Towards a Theory of the Periodical as a Publishing Genre." In *Investigating Victorian Journalism*, edited by Laurel Brake et al., 19–32. Basingstoke: Palgrave Macmillan, 1990.

Belgum, Kirsten. *Popularizing the Nation: Audience, Representation, and the Production of Identity in Die Gartenlaube, 1853–1900*. Lincoln, NE: University of Nebraska Press, 1998.

Benjamin, Walter. "The Work of Art in the Age of Its Technological Reproducibility." In *Walter Benjamin: Selected Writings*, edited by Howard Eiland and Michael W. Jennings. Translated by Edmund Jephcott, 101–33. Vol. 3: 1935–1938. Cambridge, MA: Belknap Press of Harvard University Press, 2002.

Berbig, Roland. "Das Ganze als Ganzes oder: Pastor Schmutz und Geheimrat Stiehl. Zur Rezeptionssteuerung der 'Wanderungen' durch Fontane." *Berliner Hefte zur Geschichte des literarischen Lebens* 2 (1998): 75–94.

Berbig, Roland. "'aber zuletzt – [. . .] schreibt man doch sich selbst zu Liebe'. Mediale Textprozesse. Theodor Fontanes Romanerstling Vor dem Sturm." In *Theodorus Victor. Theodor Fontane, der Schriftsteller des 19. am Ende des 20. Jahrhunderts. Eine Sammlung von Beiträgen*, edited by Roland Berbig, 99–120. Literatur – Sprache – Region 3. Frankfurt a. M.: Lang, 1999.

Berbig, Roland. "2.21 Die Gegenwart." In *Theodor Fontane im literarischen Leben: Zeitungen und Zeitschriften, Verlage und Vereine*, edited by Roland Berbig and

Bettina Hartz, 212–13. Schriften der Theodor Fontane Gesellschaft 3. Berlin: De Gruyter, 2000.

Berbig, Roland. *Theodor Fontane Chronik*. With Josefine Kitzbichler. 5 vols. Berlin: De Gruyter, 2010.

Berbig, Roland, and Bettina Hartz, eds. *Theodor Fontane im literarischen Leben: Zeitungen und Zeitschriften, Verlage und Vereine*. Schriften der Theodor Fontane Gesellschaft 3. Berlin: De Gruyter, 2000.

Berg-Ehlers, Luise. *Theodor Fontane und die Literaturkritik. Zur Rezeption eines Autors in der zeitgenössischen konservativen und liberalen Berliner Tagespresse*. Bonn: Winkler, 1990.

Beta, Ottomar. "Er hat mich bis zuletzt geottomart. Gespräche in London und Berlin." In *"Erschrecken Sie nicht, ich bin es selbst." Erinnerungen an Theodor Fontane*, edited by Wolfang Rasch and Christine Hehle, 34–43. Berlin: Aufbau, 2003.

Biernacki, Richard. "The Social Manufacture of Private Ideas in Germany and Britain, 1750–1830." In *Wissenschaftskolleg zu Berlin. Jahrbuch 1998/99*, edited by Wolf Lepenies, 221–46. Berlin: Wissenschaftskolleg zu Berlin, 2000.

Bisky, Jens. "Zur Verlagsgeschichte der 'Wanderungen durch die Mark Brandenburg' 1860–1945. Mit einer kommentierten Bibliographie." *Berliner Hefte zur Geschichte des literarischen Lebens* 1 (1996): 112–32.

Blair, Ann M. "Note Taking as an Art of Transmission." *Critical Inquiry* 31 (2004): 85–107.

Blair, Ann M. *Too Much to Know: Managing Scholarly Information before the Modern Age*. New Haven, CT: Yale University Press, 2010.

Blair, Ann M., and Peter Stallybrass. "Mediating Information, 1450–1800." In *This Is Enlightenment*, edited by Clifford Siskin and William B. Warner, 139–63. Chicago: University of Chicago Press, 2010.

Blomqvist, Clarissa. "Der Fontane-Ton. Typische Merkmale der Sprache Theodor Fontanes." *Sprachkunst. Beiträge zur Literaturwissenschaft* 35, no. 1 (2004): 23–34.

Blomqvist, Clarissa. "'Dreiviertel ist corrigiren und feilen gewesen.' Theodor Fontanes Bearbeitung eigener Texte." *Euphorion* 111, no. 1 (2017): 75–91.

Böschenstein, Renate. "Fontanes 'Finessen.' Zu einem Methodenproblem der Analyse 'realistischer' Texte" (1985). In *Renate Böschenstein: Verborgene Facetten. Studien zu Fontane*. Edited by Hanna Delf von Wolzogen and Hubertus Fischer, 85–90. Fontaneana 3. Würzburg: Königshausen & Neumann, 2006.

Böschenstein, Renate. "Namen als Schlüssel bei Hoffmann und Fontane." *Colloquium Helveticum* 23 (1996): 67–91.

Bosse, Heinrich. "Schreiben." In *Historisches Wörterbuch des Mediengebrauchs*, edited by Heiko Christians, Matthias Bickenbach, and Nikolaus Wegmann, 482–97. Cologne: Böhlau, 2015.

Bowman, Peter J. "Fontane and the Programmatic Realists. Contrasting Theories of the Novel." *Modern Language Review* 103, no. 1 (2008): 129–42.

Braese, Stephan. "Im Labyrinth des Fortschritts. Fontanes *Ein Sommer in London*." In *Realien des Realismus. Wissenschaft – Technik – Medien in Theodor Fontanes Erzählprosa*, edited by Stephan Braese and Anne-Kathrin Reulecke, 27–52. Berlin: Vorwerk 8, 2010.

Brandstetter, Gabriele, and Gerhard Neumann. "'Le laid c'est le beau.' Liebesdiskurs und Geschlechterrolle in Fontanes Roman *Schach von Wuthenow*." *Deutsche Vierteljahrsschrift für Literaturwissenschaft und Geistesgeschichte* 72, no. 2 (1998): 243–67.

Brieger, Lothar. *Theodor Hosemann. Der Maler des Berliner Volkes*. Compiled by Lothar Brieger. Munich: Delphin, 1920.
Brinkmann, Richard. "Der angehaltene Moment: Requisiten, Genre, Tableau bei Fontane." *Deutsche Vierteljahrsschrift für Literaturwissenschaft und Geistesgeschichte* 53, no. 3 (1979): 429–62.
Brückner, Wolfgang. "Trivialisierungsprozesse in der bildenden Kunst zu Ende des 19. Jahrhunderts, dargestellt an der 'Gartenlaube.'" In *Das Triviale in Literatur, Musik und bildender Kunst*, edited by Helga de la Motte-Haber, 226–54. Frankfurt a. M.: Klostermann, 1972.
Brunner, Constantin. "Die Technik des künstlerischen Schaffens. Vorläufige Mitteilung!" *Der Zuschauer* 1, no. 1 (February 15, 1893): 34.
Bürger, Peter. *Theory of the Avant-Garde*. Translated by Michael Shaw. Manchester: Manchester University Press / Minneapolis, MN: University of Minnesota Press, 1984.
Butt, John, and Kathleen Tillotson. *Dickens at Work*. London: Methuen, 1957.
Butzer, Günter. "Unterhaltsame Oberflächen und symbolische Tiefe: Die doppelte Codierung realistischer Literatur in Storms Immensee." In *Geselliges Vergnügen: Kulturelle Praktiken der Unterhaltung im langen 19. Jahrhundert*, edited by Anna Ananieva, Dorothea Böck, and Hedwig Popme, 319–46. Bielefeld: Aisthesis, 2011.
Butzer, Günter. "Von der Popularisierung zum Pop: Literarische Massenkommunikation in der zweiten Hälfte des 19. Jahrhunderts." In *Popularisierung und Popularität*, edited by Gereon Blaseio, Hedwig Pompe, and Jens Ruchatz, 115–35. Cologne: DuMont, 2005.
Byrd, Vance. "The Politics of Commemoration in Wien und die Wiener (1841–44)." *Journal of Austrian Studies* 47, no. 1 (2014): 1–20.
Byrd, Vance. "Epigraphs and the Journal Edition of Droste-Hülshoffs *Judenbuche*." *Colloquia Germanica* 49, no. 3–4 (2016): 178–99. Special Issue: Periodical Literature in the Nineteenth Century, eds. Vance Byrd and Sean Franzel.
Cahn, Michael. "Hamster: Wissenschafts- und mediengeschichtliche Grundlagen der sammelnden Lektüre." In *Lesen und Schreiben im 17. und 18. Jahrhundert. Studien zu ihrer Bewertung in Deutschland, England, Frankreich*, edited by Paul Goetsch, 63–77. Tübingen: Narr, 1994.
Campe, Rüdiger. "Die Schreibszene. Schreiben." In *Paradoxien, Dissonanzen, Zusammenbrüche. Situationen offener Epistemologie*, edited by Hans-Ulrich Gumbrecht and Karl Ludwig Pfeiffer, 759–72. Frankfurt a. M.: Suhrkamp, 1991.
Carlyle, Thomas. *Sartor Resartus: The Life and Opinions of Herr Teufelsdröckh*, edited by Charles Frederick Herold. New York: Odyssey Press, 1937.
Chaouli, Michel. "Remix: Literatur. Ein Gedankenexperiment." *Merkur* 63 (2009): 463–76.
Christians, Heiko. *Crux Scenica. Eine Kulturgeschichte der Szene von Aischylos bis YouTube*. Metabasis – Transkriptionen zwischen Literaturen, Künsten und Medien 18. Bielefeld: Transcript, 2016.
Church, Scott H. "A Rhetoric of Remix." In *The Routledge Companion to Remix Studies*, edited by Eduardo Navas, Owen Gallagher, and xtine burrough, 43–53. New York: Routledge, 2015.
Cicero, Marcus Tullius. *Brutus: Orator*. Translated by G. L. Hendrickson and H. M. Hubbell. Loeb Classical Library 342. Cambridge, MA: Harvard University Press, 1939.
Cramer, Florian, and Matthew Fuller. "Interface." In *Software Studies: A Lexicon*, edited by Matthew Fuller, 149–52. Cambridge, MA: MIT Press, 2008.

Crane, Susan A. *Collecting and Historical Consciousness in Early Nineteenth-Century Germany*. Ithaca, NY: Cornell University Press, 2000.
Cusack, Andrew. *The Wanderer in Nineteenth-Century German Literature: Intellectual History and Cultural Criticism*. Studies in German Literature, Linguistics, and Culture. Rochester, NY: Camden House, 2008.
Daston, Lorraine. "Taking Note(s)." *Isis* 95, no. 3 (September 2004): 443–8.
Denkler, Horst. *Wilhelm Raabe: Legende – Leben – Literatur*. Tübingen: Niemeyer, 1989.
Dickens, Charles. *Dickens' Working Notes for His Novels*. Edited by Harry Stone. Chicago: University of Chicago Press, 1987.
Dickens, Charles. *The Letters of Charles Dickens*. Edited by Madeline House and Graham Storey. Vol. 1 (1820–1839). Oxford: Oxford University Press, 1965.
Dilg, Peter. "Apotheker als Sammler." In *Macrocosmos in Microcosmo: Die Welt in der Stube. Zur Geschichte des Sammelns 1450 bis 1800*, edited by Andreas Grote, 453–74. Opladen: Leske und Budrich, 1994.
Dotzler, Bernhard J. "Genuine Correspondences: Fontane's World Literature." Translated by Chris Chiasson. *The Yearbook of Comparative Literature* 55 (2009): 264–99.
Downing, Eric. *Double Exposures: Repetition and Realism in Nineteenth-Century German Fiction*. Stanford, CA: Stanford University Press, 2000.
Efimova, Svetlana. "'Man hat hier alles in Bild und Schrift beisammen': Wissenserzeugung in Theodor Fontanes Notizbüchern und Werk." *Zeitschrift für deutsche Philologie* 4 (2017): 501–32.
Eisenstein, Elizabeth. *The Printing Press as an Agent of Change: Communications and Cultural Transformations in Early-Modern Europe*. Cambridge: Cambridge University Press, 1979.
Encke, Julia. *Kopierwerke. Bürgerliche Zitierkultur in den späten Romanen Fontanes und Flauberts*. Münchener Studien zur literarischen Kultur in Deutschland. Frankfurt a. M.: Lang, 1998.
Engelsing, Rolf. *Der Bürger als Leser. Lesergeschichte in Deutschland 1500–1800*. Stuttgart: Metzler, 1974.
Erickson, Lee. *The Economy of Literary Form: English Literature and the Industrialization of Publishing, 1800–1850*. Baltimore, MD: Johns Hopkins University Press, 1996.
Erler, Gotthard. "Druck- und Editionsgeschichte, Nachlaß, Forschungsstätten." In *Fontane-Handbuch*, edited by Christian Grawe and Helmuth Nürnberger, 889–905. Stuttgart: Kröner, 2000.
Ernst, Wolfgang. "Nicht Organismus und Geist, sondern Organisation und Apparat. Plädoyer für archiv- und bibliothekswissenschaftliche Aufklärung über Gedächtnistechniken." *Sichtungen* 2 (1999): 129–39.
Eschenburg, J. J. *Entwurf einer Theorie und Literatur der schönen Wissenschaften; zur Grundlage bey Vorlesungen*. Frankfurt a. M., Leipzig, 1790.
Ester, Hans. "Fontane und der Fortsetzungsroman." In *Formen ins Offene. Zur Produktivität des Unvollendeten*, edited by Hanna Delf von Wolzogen and Christine Hehle, 59–76. Untersuchungen zur deutschen Literaturgeschichte 151. Berlin: De Gruyter, 2018.
Estermann, Alfred, ed. *Inhaltsanalytische Bibliographien deutscher Kulturzeitschriften des 19. Jahrhunderts* (IBDK). Vol. 3 *Die Gartenlaube* (1853–1880); vol. 6 *Deutsche Roman-Zeitung* (1864–1880); vol. 8 *Westermanns Monatshefte* (1856–1880). Munich: Saur, 1995.

Estermann, Monika, and George Jäger. "Geschichtliche Grundlagen und Entwicklung des Buchhandels im Deutschen Reich bis 1871." In *Geschichte des deutschen Buchhandels im 19. und 20. Jarhundert*, edited by Georg Jäger, Dieter Langewiesche, and Wolfram Siemann, 17–41. Vol. 1.1. Frankfurt a. M.: MVB, 2001.

Fertig, Ludwig. "Ein Kaufladen voll Manuskripte: Jean Paul und seine Verleger." *Archiv für Geschichte des Buchwesens* 32 (1989): 273–395.

Fidicin, Ernst. *Die Territorien der Mark Brandenburg oder Geschichte der einzelnen Kreise, Städte, Rittergüter als Fortsetzung des Landbuchs Kaiser Karls IV*. 4 vols. Berlin: Guttentag, 1857–1864.

Fischer, Hubertus. "Fontanes 'Zietenhusarenschaft' – nicht nur eine Regimentsgeschichte." *Fontane Blätter* 97 (2014): 73–88.

Fleming, Paul. *Exemplarity and Mediocrity: The Art of the Average from Bourgeois Tragedy to Realism*. Stanford, CA: Stanford University Press, 2009.

Fontane, Friedrich. "Geschichten aus Mark Brandenburg. Ein Beitrag zur Fontane=Forschung." In *Ruppiner Kreiskalender* 23 (1933): 38–41.

Fontane, Friedrich. "Potsdamer Straße 134c." In *'Erschrecken Sie nicht, ich bin es selbst,'* edited by Wolfgang Rasch and Christine Hehle, 80–6. Berlin: Aufbau, 2003.

Fontane, Theodor. *A Man of Honor* [*Schach von Wuthenow*]. Translated by E. M. Valk. In *Theodor Fontane: Short Novels and Other Writings*, edited by Peter Demetz, 1–134. New York: Continuum, 1982.

Fontane, Theodor. *Before the Storm. A Novel of the Winter of 1812–13* [*Vor dem Sturm. Roman aus dem Winter 1812 auf 13*]. Translated by R. J. Hollingdale. Oxford: Oxford University Press, 1985.

Fontane, Theodor. *Briefe an Georg Friedlaender*. Edited by Kurt Schreinert. Heidelberg: Quelle & Meyer, 1954.

Fontane, Theodor. *Briefe an Mathilde von Rohr*. Edited by Kurt Schreinert. Berlin: Propyläen, 1970.

Fontane, Theodor. *Briefe an Wilhelm und Hans Hertz 1859–1898*. Edited by Kurt Schreinert. Stuttgart: Klett, 1972.

Fontane, Theodor. *Briefe Theodor Fontanes. Zweite Sammlung*. Edited by Otto Pniower and Paul Schlenther. Vol. 1. Berlin: Friedrich Fontane, 1910.

Fontane, Theodor. *Der Briefwechsel zwischen Theodor Fontane und Paul Heyse*. Edited by Gotthard Erler. Berlin: Aufbau, 1972.

Fontane, Theodor. *Die Fontanes und die Merckels. Ein Familienbriefwechsel 1850–1870*. Edited by Gotthard Erler. Vol. 1. Berlin: Aufbau, 1987.

Fontane, Theodor. "Die Technik des künstlerischen Schaffens." *Der Zuschauer* 1, no. 10 (November 15, 1893): 305.

Fontane, Theodor. *Effi Briest*. Translated by Mike Mitchell, with an Introduction by Ritchie Robertson. Oxford World's Classics. Oxford: Oxford University Press, 2015.

Fontane, Theodor. *"Eine Zeitungsnummer lebt nur 12 Stunden." Londoner Korrespondenzen aus Berlin*. Edited by Heide Streiter-Buscher. Berlin: De Gruyter, 1998.

Fontane, Theodor. *Fragmente. Erzählungen, Impressionen, Essays*. Edited by Christine Hehle and Hanna Delf von Wolzogen. 2 vols. Berlin: De Gruyter, 2016.

Fontane, Theodor. *Große Brandenburger Ausgabe*. Edited by Gotthard Erler, continued by Heinrich Detering and Gabriele Radecke. Berlin: Aufbau, 1994.

Fontane, Theodor. *Notizbücher. Digitale genetisch-kritische und kommentierte Edition*. Edited by Gabriele Radecke. https://fontane-nb.dariah.eu/index.html

Fontane, Theodor. *On Tangled Paths* [*Irrungen, Wirrungen*]. Translated by Peter James Bowman. Penguin Classics. London: Penguin, 2013.

Fontane, Theodor. Preface to *Wanderungen durch die Mark Brandenburg*. v–viii. Berlin: Hertz, 1862.

Fontane, Theodor. *Sämtliche Werke* [Nymphenburger Ausgabe]. Edited by Edgar Gross et al. Munich: Nymphenburger, 1959–75.

Fontane, Theodor. *Theodor Fontane und Bernhard von Lepel. Der Briefwechsel. Kritische Ausgabe*. Edited by Gabriele Radecke. 2 vols. Schriften der Theodor Fontane Gesellschaft 5,1; 5.2. Berlin: De Gruyter, 2006.

Fontane, Theodor. *Unechte Korrespondenzen*. Edited by Heide Streiter-Buscher. 2 vols. Schriften der Theodor Fontane Gesellschaft 1. Berlin: De Gruyter, 1996.

Fontane, Theodor. *Wanderungen durch die Mark Brandenburg. Erster Theil. Die Grafschaft Ruppin. Barnim=Teltow*. Berlin: Hertz, 1865.

Fontane, Theodor. *Wanderungen durch die Mark Brandenburg. Zweiter Theil. Das Oderland Barnim. Lebus*. Berlin: Hertz, 1863.

Fontane, Theodor. *Wanderungen durch die Mark Brandenburg. Dritter Theil. Havelland. Die Landschaft um Spandau, Potsdam, Brandenburg*. 2. verb. Aufl. Berlin: Hertz, 1880.

Fontane, Theodor. *Wanderungen durch die Mark Brandenburg. Vierter Theil. Spreeland. Beeskow=Storkow und Barnim=Teltow*. Berlin: Hertz, 1882.

Fontane, Theodor. *Werke, Schriften und Briefe* [Hanser Ausgabe]. Edited by Walter Keitel and Helmuth Nürnberger. Munich: Hanser, 1969–97.

Frank, Gustav, "Tiecks Epochalität." In *Ludwig Tieck: Leben – Werk – Wirkung*, edited by Claudia Stockinger and Stefan Scherer, 131–47. Berlin: De Gruyter, 2011.

Frank, Gustav, Madleen Podewski, and Stefan Scherer. "'Kultur – Zeit – Schrift. Literatur- und Kulturzeitschriften als 'kleine Archive.'" *Internationales Archiv für Sozialgeschichte der Literatur* 34, no. 2 (2009): 1–45.

Franzel, Sean. "Von Magazinen, Gärbottichen und Bomben: Räumliche Speichermetaphern der medialen Selbstinszenierung von Zeitschriften." In *Archiv/Fiktionen: Verfahren des Archivierens in Literatur und Kultur des langen 19. Jahrhunderts*, edited by Daniela Gretz and Nicolas Pethes, 209–31. Litterae 217. Freiburg i. Br.: Rombach, 2016.

Fricke, Hermann. "Fontanes Historik." *Jahrbuch für Brandenburgische Landesgeschichte* 5 (1954): 13–22.

Fricke, Hermann. "Das Theodor-Fontane-Archiv. Einst und jetzt." *Jahrbuch für Brandenburgische Landesgeschichte* 15 (1964): 165–81.

Friedlaender, Ernst. "Emil Gottlieb Friedlaender (1805–78)." In *Allgemeine Deutsche Biographie (ADB)*, 778–80. Vol. 48. Leipzig: Duncker & Humblot, 1904.

Furst, Lilian. "Parallels and Disparities: German Literature in the Context of European Culture." In *German Literature of the Nineteenth Century, 1832–1899*, edited by Clayton Koelb and Eric Downing, 45–62. Rochester, NY: Camden House, 2005.

Fürstenau, Jutta. *Fontane und die märkische Heimat*. Berlin: Ebering, 1941.

G. H-r. and H. B. "Und sie bewegt sich doch. Zum Jubelgedächtniß eines Erlösers der Wissenschaft." *Die Gartenlaube* 7 (1864): 100–4.

Gaethgens, Barbara. Introduction to *Genremalerei*, edited by Barbara Gaethgens, 13–46. Berlin: Reimer, 2002.

Gierl, Martin. "Kompilation und die Produktion von Wissen im 18. Jahrhundert." In *Die Praktiken der Gelehrsamkeit in der frühen Neuzeit*, edited by Helmut Zedelmaier and Martin Mulsow, 63–94. Tübingen: Niemeyer, 2001.

Gitelman, Lisa. *Paper Knowledge: Towards a Media History of Documents*. Durham, NC: Duke University Press, 2014.

Glagau, Otto (1870). "Der Colportage-Roman, oder 'Gift und Dolch, Verrath und Rache.'" In *Realismus und Gründerzeit. Manifeste und Dokumente zur deutschen Literatur 1848–1880*, edited by Max Bucher, 661–9. Vol. 2. Stuttgart: Metzler, 1981.

Gödden, Walter, and Jochen Grywatsch, eds. *'Ich, Feder, Tinte und Papier.' Ein Blick in die Schreibwerkstatt der Annette von Droste-Hülshoff*. Paderborn: Schöningh, 1996.

Goethe, Johann Wolfgang. "A. v. Arnim; C. Brentano, Des Knaben Wunderhorn." *Jenaische Allgemeine Literatur-Zeitung* 3.18 and 3.19 (January 21 and 22, 1806): 137–48.

Goody, Jack. *The Domestication of the Savage Mind*. Cambridge: Cambridge University Press, 1977.

Graevenitz, Gerhart von. "Memoria und Realismus: Erzählende Literatur in der deutschen 'Bildungspresse' des 19. Jahrhunderts." In *Memoria: Vergessen und Erinnern*, edited by Anselm Haverkamp and Renate Lachmann, 283–304. Munich: Fink, 1993.

Graevenitz, Gerhart von. *Theodor Fontane: ängstliche Moderne. Über das Imaginäre*. Konstanz: Konstanz University Press, 2014.

Graf, Andreas. "Die Ursprünge der modernen Medienindustrie: Familien- und Unterhaltungszeitschriften der Kaiserzeit (1870–1918)." In *Geschichte des deutschen Buchhandels im 19. und 20. Jahrhundert*, edited by Georg Jäger, Dieter Langewiesche, and Wolfram Siemann, 409–522. Vol 1.2. Frankfurt a. M.: MVB, 2003.

Granovetter, Mark S. "The Strength of Weak Ties." *American Journal of Sociology* 78, no. 6 (April 1973): 1360–80.

Grätz, Katharina. *Alles kommt auf die Beleuchtung an. Theodor Fontane – Leben und Werk*. Stuttgart: Reclam, 2015.

Grawe, Christian. "Der Fontanesche Roman." In *Fontane-Handbuch*, edited by Christian Grawe and Helmuth Nürnberger. Stuttgart: Kröner, 2000.

Grawe, Christian. "'Die wahre hohe Schule der Zweideutigkeit': Frivolität und ihre autobiographische Komponente in Fontanes Erzählwerk." *Fontane Blätter* 65/66 (1998): 138–62.

Greif, Stefan. "'Neid macht glücklich.' Fontanes 'Mathilde Möhring' als wilhelminische Satire." *Der Deutschunterricht* 50, no. 4 (1998): 46–57.

Gretz, Daniela, and Nicolas Pethes. Introduction to *Archiv/Fiktionen. Verfahren des Archivierens in Literatur und Kultur des langen 19. Jahrhunderts*, edited by Daniela Gretz and Nicolas Pethes, 9–31. Litterae 217. Freiburg i. Br.: Rombach, 2016.

Grimm, Jacob, and Wilhelm Grimm. *Deutsches Wörterbuch*. 16 vols. Leipzig: Hirzel, 1854–1961. http://woerterbuchnetz.de

Grimm, Jacob, and Wilhelm Grimm. "Vorrede." In *Kinder- und Hausmärchen. Gesammelt durch die Brüder Grimm*. Edited by Heinz Rölleke, V–XXVIII. Band 1. Vergrößerter Nachdruck der zweibändigen Erstausgabe von 1812 und 1815. Göttingen: Vandenhoeck & Ruprecht, 1986.

Guillory, John. "The Memo and Modernity." *Critical Inquiry* 31 (Autumn 2004): 108–32.

Gunkel, David J. *Of Remixology: Ethics and Aesthetics after Remix*. Cambridge, MA: MIT Press, 2016.

Günter, Manuela. "Die Medien des Realismus." In *Realismus: Epoche – Autoren – Werke*, edited by Christian Begemann, 45–62. Darmstadt: Wissenschaftliche Buchgesellschaft, 2007.

Günter, Manuela. *Im Vorhof der Kunst: Mediengeschichten der Literatur im 19. Jahrhundert*. Bielefeld: Transcript, 2008.

Günter, Manuela. "Realismus in Medien. Zu Fontanes Frauenromanen." In *Medialer Realismus*, edited by Daniela Gretz, 167–90. Litterae 145. Freiburg i. Br.: Rombach, 2011.

Günter, Manuela, and Michael Homberg. "'cut & paste' im 'Archiv der Massenmedien'? Theodor Fontanes Unechte Korrespondenzen und die Poesie der Zeitung." In *Archiv/Fiktionen. Verfahren des Archivierens in Literatur und Kultur des langen 19. Jahrhunderts*, edited by Daniela Gretz and Nicolas Pethes, 233–54. Litterae 217. Freiburg i. Br.: Rombach, 2016.

Hädecke, Wolfgang. *Theodor Fontane: Biographie*. Munich: Hanser, 1998.

Häntzschel, Günter. *Sammel(l)ei(denschaft). Literarisches Sammeln im neunzehnten Jahrhundert*. Freiburg: Königshausen & Neumann, 2014.

Hauff, Herrmann. "Gedanken über die moderne schöne Literatur. *Deutsche Vierteljahrs-Schrift* 11, no. 3 (1840): 244–87.

Hauff, Wilhelm. "Die Bücher und die Lesewelt." In *Sämtliche Werke*. Edited by Sibylle von Steinsdorf, 55–71. Vol. 3. Munich: Winkler, 1970.

Heine, Heinrich. *Briefe 1815–1831*. Säkularausgabe. Vol. 20. Edited by Fritz Eisner and Fritz Mende. Berlin: Akademie-Verlag, 1975.

Helmstetter, Rudolf. *Die Geburt des Realismus aus dem Dunst des Familienblattes. Fontane und die öffentlichkeitsgeschichtlichen Rahmenbedingungen des Poetischen Realimus*. Munich: Fink, 1998.

Hettche, Walter. "'Die erste Skizze wundervoll.' Zu einem Kapitel aus Theodor Fontanes Roman Vor dem Sturm." In *Schrift – Text – Edition. Hans Walter Gabler zum 65. Geburtstag*, edited by Christiane Henkes, Walter Hettche, Gabriele Radecke et al., 213–20. Beihefte zu Editio 19. Tübingen: Niemeyer, 2003.

Hettche, Walter. "Die Handschriften zu Theodor Fontanes *Vor dem Sturm*. Erste Ergebnisse ihrer Auswertung." *Fontane Blätter* 58 (1994): 193–212.

Hoenn, Georg Paul. "Bücher-Schreiber." *Betrugs-Lexikon, worinnen die meisten Betrügereyen in allen Staenden nebst denen darwieder guten Theils dienenden Mitteln entdecket*, 83–4. Coburg, 1753 (reprint: Leipzig: Zentralantiquariat der Deutschen Demokratischen Republik, 1981).

Hoffmann, Christoph. "Umgebungen. Über Ort und Materialität von Ernst Machs Notizbüchern." In *Portable Media. Schreibszenen in Bewegung zwischen Peripatetik und Mobiltelefon*, edited by Martin Stingelin and Matthias Thiele, with Claas Morgenroth, 89–107. Zur Genealogie des Schreibens 12. Munich: Fink, 2010.

Höhn, Gerhard. "Die Reisebilder: Das Gesamtprojekt." In *Heine-Handbuch. Zeit, Person, Werk*, 3rd ed., 180–91. Stuttgart: Metzler, 2004.

Holub, Robert C. *Reflections of Realism: Paradox, Norm, and Ideology in Nineteenth-Century German Prose*. Detroit: Wayne State University Press, 1991.

Horlitz, Manfred. "Fontanes Quellennutzung für seine *Wanderungen*-Texte." In *"Geschichte und Geschichten aus Mark Brandenburg." Fontanes "Wanderungen durch die Mark Brandenburg" im Kontext der europäischen Reiseliteratur*, edited by Hanna Delf von Wolzogen, 273–301. Fontaneana 1. Würzburg: Königshausen & Neumann, 2003.

Horlitz, Manfred, ed. *Vermißte Bestände des Theodor Fontane Archivs. Eine Dokumentation im Auftrag des Theodor-Fontane-Archivs*. Theodor-Fontane-Archiv, Potsdam, 1999.

Hosken, Dan. *An Introduction to Music Technology*. New York: Routledge, 2014.

Hügel, Hans-Otto. "Forschungsfeld Populäre Kultur. Eine Einführung." In *Lob des Mainstreams. Zu Begriff und Geschichte von Unterhaltung und Populärer Kultur*. Cologne: von Halem, 2007.

Hügel, Hans-Otto. "Unterhaltung durch Literatur: Kritik, Geschichte, Lesevergnügen." In *Medien zwischen Kultur und Kult. Zur Bedeutung der Medien in Kultur und Bildung. Festschrift für Heribert Heinrichs*, edited by Rudolf Keck and Walter Thissen, 95–111. Bad Heilbrunn: Klinkhardt, 1987.

Hurlebusch, Klaus. "Den Autor besser verstehen: aus seiner Arbeitsweise. Prolegomenon zu einer Hermeneutik textgenetischen Schreibens." In *Textgenetische Edition*, edited by Hans Zeller and Gunter Martens, 7–51. Tübingen: Niemeyer, 1998.

Huwer, Elisabeth. *Das Deutsche Apotheken-Museum – Schätze aus zwei Jahrtausenden Kultur- und Pharmaziegeschichte*. 2nd ed., Regensburg: Schnell und Steiner, 2008.

Immermann, Karl. *Die Epigonen. Familienmemoiren in neun Büchern. Werke in fünf Bänden*. Vol. 2. Edited by Benno von Wiese. Frankfurt a. M.: Athenäum, 1971.

Irvine, Martin. "Remix and the Dialogic Engine of Culture: A Model for Generative Combinatoriality." In *The Routledge Companion to Remix Studies*, edited by Eduardo Navas, Owen Gallagher, and xtine burrough, 15–42. New York: Routledge, 2015.

Iurascu, Ilinca. "Annoncenliteratur: Kleist, Fontane, and the Rustle of Paper." *Oxford German Studies* 43, no. 3 (2014): 246–61.

Jakobson, Roman. "On Realism in Art." In *Readings in Russian Poetics: Formalist and Structuralist Views*, edited by Ladislav Matejka and Krystyna Pomorska, 38–46. Cambridge, MA: MIT Press, 1971.

Johns, Adrian. *The Nature of the Book: Print and Knowledge in the Making*. Chicago: University of Chicago Press, 1998.

Jolles, Charlotte. "Fontane als Journalist und Essayist." *Jahrbuch für internationale Germanistik* 7, no. 2 (1975): 98–119.

Kafka, Franz. "Oxforder Oktavhefte 1&2." *Historisch-kritische Ausgabe sämtlicher Handschriften, Drucke und Typoskripte*. Edited by Roland Reuß and Peter Staengle. Basel/Frankfurt a.M.: Stroemfeld, 2006–11.

Kaminski, Nicola, Nora Ramtke, and Carsten Zelle. "Zeitschriftenliteratur/ Fortsetzungsliteratur: Problemaufriß." In *Zeitschriftenliteratur/ Fortsetzungsliteratur*, edited by Nicola Kaminski, Nora Ramtke, and Carsten Zelle, 7–40. Hannover: Wehrhahn, 2014.

Kant, Immanuel. "Fine Art Is the Art of Genius (§ 46)." In *Critique of Judgment*. Edited by Nicolas Walker. Translated by James Creed Meredith, 136–7. Oxford: Oxford University Press, 2007.

Karge, Henrik. "Poesie und Wissenschaft. Fontane und die Kunstgeschichte." In *Fontane und die bildende Kunst*, edited by Claude Keisch, Peter-Klaus Schuster, and Moritz Wullen, 267–78. Berlin: Henschel, 1998.

Keil, Ernst, and Ferdinand Stolle. "An unsere Freunde und Leser!" *Die Gartenlaube* 1 (1853): 1.

Keller, Gottfried. "Die mißbrauchten Liebesbriefe." In *Sämtliche Werke. Historisch-Kritische Ausgabe*. Edited by Walter Morgenthaler, 97–180. Vol 5.2. Basel: Stroemfeld/Verlag Neue Zürcher Zeitung, 2000.

Keller, Gottfried. *Martin Salander: Apparat zu Band 8. Sämtliche Werke. Historisch-Kritische Ausgabe.* Edited by Thomas Binder et al. Vol. 24. Basel: Stroemfeld/ Verlag Neue Zürcher Zeitung, 2004.

Keller, Gottfried. *Notizbuch Ms. GK 70. Sämtliche Werke. Historisch-Kritische Ausgabe.* Edited by Walter Morgenthaler. Vol. 16.2. Basel: Stroemfeld/Verlag Neue Zürcher Zeitung, 2001, 221–58.

Kienpointner, Manfred. "Inventio." In *Historisches Wörterbuch der Rhetorik*, edited by Gert Ueding, 561–87. Vol. 4. Tübingen: Niemeyer, 1998.

Kilcher, Andreas. *mathesis und poiesis. Die Enzyklopädik der Literatur 1600 bis 2000.* Munich: Fink, 2003.

Kirschenbaum, Matthew. *Track Changes: A Literary History of Word Processing.* Cambridge, MA: Belknap Press of Harvard University Press, 2016.

Kittler, Friedrich A. *Discourse Networks 1800/1900.* Translated by Michael Metteer, with Chris Cullens. Foreword by David E. Wellbery. Stanford, CA: Stanford University Press, 1990.

Klein, Ursula. "Paper Tools in Experimental Cultures: The Case of Berzelian Formulas." *Studies in History and Philosophy of Science* 32 (2001): 265–312.

Kleinwort, Malte. "Kafkas Querstrich – Der Schreibstrom und sein Ende." In *Schrift und Zeit in Franz Kafkas Oktavheften*, edited by Caspar Battegay, Felix Christen, and Wolfram Groddeck, 37–66. Göttingen: Wallstein, 2010.

Klünner, Hans-Werner. "Theodor Fontane im Bildnis." In *Festschrift der Landesgeschichtlichen Vereinigung für die Mark Brandenburg*, edited by Eckart Henning and Werner Vogel, 279–307. Berlin: n. p., 1984.

Klünner, Hans-Werner. "Theodor Fontanes Wohnstätten in Berlin." *Fontane Blätter* 4, no. 2 (1997): 107–34.

Knight, Jeffrey Todd. *Bound to Read: Compilations, Collections, and the Making of Renaissance Literature.* Material Texts. Philadelphia: University of Pennsylvania Press, 2013.

Koniezcny, Hans-Joachim. "Theodor Fontane und Westermann's illustrierte deutsche Monats-Hefte." *Fontane Blätter* 24 (1976): 573–88.

Kontje, Todd. "Introduction: Reawakening German Realism." In *A Companion to German Realism 1848–1900*, edited by Todd Kontje, 1–28. Rochester, NY: Camden House, 2002.

Kosch, Günter, and Manfred Nagl. *Der Kolportageroman: Bibliographie 1850 bis 1960.* Stuttgart: Metzler, 1993.

Krajewski, Markus. *Paper Machines: On Cards & Catalogs, 1548–1929.* Translated by Peter Krapp. Cambridge, MA: MIT Press, 2011.

Krämer, Sybille. "Writing, Notational Iconicity, Calculus: On Writing as a Cultural Technique." *MLN* 118, no. 3 (April 2003): 518–37.

Krause, Edith. "Domesticity, Eccentricity, and the Problems of Self-Making: The Suffering Protagonists in Theodor Fontane's *Effi Briest* and Leopoldo Alas's *La Regenta*." *Seminar* 44, no. 4 (2008): 414–32.

Krauthausen, Karin. "Vom Nutzen des Notierens. Verfahren des Entwurfs." In *Notieren, Skizzieren. Schreiben und Zeichnen als Verfahren des Entwurfs*, edited by Karin Krauthausen and Omar Nasim, 7–26. Wissen im Entwurf 3. Zurich: Diaphanes, 2010.

Krings, Dorothee. *Theodor Fontane als Journalist – Selbstverständnis und Werk.* Öffentlichkeit und Geschichte 2. Cologne: von Halem, 2008.

Kruse, Joseph. "Heines Leihpraxis und Lektürebeschaffung." In *Die Leihbibliothek als Institution des literarischen Lebens im 18. und 19. Jahrhundert: Organisationsformen,*

Bestände und Publikum, edited by Georg Jäger and Jörg Schönert, 197–227. Stuttgart: Hauswedell, 1980.

Kürschner, Joseph. *Handbuch der Presse für Schriftsteller, Redaktionen, Verleger [und] überhaupt Alle, die mit der Presse in Beziehung stehen*. Berlin: Hillger, 1902.

Ladendorf, Otto. *Historisches Schlagwörterbuch. Ein Versuch*. Straßburg; Berlin: Trübner, 1906.

Langenbucher, Wolfgang. "Die Demokratisierung des Lesens in der zweiten Leserevolution." In *Lesen und Leben: Eine Publikation des Börsenvereins des Deutschen Buchhandels in Frankfurt am Main zum 150. Jahrestag zur Gründung des Börsenvereins der deutschen Buchhändler am 30. April 1825 in Leipzig*, edited by Herbert G. Göpfert, Ruth Meyer, Ludwig Muth, and Walter Rüegg, 12–35. Frankfurt a. M.: Buchhändler-Vereinigung, 1975.

Laufer, Christel. "Der handschriftliche Nachlaß Theodor Fontanes." *Fontane Blätter* 20 (1974): 264–87.

Lausberg, Heinrich (1973). *Handbook of Literary Rhetoric: A Foundation for Literary Study*. Edited by David E. Orton and R. Dean Anderson, translated by Matthew T. Bliss, Annemiek Jansen, and David E. Orton. Leiden: Brill, 1998.

Lavater, Johann Caspar. "Genie." In *Physiognomische Fragmente zur Beförderung der Menschenkenntniß und der Menschenliebe*, 80–99. Vol. 4. Leipzig: Weidmanns Erben, 1778.

Lenman, Robin. "From 'Brown Sauce' to 'Plein Air': Taste and the Art Market in Germany, 1889–1910." In *Imagining Modern German Culture: 1889–1910*, edited by Françoise Forster-Hahn, 53–69. Hanover: University Press of New England; Washington: National Gallery of Art, 1996.

Lichtenberg, Georg Christoph. *Sudelbücher*. Edited by Wolfgang Promies. 3 vols. Munich: Deutscher Taschenbuchverlag, 2005.

Love, Harold. "Early Modern Print Culture: Assessing the Models." *Parergon* 20, no. 1 (2003): 45–64.

Luhmann, Niklas. "Kommunikation mit Zettelkästen. Ein Erfahrungsbericht." In *Universität als Milieu. Kleine Schriften*, edited by Niklas Luhmann and André Kieserling, 53–61. Bielefeld: Haux, 1992.

Lyon, John B. *Out of Place: German Realism, Displacement, and Modernity*. New Directions in German Studies 7. London: Bloomsbury Academic, 2013.

Machner, Bettina. "Potsdamer Straße 134c. Der Dichternachlaß." In *Theodor Fontane und sein Jahrhundert*, edited by Stiftung Stadtmuseum Berlin, 251–68. Berlin: Henschel, 1998.

Mainberger, Sabine. *Die Kunst des Aufzählens. Elemente zu einer Poetik des Enumerativen*. Quellen und Forschungen zur Literatur- und Kulturgeschichte 22. Berlin: De Gruyter, 2003.

Mann, Thomas. "The Old Fontane." In *Thomas Mann: Essays of Three Decades*. Translated by H. T. Lowe-Porter, 287–306. New York: Alfred Knopf, 1947.

Manovich, Lev. "What Comes after Remix?" [Typescript, 2007] http://manovich. net/content/04-projects/057-what-comes-after-remix/54_article_2007.pdf.

Marx, Karl. *Capital: A Critical Analysis of Capitalist Production*. 1867. Translated from the third German edition by Samuel Moore and Edward Aveling. Edited by Frederick Engels. Vol. I. Moscow: Foreign Language Publishing House, 1958.

May, Karl. *Mein Leben und Streben*. Volume I. Freiburg i. Br.: Fehsenfeld, o.J. [1910].

McBride, Patrizia. "Montage/Collage." In *German Aesthetics: Fundamental Concepts from Baumgarten to Adorno*, edited by J. D. Mininger and Jason Michael Peck,

204–49. New Directions in German Studies 16. London: Bloomsbury Academic, 2016.

McGillen, Petra. "Kompilieren." In *Historisches Wörterbuch des Mediengebrauchs*, edited by Heiko Christians, Matthias Bickenbach, and Nikolaus Wegmann, 352–68. Cologne: Böhlau, 2014.

McGillen, Petra. "Poetische Mobilmachung im Textbaukasten. Fontanes Listen und die Kunst der Weiterverwendung – der Fall 'Allerlei Glück.'" In *Formen ins Offene. Zur Produktivität des Unvollendeten*, edited by Hanna Delf von Wolzogen and Christine Hehle. Untersuchungen zur deutschen Literaturgeschichte 151. Berlin: De Gruyter 2018, 97–119.

McLuhan, Marshall. *Understanding Media: The Extensions of Man*. [1964.] Critical edition. Edited by W. Terrence Gordon. Corte Madeira: Ginko Press, 2003.

Mecklenburg, Norbert. *Theodor Fontane. Romankunst der Vielstimmigkeit*. Frankfurt a. M.: Suhrkamp, 1998.

Meisel, Martin. *Realizations: Narrative, Pictorial, and Theatrical Arts in Nineteenth-Century England*. Princeton, NJ: Princeton University Press, 1983.

Mellmann, Katja. "Literarische Öffentlichkeit im mittleren 19. Jahrhundert – Zur Einführung." In *Vergessene Konstellationen literarischer Öffentlichkeit zwischen 1840 und 1885*, edited by Katja Mellmann and Jesko Reiling, 1–32. Studien und Texte zur Sozialgeschichte der Literatur 142. Berlin: De Gruyter, 2016.

Meyer & Ernst. *Theodor Fontane. August von Kotzebue. Zwei deutsche Dichternachlässe sowie ausgewählte Autographen*. Katalog 35. Berlin W 35, 1933.

Meyer-Krentler, Eckhardt. "'Wir vom Handwerk.' Wilhelm Raabe als Berufsschriftsteller." In *Vom Wert der 'Arbeit' in der deutschen Literatur (1770–1930)*, edited by Harro Segeberg, 204–29. Tübingen: Niemeyer, 1991.

Meyer, Richard M. "'Vollständigkeit.' Eine methodologische Skizze." *Euphorion* 14 (1907): 1–17.

Möller, Klaus-Peter. "Eduard Handtmann – der Pfarrer von Seedorf." *Jahrbuch Ostprignitz–Ruppin* 2005: 43–54.

Möller, Klaus-Peter. "Preußisches Panoptikum mit Pfefferkuchen: Fontane-Porträts und –Bildnisse (2)." *Fontane Blätter* 78 (2004): 52–74.

Muhs, Rudolf. "*Unechte Korrespondenzen*, aber alles echter Fontane? Zur Edition von Heide Streiter-Buscher." *Fontane Blätter* 64 (1997): 200–20.

Müller-Brauel, Hans. "Erinnerungen an Wilhelm Raabe." In *Wilhelm Raabe: Gespräche. Ein Lebensbild in Aufzeichnungen und Erinnerungen der Zeitgenossen*, edited by Rosemarie Schillemeit. Sämtliche Werke (Braunschweiger Ausgabe), Ergänzungsband 4, 218–22. Göttingen: Vandenhoeck & Ruprecht, 1983.

Müller-Sievers, Helmut. *The Cylinder: Kinematics of the Nineteenth Century*. Berkeley, CA: University of California Press, 2012.

Müller, Lothar. *White Magic: The Age of Paper*. Translated by Jessica Spengler. Cambridge, MA: Polity Press, 2014.

Muth, Agathe Gisela. "Stifters Briefe an Gustav Heckenast im Zusammenhang mit ihrem ersten gemeinsame Unternehmen, *Wien und die Wiener* . . ." In *Der Brief in der österreichischen und ungarischen Literatur*, edited by András F. Balogh and Helga Mitterbauer, 130–38. Budapest: Elte, 2005.

Nasim, Omar. *Observing by Hand. Sketching the Nebulae in the Nineteenth Century*. Chicago: University of Chicago Press, 2013.

Navas, Eduardo, Owen Gallager, and xtine burrough. Introduction to *The Routledge Companion to Remix Studies*, edited by Eduardo Navas, Owen Gallager, and xtine Burrough, 1–12. New York: Routledge, 2015.

Neuhaus, Volker. *Der zeitgeschichtliche Sensationsroman in Deutschland 1855–1878. "Sir John Retcliffe" und seine Schule.* Berlin: Schmidt, 1980.
Neumann, Peter. "Industrielle Buchproduktion." In *Geschichte des deutschen Buchhandels im 19. und 20. Jarhundert*, edited by Georg Jäger, Dieter Langewiesche, and Wolfram Siemann, 170–81. Vol. 1.1. Frankfurt a. M.: MVB, 2001.
Nietzsche, Friedrich. Notizbuch N-VI-2. *Digitale Faksimile-Gesamtausgabe* (DFGA). Edited by Paolo D'Iorio, Klassik Stiftung Weimar, 2009— http://www.nietzschesource.org/DFGA/N-VI-2.
Nürnberger, Helmuth. *Fontanes Welt.* Berlin: Siedler, 1997.
Nürnberger, Helmuth. "Theodor Fontane: Leben und Persönlichkeit." In *Fontane-Handbuch*, edited by Christian Grawe and Helmuth Nürnberger, 1–89. Stuttgart: Kröner, 2000.
Nürnberger, Helmuth, and Dietmar Storch. "Brouillon." In *Fontane-Lexikon. Namen – Stoffe – Zeitgeschichte*, edited by Helmuth Nürnberger and Dietmar Storch, 76. Munich: Hanser, 2007.
Nürnberger, Helmuth, and Dietmar Storch. "Kleine und Große (das)." In *Fontane-Lexikon. Namen – Stoffe – Zeitgeschichte*, edited by Helmuth Nürnberger and Dietmar Storch, 244–5. Munich: Hanser, 2007.
Nürnberger, Helmuth, and Dietmar Storch. "Nervenpleite." In *Fontane-Lexikon. Namen – Stoffe – Zeitgeschichte*, edited by Helmuth Nürnberger and Dietmar Storch, 323. Munich: Hanser, 2007.
Offutt, Chris. "My Dad, the Pornographer." *The New York Times Magazine*, February 8, 2015, MM38.
Osterhammel, Jürgen. *The Transformation of the World: A Global History of the Nineteenth Century.* Translated by Patrick Camiller. Princeton, NJ: Princeton University Press, 2014.
Parikka, Jussi. "Copy." In *Software Studies: A Lexicon*, edited by Matthew Fuller, 70–8. Cambridge, MA: MIT Press, 2008.
Parr, Rolf. *Autorschaft. Eine kurze Sozialgeschichte der literarischen Intelligenz in Deutschland zwischen 1860 und 1930.* With Jörg Schönert. Heidelberg: Synchron, 2008.
Perthes, Friedrich Christoph. "Die Bedeutung des deutschen Buchhandels, besonders in der neuesten Zeit." In *Der deutsche Buchhandel als Bedingung des Daseins einer deutschen Literatur. Schriften.* Edited by Gerd Schulz, 49–53. Stuttgart: Reclam, 1995.
Peters, Günther. "Genie." In *Historisches Wörterbuch der Rhetorik*, edited by Gert Ueding. Vol. 3. Tübingen: Niemeyer, 1996.
Peters, John Durham. *The Marvelous Clouds: Towards a Philosophy of Elemental Media.* Chicago: University of Chicago Press, 2015.
Petersen, Julius. "Fontanes Altersroman." *Euphorion* 29 (1928): 1–74.
Pettegree, Andrew. *The Invention of News: How the World Came to Know about Itself.* New Haven, CT: Yale University Press, 2014.
Plett, Bettina. *Die Kunst der Allusion. Formen literarischer Anspielungen in den Romanen Theodor Fontanes.* Cologne: Böhlau, 1986.
Plumpe, Gerhard. Introduction to *Bürgerlicher Realismus und Gründerzeit 1848–1890*, edited by Edward McInnes and Gerhard Plumpe, 17–83. Munich: Hanser, 1996.
Poe, Edgar Allan. "The Philosophy of Composition." 1846. In *Literary Criticism of Edgar Allan Poe.* Edited by Robert L. Hough, 20–32. Lincoln, NE: University of Nebraska Press, 1965.

Polaschegg, Andrea. "Hauff im Fokus. Eine Einleitung." In *Wilhelm Hauff oder Die Virtuosität der Einbildungskraft*, edited by Ernst Osterkamp, Andrea Polaschegg, and Erhard Schütz, 7–20. Göttingen: Wallstein, 2010.
Pompe, Hedwig. "Botenstoffe. Zeitung – Archiv – Umlauf." In *Archivprozesse. Die Kommunikation der Aufbewahrung*, edited by Hedwig Pompe and Leander Scholz, 121–54. Mediologie 5. Cologne: DuMont, 2002.
Porombka, Stephan. "Der Eckermann-Workshop. Die *Gespräche mit Goethe* als Einübung in die Literatur der Gegenwart." *Politische Künste. Jahrbuch für Kulturwissenschaften und ästhetische Praxis* (2007): 183–218.
Price, Leah. "Victorian Reading." In *The Cambridge History of Victorian Literature*, edited by Kate Flint, 34–55. Cambridge: Cambridge University Press, 2012.
Quintilian. *The Orator's Education*. Vol. 5: Books 11–12. Edited and translated by Donald A. Russell. Loeb Classical Library 494. Cambridge, MA: Harvard University Press, 2002.
Raabe, Wilhelm. *Briefe 1842–1870*. Edited by William Webster. Berlin: Erich Schmidt, 2004.
Radecke, Gabriele. "Schneiden, Kleben und Skizzieren. Theodor Fontanes Notizbücher." In *'Gedanken Reisen, Einfälle kommen an.' Die Welt der Notiz*, edited by Marcel Atze and Volker Kaukoreit, 199–213. Vienna: Praesens, 2017.
Radecke, Gabriele, ed. *Theodor Storm – Theodor Fontane: Briefwechsel*. Kritische Ausgabe. Berlin: Erich Schmidt, 2011.
Radecke, Gabriele. *Vom Schreiben zum Erzählen. Eine textgenetische Studie zu Theodor Fontanes 'L'Adultera.'* Epistemata Reihe Literaturwissenschaft 358. Würzburg: Königshausen & Neumann, 2002.
Rasch, Wolfgang. *Theodor Fontane Bibliographie: Werk und Forschung*. Edited by Ernst Osterkamp and Hanna Delf von Wolzogen. 3 vols. Berlin: De Gruyter, 2006.
Rasch, Wolfgang. "Zeitungstiger, Bücherfresser. Die Bibliothek Theodor Fontanes als Fragment und Aufgabe betrachtet." *Imprimatur* 19 (2005): 103–44.
Rasch, Wolfgang, and Christine Hehle, eds. *'Erschrecken Sie nicht, ich bin es selbst,' Erinnerungen an Theodor Fontane*. Berlin: Aufbau, 2003.
Reitterer, H. "Schlesinger, Max(imilian)." In *Österreichisches Biographisches Lexikon und biographische Dokumentation 1815–1950*, 197–198. Vol. 10. Verlag der Österreichischen Akademie der Wissenschaften, 1992. http://www.biographien.ac.at/oebl/oebl_S/Schlesinger_Max_1822_1881.xml.
Requate, Jörg. *Journalismus als Beruf. Entstehung und Entwicklung des Journalistenberufs im 19. Jahrhundert – Deutschland im internationalen Vergleich*. Göttingen: Vandenhoeck & Ruprecht, 1995.
Reuter, Hans-Heinrich. *Fontane*. 2 vols. Munich: Nymphenburger Verlagshandlung, 1968.
Reuveni, Gideon. *Reading Germany: Literature and the Consumer Culture in Germany before 1933*. New York: Berghahn, 2006.
Rösch, Gertrud. *Clavis Scientiae. Studien zum Verhältnis von Faktizität und Fiktionalität am Fall der Schlüsselliteratur*. Studien zur deutschen Literatur 170. Tübingen: Niemeyer, 2004.
Rost, Wolfgang E. *Örtlichkeit und Schauplatz in Fontanes Werken*. Berlin: De Gruyter, 1931.
Salmen, Walter. "'Am Sylvester war Ressourcenball. . .': Tänze und Bälle bei Theodor Fontane." *Fontane Blätter* 88 (2009): 104–26.
Salomon, Ludwig. *Geschichte des deutschen Zeitungswesens. Von den ersten Anfängen bis zur Wiederaufrichtung des deutschen Reiches*. Vol. 3. Das

Zeitungswesen seit 1814. Neudruck der Ausgabe Oldenburg 1906. Aalen: Scientia Verlag, 1973.

Schacht, Gertrud. "'Kind, du darfts kommen!'" In *'Erschrecken Sie nicht, ich bin es selbst.' Erinnerungen an Theodor Fontane*, edited by Wolfgang Rasch and Christine Hehle, 260–64. Berlin: Aufbau, 2003.

Scherer, Stefan. "Dichterinszenierung in der Massenpresse. Autorpraktiken in populären Zeitschriften des Realismus – Storm (C. F. Meyer)." In *Schriftstellerische Inszenierungspraktiken: Typologie und Geschichte*, edited by Christoph Jürgensen and Gerhard Kaiser, 229–49. Beihefte zum Euphorion 62. Heidelberg: Winter, 2011.

Scherer, Stefan, and Claudia Stockinger. "Archive in Serie. Kulturzeitschriften des 19. Jahrhunderts." In *Archiv/Fiktionen. Verfahren des Archivierens in Literatur und Kultur des langen 19. Jahrhunderts*, edited by Daniela Gretz and Nicolas Pethes, 255–77. Litterae 217. Freiburg i. Br.: Rombach, 2016.

Schobess, Joachim. "Fontanes Apothekerlaufbahn und ihr Einfluss auf sein literarisches Schaffen." *Die Pharmazie* 9 (1958): 588–94.

Schrader, Hans-Jürgen. "Autorfedern unter Preß-Autorität: Mitformende Marktfaktoren der realistischen Erzählkunst – an Beispielen Storms, Raabes und Kellers." *Jahrbuch der Raabe-Gesellschaft* (2001): 1–40.

Schrader, Hans-Jürgen. "Editionsgeschichte und Nachlass." In *Raabe-Handbuch. Leben – Werk – Wirkung*, edited by Dirk Göttsche, Florian Krobb, and Rolf Parr. Stuttgart: Metzler, 2016.

Schumacher, Eckhard. "Aufschlagesysteme 1800/2000." In *Literatur als Blätterwerk. Perspektiven nichtlinearer Lektüre*, edited by Jürgen Gunia and Iris Hermann, 23–45. St. Ingbert: Röhrig, 2002.

Siegert, Bernhard. *Cultural Techniques: Grids, Filters, Doors, and Other Articulations of the Real*. Translated by Geoffrey Winthrop-Young. New York: Fordham, 2015.

Siegert, Bernhard. *Relays: Literature as an Epoch of the Postal System*. Translated by Kevin Repp. Writing Science Series. Stanford, CA: Stanford University Press, 1999.

Sina, Kai, and Carlos Spoerhase. "Nachlassbewusstsein. Zur literarischen Erforschung seiner Entstehung und Entwicklung." *Zeitschrift für Germanistik* 23, no. 3 (2013): 607–23.

Sommer, Manfred. *Sammeln. Ein philosophischer Versuch*. Frankfurt a. M.: Suhrkamp, 1999.

Spang, Karl. "Dreistillehre." *Historisches Wörterbuch der Rhetorik*, edited by Gert Ueding, col. 921–72. Vol. 3. Tübingen: Niemeyer, 1996.

Spielhagen, Friedrich. "Finder oder Erfinder." In *Beiträge zu einer Theorie und Technik des Romans*, 1–34. Nachdruck der 1. Aufl. Leipzig 1883. Göttingen: Vandenhoeck & Ruprecht, 1967.

Spies [McGillen], Petra. "A Creative Machine: The Media History of Theodor Fontane's Library Network and Reading Practices." *The Germanic Review* 87, no. 1 (2012): 72–90.

Spies [McGillen], Petra. "Original Compiler. Notation as Textual Practice in Theodor Fontane." Ph.D. diss., Princeton University, 2012.

Stalder, Felix. "Neun Thesen zur Remix-Kultur." In *Der Autor am Ende der Gutenberg Galaxis*, 29–83. Zurich: Buch & Netz, 2014.

Stallybrass, Peter. "Books and Scrolls: Navigating the Bible." In *Books and Readers in Early Modern England: Material Studies*, edited by Jennifer Andersen and Elizabeth Sauer, 42–79. Philadelphia: University of Pennsylvania Press, 2002.

Stanitzek, Georg. "Brutale Lektüre um 1800/heute." In *Poetologien des Wissens*, edited by Joseph Vogl, 249–65. Munich: Fink, 1999.

Sternfeld, Richard. "Fontane als Historiker." In *'Erschrecken Sie nicht, ich bin es selbst.' Erinnerungen an Theodor Fontane*, edited by Wolfgang Rasch and Christine Hehle, 163–67. Berlin: Aufbau, 2003.

Stifter, Adalbert. *Wien und die Wiener, in Bildern aus dem Leben. Adalbert Stifter: Werke und Briefe. Historisch-kritische Gesamtausgabe*. Edited by Alfred Doppler and Hartmut Laufhütte. Vol 9.1. Stuttgart: Kohlhammer, 2005.

Streiter-Buscher, Heide. "Die politische Journalistik." In *Fontane-Handbuch*, edited by Christian Grawe and Helmuth Nürnberger, 788–806. Stuttgart: Kröner, 2000.

Streiter-Buscher, Heide. "Gebundener Journalismus oder freies Dichterleben? Erwiderung auf ein Mißverständnis." *Fontane Blätter* 64 (1997): 221–44.

Streiter-Buscher, Heide. Introduction to *Theodor Fontane: Unechte Korrespondenzen*, 1–66. Vol. 1. Berlin: De Gruyter, 1996.

Streiter-Buscher, Heide "'...und dann wieder jahrelang unechter Korrespondent': Der Kreuzzeitungsredakteur Theodor Fontane." *Fontane Blätter* 58 (1994): 89–105.

Strowick, Elisabeth. "'Mit dem Bazillus is nicht zu spaßen.' Fontanes 'Finessen' im Zeichen der Infektion." *Der Deutschunterricht* 55 (2003): 43–50.

Sullivan, Hannah. *The Work of Revision*. Cambridge, MA: Harvard University Press, 2013.

Sulzer, Johann Georg. "Originalwerk." In *Allgemeine Theorie der schönen Künste*, 863–4. Vol. 2. Leipzig: Weidmann, 1774.

Sutherland, John. "The Victorian Novelists: Who Were They?" In *The Book History Reader*, edited by David Finkelstein and Alistair McCleery, 2nd ed., 345–353. New York: Routledge, 2006.

Tatlock, Lynne. Introduction to *Publishing Culture and the "Reading Nation." German Book History in the Long Nineteenth Century*, edited by Lynne Tatlock, 1–21. Rochester, NY: Camden House, 2010.

te Heesen, Anke. *Weltkasten. Die Geschichte einer Bildenzyklopädie aus dem 18. Jahrhundert*. Göttingen: Wallstein, 1997.

te Heesen, Anke. "Die doppelte Verzeichnung. Schriftliche und räumliche Aneignungsweisen von Natur im 18. Jahrhundert." In *Gehäuse der Mnemosyne. Architektur als Schriftform der Erinnerung*, edited by Harald Tausch, 263–86. Göttingen: Wallstein, 2003.

Theisohn, Philipp. *Plagiat. Eine unoriginelle Literaturgeschichte*. Stuttgart: Kröner, 2009.

Trommsdorff, Johann Bartholomäus. *Systematisches Handbuch der Pharmacie für angehende Aerzte und Apotheker, zum Gebrauche academischer Vorlesungen, und zum Unterrichte angehender Pharmaceuten*. Zweyte, völlig umgearbeitete Ausgabe. Vienna: Aloys Doll, 1816.

Turner, Mark W. "The Unruliness of Serials in the Nineteenth Century (and in the Digital Age)." In *Serialization in Popular Culture*, edited by Rob Allen and Thijs van den Berg, 11–32. New York: Routledge, 2014.

Vellusig, Robert. "'Ein Widerspiel *des* Lebens, das wir führen.' Fontane und die Authentizität des poetischen Realismus." *Zeitschrift für deutsche Philologie* 125, no. 1 (2006): 212.

Vincent, David. *The Rise of Mass Literacy: Reading and Writing in Modern Europe*. Cambridge, MA: Polity Press, 2000.

Vismann, Cornelia. *Files: Law and Media Technology*. Translated by Geoffrey Winthrop-Young. Meridian: Crossing Aesthetics. Stanford, CA: Stanford University Press, 2008.

Vismann, Cornelia. "Cultural Techniques and Sovereignty." *Theory, Culture and Society* 6 (2013): 83–93.

Voss, Lieselotte. *Literarische Präfiguration dargestellter Wirklichkeit bei Fontane. Zur Zitatstruktur seines Romanwerks*. Munich: Fink, 1985.

Wandrey, Conrad. *Theodor Fontane*. Munich: C. H. Beck, 1919.

Wegmann, Nikolaus. *Bücherlabyrinthe. Suchen und Finden im alexandrinischen Zeitalter*. Cologne: Böhlau, 2000.

Wegmann, Nikolaus, and Matthias Bickenbach. "Herders Reisejournal. Ein Datenbankreport." *Deutsche Vierteljahrsschrift für Literaturwissenschaft und Geistesgeschichte* 73, no. 1 (1997): 397–420.

Wiedenroth, Hermann. "XI. Fragmente, Entwürfe und Pläne." In *Karl-May-Handbuch*, edited by Gert Ueding, 2. erw. Aufl., 488–91. Würzburg: Königshausen & Neumann, 2001.

Wildmeister, Birgit. *Die Bilderwelt der Gartenlaube: Ein Beitrag zur Kulturgeschichte des bürgerlichen Lebens in der zweiten Hälfte des 19. Jahrhunderts*. Würzburg: Bayerische Blätter für Volkskunde, 1998.

Windfuhr, Manfred. "Fontanes Erzählkunst unter den Marktbedingungen ihrer Zeit." In *Formen realistischer Erzählkunst*, edited by Jörg Thunecke, 335–46. Nottingham: Sherwood Press, 1979.

Wittmann, Reinhard. *Geschichte des deutschen Buchhandels*. 3rd ed. Munich: C.H. Beck, 2011.

Woodford, Charlotte. Introduction to *The German Bestseller in the Late Nineteenth Century*, edited by Charlotte Woodford and Benedict Schofield, 1–18. Rochester, NY: Camden House, 2012.

Wruck, Peter. "Fontane als Erfolgsautor: Zur Schlüsselstellung der Makrostruktur in der ungewöhnlichen Produktions- und Rezeptionsgeschichte der Wanderungen." In *"Geschichte und Geschichten aus Mark Brandenburg": Fontanes "Wanderungen durch die Mark Brandenburg" im Kontext der europäischen Reiseliteratur*, edited by Hanna Delf von Wolzogen, 373–93. Fontaneana 1. Würzburg: Königshausen & Neumann, 2003.

Wuttke, Heinrich. *Die deutschen Zeitschriften und die Entstehung der öffentlichen Meinung. Ein Beitrag zur Geschichte des Zeitungswesens*. 3rd ed. Leipzig: Krüger, 1875.

Young, Edward (1759). "Conjectures on Original Composition." In *Critical Theory Since Plato*, edited by Hazard Adams, 329–37. New York: Harcourt Brace Jovanovich, 1971.

Zapp, Arthur. "Schriftstellerleiden." *Die Zukunft* 25 (1898): 299–305.

Zedler, Johann Heinrich. "Papiermacher." In *Großes vollständiges Universal-Lexicon aller Wissenschafften und Künste*, col. 646–7. Vol. 26. P–Pd. Halle; Leipzig: Zedler, 1740.

Index

Note: Italic numbers refer to figures.

additive strategy, of publishing 64
L'Adultera 187, 233, 255
advertising, the Prussian state and 39
aesthetic strategies, of Fontane 187
affect, reading and 174
agency, of the market 91, 183–9, 190, 191
Die Ahnen 246
Allerlei Glück 206, 255
Allgemeine Theorie der prosaischen Schreibart (General Theory of the Prosaic Manner of Writing) 245
Allgemeine Zeitung 41, 84
allusion, art of 107
amanuenses 5
antiquarian objects and notes, of Fontane 166–7, 172
archiving
   of Fontane 31, 122–4, 140, 142, 143–4, 145, 149, 150
   media theory of archives 146
   sampling from Fontane's archive 165–73
   studies based on archival work 29
   term 'archive' 122n.4
Arnim, A. v. 126
art, the task of 12–13

art of chatter (*Plauderkunst*) 182
Assmann, Aleida 144
attentiveness, reading and 45
audiences, inclusion of in the creative process 253 (*see also* readers)
authors (*see also* writers)
   authorial image of Fontane 115–16
   foreign-language 61
   imaginative projections/PR stunts of 21
   income of 190, 205, 206
   Kolportage 10
   lack of control of 56
   mass production of literature and 37, 60–9
   pressures of serialization and 57–8
authorship
   compiling as 5
   of Fontane 6, 19, 20, 145
   as inspired genius 9
   Romantic models of 8–9, 11
autobiographical writings 76, 78, 116–17

Bahr, Hermann 179
Barthes, Roland 102
Beetham, Margaret 223

Before the Storm (*Vor dem Sturm*)
  32, 58, 85, 161, *162*, *180*, 192,
  211–17, 218–22, 224, 253
Berbig, Roland 128
Berlin novels 254, 270, 271
Berliner Illustrirte 11
"Berliner Zuschauer" ("Berlin
  Spectator") 112
bestsellers 64
Beta, Ottomar 81
Betrugs-Lexikon 8
Biernacki, Richard 37
Bisky, Jens 204
Book of Memoranda 226
bookbinding, of source materials
  176–7
books
  book history 25
  book sales 127–8
  industrialization and 39–40,
    42–3
  marginalization of 48
  standards for book production
    73
Böschenstein, Renate 215
Bosse, Heinrich 59
Bratring, F.A.W. 139
The Breaking of the Storm
  (*Sturmflut*) 64
Brentano, C. 126
Briefe an Georg Friedlaender 105–6,
  151–2
Briefe an Wilhelm und Hans Hertz
  2, 3
*Der Briefwechsel zwischen Theodor
  Fontane und Paul Heyse*
  158–9, 177
Brinkmann, Richard 172
Brunner, Constantin 179
brutal reading 173–4, 175–7
"Die Bücher und die Lesewelt"
  ("Books and the World of
  Reading") 33–4, 36–8, 68,
  204

Bullock, William 40, 41
business model of subscription
  43–4 (*see also* subscription)
Butzer, Günter 43
Byrd, Vance 56

capitalism 13
Carlyle, Thomas 51
censorship 56n.87, 107
Chaouli, Michel 17–18
characters
  Fontane's construction of 262
  individualization of 223, 224,
    226
  social types of 222–3, 247–8
  speaking styles of 243
  typified 218–30
Children and Household Tales
  (*Kinder- und Hausmärchen*)
  126, 131
chronique scandaleuse 151
Cicero 245
class
  Fontane and 160
  literacy and 42
  middle classes 12, 13, 224
  periodicals and 48, 50
  subscriptions and 44
collage 115
collecting, concept of 132–6
comic strips 56
compilation
  bias against 7–12, 118–19
  the compiler's task 99
  from compiling to remixing
    12–21
  early modern period 72, 75
  editors of newspapers and 102
  emergence of compilers 74
  fiction and 10
  Fontane and 4–7, 30, 66–9, 71–2,
    75, 91–2, 115, 119, 154–5
  intertextuality and 74–5
  material practices needed 77

newspaper editors and 75,
83–99, 102
newspapers and 10, 75
nineteenth century 7–12, 76
periodical industry and
16–17, 67
poetic features of Fontane's
100–7
Renaissance and 72, 74
sourcing materials. *See* source
materials
status of 101
consumption, of printed matter 43
contextualization, of notebooks
27–8
copy-and-pasting 6, 7, 20 (*see also*
cut-and-paste)
copying 5
copyright law 56n.87, 61, 62
costs, printing 41
Cotta 41, 84, 192
Cramer, Florian 190
creative process
of Fontane 1–2, 3–4, 145,
179–80, 182, 187–9, 192–3,
211–12, 234, 244, 255–6, 260,
273, 274
idealization of 101, 116
including the audience in
253
on method and the
reconstruction of 21–9
of Poe 186
creativity
archiving and 146
technology and 18
crowdsourcing 31, 122, 124,
125–32
cultural dimension, of Fontane's
work 169
cultural memory 144
cultural practices
remixing as 15
writing as a 189

cultural usage, material medium
and 26
cut-and-paste 24, 31, 82 (*see also*
copy-and-pasting)

Daheim 47, 58
Der Dämon (The Demon) 52, 56
Daston, Lorraine 195
data-mining 156
David Copperfield 227–8
deadlines, hard 145, 183–4
Debit and Credit (Soll und Haben) 64
decoding, reading and 225
Defregger, Franz 211
demand, for fiction 37
Depeschenbureau 63
Der Deutsche Krieg 1866
(The German War of 1866)
80
Deutsche Roman-Zeitung 171
Deutsche Rundschau. *See Rundschau*
*Die deutschen Zeitschriften (German
Periodicals)* 86
diagrams 198, 199–200, 203
Dickens, Charles 207–8, 210,
226–9, 254
discontinuous reading 124, 173,
179–80, 180–2
discourse, use of direct and
indirect 232, 236–7
discursive sound bites 230–43
drafting process
of Fontane 251–2, 255
novels 210, 212, 218, 226
drawings 198–203
Dreyfus affair 109
Droste-Hülshoff, Annette von 56,
250, 251

early modern period, compilation
and 72, 75
editing, nonlinear 250, 251
editorial journalism 83–4
editorial offices 56

editors of newspapers, compilation and 75, 83–99, 102
effect
    category of the 28
    writing and 186–7
Effi Briest 2, 169, 270–3
"An Electric Girl" 171
emulation 20, 249
"Endlose Dichtkunst" ("Infinite Poetry") 64, *65*
entertainment
    fiction as 34
    Fontane and 113
    periodicals and 39, 45, 46–7
envelopes (newspaper) 71–2, 81–2
Die Epigonen (*The Epigones*) 60, 67
epigones 59–60, 68
Erickson, Lee 64
Ernst, Wolfgang 29
eroticism
    in novels 111–12
    social news and 169–70
Eschenburg, J.J. 245

Falk, Victor von 109
false foreign correspondences 30–1, 88–99, 100, 107, 264
family magazine novel (*Familienblattroman*) 50, 170–1
La faute de L'Abbé Mouret 260
fiction (*see also* novels; periodicals)
    compiling and 10
    demand for 37
    as entertainment 34
    of Fontane 14, 111, 172
    foreign-language 34–5, 61
    formulaic nature of 61
    periodicals 11
    serialized 39 (*see also* serialization)
Fidicin, Ernst 127
Finessen 270

Fischer, Hubertus 6
Fleming, Paul 13, 60
Fliegende Blätter 64
folklore 167, 171
Fontane, Emilie 5, 80, 149
Fontane, Friedrich 5, 6, 81, 144–5
Fontane, Martha 5, 6, 82
Fontane, Theodor
    early career of 75, 76–7, 81–2, 110–11
    false foreign correspondences of 30–1, 88–99, 100, 107, 264
    at his desk *1*
    output of 69
    as a pharmacist 75, 76–83
    self-fashioning of 115–16, 118
    style of 243
    working methods of 144–5, 187–9, 274
foreign-language fiction 34–5, 61
form, format and 57
Fragmente 24n.68
frame of reference, for collecting 133
Frank, Gustav 190
Frau Jenny Treibel 229
Freytag, Gustav 64, 246
Friedlaender, Georg 105, 106, 151–2, 154, 204
Fuller, Matthew 190
functional memory 144, 145
Fünf Schlösser. Altes und Neues aus Mark Brandenburg (*Five Castles. Old and New in Mark Brandenburg*) 150
Fürstenau, Jutta 129

Gartenlaube 45–6, 47, *49*, 50–1, 52, 54, 57, 73, 171, 224, 254
Die Gegenwart 48
Genoux, Claude 61
genre imagery 54–5, 172, 211–18
genus grande/ genus humile/ genus medium 244–55

German literature,
  historiographies of 12, 13
German media theory 25
Geschichte des deutschen Zeitungswesens (*History of the German Press*) 52, 61
"Gesetz zum Schutze des Eigenthums an Werken der Wissenschaft und Kunst gegen Nachdruck und Nachbildung" ("Law for the protection of property in works of scholarship and art from reprinting and imitation") 62
Ghost stories (*Spukgeschichten*) 171
Glagau, Otto 110
Glaser, Adolf 57, 58
Goedsche, Hermann 19, 112–13
Goethe, Johann Wolfgang von 147, 174–5
Graevenitz, Gerhart von 200, 217, 218
Graf Petöfy 254
Granovetter, Mark S. 155
Great Fire of London 91–6 (*see also* "Das große Feuer und die Taschendiebe")
Grete Minde. Nach einer altmärkischen Chronik (*Grete Minde: After an Altmark Chronicle*) 146, 200–3, 206
Grimm, Brothers' 126, 131
Grönländische Prozesse (*The Greenland Lawsuits*) 175
Große Brandenburger Ausgabe 23
"Das große Feuer und die Taschendiebe" ("The Great Fire and the Pickpockets") 91, 92–8, 100, 102, 103
Grosser, Julius 205
Günter, Manuela 73
Gutenberg's letterpress 40
Gutzkow, Karl 39

Hackländer, F.W. 52
Hagen, Karl Gottfried 78, 82
Handbuch der Presse 63
handpresses 73
Hans Lange 158
Hauff, Hermann 13
Hauff, Wilhelm 33–4, 36–8, 41, 42, 55, 68, 203–4
Heckenast, Gustav 134
Heine, Heinrich 130, 157–8
Helmstetter, Rudolf 50, 51, 100, 118
Hertz, Hans 2, 47
Hertz, Wilhelm 129, 130, 135, 145, 146, 159
Hesekiel, George 19, 88, *89*
Heyse, Paul 158
historical collecting 126, 130
Historisches Schlagwörterbuch (*Historical Dictionary of Phrases*) 9
Hoffmann, Christoph 252
Horlitz, Manfred 118
Hosemann, Theodor 218
Hügel, Hans-Otto 45
humor, use of by Fontane 168–9
Hunger-Pastor (*Der Hungerpastor*) 57, 58

Ibsen, Henrik 82
Ideen-Assoziazion 178
illustrated family magazines 45–7, 48–9, 50–1
image factories (Bilderfabriken) 62
images, space dedicated to 52
Immermann, Karl 60, 67–8
individualization of characters 223, 224, 226
industrial age of print, term 7n.8
industrialization, of print/printing 9–10, 13, 37, 39–40
intellectual property rights 62
interfaces 25, 190–203

intertextuality
    of Fontane's library 161–2, 165
    nineteenth century 75
    Renaissance 74
inventio 100–7, 178
Irretrievable (Unwiederbringlich) 192
Iurascu, Ilinca 160

Jakobson, Roman 102
Janke, Otto 57
The Jew's Beech (Die Judenbuche) 56
journalism
    editorial 83–4
    of Fontane 30–1, 75–6, 84–99, 107, 116–17
    Fontane's novels and 232–3
    notebooks and 27
    journals, genre images in 55

Kasten 78
Keil, Ernst 50
Keller, Gottfried 60, 183–4
Kilcher, Andreas 178
Kittler, Friedrich 37
Kletke, Hermann 37
Knight, Jeffrey Todd 73, 74, 75
knowledge
    oral knowledge 167
    organization of 74
    rhetorical 28
    sociological of readers 253–4
Koenig, Friedrich 40, 41
Kolportage novels 10, 19, 75, 107–15
Kolporteure 44
Korrespondenz 63
Kosch, Günter 108–9, 110
Krämer, Sibylle 193
Kräuter, Friedrich Theodor 147
Krauthausen, Karin 27
Kreuzzeitung 31, 75, 76, 83, 84, 85–99, 112, 115, 116–17, 128, 135
Kruse, Joseph 158

"Die Kunst des Erzählens" ("The Art of Storytelling") 208, 247
Kürschner, Joseph 63, 84, 102

labor, division of 36
Ladendorf, Otto 9
"Lament" 106
Das Ländchen Friesack und die Bredows (The Little Country of Friesack and the Bredow Family) 150
Leben Fibels (The Life of Fibel) 178
legacy, the shaping of 146–8
legends 167
Lehrbuch der Apothekerkunst (Textbook of the Pharmacist's Art) 78
Leipziger Illustrirte Zeitung 62
Lepel, Bernhard von 156
letter writing 154
library connections 150–1, 158, 161
library, of Fontane 152, 165
Lichtenberg, Georg Christoph 101
Lindau, Rudolf 206
list-making 26, 193–7, 219, 222, 226
literacy, mass 42
literary poetics, of Fontane 107
literary production
    an alternative historiography of 12–21
    literary mass production 33–6, 37
    mass media and 30, 38–9, 48
    mass-produced images and 55
    moral codes and 51
literary rhetoric 28
literary sensationalism 112–13
literature
    the authority of the periodical 48–58
    factory made 36–8
    historiographies of German 12, 13
    the image world and 54–5

literary innovation of Fontane 274
literary marketplace 17
mass media and 65
mass production of 37, 60–9
Little Dorrit 254
"little pictures" (*kleinen Bildern*) 55
Lübke, Wilhelm 79–80

Mach, Ernst 252
magazines (*see also* periodicals)
  conservative family 217
  illustrated family magazines 45–7, 48–9, 50–1
A Man of Honor (*Schach von Wuthenow*) 32, 205–6, 229, 234–42, 248
manifoldness 131–2
Mann, Thomas 118
market(s)
  agency of the 91, 183–9, 190, 191
  Fontane and 185–6
  literary marketplace 17
  mass markets 44
Martin Salander 183
The Marvelous Clouds 189
mass audiences, women as 51
mass media
  communicative framing of 50
  and Fontane's output 172–3
  image flood in 54–5
  literary production and 30, 38–9, 48
  literature and 65
  marketplace 64
  redundancy and imitation and 66–7
mass-produced images, literary production and 55
mass production, literary 33–6, 37
mass readership 42, 48, 51
material evidence 22, 29

material media theory 25
material medium, cultural usage and 26
material practices, internalization of 76
materials, reuse of 146
Mathilde Möhring 32, 172, *188*, 257–74
May, Karl 10, 108, 110
McLuhan, Marshall 189, 209–10, 244, 250
Mecklenburg, Norbert 230, 231, 233, 239, 242
media constructivism 109, 111
media history 26
media landscape 27
media objects, remixing and 16
media realism 14, 18, 31, 103, 105–6, 217
media theory
  of archives 146
  German 25
  writing and 209–10
Mein Leben und Streben (*My Life and My Efforts*) 10
Meine Kinderjahre (*My Childhood Years*) 78
memory 144, 145
Merckel, Wilhelm von 115, 156
Merle, Eugène 21
method, reconstructing a creative process 21–9
Meyer, Carl Joseph 56n.87
mimesis 249
Die mißbrauchten Liebesbriefe (*The Misused Love Letters*) 60
montage 16
moral codes, *Gartenlaube's* 50–1
Morgenblatt für gebildete Stände 42, 192
Moser, Johann Jacob 121
Müller, Lothar 39
Müller-Sievers, Helmut 39

Index

Nachlass 22, 115, 140, 142, 147, 166, 218, 230
Nagl, Manfred 108–9, 110
narrative genre scenes, novels 211–18
narrative strategies, drawings and 200
Nena Sahib, oder Die Empörung in Indien (Nena Sahib, or the Indian Revolt) 112
networks
   of Fontane 124, 150–1, 155–6, 158–60, 253
   postal library network 150–65
   social networks 31
Neue Preußische (Kreuz-) Zeitung 231, 232
Neue Zürcher Zeitung 183
Neueste Weltkunde 84
Neuhaus, Volker 113
new technologies, newspapers and 41
newspaper editors
   compilation and 75, 83–99, 102
   Fontane as 75–6
newspapers
   compiling and 10, 75
   false foreign correspondences 30–1, 88–99, 100, 107, 264
   new technologies and 41
   oral knowledge and 167
   redundancy, imitation and 63–4
   serialized fiction in 39
   use of direct and indirect discourse 232
Nicholas Nickleby 207
Niedner, Julius 66
nobility, contacts with 156
nonlinear editing 250, 251
Nord und Süd 205
notational forms
   discrete bounded entries 197–8
   list-making 26, 193–7, 219, 222, 226
note-taking 26–7, 29
   types of 32, 192–3
notebooks
   capturing the *zeitgeist* 168
   contextualization of 27–8
   discontinuous reading and 180–2
   drawings 198–203
   of Fontane 3, 4, 19, 22–7, 137–40, 142–3
   and Fontane's output 185
   the formatting of Fontane's notes 190–203
   as interfaces 191–203
   lists *194*
   modular entries *197*
   reading/analysis of 25–6
   sensationalism/eroticism and occultism in 170–1
   source materials and 162–5
   Before the Storm (Vor dem Sturm) 219, 220–1
   Wanderungen project and 166–7
novellas 37, 47, 200–1
novels
   Berlin novels 254, 270, 271
   compositional process for 6, 208–11
   discursive sound bites 230–43
   drafting process 210, 212, 218, 226
   as entertainment 34
   family magazine novel (*Familienblattroman*) 50, 170–1
   of Fontane 20, 100, 160, 186–7, 207, 247
   Kolportage 10, 19, 75, 107–15
   Münchmeyer 10
   narrative genre scenes 211–18
   ordinary print runs of 47
   realist 124, 247
   Retcliffe 112–13

sexuality in 111–12
typified characters 218–30

Oberländer, Alfred 64, 65
occultism, social news and 169, 170–1
"The Old Fontane" ("Der alte Fontane") 118
"On Realism in Art" 102
On Tangled Paths (*Irrungen, Wirrungen*) 111, 160, 226
Ong, Walter 189
oral knowledge 167
orality
  production process of Fontane and 112
  secondary 167
oratorical ornament (*Redeschmuck*) 245
The Orator's Education 245
original work 8–9
originality, reproduction and 60–1, 64

packets (newspaper) 71–2, 81–2
paper, history of 26
paper sleeves (*Banderolen*) 26, 137, 140, 142, 144, 145–6, 148
paper tools
  of Fontane 4, 18, 19
  as interface 190–203
papermaking 40–2
Parerga and Paralipomena 174, 175
patriotism 126–7, 132
Paul, Jean 56, 175–6, 178
percursio 177–8, 179, 182
periodicals
  the authority of the 48–58
  books and 127–8
  class and 48, 50
  compilation and 16–17, 67
  creation of continuities and 48
  Die deutschen Zeitschriften (*German Periodicals*) 86

entertainment and 39, 45, 46–7
fiction and 11
Fontane and 30
Fontane's use of in his novels 100
the illustrated family magazine/universal culture magazine (*Rundschauzeitschrift*) 45, 48–9, 50–1, 217, 224
negative stance towards 14–15
papermaking and 41–2
positioning and 48
pricing of 44
reader feedback 56–7
reproduction of elements within 223
serialization 55–7, 183–4
space dedicated to images 52
subscription and 43–4, 47
text-image interactions in 52–3
Peters, John Durham 189, 251
pharmacist, Fontane as a 75, 76–83
Philadelphia Public Ledger 41
"Philosophy of Composition" 186
"Pigment Rot and Bleeding Hosts (*Hostien*)" 171
plagiarization 61
Platen, August von 106
Plumpe, Gerhard 105
Poe, Edgar Allan 186
Poesie, Prosa and 263, 264
poetics
  poetic features of Fontane's compilations 100–7
  poetics of realism 28, 32
  workshop 27–8
political engagement 14
pornography 113
Porombka, Stephan 27–8
positioning, periodicals and 48
"The Possessed Boys of Illfurth" 171
postal library network 150–65

practice-driven approach 26–7
Preußische Jahrbücher 128
pricing, of periodicals 44
printing
  costs 41
  evolution of the printing press 30
  Gutenberg's letterpress 40
  handpresses 73
  industrialization of 9–10, 13, 37, 39–41
  production procedures/ processes 28, 37
productivity, of Fontane 205–6
Prosa, Poesie and 263, 264
Prussian Communications Department 85
Prussian Ministry for Affairs of Religion, Education, and Medicine 126
Prussian postal system 31, 153–4
Prussian state, advertising monopoly of 39
publication, part-issues 56n.87
publishing, additive strategy of 64
purification (*Läuterung*) 104

questionnaires 135
quill pens 59
Quintilian 245

Raabe, Wilhelm 11, 57–8, 66, 73, 111, 147
Radecke, Gabriele 23, 187
Räsonnement 83–4
readers
  contributing materials 31, 122, 128, 134, 135–6
  mass readership 42, 48, 51
  novels and 209
  reader feedback 56–7
  sociological knowledge of 253–4

reading
  affect and 174
  attentiveness and 45
  brutal 173–4, 175–7
  as a creative process 182
  decoding and 225
  discontinuous 124, 173, 179–80, 180–2
  for entertainment 45
  first/second reading revolutions 42
  of Fontane 154–5, 173–82, 268
  women and 51
realism
  defined 104
  of Fontane 14, 20, 28, 102–7, 212, 230, 244–55, 275
  German 13–14
  media realism 14, 18, 31, 103, 105–6, 217
  of the middle 248–9, 256
  poetics of realism 28, 32
  realist novels 124, 247
  reality effects 28–9
recollection, modes of 144
recycling of material 206
Redakteure 84
redundancy work 102
Reisebilder 130
"Remix: Literatur. Ein Gedankenexperiment" 17–18
remixing
  from compiling to 12–21
  as a defined artistic practice 15–16
  of Fontane 17, 18, 19, 20
  remix artists 114–15
Renaissance, the 72, 73, 74
reproduction
  images and reproduction practices 62–3
  originality and 60–1, 64
research strategies 159–60

Index   307

Restless Guests (*Unruhige Gäste*) 73
Retcliffe novels 112–13
rhetoric 178, 244
rhetorical knowledge 28
Die Ritter vom Geiste (*The Knights of the Spirit*) 39
Robert, Louis-Nicolas 40
Rodenberg, Julius 183, 184, 254
Rohr, Georg Moritz von 222
Rohr, Mathilde von 135, 156, 170
roman à clef 225
Romantic models, of authorship 8–9, 11
Romanzeitung 57
Rost, Wolfgang 199
rotational presses 40
rumors 167–8
Rundschau 57, 183–4

Salomon, Ludwig 52, 61
scandals 151–2
scene of writing 22n.58
Scheerau factory 35–6
Scherer, Stefan 223
Schiller, Friedrich 174–5
Schlenther, Paul 226
Schlesinger, Max 86, *87*, 91
Schloß, Michael 158
Schnaase, Karl 126–7
scholarship, Fontane 23
Schopenhauer, Arthur 174–6
Schubkasten 78
Schücking, Levin 52, 56
Schumann Brothers 37
Schwartz, Wilhelm 128, 136
Schwerin, Sophie von 170
science, history of 25
Scott, Walter 35, 37
self-fashioning, of Fontane 115–16, 118
semiotic systems, competing 52
sensationalism
   literary 112–13
   social news and 169–70, 172

serialization 39, 55–8, 183–4, 207–8, 212
sexuality, in novels 111–12
Shaw, George Bernard 210
Siegert, Bernhard 26
Simenon, Georges 21
sketches 198, 199
Sochaczewsky, Heinrich 109
social capital 159
social criticism 14
social distance, postal library network and 150–65
social distinctions, staging of 231
social gossip 151–2
social groups, periodicals and 48
social networks 31
social news
   occultism and 169, 170–1
   sensationalism and 169–70, 172
social tagging 156–7
social types, of characters 222–3, 247–8
socio-cultural patterns 230
sociological knowledge, of readers 253–4
Sommer, Manfred 153
source materials
   bookbinding of 176–7
   compilation and 86, 121–4
   of Fontane 150, 161–5, 172–3
   journalistic skills and 107
   manipulation of 97
   Redakteure and 84
   transformations of 242
   Wanderungen durch die Mark Brandenburg 165–73
Spielhagen, Friedrich 64, 225
Statistisch-topographische Beschreibung der gesammten Mark Brandenburg 139
The Stechlin (*Der Stechlin*) 250–1, 252
stereotyping, technology of 61
Stifter, Adalbert 133–4

Stine 205
stock images/texts 61
Stockinger, Claudia 223
Stolle, Ferdinand 50
storage memory 144, 145
storage, of materials 78, 79–81, 121–2, 136–50, 184–5, 191
Storm, Theodor 66, 176
Streiter-Buscher, Heide 91, 116
Strowick, Elisabeth 259, 270
subscription 43–4, 47, 128, 253
Sullivan, Hannah 8
Sulzer, Johann Georg 8
Systematisches Handbuch der Pharmacie für angehende Aerzte und Apotheker (*Systematic Handbook for Trainee Physicians and Pharmacists*) 78

tags 231, 233
Tangermünde castle *201*, 202–3
technology
  creativity and 18
  newspapers and 41
Telegraphenbureau 63
Die Territorien der Mark Brandenburg 127
text-image interactions, in periodicals 52–3
text production
  compiling 4–6
  as a craft or industry 101
  drawings and 199–200
  of Fontane 17, 24, 185
  methods of flexible 203–8
  Renaissance 73
  textual reconfiguration 74
texts, as entertainment 45
textual practices, of Fontane 76, 92, 195–7, 262–3
theater, Fontane's use of in his novels 231

Theatrum vitae humanae 121
Theodor-Fontane-Archiv 142, 152
Theodor Fontane: Fragmente. Erzählungen, Impressionen, Essays 208–9
Theodor Fontane: Große Brandenburger Ausgabe 6, 80, 99, 116–17, 125, 156–7, 202, 216, 236–7, 238–9
Theodor Fontane: Werke, Schriften und Briefe 205–6, 246
Tieck, Ludwig 190
time-axis manipulation 251
time, periodicals and 55
Times, The 41, 92
translations, of foreign-language fiction 34–5
Trommsdorff, Johann Bartholomäus 78
Tunnel über der Spree 156
typewriters 59

Ueber Land und Meer 46, 47, 52, *53*, 56, 190, 254
Understanding Media 209
universal culture magazine (*Rundschauzeitschrift*) 45–7, 51
Universal-Lexicon Aller Wissenschafften und Künste (*Universal Encyclopedia of All Sciences and Arts*) 40
Universal Postal Union 153
"Unsere lyrische und epische Poesie seit 1848" ("Our lyric and epic poetry since 1848") 104
Unterm Birnbaum 229

verisimilitude, effects of 32
Vermißte Bestände (*Lost Holdings*) 142
violence, literary 113

visiting card strategy 129
Vismann, Cornelia 146, 147
Von Zwanzig bis Dreißig (*From Twenty to Thirty*) 31, 71, 78, 116, 148
Vorschule der Ästhetik (*Introduction to Aesthetics*) 178
Vossische Zeitung 6, 37

Walter, John 41
Wanderungen durch die Mark Brandenburg (*Walks through Mark Brandenburg*)
  as an archive 123–4
  closing of the project 149–50
  compilation and 118–19
  crowdsourcing of 31, 122, 125–32
  note-taking and 29
  readers sending materials 31, 122
  source materials 165–73
  starting of the project 85
  storage of media 136–50
  text generation and 204
Westermanns Monatshefte 47, 57
Wien und die Wiener, in Bildern aus dem Leben (*Vienna and the Viennese in Pictures Drawn from Life*) 133
Wohlfeile Ausgabe 150
women, reading and 51
wood engravings 62–3
workshop poetics 27–8

writers (*see also* authors)
  German 13
  of *Kolportage* novels 108–9
writing
  as a cultural practice 189
  effect and 186–7
  of Fontane 189, 251
  heavy materiality of the writing process 59, 68
  as intellectual work 101
  letter writing 154
  media theory and 209–10
  as a nonlinear recording medium 251
  Romantic notions of 101
  scene of writing 22n.58
  with scissors and glue 9, 11, 21
Wuttke, Heinrich 86

xylography 55

The Youth's Magic Horn (*Des Knaben Wunderhorn*) 126

Zedler, Johann Heinrich 40
Zeitgeist 168
Zeitschriftenliteratur 171
"Das Zietensche Husarenregiment von 1730 bis 1880" (The Regiment of the Zieten Hussars from 1730 to 1880) 6
Der Zuschauer 179
Zwickau translation factory 37
Zwinger, Theodor 121